COMPLETELY Alive

A YEAR OF DAILY DEVOTIONS

Alive 1 and *Alive 2*
Now in One Complete Edition

S. RICKLY CHRISTIAN

ZondervanPublishingHouse
Grand Rapids, Michigan

A Division of HarperCollins*Publishers*

Requests for information should be addressed to:

■ ZondervanPublishingHouse
Grand Rapids, Michigan 49530

Library of Congress Cataloging-in-Publication Data

Christian, S. Rickly (Scott Rickly)
  [Alive 1]
  Completely alive : a year of daily devotions / S. Rickly Christian
    p.   cm.
    First work previously published: Alive 1. Rev. ed. ©1995. 2nd work
previously published: Alive 2. Rev. ed. ©1995.
    Summary: Daily readings for high school students, using Scripture as a
springboard to reflect on God and Christianity in school life, dating, sex, parental
relations, fears, peer pressure, and more.
    ISBN: 0-310-20966-8
    1. Teenagers—Prayer-books and devotions—English. 2. Devotional calendars.
[1. Prayer books and devotions. 2. Christian life.] I. Christian, S. Rickly (Scott
Rickly) Alive 2. II. Title.
BV4850.C53   1996
242'.63—dc 20
                                                                    96-24536
                                                                        CIP
                                                                         AC

Interior design by Sue Vandenberg Koppenol

Printed in the United States of America

---

96 97 98 99 00 01 02 /❖ DH/ 10 9 8 7 6 5 4 3 2

For Andrea, Bradley, and Tyler,

citizens of high heaven and each an original.
You make me feel such joy, fill me with such pride.

Live creatively.
Don't waver.
Stay on track, steady in God.
May what he gives freely
    be deeply and personally yours.
Pure grace and nothing but grace be with you.

INTRODUCTION

From one day to the next, one year to the next, newspaper headlines and CNN broadcasts don't seem to change. Armies invade neighboring countries. Suicide bombers blow up a bus. Assassins topple governments. Earthquakes level major cities. Politicians steal the public blind. Something else causes cancer. Another Hollyweirdo ODs on drugs. And some lunatic is loose in public.

Things aren't much better at school. Fights break out almost daily. A major drug raid leads to seventeen student arrests. The homecoming queen gets pregnant. The football coach keels over with a heart attack. The Coke machine is busted into again. Your main squeeze begins dating someone else. And you flunk an algebra test.

On the home front, your parent's best friends announce their pending divorce. Your sister hogs the bathroom. Your brother is his usual slob self. Your aunt with her armpit hair of a dog comes to stay on one day's notice. And you get laid off at work.

If you're anything like me, you sometimes feel overwhelmed by the chaos of life and people around you. There are days when nothing or nobody makes sense, and you're convinced you're the last surviving sane person.

On days when I feel like that, it helps me to tell God and get the burden off my shoulders. That doesn't mean things will change overnight . . . or necessarily at all. It just makes me feel better to know God understands how I feel.

That God understands and cares about the intimate details of our lives is made clear in the Bible, a sort of "Owner's Manual" for the human race. It is not, however, a technical manual of schematic diagrams and charts, nor a cold, dead, dated document. It's at once a love story, autobiography, biography, self-help text, poetry anthology, compilation of personal letters, songbook, log of genealogy, how-to manual, and collection of prophecy.

It contains stories from men and women who have trusted God completely—providing guidance and inspiration for you—and details life histories of people who have just as completely disregarded God—giving you fair warning.

Above all, the Bible is God's way of stepping out of the shadows and making himself known. It tells us exactly what he's like, what he expects of us, why things aren't the way they ought to be, and what he intends to do about it.

It is my hope that this book, *Completely Alive*, will help you better understand God and the Bible, which is his final word on how to experience a full, rich life. It guides you and helps you maneuver through every difficulty, whether it's your fears about next year or your tears about a broken relationship. God knows and cares about these matters and more.

In James 4:8 the Bible says, "Come near to God and he will come near to you." *The Message* puts it this way: "Say a quiet *yes* to God and he'll be there in no time." So take God up on the promise by spending time together on those days you feel like a human hockey puck. It's a great relief to sense God's presence. As you'll discover in coming days and weeks as you read this book, God wants to be the still point of your turning, twisting, ever-changing world. You've got his word on it.

S. Rickly Christian
Colorado Springs, Colorado

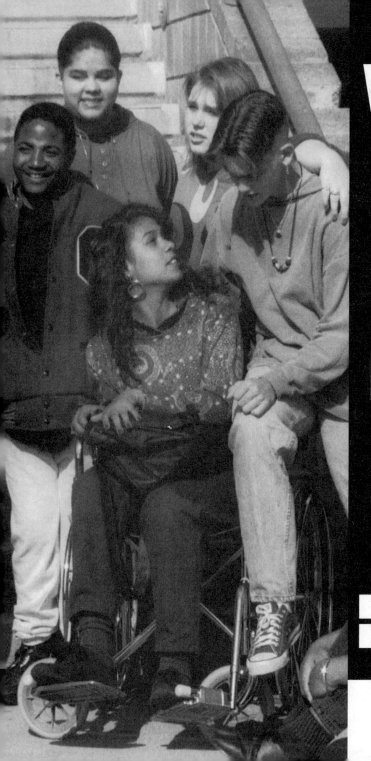

WEEK 1

▪▪ THE PERSONAL TAG

Rejoice that your names are written in heaven.

LUKE 10:20

I have a strange habit. Whenever I travel, the first thing I do upon checking into a hotel or stopping for gas is to open the local phone book. I want to know whether anyone else has my name. So far, no one has. But then, I have an unusual name: S. Rickly Christian.

That name, assigned by my parents, was written on a blue plastic bracelet and attached to my arm shortly after birth. These bracelets, given to all babies, were the hospital's way of ensuring that newborns wouldn't accidentally get switched.

Later, that name was the first word I learned to scribble with crayons. It became the name my friends used when they shouted for me down a crowded locker hall; the name my coach bellowed when I didn't swim fast enough; the name my girlfriend whispered in my ear, causing goose bumps on my neck.

More than any other label, my name symbolizes who I am: my personality, my dreams, my failures, my successes. And it's such a personal tag that my ears pop when I hear my name mentioned in conversation.

To know that my name, according to Luke, is a matter of celestial chitchat causes my *mind* to pop! Are you sure, Luke? My *name* recorded in God's Book of Life? I suppose God could keep roll more efficiently by using my social security number or bank access code. Numbers are easier to program, but God evidently prefers to use names.

That preference, I think, reflects the kind of personal relationship he wants to build with me. It's his way of assuring me that I matter; I'm not just some insignificant blip or digit code in the far corner of the universe.

Perhaps that is why the Bible is so full of long genealogies— God didn't want to miss a single name!

God's use of my name also signals his concern for the things my name represents: everything from my biggest hurts to my highest hopes. My name in my yearbook reminds my friends of such things as the day we shared together at the beach, the time we cried when we learned of another friend's cancer, the times we belly-laughed at a good joke.

My name, I believe, triggers the same kinds of memories in God's mind: the times we talked together in prayer, the time he comforted me during my mom's illness, the time I was dazzled by the splash of color he gave a peacock.

Looking back, those were special times, times of getting to know each other on a first-name basis.

See also: 1 Chronicles 1–9; Matthew 1:1–17

∷ "THEY SAID..."

Consider what a great forest is set on fire by a small spark. The tongue also is a fire, a world of evil among the parts of the body. It corrupts the whole person, sets the whole course of his life on fire, and is itself set on fire by hell.

JAMES 3:5–6

A few years ago, officials at McDonald's headquarters in Oak Brook, Illinois, became very sensitive about the topic of *earthworms.*

If you had mentioned the subject in the office, chances were good you'd have been tackled by a wart-faced fry cook and gagged with a half-dozen sesame seed buns. The reason: Ronald McDonald and his Golden Arch cohorts were fighting a rumor that they used the creepy crawlers as protein substitute in their burgers.

The rumor spread across America like ... well, like earthworms after a spring rain. Sales slumped, and the king of the burger was forced to launch a lavish campaign to regain its reputation.

Rumors usually don't reach such proportions. Often they just circulate among a close circle of friends in places like school locker halls and cafeterias. And generally the rumors damage lives and individual reputations, not those of corporations.

Such was the case when the new girl moved to town from Florida. Other girls at school felt threatened. They didn't have her cover-girl looks or *Seventeen* wardrobe. So they protected themselves by talking behind her back.

"You're kidding! I never knew *that*," said one girl. And before long tongues were wagging all over campus. To make the story *really* juicy, they'd pad the tale a little here, stretch a bit there. Soon, this poor girl's life was on the rocks—shipwrecked.

The anguish she must have felt and tears she must have cried are probably similar to a case I read about in which a woman's suicide note simply read, "They said . . ."

She didn't complete the sentence. Something "They said" killed her.

See also: Psalm 140:1–3; Romans 1:29–32; 1 Peter 3:8–12

:: THE EXCHANGE

> *I pray that you, being rooted and established in love, may have power, together with all the saints, to grasp how wide and long and high and deep is the love of Christ.*

> EPHESIANS 3:17–18

Imagine this scene. You've just been born and are taking your first breaths outside your mother's womb. The obstetrician and nurse are smiling, but your parents are strangely smug. They confer quietly to themselves, ignoring your cries.

"Doctor," your father says, turning to the physician, "would you mind holding the baby up again so we can better decide?"

"Decide what?" the doctor asks, lifting you up into the light.

"We just want to be sure the child's *right* for us," your father says. "We saw another baby in the nursery that seemed to have, well, a little more promise. This one here is too ruddy, and the eyes are the wrong color. We wanted a child with blue eyes and, you know, a shorter nose."

He whispers something in your mother's ear, and then motions the obstetrician closer.

"Doctor, I'm sure we could eventually learn to love this little one, but we have our hearts set on that cute blond baby. My wife and I have discussed this, and we'd like to work out an exchange. The hospital said we could pay the transfer fee with our Visa card."

This scenario is understandably absurd. When you were born, your parents accepted you into their family without qualifications. Their love was not based on your looks or performance. Not even your drooling mattered. They loved you simply because you were their child. Granted, their love at times was not perfect. There were times they withheld their affection—like the time you wrecked the family car or the night you missed your curfew by three hours. So while a parent's love is great, it does have limits.

But God's love has no bounds. You're loved because you're his child, and nothing you ever do will make him love you any more or less. His love is unconditional. As the apostle Paul wrote, "Neither death nor life, neither angels nor demons, neither the present nor the future, nor any powers, nor height nor depth, nor anything else in all creation, will be able to separate us from the love of God that is in Christ Jesus our Lord" (Romans 8:38–39).

When you realize you're loved that much, you begin to feel like you're worth loving ... and begin loving others in the same way, because God loves even the most unlovable as much as he loves you.

See also: Romans 8:31–39; 1 John 4:19–21

██ CARBON COPYING

If anyone is in Christ, he is a new creation; the old has gone, the new has come!

2 CORINTHIANS 5:17

I always thought of myself as a lot like Frank. Or maybe I just tried to be like him. When he went out for the swim team, I went out for the swim team. When he dropped that for the tennis team, I was right behind him.

We were both journalism junkies and wrote for the school paper. We both got involved in student-body politics. We liked the same kind of music, disliked the same teachers for the same reasons, wore the same style of jeans, went to the same parties, body-surfed at the same beach, and even dated some of the same girls.

But things began to change when I became a Christian. I decided to let God take control of my life, and I thought Frank eventually would, too. But that never happened. The "big" questions about life that drew me closer to God—Why do I exist? What happens after death? Were Jesus' claims valid? What purpose is there in life?—didn't seem to phase Frank.

When I'd try to talk to him about these things, he'd brush me off. "You're getting all philosophical, and it's just not where I'm at," he'd say. End of conversation.

Slowly I began to notice we were going in different directions. Parties that once seemed fun began feeling like an empty waste of time. Getting drunk seemed pointless. Jokes I once thought were funny seemed crude and prejudiced—the laugh was always at someone else's expense.

God began to instill in me value for other people. They took on new importance because of *who* they were (unique creations of God) rather than for *what* they were (good-looking, smart, funny, etc.). Members of the opposite sex became more than just "bodies." My parents and teachers became more than just authorities. In them I discovered people with many of the same needs I had—but I'd never noticed before.

When I think of Frank, I feel how a pardoned criminal probably feels toward buddies left behind in prison. You'd love for them to join you on the outside, yet the bars are all they know. And they only laugh when you tell them that the warrant for release—the pardon—has already been signed.

Becoming a Christian is an acceptance of that fact. It's not an effort, a striving, a ceaseless seeking, as one writer said. It's a letting go. And slowly you begin to notice that Christ is working on you from the inside out to give you new purpose, new values . . . and a new pattern for life.

See also: Ephesians 4:17–24; 6:10–18

■■ THE VISIBILITY FACTOR

> *A city on a hill cannot be hidden. Neither do people light a lamp and put it under a bowl. Instead they put it on its stand, and it gives light to everyone in the house. In the same way, let your light shine before men, that they may see your good deeds and praise your Father in heaven.*
>
> **MATTHEW 5:14–16**

Melinda was a typical case of what John Stott calls a "rabbit-hole Christian." She'd bounce out her front door in the morning after a mere grunt at her parents, scurry to school, and then race from the parking lot looking for her usual clique of Christian friends. Their favorite hangout before class: a bank of lockers, plastered with Christian stickers.

When the bell rang, she'd proceed with her holy huddle to journalism, where they'd sit together in the back corner by the window. Often they'd pass notes back and forth and giggle quietly about some hidden joke. When lunch arrived, Melinda would make a mad dash to the cafeteria and lay her books and sweater across a large table to reserve it for other Christians. They'd talk about God and how messed up their families were, and then retreat outside together for some informal Bible reading on the lawn.

After class, she'd buzz home, snort dinner, and then drive across town to pick up fellow Christians, sometimes for a Bible study at church, where they'd pray for God's help in witnessing to nonbelievers at school. After the final prayers, she'd scurry back home, wave to her parents in passing, and then disappear into her room where she'd mumble a few "bless 'ems" before falling asleep. And upon waking in the morning, she would begin her harried, holy pace all over again.

As Christians, we can't be lights of the world if our only contacts with unbelievers are those mad blitzes to and from Christian gatherings. We can't withdraw—we must penetrate darkness with the light of God's love. And it's hard to generate much brightness from rabbit holes.

See also: Matthew 28:18–20; Mark 1:17; John 8:12

:: HOLY HYPE

If anyone considers himself religious and yet does not keep a tight rein on his tongue, he deceives himself and his religion is worthless.

JAMES 1:26

I earned decent grades in most classes, but was less than a scholar with foreign languages. I took three years of Spanish in high school, yet scored 17 out of 150 points on a college proficiency test. And if I tried to converse with a native in Tijuana today, I probably couldn't get much further than ¿Como tu frijole? *How you bean?*

I switched to French in college. The result? I can count to ten, barely, and can pronounce "lingerie," "crepe," and "toilet" without looking in a dictionary. In other languages I can, let's see ... say "love you" in Tagalog and Japanese; I can remember a few words in Italian like "spaghetti," "ravioli," and "lasagna"; and I can hold my own in Australia, Ireland, and Kentucky, though the foreign accents trouble me.

With such a background, I sympathize with people who understandably scratch their heads when Christians convene their holy huddles and start rambling about things like redemption, agape love, trinity, rapture, and being saved by the blood.

One writer has said the world is bombarded with a mishmash of religious gobbledygook from people like "Theodore Theologian" with his pointy-headed talk about glorification, justification, and sanctification ... and his counterpart, "Rev. Pat Popcorn," with his holy hype about "Praise Gawd! Jump for joy! I see those hands! Pass the plate! Amen!"

Actions speak louder than words, it is said. Perhaps that is why the apostle Peter, in writing to Christian women married to unbelievers, urged the wives to let their godliness be demonstrated by their lives, not their words: "They [the husbands] may be won over *without words* by the behavior of their wives."

The apostle James was adamant that Christians "keep a tight rein on their tongues"—that they be "slow to speak" and instead show their faith by good life and deeds.

You see, it's much easier to *sound* spiritual and gush "Praise the Lord!" than it is to *be* spiritual. That's the problem Christ found with the Pharisees, religious leaders who talked godly but lived godlessly.

With that in mind, try an experiment: See what happens when you stop just *telling* people you're a Christian and start *showing* them. It can be a very radical way of living.

See also: 1 Peter 3:1; James 3:13; 1 John 3:18

POINTS TO PONDER–CHRISTIANITY

You are the light of the world.

MATTHEW 5:14

He is no fool who gives what he cannot keep to gain what he cannot lose.

JIM ELLIOT

There is one single fact which we may oppose to all the wit and argument of infidelity, namely, that no man ever repented of being a Christian on his death bed.

HANNAH MORE

It is so hard to believe because it is so hard to obey.

SÖREN KIERKEGAARD

If your father and mother, your sister and brother, if the very cat and dog in the house, are not happier for your being Christian, it is a question whether you really are.

HUDSON TAYLOR

Christian: one who believes that the New Testament is a divinely inspired book admirably suited to the spiritual needs of his neighbors.

AMBROSE BIERCE

Jesus Christ will never strong-arm his way into your life.

GRADY B. WILSON

Being a Christian is more than just an instantaneous conversion– it is a daily process whereby you grow to be more and more like Christ. Jesus Christ is the man God wants every man to be like.

BILLY GRAHAM

Christianity is the land of beginning again.

W. A. CRISWELL

A Christian is one who is on [Christ's] way, though not necessarily very far along it, and who has at least some dim and half-baked idea of whom to thank. A Christian isn't necessarily any nicer than anybody else. Just better informed.

FREDERICK BUECHNER

Take the case of a sour old maid, who is a Christian, but cantankerous. On the other hand, take some pleasant and popular fellow, but who has never been to Church. Who knows how much more cantankerous the old maid might be if she were *not* a Christian, and how much more likable the nice fellow might be if he *were* a Christian? You can't judge Christianity simply by comparing the *product* in these two people; you would need to know what kind of raw material Christ was working on in both cases.

C. S. LEWIS

When a Christian is in the wrong place, his right place is empty.

T. J. BACH

If you were arrested for being a Christian, would there be enough evidence to convict you?

DAVID OTIS FULLER

A person may go to heaven without health, without riches, without honors, without learning, without friends; but he can never go there without Christ.

JOHN DYER

Those who live in the Lord never see each other for the last time.

GERMAN MOTTO

See also: Matthew 5:13; Colossians 3:1–17

WEEK 2

■ SOUNDS OF SILENCE

Be still before the Lord and wait patiently for him.

PSALM 37:7

Yesterday, O Lord, was a frantic day—
of running and driving and chasing;
A 24-hour blur of sights and sounds.
Your calm, Your still, small voice
Was drowned by the rumble of traffic,
The boom of stereo loudspeakers,
The drone of gossip,
The blast of coaches' whistles,
The scream of family arguments,
The blare of prime-time television,
The ring of telephones,
The crash of locker doors,
The pound of headaches that beat like bass drums.
Lost in the circus of sounds, O Lord,
Was Your golden voice that was meant to whisper
Your comfort as softly as a forest breeze,
As softly as a kitten's purr, a lover's kiss, a child's embrace.
Buried amidst the cacophony of noise, O Lord,
Was Your calm assurance that was intended to come
As silently as a cloud sailing the sky,
As silently as a smile, a ray of light, a bird in flight.
Help me today to rediscover Your nearness—
To quiet my soul and hear You speak,
To shut out the high-decibel sounds of people, and traffic,
and music;
That I may again hear the sounds of Your silence
So deep, deep within my heart.

See also: Psalm 46:10; 131:2; Isaiah 32:17; Zephaniah 3:17

■■ PEER PRESSURE

Do not conform any longer to the pattern of this world, but be transformed by the renewing of your mind.

ROMANS 12:2

Mark was the kind of guy you loved to hate. He wore wing-tip shoes and sport coats to class, played electronic chess during lunch, published research papers on sixteenth-century Huguenots in history journals, and debated the science teacher about obscure textbook facts.

Everyone figured he'd be the school valedictorian, attend an Ivy League university, and win the Nobel Prize or something similar down the road.

But that never happened. In his junior year, Mark got tired of everyone thinking he was different from them. He wanted friends to hang around with, friends to joke with, friends to go to parties with. He wanted to be just a regular guy. And in his mind, regular meant drinking, smoking, fast cars, and fast girls.

It was really a surprise when Mark showed up at a basketball game drunk. And he created shock waves among faculty members when he was suspended for smoking pot in the bathroom. He started playing dumb in class, exchanged his calculator for a pack of Marlboros, and studied Zen instead of Huguenots and inert gases.

Even though I'd resented Mark for distorting the class grading curves, I felt sad watching him succumb to peer pressure. He quickly became just another face in the crowd. I kept hoping he'd come around and regain his sense of individuality, but that never happened. He never took the SAT college entrance exam, and Arlene Schneider beat him out as valedictorian. (Actually it wasn't even close. He dropped to the 38th position in our graduating class.)

Instead of pursuing a brilliant career, he took a job at a beach snack shop. And whenever I think of peer pressure and its effects, I think of Mark sitting in his stand, selling rainbow-colored snow cones for a buck twenty-five.

See also: Galatians 5:16–26; 6:7–10; 1 Peter 1:13–16

:: THE LONELINESS DISEASE

Be devoted to one another in brotherly love.

ROMANS 12:10

Anne thought there was something wrong with her. There was. She had the loneliness disease.

She probably had dozens of friends, but often moped about how she never dated and led a genuinely boring life compared with _____. She filled in the blank with any number of people.

Everyone knew why Anne didn't have close friends. It was because she constantly jabbered about her loneliness. The result: She was as depressing to be around as late-night talk radio.

Loneliness, I suppose, is one of the inevitable facts of being human. We all feel it: standing in line surrounded by unfamiliar faces; waiting for the phone to ring; leaving home. Even in a crowd of friends we can feel lonely. It's a universal feeling. But Anne thought it was some rare phenomenon that affected only her.

"The only way to have a friend," wrote Ralph Waldo Emerson, "is to be one." Somewhere along the line, Anne realized that principle. Over a period of months I noticed a change had come over her. She often ran errands for people, picked them up when their car was stranded, helped with their homework. She genuinely and lovingly *devoted* herself to others.

Later that year Anne started coming to workdays sponsored by our youth group. One such Saturday I spotted her atop a ladder with a bucket of paint. Her face was sunburned, and her hair was covered with blue Ultra Hide flat latex. But the most noticeable thing was her huge, bright smile. She had learned to reach out to others, thereby discovering the cure to her loneliness disease.

God reached out to us. Nowhere does the Bible say anyone beat a path to heaven to seek his friendship. Adam and Eve even hid from him. So Jesus took the first step toward us. He built a bridge where we had constructed walls. And his example, I believe, provides the guideline for us: "The only way to have a friend is to be one."

See also: Luke 6:38; Philippians 2:4

■■ FUTURE FRENZY

"I know the plans I have for you," declares the Lord, "plans to prosper you and not to harm you, plans to give you hope and a future."

JEREMIAH 29:11

Your best friend was accepted for the biochemistry program at Stanford University. Your brother was hired as special features writer for the local newspaper. Your girlfriend has an internship with the hospital.

Everyone you know is either going to college, working a good job, or getting married. It feels like you're the only person on Planet Earth who is honestly, desperately mixed up about the future.

Whenever your parents' friends come over, they always ask you the same question: "By the way, have you decided what you're going to *do?*"

You feel that same familiar pressure creeping over you, that knot of tension in your gut. Everyone expects you to know what you'll be doing for the rest of your life. But you don't even know what you'll be doing next year.

Thinking of the future can be scary. But the fear is not necessary. "When you worry, you pay interest on debts you don't owe," someone once said. That's especially true for Christians. God knows the desires of your heart and your uncertainties. And he promises not to leave you stranded without hope. You can relax in the knowledge that God has a unique plan for your life—a plan more fulfilling and a life more abundant than anything you could dream for yourself.

But his plan doesn't just happen by magic. You discover it as you draw closer to God each day. As you get to know him better and start making decisions affecting your future, his plans for your life will be made clear. He guarantees it.

See also: Psalm 37:4; 139:1–16

▪▪ THE GREAT OBSCENITY

Watch out! Be on your guard against all kinds of greed; a man's life does not consist in the abundance of his possessions.

LUKE 12:15

The media bombardment began when you were barely beyond the goo-goo stage and still in diapers. If you were like most infants, one day you blurted out something profoundly silly, such as "Cocoa Puffs!"

It meant nothing to you—you were merely repeating something you'd heard during Saturday-morning cartoons. But your parents were so amused they bought you a box. And soon you were blurting other things, such as "Honey Comb!" and "Lucky Charms!"

Your desires have been greatly inflamed since then, thanks to media hucksters who create "need" for their products. To illustrate, when I recently heard a commercial for a new bubble gum, I thought, "Kid stuff!" Besides, chewing bubble gum makes my jaw ache. But the new product stuck in my mind, and I even caught myself singing the company's commercial jingle in the shower. Before long, my response changed from "How dumb!" into "Maybe it's not so dumb!" and then into "It's probably worth the money!" and finally into "I need some now!"

The problem is, the world teaches just the opposite of what Luke says in the verse above: your life *does* consist of your possessions. You see this when people try to define your life by the price of your clothes, the brand of your stereo, the age of your car, etc. Along the way, we're led to believe we need what we don't need at all. The result: Not only do we have many needless possessions, but our possessions have us.

When Jesus told us to store treasures in heaven rather than on earth, he added: "For where your treasure is, there your heart will be also" (Luke 12:34). As Richard Foster points out in *Freedom of Simplicity*, Christ wasn't saying your heart should or should not be where your treasure is; he was saying it *will* be.

At some point, we need to unplug today's propaganda machine that bombards us with the four-letter obscenity, "More!" And we need to discard the "shopping-cart attitude" toward life.

You might start by playing devil's advocate with today's commercials and advertisements. Will having that new pair of $95 shoes, the latest CD, or the "Super! New! Improved!" product really make you more popular, happy, and whole? Of course not. *Having* doesn't bring happiness—it just brings a desire to have more.

See also: Matthew 6:19–34

:: FRIENDS WHO GO BUMP

Let us not love with words or tongue but with actions and in truth.

1 JOHN 3:18

I was walking through the crowded locker hall when I felt a hand on my shoulder. Whipping around, I saw that it was Donna.

"Hey, did you hear about Jim?" she asked.

"What about him?" I'd just spent time with him the day before and things seemed okay. But as the news of his bust cascaded from her mouth, I shook my head. "No kidding! That doesn't even sound like Jim."

Jim was a close friend, at least as I measured closeness. We jogged together twice weekly, and had gone to school together since junior high. What was this talk now of drugs? The thought seemed insane. Maybe that's because I only knew the shell—the smiling, good-looking, always-joking Jim—but was oblivious to the subsurface erosion in his life. We'd never discussed our inner needs, doubts, or failings. So I naively assumed he didn't have any. Meanwhile, he was crumbling before my eyes.

Now that I think about it, that's pretty much how most of my friendships have been—nothing more than billiard-ball relationships. We would ricochet back and forth, but never connect in any meaningful way:

"How's it going?" *Bump.*

"Fine." *Bump.*

"Catch you later." *Bump.*

Somewhere along the line, friends become acquaintances—people to wave at, but not to get intimately involved with. We want to know what they're doing this weekend, but not about their needs and problems. When we ask how someone is doing, we *expect* a cursory "Fine!" or "Great!" or "Not bad, how about you?"

It's hard to imagine our reaction if someone instead responded, "Oh, pretty lousy actually. I woke up this morning not feeling much like a Christian. My parents were all over my back, and with the pressures I'm facing at school and work, I feel tempted to smoke some dope."

But that will never happen, because no one gets close enough to risk breaking through the high-gloss facades, to dare shattering the ceramic smiles. Nobody will burst into that inner shadow chamber where we sometimes think, feel, and act awfully desperate and very lonely. It's easier to wave and bump than to sit down and listen or confront.

The end result of all of this bumping is that we're appalled when someone stumbles and behaves like a real-life, imperfect human being. We act very surprised by their fall, and think it all happened overnight. But erosion of the heart is a slow process; we just never take time to notice.

See also: Hebrews 3:12–13; 10:24–25

▪▪ POINTS TO PONDER – SELF

> *Let another praise you, and not your own mouth; someone else, and not your own lips.*
>
> **PROVERBS 27:2**

The highest and most profitable reading is the true knowledge and consideration of ourselves.

THOMAS À KEMPIS

The foolish man is full of selfishness; he toils day and night, greedy for wealth, as if he will never grow old, or die.

RUSSIAN SAYING

There is no room for God in him who is full of himself.

SERVICE OF THE HEART

I would prefer to combat the "I'm special" feelings not by the thought "I'm no more special than anyone else," but by the feeling, "Everyone is as special as me."

C. S. LEWIS

The man who lives for self alone, lives for the meanest mortal known.

JOAQUIN MILLER

Be not like a cock who thought the sun had risen to hear him crow.

GEORGE ELIOT

There are few people who are more often in the wrong than those who cannot endure to be thought so.

FRANÇOIS DUC DE LA ROCHEFOUCAULD

When a person feels disposed to overestimate his own importance, let him remember that mankind got along very well before his birth, and that in all probability they will get along very well after his death.

CHARLES SIMMONS

We are very apt to be full of ourselves, instead of Him that made what we so much value, and but for whom we have no reason to value ourselves. For we have nothing that we can call our own, no, not ourselves; for we are all but tenants, and at will too, of the great Lord of ourselves, and of this great farm, the world that we live upon.

WILLIAM PENN

The less a man thinks or knows about his virtues the better we like him.

RALPH WALDO EMERSON

See also: Mark 8:34–38, 10:42–45; John 15:13

WEEK

3

■■ BETHLEHEM, USA

Your attitude should be the same as that of Christ Jesus: Who, being in very nature God, did not consider equality with God something to be grasped, but made himself nothing.

PHILIPPIANS 2:5–7

If Christ were reborn in the United States this month, I wonder how things would be different?

Would his birth warrant a blurb in *The New York Times*? Would CNN crews poke cameras in his face? Would an agent get him a Pampers commercial? Would he watch "Sesame Street" and "Mr. Rogers"?

Where would he grow up? In Malibu? In Boulder? In Boston? Or would he hang out in a Watts ghetto, just to be different? Would he attend a public school? A private academy? Or would he be home schooled by his parents? Would he go out for football or play in the band? Would he own the latest computer gizmo? Would he work after school and get yelled at by his boss?

Later on, where would he go to recruit his apostles? From corporate management programs? From Stanford Law School? From the wharf in San Francisco? Would he want you if you were black? Or gay? Or crippled?

Would he hold summer revival meetings and stay in Hiltons? Would he pass out tracts at beaches and airports? How would he respond to Hare Krishnas? To Southern Baptists? I wonder if he'd play pool in a bar? Would he come home at night and watch himself on the "CBS Evening News"?

Would he join a church? Become a pastor? How would he treat people with AIDS? And what would he wear: Levis with Nikes or an Armani suit with Italian loafers? Would he drive a truck or something red and fast? Would he fly first-class or coach?

I wonder if we'd recognize him? And if so, would we shout him down with racial slurs? Would we crucify him on an aluminum cross? Or would he get a life sentence and be paroled after seven years?

See also: Mark 10:35–45; John 13:1–17

■■ FACE TO FACE

Jesus entered Jericho and was passing through. A man was there by the name of Zacchaeus; he was a chief tax collector and was wealthy. He wanted to see who Jesus was, but being a short man he could not, because of the crowd. So he ran ahead and climbed a sycamore-fig tree to see him, since Jesus was coming that way. When Jesus reached the spot, he looked up and said to him, "Zacchaeus, come down immediately. I must stay at your house today."

LUKE 19:1–5

The crowd was lined up three and four deep along the curb fronting Jericho's main drag, abuzz with anticipation as Jesus neared. On the edge of the parade throng, perched on tiptoes, stood Zacchaeus, a pint-sized swindler who was the district's IRS honcho. He was the kind of guy who, if he came through your front door, you'd run out the back—a man who, following the custom of his day, inflated people's tax bills and pocketed the difference.

From where he stood, craning his neck, Zacchaeus couldn't see a thing. So he shinnied up a tree for a better look, just as a wild roar rose from the streets. Suddenly Christ rounded the corner and stopped.

Distracted by a flash of bright clothing in the curbside tree, Jesus forgot about those on street level and turned his attention to Zacchaeus. You could have heard a pin drop. And when Jesus called for the crook to hop down, people could hardly wait for what would happen next. Jesus would probably make an example of Zacchaeus, as he did with the Pharisees: *You snake! You brood of vipers! You'll rot in hell!*

Zacchaeus knew better than anyone that that's what he deserved, and Jesus did, too. But that's not what happened. Jesus simply invited himself to be Zacchaeus's houseguest. Jumping from the tree, Zacchaeus pumped Christ's hand and blabbed excitedly about how he'd give half his belongings to Goodwill and pay people quadruple what he had cheated in tax surcharges. And that made Christ smile. But everyone else grumbled about how Jesus was berserk to even think of associating with someone like Zacchaeus.

Of course, Christ didn't think it was so crazy. After all, that's what usually happens when he meets sinners face-to-face. They receive just the opposite of what they deserve. The same thing happened to you and me. And that's what grace is all about. The world hasn't gotten over it yet.

See also: Romans 5:20; Ephesians 2:8–10; Revelation 3:20

▪▪ SIDE BY SIDE

I will never leave you nor forsake you.

JOSHUA 1:5

I once read a story about a young man whose life was marked by repeated heartaches and discouragements. Several of his closest friends and family members died; his life goals were never attained; and financial trouble plagued him. Each day brought nothing but hardship and lonely times of crisis.

And then one night he had a vivid dream in which he saw himself walking along a windswept beach with the Lord. As they strode together against the gale, scenes from the young man's life flashed like lightning across the sky. Each scene, he noticed, was also depicted behind them in the sand as footprints—one set belonging to him, the other to the Savior.

When the last scene from the young man's life had lit up the evening sky, he turned and looked back at the ribbons of footprints crossing the shore. Something seemed odd. He dropped to his knees to examine the tracks more closely. Then he traced them back, remembering the scenes they corresponded with in his life.

Usually there was a double set of footprints, but at other times—often when he faced his biggest hardships—the second pair of footprints mysteriously disappeared. Confused, he turned to the Lord.

"I'm sorry, but none of this makes sense," he stammered. "We've walked together for a long time now, but I notice that during some of the roughest, most grueling moments of my life there is only one set of footprints in the sand. Why, Lord . . . ," he fumbled for words, "how could you desert my side when I needed you the most?"

"My dear, precious child," the Lord said, drawing the young man close to his body, "I promised I would never leave your side no matter what. The double set of footprints assures you of that."

"But ...," the young man began, pointing his finger behind him.

"When you look back and see just one pair of footprints," the Lord said, "it was then that I carried you."

See also: Psalm 23; 46; Matthew 11:28; John 14:27

■■ THREE LOVES

You have heard that it was said, "Love your neighbor and hate your enemy." But I tell you: Love your enemies and pray for those who persecute you.

MATTHEW 5:43–44

"*If love*" is conditional love. It says, I love you ...

if you run with the right crowd.
if you let me borrow your car this weekend.
if you will go to bed with me.
if you wear the latest styles and like loud music.
if you let me see your answers when I'm stumped.
if you don't hassle me with your problems.
if you loan me money for a pizza.

"*Because love*" is easy love. It says, I love you ...

because you were "most-valuable player" in last week's game.
because you voted for me as class president.
because you're crazy and make me laugh.
because you throw wild parties and like rock 'n' roll.
because your character-reference letter helped me get accepted to college.
because you have a great body and nice hair.
because you are basically a lot like me.

"*Anyhow love*" is hard, unconditional love. It says, I love you ...

anyhow, even if you ignore me when I talk.
anyhow, even if you judge me unfairly and gossip behind my back.

anyhow, even if you like classical music.

anyhow, even if you don't have a car.

anyhow, even if you have a fresh outbreak of acne.

anyhow, even if you grew up on the wrong side of the tracks.

anyhow, even if you don't understand me and my lifestyle.

Yes, I love you anyhow ... because that's how God loves me. And I'm trying to learn to love you the same way.

See also: Luke 6:27–36; John 21:15–17; Philippians 2:1–4

:: SHOUT OF LOVE

Love is patient, love is kind. It does not envy, it does not boast, it is not proud. It is not rude, it is not self-seeking, it is not easily angered, it keeps no record of wrongs. Love does not delight in evil but rejoices with the truth. It always protects, always trusts, always hopes, always perseveres.

1 CORINTHIANS 13:4–7

If I speak with the ease of a radio DJ and sing like a superstar, but don't have love, my words are like the grating whine of a woodshop buzz saw.

If I know my way through cyberspace and can program better than my computer teacher, if I memorize Genesis and can read Leviticus without falling asleep, or if I can even see the future and know everything about everything like some latter-day Wizard of Oz ... but have not love, my value to others is as sawdust.

If I donate my designer jeans to the Salvation Army and let my brother use my car, if I serve as a missionary to cannibals in Borneo, or if I give my body to science ... but don't have love, my contribution is worthless.

Love is patient—even if it means going to the beach with my mom or waiting quietly until my sister is finished primping in the bathroom.

Love is kind—it shares a table with the lonely boy at lunch and consoles the new girl who just moved to town from Kansas.

love does not envy the student-body president, the hockey the cheerleader, or even the blonde who has the world's most even tan.

Love doesn't boast about admittance to Harvard University or a science fair blue ribbon. Love isn't snooty about a new dress or a custom-built house on the right side of town.

Love doesn't jeer at the girl who weighs two hundred and plenty pounds and doesn't vie to be first in line. Love is cool as ice—even when provoked by the rival gang.

Love doesn't cheat when the teacher isn't looking or stop by the racks for a quick peek at *Penthouse* magazine. Love roots for what's right and shouts "Whoopee!" when the good guy wins. Love never quits.

Love isn't like a cheap stereo from the discount store. It never fails. Its power source is God, so it will last forever.

See also: John 3:16; John 13:34–35; 1 John 3:11–18

■■ LOVE IS ...

Do everything in love.

1 CORINTHIANS 16:14

Love is one of those words that is difficult to define. Maybe that's because its meaning has become twisted over time.

You can say that you *love* your girlfriend or boyfriend ... but you can also say you *love* going to basketball games. You can *love* pizza, you can *love* gymnastics, you can *love* rock 'n' roll or a good movie. And then, you can *love* God.

But what is love? The apostle Paul did his best to define it in the so-called "Love Chapter" of 1 Corinthians 13. We read about that yesterday.

Try writing a few practical definitions of your own. Relate these definitions to people and things around you, your friends, and family. For example, you might say, "Love is the patience my friend displayed when I was late getting ready last Friday night." Or, "Love is the kindness I showed when I gave up my seat on the bus yesterday." Be original:

Love is _____

Love is _____

Love is _____

Love is _____

Love is _____

Love is _____

Love is _____

See also: Luke 10:25–37; 1 Peter 4:8

■■ POINTS TO PONDER–LOVE

A new commandment I give you: Love one another. As I have loved you, so you must love one another. By this all men will know that you are my disciples if you love one another.

JOHN 13:34–35

Love is not only something you feel. It's something you do.

DAVID WILKERSON

Joy is love exalted; peace is love in repose; long-suffering is love enduring; gentleness is love in society; goodness is love in action; faith is love on the battlefield; meekness is love in school; and temperance is love in training.

D. L. MOODY

I never knew how to worship until I knew how to love.

HENRY WARD BEECHER

We are shaped and fashioned by what we love.

JOHANN WOLFGANG VON GOETHE

Love is not blind—it sees more, not less. But because it sees more, it is willing to see less.

RABBI JULIUS GORDON

There is a land of the living and a land of the dead and the bridge is love, the only survival, the only meaning.

THORNTON WILDER

Tell me how much you know of the sufferings of your fellow men and I will tell you how much you have loved them.

HELMUT THIELICKE

The rule for all of us is perfectly simple. Do not waste time bothering whether you "love" your neighbor; act as if you did. As soon as we do this we find one of the great secrets. When you are behaving as if you loved someone, you will presently come to love him. If you injure someone you dislike, you will find yourself disliking him more. If you do him a good turn, you will find yourself disliking him less.

C. S. LEWIS

It is better to have loved and lost, than not to have loved at all.

ALFRED LORD TENNYSON

Love must be learned and learned again and again; there is no end to it. Hate needs no instruction, but waits only to be provoked.

KATHERINE ANNE PORTER

Our Lord does not care so much for the importance of our works as for the love with which they are done.

TERESA OF AVILA

The waste of life lies in the love we have not given, the powers we have not used, the selfish prudence which will risk nothing and which, shirking pain, misses happiness as well.

UNKNOWN

He that falls in love with himself will have no rivals.

BENJAMIN FRANKLIN

See also: Matthew 5:43–44; 1 Corinthians 13

WEEK

4

:: THE SIX-MILLION-DOLLAR MAN

I praise you because I am fearfully and wonder-fully made.

PSALM 139:14

Everyone talks about the infinite preciousness of human beings, but one Yale University biochemist set out to prove it. Working with a chemistry supply company's catalog a few years ago, Harold J. Morowitz began tabulating the exact value of the human body.

At that point, hemoglobin ran $285 a gram; insulin, $47.50 a gram; human DNA, $76; collagen, $15; and alkaline phosphatase, $225, among others. On the more expensive side were such chemicals as bradykinin, which sold for $12,000 per gram; follicle-stimulating hormone, $8 million a gram, and prolactin, the hormone that stimulates female milk production, $17.5 million per gram.

When the price list was completed, Morowitz calculated how much of each chemical was in the human body and came up with an average value per gram of human body at $245.54. Multiplying that by his dry weight (68 percent of the body is water), he tallied his final value: $6,000,015.44.

Our test-tube value reflects the fact that God splurged on his Human Project. He could have kept things simple, as he did with his Tree or Rock Project. But he chose to make us more lavish, a fact mirrored in everything from our hearts (an "engine" that typically runs without rest or repair for 70+ years) to something as extravagantly ordinary as our skin. (This self-healing outer sheathing is tough and resilient, yet responds to minute changes in temperature, and reacts like Fourth of July sparklers when stroked by one's love.)

My problem is that I'm generally not aware of my six-million-dollar body. Sure, I notice it when I'm clogged with a cold. Or when I get BO. But then I just swallow some colored pills, or switch deodorants . . . and forget about me.

A unique, miraculous creation of God? Oh, I suppose. But on a day-to-day basis, I'm more awestruck by the apparent miracles of architects and engineers who build skyscrapers and space shuttles. When I look in the mirror each morning, I don't think, "Wow, God, thanks for splurging on my body!" Instead I think, "If I could just get rid of the zit on my nose . . ."

And if God were to open the door for body alterations, I'd elbow my way to the front of the line.

See also: Genesis 1:26–31; Matthew 6:25–34

■■ COURAGE TO CONTINUE

Be strong and courageous. Do not be terrified; do not be discouraged, for the Lord your God will be with you wherever you go.

JOSHUA 1:9

The story of Kathy Miller didn't begin the day she was born. It really started the March afternoon she darted across the four-lane highway near her home in Scottsdale, Arizona. One of the drivers hit his brakes to avoid her. The car skidded. There was a scream. Many thought Kathy Miller was dead.

The report from hospital neurosurgeons was grim. She not only had compound fractures of one leg, but severe brain injuries as well. She lapsed into a coma—like a deep sleep from which she would never awaken. Days stretched into weeks with no sign of improvement. She dwindled from 110 to 55 pounds. It wasn't until late May that she could open her eyes. Even that was a miracle.

When she was finally released in June to go home, she couldn't talk or walk. She wore diapers and acted like an infant. She could barely even grunt out the word *Mama*. But Kathy had a strange idea. She wanted to run. Not just walk, but run—and run in a mini-marathon. She trusted God for courage to try.

Long, agonizing months passed as Kathy tried to regain coordination. She would shuffle a few steps, then catch hold of a wall or door. The first time she tried to jog a few steps she fell flat on her face, fracturing her nose. But she got up and kept trying, day after day. She fell again and again. But she kept getting up, determined to regain coordination.

And then on a crisp November day, eight months after her accident, Kathy entered the 10,000-meter North Bank Run in Phoenix.

She didn't come close to finishing first. In fact, the thousands of other runners were far ahead by the time she'd managed to go a block. But she won *her* race, because she finished. She went the distance.

When failure or unfortunate incidents occur in your life, you have a choice. You can shake your fist and blame God—that is, you can *give up*. Or, you can *grow up*—you can trust God to help you fight off the discouragements and, like Kathy, take that one step at a time to regain your footing.

When down times come, remember that you are not alone: "For the LORD your God will be with you wherever you go." That encouragement is echoed in Isaiah 40:30–31: "Even youths grow tired and weary, and young men stumble and fall; but *those who hope in the LORD* will renew their strength. They will soar on wings like eagles; they will run and not grow weary, they will walk and not be faint."

So, best wishes. Not for your future success, but for your future misfortune. And may these adverse times be extravagant and enormously, outrageously joyful—for it's at these very moments Christ's strength moves in on your weakness. It's his way of helping you grow up.

See also: 2 Corinthians 12:9; Hebrews 12:1–11; James 1:2–4

∷ STRANDED

God is our refuge and strength, an ever-present help in trouble.

PSALM 46:1

I was in an unfamiliar city, and it was starting to snow as I pulled onto the expressway. Merging into the rush of late-night traffic, my engine suddenly lost power. I pulled over in a panic. I was stranded in sub-zero weather, stuck in a section where the road curved drunkenly toward the sleazy downtown district. I waited for someone to stop, but no one did. They'd read too many newspaper stories.

I felt as insignificant as a piece of discarded roadside litter as I waited in the shadow of the lonely city on that black, snowy night. I was scared; I was cold. So I did the only thing I could think of: I told God I needed help. I asked him to ease my anxieties, and thanked him that he knew exactly where I was.

As cars hurtled past, I realized I had no choice but to trust God. And in that moment I became aware that God was enough. I then tried to think of Bible verses I knew: *"Never will I leave you; never will I forsake you."* It was a promise of God's I could count on—regardless of what happened. *"The Lord is my helper; I will not be afraid."* It was an assurance God could be trusted—regardless of the outcome.

At that moment, a sense of God's peace overwhelmed me. Praying to him was like talking with a best friend. And a few minutes later a sort of miracle happened. A car pulled over to help.

It's often true that when I dwell on myself and my problems, my troubles seem to grow. But when I dwell on God, my troubles seem to go. That doesn't mean things are always bright and rosy. Christians aren't immune to hurt and heartache. Yet God gives us a special capacity to cope with such times.

Chet Bitterman, a young missionary slain by Colombian terrorists, was probably praying for God's help up until the moment a bullet entered his head. God may have *seemingly* not been there. But he is *always* there. It's just that for a reason only God knows, he sometimes chooses not to intervene directly in human affairs. He saved Daniel in the lion's den. But he didn't save Christ on the cross. Does that mean God was dozing or negligent? No. He had other plans.

In my case I was saved. I was rescued. I know that others sometimes are not. Christians die every day. Yet even at that moment of death, Christ is there—offering a harbor in heaven for the storm-tossed vessel. And even there—yes, especially there—God is our refuge and our strength.

See also: Psalm 23; Hebrews 13:5–6; Revelation 21:4

▪▪ THE QUITTING COMPLEX

> *See to it that you complete the work you have received in the Lord.*

> COLOSSIANS 4:17

Tom had big dreams for a quitter. His problem was he never stuck with anything past the dream stage.

He had the voice to become another Michael W. Smith and talked about how he'd cut an album by his twenty-first birthday. But when he quit his band over a dispute with another member, he never much mentioned music anymore. Instead, Tom said he'd run for the city council after graduation as the "youngest-ever" representative. But that dream was aborted when he couldn't even get elected class treasurer his senior year.

In view of his past, I was a bit cynical when Tom became a Christian. I figured it would be just like everything else in his life. And it was. A couple of months later he "gave up on God" and started turning up stoned at football games.

"The Christian thing just didn't work out," Tom said when I asked him about it. "I'm tired of being all goody-goody. You know, playing Mister Nice Guy all of the time."

Tom was not some strange, abnormal, butterfly-type person who always flits from one thing to another. Sure, he quit a lot. But probably no more than you or I do, if we're counting. We all have dreams and goals that we don't follow through on. And if we don't actually "quit" being Christians, we're all pretty good at dragging our feet.

I sometimes feel a lot like Tom—that I'm just playacting as a Christian and pretending I'm nice and good and loving, when I know inside I'm not that way at all. The Russian writer Turgenev said it best when he wrote, "I don't know what the heart of a bad man is like, but I do know what the heart of a good man is like—and it's terrible."

I think the writers of the Bible knew the same feelings at times. That's why, in talking about the Christian faith, they use hard words like *struggle*, *race*, *battle*. Paul says we should "work out" our battle with sin daily. He knew what he was talking about: the battle against sin is just that, a bloody, never-ending battle. It's not easy to be a Christian in a non-Christian world. Even faith is not easy. When Christ said your faith could move mountains, he didn't mean it was as simple as saying "Presto-chango!" He meant that faith that moves mountains always carries a pick.

See also: Galatians 5:7; Philippians 2:12

:: IT IS FINISHED!

I press on toward the goal to win the prize for which God has called me heavenward in Christ Jesus.

PHILIPPIANS 3:14

When Christ died on the cross, his last words were, "It is finished!" There was nothing he left undone. He met his every goal on earth.

That seems unusual today, because many people's goals are never realized. They either don't pursue them or ditch the effort partway through. These might be such everyday goals as perfecting a serve in tennis or eating fewer Twinkies and losing twenty pounds. Your goals could be to get straight A's and earn a college scholarship. Or they may focus on the spiritual areas of your life, such as quitting a bad habit or rededicating your life to God.

Take a few minutes and think about what's holding you back from starting to work on—and finishing—the goals you've set in your own life. Write your reasons below:

I haven't _____

because _____.

I haven't _____

because _____.

I haven't _____

because _____.

If you've never thought much about setting goals before, consider making some for each of the different areas of your life: social, physical, mental, *and* spiritual. And then post them where you'll see them daily, perhaps on your locker door. When tempted to waver, try letting God restimulate you to *keep on* instead of giving up. Read the verse above slowly. Paul was determined not to quit on God. He had his eye on the goal, where God is beckoning us onward—to Jesus. He was off and running, and wasn't about to turn back. (Read 2 Corinthians 11:24–33 to better understand what this goal entailed for him.)

Now, rewrite the passage (Phil. 3:14) in your own words, relating it to your personal situations: _____

_____

_____

See also: 1 Corinthians 9:24–27

▪▪ COVER-UP

When Mary reached the place where Jesus was and saw him, she fell at his feet and said, "Lord, if you had been here, my brother would not have died." When Jesus saw her weeping, and the Jews who had come along with her also weeping, he was deeply moved in spirit and troubled. "Where have you laid him?" he asked. "Come and see, Lord," they replied. Jesus wept.

JOHN 11:32–35

When I was a new Christian, I got the impression it was important not to be overly emotional. Other Christians I knew seemed to be always happy and controlled no matter what. If they did poorly on a test, they smiled and praised God. If a relative died, they smiled and praised God.

The message was clear: God has given Christians a special ability to cope with life. You know, Romans 8:28. And if you express deep, personal feelings such as grief, anger, or despair, well, it's obvious you're not behaving as a mature Christian should—that you've lost control and don't have enough faith.

So I tried to suppress my feelings when I learned a close friend had been operated on for cancer and wasn't expected to live another year. I fought to remain levelheaded, neutrally pleasant, and emotionally unexpressive—to act like I thought a good Christian should. But it was like trying to keep an inner tube under water. The suppressed feelings just resurfaced as tension, and I couldn't sleep nights.

I was surprised when I first read in the Bible how Jesus reacted when his good friend died. He didn't erupt with pious clichés about Lazarus being in heaven with God. He wept. And when he encountered money changers in the temple, he didn't politely ask them to pack their bags and set things up down the block. No, he chased them out and kicked their tables over.

Reading things like those, I realized if Jesus didn't flaunt an attitude of spiritual self-sufficiency, I shouldn't. If I always try to seem strong to others, who am I fooling? God created me with the capacity for strong, spontaneous emotions. And he can spot a cover-up a mile away.

See also: Mark 11:15–18; Luke 19:41; Romans 12:15

▪▪ POINTS TO PONDER– HYPOCRISY

Rid yourselves of all malice and all deceit, hypocrisy, envy, and slander of every kind. Like newborn babies, crave pure spiritual milk, so that by it you may grow up in your salvation, now that you have tasted that the Lord is good.

1 PETER 2:1–2

If the devil ever laughs, it must be at hypocrites; they are the greatest dupes he has; they serve him better than any other, but receive no wages. Nay what is still more extraordinary, they submit to greater mortifications to go to hell, than the sincerest Christian to go to heaven.

CALEB C. COLTON

Hypocrisy—prejudice with a halo.

AMBROSE BIERCE

How difficult it is to avoid having a special standard for oneself!

C. S. LEWIS

Don't stay away from church because there are so many hypocrites. There's always room for one more.

A. R. ADAMS

A bad man is worse when he pretends to be a saint.

FRANCIS BACON

Hypocrisy, the only evil that walks invisible, except to God alone.

JOHN MILTON

No man can, for any considerable time, wear one face to himself, and another to the multitude, without finally getting bewildered as to which is the true one.

NATHANIEL HAWTHORNE

A man who hides behind the hypocrite is smaller than the hypocrite.

W. E. BIEDERWOLF

Some people speak as if hypocrites were confined to religion; but they are everywhere; people pretending to wealth when they have not a sixpence, assuming knowledge of which they are ignorant, shamming a culture they are far removed from, adopting opinions they do not hold.

ALBERT GOODRICH

The wolf in sheep's clothing is a fitting emblem of the hypocrite. Every virtuous man would rather meet an open foe than a pretended friend who is a traitor at heart.

H. F. KLETZING

Hypocrisy can afford to be magnificent in its promises; for never intending to go beyond promises, costs nothing.

EDMUND BURKE

See also: Matthew 7:1–5, 23:1–33; 1 Timothy 4:1–5

WEEK

5

:: A BROAD PERSPECTIVE

You are familiar with all my ways.

PSALM 139:3

The stewardess is saying something about seat belts, but no one is listening. They're glancing at watches, reading magazines, peering about as if they expect their boss or worst teacher to walk down the aisle at any moment.

Like them, I am still recovering from the whirl of last-minute details, my race-car rush to the airport, my dodging, darting dash to gate 33. My nerves, strung tighter than Steinway strings, begin to loosen only when the plane hurtles skyward after a screaming, bounding sprint down the rubber-streaked runway.

I glance out the fishbowl window at the shrinking landscape and feel my concerns drop away with the houses, cars, and people below. Loosening my seat belt, I watch quietly as my hurricane-paced world disappears and then peekaboos through the lace cover of clouds. Lakes glisten like jewels on the patchwork quilt of countryside, now 36,000 feet below.

At moments like this, I sense God views my life like I view the world that spreads now from horizon to horizon. Not that he's tucked, snoozing, beneath a blanket of clouds, unconcerned with life below. No, he's *personally* concerned because he has sampled our anxieties, hurts, and loneliness. *He has lived as one of us.*

Because of that, he can view my life personally and totally. He sees the roads I roam—where I've been and where I'm headed. He sees the valleys I must travel through, the mountains I must cross, the lonely plains I must necessarily rove. He knows where the detours are. He knows everything because he has a broad perspective.

But God doesn't just watch—he *directs.* I'm not an ant swallowed up in the vastness of the planet. To him I'm a unique creation of his that he will lovingly and individually guide through every detour and over every hill. He knows whose paths will intersect my own, and when. Marriage? College? Career? God has it all planned.

People seek release from their pressures in many different ways. Some calm their nerves with a six-pack or shot of whiskey. A line of coke or a couple of pills might do it for others. And then there are those who seek release sexually.

For me, it's enough to periodically soar skyward, to rocket above my world and view life from a new perspective. God's perspective. It's a high that stays with me long after I am back on the ground.

See also: Psalm 23; Isaiah 42:16; 46:10; Matthew 6:25–34

WHAT WILL YOU DO?

"What shall I do, then, with Jesus who is called Christ?" Pilate asked. They all answered, "Crucify him!"

MATTHEW 27:22

Much of human communication is based on questions. Among the dozens you hear every day are: "What time do we eat?" "Where do you want to go Friday?" "When is the next home game?" and "Do you need a lift?"

More momentous questions include: "Will I get well?" "Can you raise my grade?" "Will you marry me?" and "Can I borrow the car?"

Some of the Bible's most notable passages are questions. The first recorded question occurred when the serpent in the Garden of Eden raised a doubt in Eve's mind by asking, "Did God *really* say, 'You must not eat from any tree in the garden'?"

Other key questions from Scripture include: "Will a man rob God?" "Who do people say the Son of Man is?" "What good thing must I do to get eternal life?" "My God, my God, why have you forsaken me?" and "What can a man give in exchange for his soul?"

But one of the Bible's most memorable questions came from the lips of Pontius Pilate, an up-and-coming politician who was sent by Roman authorities to be governor of Palestine. He was in his Jerusalem chambers one day when some hot-under-the-collar Jews stormed in, demanding the execution of Jesus, who was then but 33.

Pilate had heard about Christ—the miracles and the bizarre claims of being God's only son. News like that makes headlines. So he spent a few minutes questioning Jesus about these things and quickly determined that he had committed no capital offense. But

Pilate didn't know what to do next. He couldn't just ignore Jesus. And because he was a politician, dependent on public opinion, he could hardly ignore the crowd either.

So he asked the masses, "What shall I do with Jesus who is called Christ?" Their predetermined response: "Crucify him!"

After some two thousand years, Pilate is remembered as the man who washed his hands of Christ by abandoning him to mob fury. That action, in itself, was a choice. Over the centuries, Pilate's question has also not been forgotten. It still rings today. You, too, must decide what you will do with Christ.

As Christians, we face that choice every day in how we respond to other people, circumstances, and temptation. You know Christ can't be ignored. But will you abandon him? Follow him? Recrucify him? You've got Christ on your hands. *What will you do with him?*

See also: Joshua 24:15; Matthew 16:13–16

▪▪ IT'S A MAD, MAD WORLD

Come to me, all you who are weary and burdened, and I will give you rest.

MATTHEW 11:28

From one day to the next, one year to the next, newspaper headlines and CNN broadcasts don't seem to change. Armies invade neighboring countries. Assassins topple governments. Earthquakes level major cities. Politicians steal the public blind. Something else causes cancer. Another rock idol ODs on drugs. And some lunatic is loose in public.

Things aren't much better at school. Fights break out almost daily. A major drug raid leads to seventeen student arrests, including my good friend. The homecoming queen gets pregnant. The football coach keels over with a heart attack. The Coke machine is busted into again. My girlfriend begins dating someone else. And I flunk an algebra test.

On the home front, some of my parents' best friends announce their pending divorce, my dad gets on me about mowing the lawn, and my mom never stops harping about my homework. My sister hogs the bathroom. My brother is his usual slob self. My aunt comes to stay on one day's notice. And I get laid off at work.

If you're anything like me, you sometimes feel overwhelmed by the chaos of life and people around you. There are days when nothing or no one makes sense, and you're convinced you're the last surviving sane person. On days when I feel like that, it helps me to tell God and get the burden off my shoulders. That doesn't mean things will change overnight ... or necessarily at all. It just makes me feel better to know God understands how I feel.

In James 4:8 the Bible says, "Come near to God and he will come near to you." *The Message* puts it this way: "Say a quiet *yes* to God and he'll be there in no time." So take God up on the promise by talking to him on those days you feel as helpless as a wind-tossed rag. It's great relief to sense God's presence. He wants to be the still point of your turning, twisting, ever-changing world.

See also: Jeremiah 31:25; Matthew 24:4–33; John 7:37

▪▪ WEIGHT LIFTER

If my people, who are called by my name, will humble themselves and pray and seek my face and turn from their wicked ways, then will I hear from heaven and will forgive their sin and will heal their land.

2 CHRONICLES 7:14

There are days when I feel that awful weight
    Dragging me, slowing me, nearly drowning me
As if I'm swimming with all my clothes on.
    With each stroke I grow more weary and think,
"If only I had a rock to cling to...."
    Such is the weight of unforgiven sin in my life.
And then I hear God's still small voice
    Whispering that he is that rock—
Able to greatly forgive because he greatly loves.

"So you think you've really blown it?" the Lord kindly asks,
  "You think there's no hope for you this time?" he gently breathes.
And then he urges me to consider how:
David must have felt when he tried to hide
  His infidelity by killing his lover's husband;
Abraham must have felt when he sacrificed
  His wife's chastity to save his own neck;
Peter must have felt when he denied
  That he'd ever known or followed Christ;
Sarah must have felt when she laughed
  At God for making a promise she thought he couldn't keep;
Esau must have felt when he traded
  His birthright for a hot bowl of chili;
Rahab must have felt when she flopped
  Into bed after bed after bed, playing the prostitute;
And the list goes on and on and on . . .
  But God graciously allows people new beginnings
When they realize they need help—and a rock to cling to.
  Be that rock, dear Lord, for me today.

See also: 1 John 1:5–10; 2:1–6

:: THE SEX TRAP

> **Flee from sexual immorality. All other sins a man commits are outside his body, but he who sins sexually sins against his own body. Do you not know that your body is a temple of the Holy Spirit, who is in you, whom you have received from God?**
>
> 1 CORINTHIANS 6:18–19

I had dated Sandy nearly a year when she broke up with me and started going out with Dave. It hurt to see her with someone else, but I felt crushed when I learned they were having sex.

When we were going together, Sandy always talked about how God was No. 1 in her life. We were active in church, and there was never any question about her stand on sex. She knew the Bible said it was wrong outside of marriage.

I lost track of her when I went away to college ... until a mutual friend said he'd heard Sandy had gotten pregnant and had a baby. Then one day I was home on break and bumped into her in the post office. Her little boy was screaming. I didn't really know what to say, so I mumbled something about her kid having a good set of lungs. She laughed. Then I asked about Dave.

"We broke up shortly after I got pregnant," she said, nodding at her toddler. "Dave didn't want the responsibility. So I've got it all." She forced a smile, then shook her head. "You know, I never thought it would be this way. When Dave was still around, I felt like such a hypocrite. I guess that's why I dropped out of church. It was easier not thinking about God. But I got things straightened out with God when Jason was born, and I'm going to church again."

I was glad to know she was doing better spiritually. Yet it was still sad to hear the tone of regret in her voice. I realized as I stood there that while God's forgiveness relieves the guilt, it doesn't always erase the consequences of sin. Sandy's trying to raise little Jason alone was proof of that.

See also: Romans 6:11–23; Galatians 6:7–10

▪▪ FAULT FINDERS

He who conceals his sins does not prosper, but whoever confesses and renounces them finds mercy.

PROVERBS 28:13

Whenever Judy blew it, she always blamed others. When I picked her up for a date and had to wait thirty minutes, she never even said she was sorry.

"My brother hogged the shower," was the best she could do.

In a history class we shared, she never accepted the responsibility for her low grades. Whenever she botched a test, it was because "I can't *believe* the picky details that dumb teacher expects us to know!" Or "None of this stuff is important anyway. Who cares about ancient history two hundred years ago." Or "I really tried to study for this one, but my parents' gabby friends stopped by."

It was the same in other areas of her life. When she forgot to add chocolate chips to the cookie dough, it was because I had distracted her. And one day when she ran out of gas and was late for work, she blamed her dad for not filling the tank the day before. Finally I lost my patience with her.

"No matter what happens, it's always someone else's fault," I said. "Are you perfect or something? Have you ever told anyone you were sorry?"

When I thought about Judy after we'd broken up, I realized the basic difference between us was simply that she verbalized the kinds of excuses I often just mumbled silently to myself. "*I was blinded by the sun,*" I'd think when I fumbled an easy pass reception in PE. "*If that jerk only knew how to drive!*" I'd quietly curse when the driver I was tailgating braked suddenly. I always had ways to explain away my mistakes.

I have a tendency to want to do the same with sin. I can blame away sin, I can ignore sin, I can conceal sin—all in an effort to look good to God. Trouble is, God sees through our shallow cover-ups. Before him, we're as guilty as the worst criminal. We've all been caught. But he has promised to forgive us and erase our record if we "come clean" and confess our sin. That's the key. The only way to look good before God is to admit our absolute worst.

See also: Isaiah 1:18; 1 John 1:8–10

▪▪ POINTS TO PONDER–SIN

> **For the wages of sin is death, but the gift of God is eternal life in Christ Jesus our Lord.**
>
> **ROMANS 6:23**

Even in this age of inflation, the wages of sin remain the same.

ANONYMOUS

There are only two kinds of people: the righteous who believe themselves sinners, and the rest, sinners who believe themselves righteous.

BLAISE PASCAL

Hate the sin, but love the sinner.

THOMAS BUCHANAN READ

Christians who get involved in sin are miserable. They've closed the door on sin and then spend their lives looking through the keyhole.

JAY KESLER

As Chesterton pointed out, the Fall of Man is only the banana-skin joke carried to cosmic proportions.

MALCOLM MUGGERIDGE

Adam ate the apple, and our teeth still ache.

HUNGARIAN PROVERB

People are not punished for their sins, but by them.

ELBERT HUBBARD

The sins of the flesh are bad, but they are the least bad of all sins. All the worst pleasures are purely spiritual: the pleasure of putting other people in the wrong, of bossing and patronizing and spoiling sport, and back-biting; the pleasures of power, of hatred.... That is why a cold, self-righteous prig who goes regularly to church may be far nearer to hell than a prostitute. But, of course, it is better to be neither.

C. S. LEWIS

One reason sin flourishes is that it is treated like a cream puff instead of a rattlesnake.

BILLY SUNDAY

Man calls it an accident; God calls it an abomination. Man calls it a blunder; God calls it a blindness. Man calls it a defect; God calls it a disease. Man calls it a chance; God calls it a choice. Man calls it an error; God calls it an enmity. Man calls it a fascination; God calls it a fatality. Man calls it an infirmity; God calls it an iniquity. Man calls it a luxury; God calls it a leprosy. Man calls it a liberty; God calls it lawlessness. Man calls it a trifle; God calls it a tragedy. Man calls it a mistake; God calls it a madness. Man calls it a weakness; God calls it willfulness.

MOODY MONTHLY

The sin they do by two and two they must pay for one by one.

RUDYARD KIPLING

My sins don't make me a sinner. They're just the evidence.

S. RICKLY CHRISTIAN

Sin is energy in the wrong channel.

AUGUSTINE OF HIPPO

Sin may be clasped so close we cannot see its face.

RICHARD CHENEVIX TRENCH

We shall never understand anything of our Lord's preaching and ministry unless we continually keep in mind what exactly and exclusively his errand was in this world. Sin was his errand in this world, and it was his only errand. He would never have been in this world, either preaching or doing anything else but for sin. He could have done everything else for us without coming down into this world at all; everything else but take away our sin.

ALEXANDER WHYTE

See also: Psalm 51:1–17; Isaiah 1:18; Matthew 9:10–12

WEEK

6

■ CONTAGIOUS OR CONTAMINATED?

"God's name is blasphemed ... because of you."

ROMANS 2:24

Tom grew disenchanted with Christianity when he took a hard look at Christians around him. His Bible study leader was having an affair with a married woman. Another Christian leader he trusted had refused to sell his house to a couple ... just because they were black. One of the regulars at church, the mother of his friend, practically had an IV hooked up to a gin bottle.

"If *they* call themselves Christians," he said, "count me out."

Hypocrisy has been a stumbling block for non-Christians since the days of the early church. In writing to the Roman church about Jews, Paul turned on the heat. He charged that their belief had turned to legalism and their commitment to God had become a "form of religion." Sure, they seemed good enough in their own eyes. They prayed and read Scripture. They tithed their money, fasted, and attended their churches and synagogues often enough to be labeled "active" and "faithful." But something was drastically wrong. They knew *what* they believed, but none of it affected their day-to-day living.

"You who teach others, do you not teach yourselves?" Paul wrote. "You who preach against stealing, do you steal? You who say that people should not commit adultery, do you commit adultery? You who abhor idols, do you rob temples? You who brag about the law, do you dishonor God by breaking the law?" (Rom. 2:21–23).

Yes to all of the above. The result: their "churchianity" and "religiosity" had turned people away from the Lord. "God's name is blasphemed because of you!" Paul blasted.

In a letter sent to the Corinthians, Paul describes Christians as "Christ's ambassadors." He also notes that God has "committed to us the message of reconciliation." In other words, God uses Christians to reach nonbelievers. We are his mouthpiece, his arms, his means of conveying love. And when that message is corrupted by our actions, others notice. They see through the phoniness of religion.

The easy solution is just to warn people that Christians are human and fallible—and urge them to judge God only by himself. That's true, of course. But the fact is, God has established us as his representatives. And if our Christianity isn't contagious, it very likely is contaminated.

See also: 2 Corinthians 5:17–21; James 1:22–25

■■ THE BUCK STOPS HERE

It is more blessed to give than to receive.

ACTS 20:35

One day I became curious about where my money was disappearing. I didn't make much working part-time after school at the box company, so I wasn't exactly loaded. But I earned enough to know I shouldn't be constantly broke.

To solve the mystery, I got out my checkbook and started flipping back through all the little scribble notes I had made when I wrote each check: the data that tells me *when* and *where* I spent *how much* for *what*.

The Timberland boots ate a wad. And it was hard to believe I'd spent $136 on gas in one month. The amount I paid for new Michelin radials made me wince. But like I told Dad, the guys at school would laugh me off campus if I drove on Tijuana retreads. There was the day I bombed my history exam and got wasted on waffle cones at TCBY; the pair of Nikes (because I felt pig-guilty about TCBY); the $37 blown on a lousy date with that dumb sophomore; three new CDs and a new compact player to better enjoy them. The list became a blur of jots and figures as I flipped faster.

It's odd, but I'd always thought of myself as a caring person, one who was concerned about others. But the truth is, I was *most* concerned about myself. My checkbook proved it. Priorities are generally mirrored by how you spend your money. Is it always for yourself? Or do you consider how you can meet others' needs?

What are some of those needs? Well, I'd ignored several just in the previous month. I thought of the family that got burned out of their house and lost *everything*. Maybe I could have made them a meal or bought them a sack of burgers. I could have done something similar for the homeless guy on the corner who looked like he was starving. Instead I walked around him. A flower would have brightened the day of the elderly lady next door. Maybe I could have spent *my time*—just ten minutes to help Mom with the dishes, call my grandfather, or clean Dad's brush after he painted the living room. I had the time to go with our youth group to the orphan home, but I'd opted for the beach.

Sometimes it's hard to change selfish habits. But the task is made easier when I consider that everything I have is a gift from God. Freely I have received, so freely should I give.

See also: Matthew 25:31–46; Mark 12:41–44

:: HEART TREASURES

Where your treasure is, there your heart will be also.
MATTHEW 6:21

I was watching CNN when scenes of a Southern California fire flashed across the TV. The windswept inferno had destroyed million-dollar estates on its flaming rampage through the bushy hillsides of Los Angeles. A reporter interviewed a man who, hours earlier, had lost his home. He described how he'd only had a couple of minutes to grab a few belongings, stash them in his minivan, and escape with his life.

What would you do in a similar situation? You're awakened in the middle of the night by a sheriff's deputy who tells you to evacuate immediately—a fire is sweeping toward your home and will engulf it within minutes. You can salvage only 10 belongings. What would they be? Write down the first items that come to mind:

1. _____

2. _____

3. _____

4. _____

5. _____

6. _____

7. _____

8. _____

9. _____

10. _____

Now review the list. The Bible says the things you treasure reveal a lot about you and your values. What kinds of things did you value enough to risk your life retrieving? What did you grab first? Last? What did you leave behind? What does all this say about the values you live by?

See also: Colossians 3:1–3

■■ HEMMED IN

> *You hem me in—behind and before; you have laid your hand upon me. Such knowledge is too wonderful for me, too lofty for me to attain.*

PSALM 139:5–6

There is generally nothing positive about being "hemmed in." The term makes you think of those hot-tempered, "GET-OFF-MY-BACK!" confrontations with your parents or those high-decibel, "GET-OUT-OF-MY-ROOM!" face-offs with your kid brother. Being "hemmed in" is a claustrophobic, itchy, cornered kind of feeling that usually makes you want to slam the door and crank up the stereo.

But when David uses the phrase pertaining to God, he doesn't shake his fist and scream skyward. Instead he gets real gushy and says, in effect, "I see you, God, everywhere I look: before me, behind me, and right next to me. I'm amazed—that's almost too wonderful to believe!" Why isn't David threatened? Because God's closeness isn't meant to be stifling.

God stands behind you. David's words, "You hem me in—behind," are similar to Isaiah's: "God . . . will be your rear guard." This is army talk. It refers to the group of soldiers that follow the main regiment, helping stragglers and more or less picking up the pieces. God is that way—he follows behind, mending and restoring your hurts and sorrows. He forgives your sin and helps you back on your feet. He picks up the pieces of your life, creating positive results from negative incidents.

God stands before you. We don't know what challenges we'll face next week, next month, next year. We don't know where our future leads. But God does, because he's scouted up ahead. "The LORD himself goes before you," says Moses in Deuteronomy. It's a promise you can count on.

God stands with you. As David writes here, "You have laid your hand upon me." It's his way of saying God doesn't just stand back and watch from a distance the goings-on in your life. He's at your side, encouraging and challenging—helping you through the rough times and celebrating with you during the high times.

Yes, you are hemmed in by God. But like David, you can be hemmed in . . . and happy!

See also: Deuteronomy 31:8; Isaiah 52:12; Jeremiah 29:11

:: THOSE WERE THE DAYS

> *As God's chosen people, holy and dearly loved, clothe yourselves with compassion, kindness, humility, gentleness and patience. Bear with each other and forgive whatever grievances you may have against one another. Forgive as the Lord forgave you. And over all these virtues put on love, which binds them all together in perfect unity. Let the peace of Christ rule in your hearts, since as members of one body you were called to peace. And be thankful.*
>
> COLOSSIANS 3:12–15

On a shelf in my closet is a stack of school yearbooks going back to junior high. My parents didn't shoot videos, so the yearbooks are the only record of who I was and what I was like back then. They contain those years in pictures: the candid moments, the formal try-and-look-studly shots, the best of times, the worst of times.

What the school photographer couldn't or didn't capture, my friends often did. They scribbled comments in the margins about the times we shared: "Remember when ..." or "I'll never forget the time when ..." Some said things like, "I wish we could have gotten to know each other better, but ..."

Reviewing old yearbooks is sort of like entering a time warp. You aren't the same person you were back then. Times have changed. And you have, too.

Take a slug of nostalgia sometime today and dig out your yearbooks. Read what people wrote about you. What adjectives surface most frequently in their descriptions of you? Nice? Bodacious? Crazy? Party animal? Quiet? Brainy? Driven? Funny?

As you flip through the pages, keep track of the descriptions that surface most frequently. Are any of the adjectives like those Paul used in the verse above to describe Christians: compassionate, kind, humble, forgiving, loving, thankful?

Christ said each of us is to be a light to our own corner of the world. You should be the bright spot in people's lives. If you truly are, you'll read about it in your yearbooks.

See also: Matthew 5:13–16; 28:18–20; Galatians 5:22–25

▪▪ THE MULTIPLICATION FACTOR

> *As evening approached, the disciples came to him and said, "This is a remote place, and it's already getting late. Send the crowds away, so they can go to the villages and buy themselves some food." Jesus replied, "They do not need to go away. You give them something to eat."*

> MATTHEW 14:15–16

When this bit of dialogue took place, dusk was settling over the Sea of Galilee. The thousands of people tagging along after Jesus were hungry, and there was no McDonald's nearby. The disciples could hear the thousands of children begging to go home to eat. So they urged Christ to adjourn the waterfront meeting. Their solution was to let the people fend for themselves: "Send the crowds away!"

But Jesus shook his head. "They do not need to go away," he said. "*You* give them something to eat."

I imagine some of the twelve disciples glanced at each other and rolled their eyes. It had been a long, hot day. *Sure, Jesus,* Peter may have giggled at Christ's seemingly absurd suggestion. There simply was nothing to eat—nothing, that is, except a sack lunch donated to the cause by a kid who undoubtedly had overheard Christ talking with the disciples.

The child didn't have much—just a few pieces of bread and some fish—but he gave what he had. One of the disciples, Andrew, counted the bread and fish, then shrugged. "Here is a boy with five small barley loaves and two small fish, but how far will they go among so many?" The question was not unreasonable. But Andrew forgot he was talking to Christ, who once declared: "I am the bread of life. He who comes to me will never go hungry."

Each day we face similar situations. Christ has asked of us the apparently impossible: to be his ambassadors in a dying world; to be his witnesses at home, at work, at school; to *give people something to eat.*

That entails things like reaching outside of your clique for friends, being more open about sharing your faith, setting a positive example by not gossiping or lying. In other words, it means *living* the gospel—*being* the "Good News." We can analyze the odds against us, and shrug off the task because of our limited talent, time, and money. Like Andrew, we can focus on our *insufficiency.*

Or, like the young boy, we can focus on Christ's *sufficiency.* When we give Christ what little we have, he will take it and multiply it. The result now, as then, will be abundantly beyond what anyone can ask or dare think.

See also: Matthew 19:26; Mark 1:17; John 6:35

⠿ POINTS TO PONDER – POPULARITY

> *How can you believe if you accept praise from one another, yet make no effort to obtain the praise that comes from the only God?*

> **JOHN 5:44**

Popularity is what men and women think of us; character is what God and angels know of us.

THOMAS PAINE

Popularity is evanescent; applauded today, forgotten tomorrow.

EDWIN FORREST

Popular opinion is the greatest lie in the world.

THOMAS CARLYLE

Avoid popularity; it has many snares, and no real benefit.

WILLIAM PENN

Seek not the favor of the multitude; it is seldom got by honest and lawful means. But seek the testimony of the few; and number not voices, but weight them.

IMMANUEL KANT

Those who are commended by everybody must be very extraordinary men, or, which is more probable, very inconsiderable men.

LORD GRÉVILLE

The love of popularity seems little else than the love of being beloved; and is only blamable when a person aims at the affections of a people by means in appearance honest, but in their end pernicious and destructive.

WILLIAM SHENSTONE

The greatness of a popular character is less according to the ratio of his genius than the sympathy he shows with the prejudices and even the absurdities of his time.

ALPHONSE DE LAMARTINE

The way to gain a good reputation is, to endeavor to be what you desire to appear.

SOCRATES

The common people are but ill judges of a man's merits; they are slaves to fame, and their eyes are dazzled with the pomp of titles and large retinue. No wonder, then, that they bestow their honors on those who least deserve them.

HORACE

Admiration is a very short-lived passion that immediately decays upon growing familiar with its objects.

JOSEPH ADDISON

Men think highly of those who rise rapidly in the world; whereas nothing rises quicker than dust, straw, and feathers.

JULIUS CHARLES HARE

The idol of today pushes the hero of yesterday out of our recollection; and will, in turn, be supplanted by his successor of tomorrow.

WASHINGTON IRVING

Reputation is rarely proportioned to virtue. We have seen a thousand people esteemed, either for the merit they had not yet attained or for what they no longer possessed.

CHARLES DE SAINT DENIS EVREMOND

See also: Exodus 23:2; Proverbs 27:21; Matthew 7:13–14, 8:18

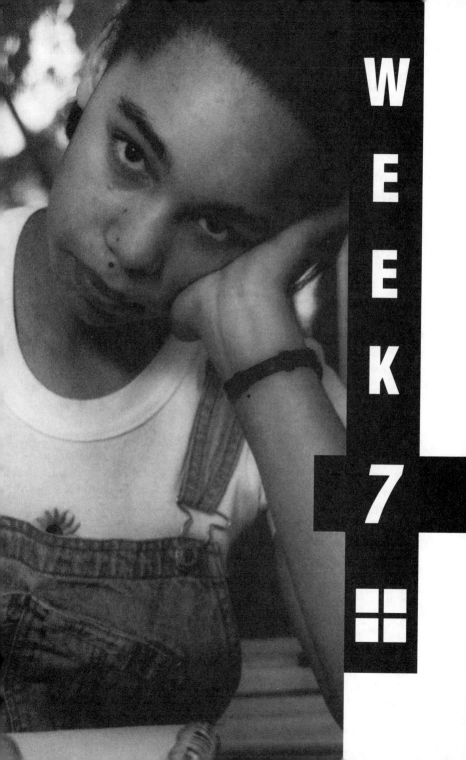

WEEK

7

■■ DOWN, BUT NOT OUT

Be still, and know that I am God.

PSALM 46:10

Sometimes adults act as if stress affects only men and women who juggle jobs and kids and mortgages. They forget what it feels like to wander from classroom to classroom with your guts in a knot and your nerves stretched tighter than violin strings.

Stress: Your teacher calls on you for an answer you don't know. Heads turn, eyes wait. Your skin flushes and suddenly you feel very hot and very dumb.

Stress: You've been trying to get the courage to ask the new girl out. Will she even know who you are? Your hands go clammy as you dial her number. The phone rings and someone—must be her mother—answers. "Is Diane there?" you ask. "Yes, could I tell her who's calling?" the voice says. "Uh, no . . . I mean, I think I've—like—got the wrong number," you blurt as you suddenly hang up.

Stress: Classmates treat you like a leper since you became a Christian. Even your best friend ignores you.

Stress: After twenty-two years of marriage, your parents announce they no longer love each other and are filing for divorce.

Stress: Your team could tie the game with a field goal, but the coach wants to gamble on fourth down and go for the win. He decides on a run and fingers you to carry the ball. You take the handoff and slam straight ahead. A helmet smashes into your ribs and the ball pops loose. "FUMBLE: NUMBER 26," the loudspeakers boom. The stands erupt with a low-pitched razz of boos, and humiliation grips you like a coronary.

You try to pretend these things don't matter, but that ache inside tells you they *do*. Your mind taunts you with slow-motion, instant replays, eroding your self-confidence with each showing. You can bite your nails to the knuckle, but if you'd force yourself to stop, be still, and get reoriented, you'd discover God is close at hand.

That's what Psalm 46:1 is all about: God offers instant help when you face the big squeeze of stress and heartache. The ultimate security is knowing he is there . . . and always will be. He's given his spirit to guide, strengthen, and help you respond to whatever comes up, because you're part of his family. And as a member of it, you also have other Christian brothers and sisters to support you.

"I am God," the last three words in the verse say. That gives you certain bragging rights—the right to say, "I am God's child."

Stop what you're doing right now. No matter what is going on around you or inside you, put it all out of your mind. Clear your head. Pause a moment and blurt it out: "*I am God's child.*"

Say it again, this time with an exclamation point.

Try it different ways: "*I* am God's child!" "I am *God's* child!" "I am God's *child!*" And smile when you say it.

You're not just another somebody on the treadmill of life. You're not a street orphan. You're *somebody.* You have the benefit of a rich and royal heritage, of being linked directly to the King of kings.

Knowing that, there's one thing you need to do. You need to start living like it.

See also: Matthew 11:28–30; John 14:27; 1 Thessalonians 5:10–11

✚ THE SINGLE LIFE

> *I would like you to be free from concern. An unmarried man is concerned about the Lord's affairs— how he can please the Lord. But a married man is concerned about the affairs of this world—how he can please his wife—and his interests are divided. An unmarried woman or virgin is concerned about the Lord's affairs: Her aim is to be devoted to the Lord in both body and spirit. But a married woman is concerned about the affairs of this world—how she can please her husband.*
>
> 1 CORINTHIANS 7:32–34

I am married. Many of my friends are married. And most of my friends who aren't, want to be. One of these single friends feels very bad that Mr. Right has yet to cross her path. When she didn't marry within a reasonable amount of time after graduation, she began to wonder what was wrong with her. Unfortunately, she views singleness like a disease. And every time she attends a wedding, she feels a little discarded, hurt, and bitter. She thinks God owes her a husband . . . and has never considered that he could have other, better plans for her life.

In contrast, I have another friend who developed such a love relationship with God that he has purposely not married. He knows how much time and energy marriage demands. He knows the personal and financial matters he'd face with a wife and kids. So he chose not to split his loyalty and love to God. Today, his "family" consists of hundreds of orphans living in the shantytowns of Mexico. Having quit his job and sold his possessions, he's free from outside concerns and has dedicated his entire life to serving these young poor — in a way that no married man or woman could.

The institution of marriage began when God created Eve for Adam. "It is not good for the man to be alone," God said. That's not the case for *every* man or woman — singleness is just the thing for some. Christ (a bachelor) indicated that some people are specifically called to the single life, and "have renounced marriage because of the kingdom of heaven" (Matt. 19:12). Paul (also a bachelor) later wrote, "It is good for a man not to marry" (1 Cor. 7:1).

They wanted people to know that marriage is an *option* — it's not for everyone — and that there are some very good things awaiting those who pursue God's calling to the single life.

See also: 1 Corinthians 7:8–9, 26–31

:: DEAR DIARY . . .

> *Let the word of Christ dwell in you richly as you . . . sing psalms, hymns and spiritual songs with gratitude in your hearts to God.*

> COLOSSIANS 3:16

Some people keep daily journals or diaries in which they chart their innermost thoughts and feelings. My sister had one. It was pink and flowery, with a little gold lock. She thought she had the only key. She did. But I had a paper clip that worked just as well.

In the Bible, many of the psalms are so personal that reading them feels as if you were snooping in someone's diary. Take

Psalm 51, for example. Written by King David, it records his deepest sorrows after he had an affair with a neighbor and then killed her husband. Other psalms are just as autobiographical and personal.

Try your hand at writing a psalm, patterned after those in the Bible. Keep it as personal as a diary. When finished, rewrite the words on a 3 x 5 card and tape it in your Bible as Psalm 151.

O Lord, you know me inside out.

> *When I feel* _____

> *Or think* _____

Even then I know you will understand.

My future is laid bare before you.

> *You know my concerns about* _____

> *And how I worry about* _____

But I know I can trust you to guide me.

I give thanks to you, O Lord,

> *Even though* _____

> *And even when* _____

Because I know you are in control, no matter what.

You are the stronghold of my life.

> *I shall not fear* _____

> *Or concern myself with* _____

For you will hold me, protect me, and comfort me
All the days of my life.

See also: Psalm 33:3; Ephesians 5:19; James 5:13

:: JUST LIKE YOU

The Lord your God goes with you; he will never leave you nor forsake you.

DEUTERONOMY 31:6

There was a time when Paula knew her father. It was back when she was about twelve. He seemed like the perfect father: he coached her softball team, took the family on long vacations, and kissed her mother each day before leaving for work.

But he changed over the years. He sometimes didn't come home at night. And each week there seemed to be more empty booze bottles in the trash. She didn't know what caused the changed behavior; all she knew was that he'd become unrecognizable as the father she once knew and trusted.

Then, a month before she left for college, she watched as he loaded his belongings into a U-Haul trailer and left to start a new life with his secretary, who was barely older than Paula herself. He seemed like a forty-one-year-old fool, she thought, and then burst into tears. She'd always looked to her father for guidance in the past. Whatever he did was right ... if only because he was grown up. But as she discovered, there is no such thing as a grown-up person.

It's a dramatic moment when you first discover your parents have major character flaws and failings. Perhaps it hit you when your mom or dad, tired from a long day, lashed out at you with uncharacteristic anger. You might have done nothing to provoke them, aside from being in the same room at the wrong time. Yet they bombarded you with hurtful, howitzer words.

There are days when you probably feel more shocked than angry at their behavior. But you really shouldn't be too surprised, because the Bible says that such actions are what mark us as people. "*All* have sinned and fall short of the glory of God" leaves no one out, including parents. So if you expect them (or anyone else, for that matter) *not* to let you down, you can expect to be disappointed.

People never act like you want them to. Teachers and bosses can be unfair and overly demanding. Family members can be rude and selfish. Even friends can be biting and cruel. But then, you have your failings, too. Like your parents, you are not immune from that "mark of humanity." You, too, respond to others in hurtful, negative ways.

At such times, God doesn't hold a grudge or twist your arm until you act better. He simply waits for you to realize your sin, and then he wipes it from his memory. And he expects the same of us. As Christ said, "If you have anything against someone, *forgive*—only then will your heavenly Father be inclined to also wipe your slate clean of sins" (Mark 11:25 *The Message*).

That means you must recognize that your parents aren't "grown up" or perfect. You need to accept them for who they are: people who are basically *just like you.*

See also: Mark 11:25; Romans 3:23

▪▪ THE BIG KAHUNA

You know that those who are regarded as rulers of the Gentiles lord it over them, and their high officials exercise authority over them. Not so with you. Instead, whoever wants to become great among you must be your servant, and whoever wants to be first must be slave of all. For even the Son of Man did not come to be served, but to serve, and to give his life as a ransom for many.

MARK 10:42–45

I once had a boss who treated everyone like dirt. She barked orders louder than a Marine drill sergeant and screamed hysterically at the least provocation. "Do this!" "Do that!" She wanted no one to forget that she was the boss.

I was unlucky enough to report directly to her, and my office was just down the hall. So my head was on the chopping block daily. My only reprieve was when she left town.

One day when my boss was on a business trip, I entered her cavernous office and glanced around quickly to make sure no one else was nearby. Then I slipped into her big, comfortable chair, leaned back and propped my feet on her sprawling desk.

"Someday," I thought, "I'll be in charge. I'll say 'Jump!' and they'll jump."

This attitude of wanting to be in control is, I suppose, natural enough. We want to be the Big Kahuna and give orders rather than take them. We want to be honored and esteemed. We'd like strangers to know our name and recognize us on the street. We tire of being pawns on someone else's chessboard, and would like to wield a little power ourselves for a change.

The Bible, however, has quite a different emphasis. "Whoever wants to become great among you must be your servant," said Christ, adding that he himself vacated heaven not to be a ruler of the masses, but to be a servant of many. He daily demonstrated this when he befriended the sick, the poor, the homeless. He washed a lot of feet. He demonstrated his Lordship by *not* lording.

"In humility consider others better than yourselves," Paul writes to the Philippians, adding: "Your attitude should be the same as that of Christ Jesus." The rub is that we are followers of a man whose attitude didn't get him crowned. It got him killed.

See also: Matthew 25:31–46; Philippians 2:1–11

▪▪ CLEARING THE ROADS

Bear with each other and forgive whatever grievances you may have against one another. Forgive as the Lord forgave you.

COLOSSIANS 3:13

What starts as a light snow of lace-like flakes suddenly turns to a blizzard. What seems beautiful—a backdrop for a picture-perfect postcard—suddenly rages. Driving snow slashes with an arctic wind, obscuring vision and deepening drifts.

School loudspeakers blare: classes are immediately dismissed. You bundle up and trudge to your car as others scramble for the bus. You arrive home just as the streets become impassable and the city shuts down.

Eventually the snowplows come, heaving great plumes of snow skyward, pushing the snow back to once again allow traffic through. The barrier is removed. A city once paralyzed becomes a city revived.

When we hold grudges—refusing to forgive *and* forget—we block the communication between ourselves and God. Drifts of unfeeling concern pile up inside of us, chilling our hearts. But forgiveness is like the snowplow—once again opening the roadway. It sweeps the barriers aside and allows communication to be restored.

The Bible tells us to forgive whatever grievances we have ... as the Lord forgave us. His forgiveness of us is often linked to our forgiveness of others. "But you don't know the hurt I've faced," you charge. "I was knifed in the back by someone I thought was my friend. Forgive? You've got to be crazy! Forget? Never!"

Such thoughts were probably not far from Peter's mind when he came to Jesus and asked, "Lord, how many times shall I forgive my brother when he sins against me?" He mentally ran down the list of wrongs others had done him. "Up to seven times?" he probed, probably hoping that Jesus would say, "Don't be silly—you've got rights, too. Let others do you in two, maybe three times at most ... and then get them back." But Jesus actually answered, "I tell you, not seven times, but seventy-seven times."

In other words, as long as it's snowing, keep the snowplows moving.

See also: Matthew 6:14–15; 1 Corinthians 13:4–5

:: POINTS TO PONDER– FORGIVENESS

If you forgive men when they sin against you, your heavenly Father will also forgive you. But if you do not forgive men their sins, your Father will not forgive your sins.

MATTHEW 6:14–15

It took me a long time to learn that God is not the enemy of his enemies.

MARTIN NIEMOLLER

I think I may have to go through the agony of hearing all my sins recited in the presence of God. But I believe it will be like this—

Jesus will come over and lay his hand across my shoulders and say to God, "Yes, all these things are true, but I'm here to cover up for Peter. He is sorry for all his sins, and by a transaction made between us, I am now solely responsible for them."

PETER MARSHALL

"I can forgive, but I cannot forget," is only another way of saying, "I will not forgive."

HENRY WARD BEECHER

A Christian will find it cheaper to pardon than to resent. Forgiveness saves the expense of anger, the cost of hatred, the waste of spirits.

HANNAH MORE

Forgiveness: the odor of flowers when they are trampled on.

ANONYMOUS

Always forgive your enemies—nothing annoys them so much.

OSCAR WILDE

If we refuse mercy here, we shall have justice in eternity.

JEREMY TAYLOR

There is no use in talking as if forgiveness were easy. We all know the old joke, "You've given up smoking once; I've given it up a dozen times." In the same way I could say of a certain man, "Have I forgiven him for what he did that day? I've forgiven him more times than I can count." For we find that the work of forgiveness has to be done over and over again.

C. S. LEWIS

Good to forgive; best to forget.

ROBERT BROWNING

See also: Isaiah 1:18; Matthew 6:12; 18:21–35; 1 John 1:9

WEEK 8

■ SPARK

> *You will receive power when the Holy Spirit comes on you; and you will be my witnesses in Jerusalem, and in all Judea and Samaria, and to the ends of the earth.*
>
> ACTS 1:8

I know that some people laugh at my idealism—
　At my effort to be a "light of the world,"
　　At my eager, though often meager, attempt to
Shine a ray of brightness into an otherwise
　Dark, dank world.
There are times when I understand why people laugh and ridicule.
　I mean, how dumb can I possibly be
　　To think my life really matters amidst
Four billion other people on this cinder speck of a planet
　In this distant corner of the spinning, reeling universe.
Dear God, sometimes my light seems no brighter
　Than the lambent glow of a single lightning bug
　　On a very cold, black night—
　　Barely a flicker, just a quick spark
　Amidst darkness deeper than shade of a shadow.
Yet a spark, just a solitary spark is all it takes
　To get a bonfire flashing and flaming, burning and blazing.
So, dear God, help me realize my life does matter,
　That being a Christian matters,
　　That telling others about your greater light matters.
Teach me the secret of high-voltage living
　So that I might be your light in my world,
　　Beginning at home and spreading
　　To everyone within my circle of influence.
Dear God, renew in me your Holy Spirit power—
　That heavenly charge that enables mere lightning bugs
　　To flame bright as lightning bolts.

See also: Matthew 5:14–16; John 14:12–14

:: HEALTHY HATE

Love must be sincere. Hate what is evil; cling to what is good.

ROMANS 12:9

Shortly after I became engaged to be married, panic struck. I was in love with one girl—desperately in love. Yet never before had so many other girls appealed to me. I felt like I do in a restaurant: every dish on the menu looks good, but I can have only one.

That moment was the beginning of my realization that to say yes to one girl meant I had to necessarily say no to all others. I had to wrench my affections from all who were not worthy of my complete love. And that's exactly what I did on my wedding day when I vowed to take my fiancé "to be my lawfully wedded wife and, *forsaking all others*, love her until death would us part."

The decision to "forsake all others" is central to a happy marriage. It is also central to a fulfilling relationship with God. "No one can serve two masters," Christ said. "Either he will hate the one and love the other, or he will be devoted to the one and despise the other." If our love for God is sincere, we must despise all else that hinders our relationship.

Malcolm Muggeridge describes the concept this way: "To believe greatly, it is necessary to doubt greatly." That is, if we believe in God, we must develop a radical skepticism toward all that is not godly. We must be great doubters of all that is evil if we are to be true lovers of that which is good.

To say yes to God means we must comparatively say no to *everything*, even very good things: to the United States of America, Frisbees, Julia Roberts, *Vogue*, the Ford Mustang, Sunset Beach, Brad Pitt, waffle cones, the Super Bowl, hot tubs, the Yankees, Algebra I, bubble gum. It means we must say no to our families and, yes, especially ourselves. We can gain life only after we lose it.

"To believe greatly, it is necessary to doubt greatly." In his book *Wishful Thinking*, Frederick Buechner calls our doubts "the ants in the pants of faith." Doubts keep faith active. Doubts keep that which is unworthy of it. Doubts keep our

-38; Luke 10:25–27; Titus 2:11–14

..LK

You are the body of Christ, and each one of you is a part of it.

1 CORINTHIANS 12:27

As a Christian you are a member of the worldwide family of God. Some people call this family the "universal church," consisting of believers from your classroom to the shanty huts of Nigeria. The apostle Paul calls it the "body of Christ."

Jesus is the head of this spiritual body which, like a human body, consists of hands and feet and noses and muscles and bones. Each one of us is a different part or organ, with a specific role to play.

As a writer, I may be a hand, etching out ideas on blank sheets of paper. I could start feeling inferior because I'm not as glamorous as a mouth or as critical to the body's health as a heart. On the other hand, I could feel very snooty that at least I'm not a toe, tucked inside a sweaty sock and stuffed in a shoe. But the way Paul talks, no single part is more important than any other one.

"If the whole body were an eye," Paul writes, "where would the sense of hearing be? If the whole body were an ear, where would the sense of smell be? But in fact God has arranged the parts in the body, every one of them, just as he wanted them to be."

Admittedly, Paul is no David Letterman. But I think he's trying to be funny here by saying, in effect: If you woke up one morning with a body shaped like a 150-pound ear or a monster eyeball, you'd be good for little more than the freak-show circuit. You could get a job at the circus. But the fact is, no part of the body stands alone. Every part is critical to the *whole*.

"The eye," continues Paul, "cannot say to the hand, 'I don't need you!' And the head cannot say to the feet, 'I don't need you!'"

Some of the most vital organs of the body remain out of sight—tucked deep beneath layers of skin, veins, and muscle. Yet your body would suffer greatly without them. The same is true of the body of Christ. A church with just a pastor and organist wouldn't be much of a church. The body of Christ needs *you* if it's to operate as God intended it to. If you start feeling your work is always done in the background without notice, realize that you're probably right where God wants you.

You may feel less useful than What's-his-name, but that inferiority is in your eyes only. Remember, it's *God* who "arranged the parts in the body . . . just as he wanted them to be."

See also: Romans 12:3–8; 1 Corinthians 12:12–26

■■ POVERTY

> *I was hungry and you gave me nothing to eat, I was thirsty and you gave me nothing to drink, I was a stranger and you did not invite me in, I needed clothes and you did not clothe me, I was sick and in prison and you did not look after me.*

MATTHEW 25:42–43

For most of us, "being poor" is simply not having enough money to go out on Friday night. But there's another side, told by a young mother from Tennessee.

Here I am, dirty, smelly, with no proper underwear beneath this rotting dress. I don't know about you, but the stench of my teeth makes me half sick. They're decaying, but they'll never be fixed. That takes money.

What is poverty? Poverty is getting up every morning from a dirty and illness-stained mattress. Sheets? There are no sheets. They have long since been used for diapers, for there are no real diapers here, either. That smell? That *other* smell? You know what it is—plus sour milk and spoiled food. Sometimes it's mixed with the stench of onions cooked too often. Onions are cheap. What dishes there are, I wash in cold water. Why don't I use hot water? It takes money to heat it. Hot water is a luxury. We don't have luxuries.

Poverty is watching gnats and flies devour my baby's tears when he cries, which is much of the time. Poverty is children with runny noses, even in the summer. Paper handkerchiefs take money, and you need all your rags for other things. Antihistamines are for the rich.

Poverty is dirt. Every night I wash every stitch my school-aged child had on and just hope that the clothes will be dry enough to wear when morning comes.

Poverty is remembering—remembering quitting school in junior high because the nice children from nice homes were so cruel about your clothes and your smell.

My daughter? She'll have a life just like mine, unless she's pretty enough to become a prostitute. My boys? I can already see them behind prison bars, but it doesn't bother me as it would you. They'll be better off behind prison bars than behind the bars of my poverty. And they'll find the freedom of alcohol and drugs—the only freedom they'll know.

I leave my despair long enough to tell you this: I did not come from another place, and I did not come from another time. I'm here now, and there are others like me all around you. (Abridged from an article by C. E. Jackson, Jr. Copyright *Christian Herald*. Used by permission.)

That woman has this feeling. She thinks you're probably not interested in her life and problems. Perhaps you'd like to prove her wrong.

See also: Proverbs 31:8–9; Matthew 25:31–46; 2 Corinthians 9:6–15

:: DIRTY HANDS

Jesus said, "Simon son of John, do you truly love me?" He answered, "Yes, Lord, you know that I love you." Jesus said, "Take care of my sheep."

JOHN 21:16

Everyone has dreams. You might dream of the time you reach a certain goal or overcome a certain problem. You might dream of the time your family all become Christians, or the time Jesus returns to earth.

The lady you read about yesterday also has dreams—dreams for the time there will be money enough for the right kind of food, for medicine, for a toothbrush, for needles and thread and . . . but she knows it's just a dream, just like you know it's a dream when you see yourself as the Super Bowl MVP or the President.

Maybe you're like me. When I first read about the woman, I tried to put her out of my mind. She made me feel uncomfortable. She gave poverty a face, a personality. She gave poverty an odor. I could *smell* her life—the sour milk and spoiled food. I could smell the stink of onions cooked too often. Onions are cheap. And I could smell that *other* stench. Sure, I felt pity for her, but I knew pity wouldn't feed her children. So I simply turned the page.

But the lady never went away. Every time I opened my Bible, she was never far away. I thought of her when Jesus told Simon Peter to "Take care of my sheep." I thought of her when Jesus said, "Whatever you did for one of the least of these brothers of mine, you did for me." Yet I didn't know what to do. Should I call Goodwill and donate my bed? Should I give my lunch or movie money to those starving-children organizations? Would anything I do *really* matter?

Most of my crusades are like New Year's resolutions—somewhere along the line the promise dies. But then I got to reading in Romans and caught a glimpse of what being a Christian is all about. In Romans 8:29 Paul talks about how we're supposed to be "conformed to the likeness" of Jesus. And who was Jesus? He was proof that God didn't just feel sorry for our problems. He didn't just pat us on the head and say he cared. He put his life where his mouth was. A father may say to his sick child, "I'd do *anything* to make you better," but God actually did it.

Part of Christ's reason for coming to earth was to raise up people for whom living for others would not just be a short-term crusade, but a way of life. He sought to duplicate himself in us—to create people who would give *love* a face, a personality; people dedicated to helping dreams come true.

See also: Isaiah 53; Matthew 25:31–46; James 2:14–26

▪▪ THE RISK WORTH TAKING

A crushed spirit who can bear?

PROVERBS 18:14

I grew up in San Diego where there is an abundance of beaches, and always loved the water. Sometimes I even skipped school to go surfing. And when the summer Olympics were on TV, I'd watch the swim meets for hours.

When I entered high school, I wanted to be the star swimmer on the varsity team. So I bought a pair of goggles and a bun-hugger suit, and showed up for workouts one day. But I wasn't prepared for the kind of endurance swimming the coach expected, and I nearly drowned. I eventually swam breaststroke in junior varsity meets, but even then I generally finished last. I wasn't very good at accepting failure and quit out of embarrassment.

I later tried the water polo team, but that was an equally dismal failure. I was virtually paralyzed with muscle cramps during workouts, and was cut from the tryout roster after the second week.

It wasn't until my freshman year in college that I got over the humiliation and tried out for another athletic team. At the urging of a friend, I went out for the crew team and — miraculously — discovered I was good at it. I even earned a varsity letter my first year. And that taught me something important about failure: If I hadn't tried (and risked) failure, I'd never have known my limitations or capabilities. I didn't do well at swimming or polo, but I gave athletics another chance and discovered what I could do.

That has helped me in other areas. I try not to back off from doing something because it appears too difficult or because I don't do well the first time around. When I do fail, it's an indicator I may not have talent in that specific area. But it's also an encouragement to try something else.

See also: Ecclesiastes 9:10; Isaiah 40:28–31; Hebrews 12:1–3

■ POINTS TO PONDER – PERSEVERANCE

Since we are surrounded by such a great cloud of witnesses, let us throw off everything that hinders and the sin that so easily entangles, and let us run with perseverance the race marked out for us.

HEBREWS 12:1

By perseverance the snail reached the ark.

CHARLES SPURGEON

I know of no more encouraging fact than the unquestionable ability of man to elevate his life by a conscious endeavor.

HENRY DAVID THOREAU

It is not necessary to hope in order to undertake, nor to succeed in order to persevere.

CHARLES THE BOLD

There is no royal road to anything. One thing at a time, all things in succession. That which grows fast withers rapidly; that which grows slowly endures.

J. G. HOLLAND

Victory belongs to the most persevering.

NAPOLEAN

He that has patience can have all that he will.

BENJAMIN FRANKLIN

Great works are performed, not by strength, but by perseverance. He that shall walk, with vigor, three hours a day, will pass, in seven years, a space equal to the circumference of the globe.

SAMUEL JOHNSON

No road is too long to the man who advances deliberately and without undue haste; and no honors are too distant for the man who prepares himself for them with patience.

JEAN DE LA BRUYÈRE

The virtue lies in the struggle, not in the prize.

RICHARD MILNES

There are two ways of attaining an important end—force and perseverance. Force falls to the lot only of the privileged few, but austere and sustained perseverance can be practiced by the most insignificant. Its silent power grows irresistible with time.

MADAM SWETCHINE

The conditions of the conquest, are always easy. We have but to toil awhile, endure awhile, believe always, and never turn back.

WILLIAM GILMORE SIMMS

See also: Romans 5:1–5; James 1:2–4; 2 Peter 1:5–9

WEEK 9

▪▪ THE BIG SQUEEZE

Where sin increased, grace increased all the more.

ROMANS 5:20

I feel the same familiar pressure creeping over me today, Lord. It squeezes me from the outside and eats me from the inside ... until I feel my life would be a lot less complicated if I weren't a Christian. Nothing personal, Lord, but following you is the hardest thing I've ever attempted.

Sometimes I get tired of having to make so many choices— choices between what I want and what I think you want for me. Should I or shouldn't I wander over to that magazine rack and thumb through the latest *Playboy?* Should I or shouldn't I eat another doughnut? Should I or shouldn't I return the extra dollar the store clerk mistakenly gave me? Should I or shouldn't I join in the fun when the guys start joking about the fat girl in history class? Should I or shouldn't I have a couple of drinks at the party Friday night? Or for that matter, should I even go to the party?

All of these choices are getting to me, Lord. I mean, what do you expect? Perfection? That's kind of silly, because I don't even come close. I figure I must be just a big goof in your eyes. But then I'm confused, because the Bible is full of stories about people who even out-gross me. Your Word reads like a document of depravity, yet the losers generally come out the winners.

Rahab, the prostitute, is commended by Paul and James for her great faith. Solomon, who broke every rule in the book, later became known as the wisest man in the Bible. Moses and David were both cold-blooded killers; Noah occasionally got plastered; Peter turned his back on Christ; Sarah laughed in your face, and, well ... talk about surprise endings!

Lord, my pressures aren't eased by knowing someone in ancient history committed murder or adultery and then went on to be listed in the Bible's Hall of Faith. But it helps me greatly to know you didn't write them off as failures just because they failed. In all their struggles and sin, they were driven back to you.

Help me do the same. Draw me back with your love when I feel like turning away and fleeing. And overwhelm me with your grace as you must have also overwhelmed Rahab, Solomon, Moses, David, Noah, Peter, Sarah, and all your other tired, life-worn, bedraggled followers.

See also: Romans 7:14–25; 2 Corinthians 4:16–18; 12:7–9

IF I HAD MY LIFE TO LIVE OVER AGAIN

Be still, and know that I am God.

PSALM 46:10

Advice from adults often begins the same way: "When I was your age . . ." They somehow expect you to follow in their footsteps. But the perspective on life offered below is not so . . . well, so pre-historic, and it may help you realize there are greater powers than your history teacher, who expects your oral report and 10-page paper by tomorrow. It was written late in life by an anonymous friar in a Nebraska monastery, but don't let that turn you away:

If I had my life to live over again, I'd try to make more mistakes next time. I would relax, I would limber up, I would be sillier than I have been this trip.

I know of very few things I would take seriously. I would take more trips. I would be crazier. I would climb more mountains, swim more rivers, and watch more sunsets.

I would do more walking and looking. I would eat more ice cream and less beans. I would have more actual troubles, and fewer imaginary ones.

You see, I'm one of those people who lives life prophylactically and sensibly hour after hour, day after day. Oh, I've had my moments, and if I had to do it over again I'd have more of them.

In fact, I'd try to have nothing else, just moments, one after another, instead of living so many years ahead each day. I've been one of those people who never go anywhere without a thermometer, a hot-water bottle, a gargle, a raincoat, aspirin, and a parachute.

If I had to do it over again I would go places, do things, and travel lighter than I have.

If I had my life to live over I would start barefoot earlier in the spring and stay that way later in the fall. I would play hooky more. I wouldn't make such good grades, except by accident.

I would ride on more merry-go-rounds.

I would pick more daisies.

See also: Psalm 39:4–7; 100:3; Matthew 6:25–34

▪▪ "NOBODIES" WANTED

The word of the Lord came to me, saying, "Before I formed you in the womb I knew you, before you were born I set you apart; I appointed you as a prophet to the nations." "Ah, Sovereign Lord," I said, "I do not know how to speak; I am only a child."

JEREMIAH 1:4–6

God had big plans for Jeremiah, as he does for each of us. That doesn't mean God has fingered you to be another "prophet to the nations," a worldwide evangelist, or a best-selling gospel singer. But he has big plans for you, nevertheless. And that may simply mean staying right where you are and being that spark of life, that ray of hope in your classroom, at home, on the racquetball court, or behind the grill flipping hamburgers for minimum wage.

With God, the size of your ministry is not important—it's your attitude toward service that matters. Are you willing to do whatever the Lord wants you to do, go wherever he wants you to go, speak to whomever he brings into your path—even if it's only the fry cook who shares your shift?

The idea of being that open to God scared Jeremiah. When God unfolded his plan for Jeremiah's life, the young man's knees rattled. He felt insecure and unqualified. He felt God had made a mistake. "I'm just a sophomore!" he might as well have said. "This is a great compliment and all, but you've got the wrong person for the job. I've never done anything like this before. Besides, I can't even talk correctly. I garble my words, mix metaphors, and st-st-stutter. Sorry, God, but it sounds like you want a superstar. I'm a nobody."

The Lord's response? "Do not say, 'I am only a child.' You must go to everyone I send you to and say whatever I command you. Do not be afraid of them for I am with you."

In a sense, none of us will ever measure up to what we *think* God needs in us. There will always be someone older, flashier, prettier, smoother—someone who could *really* win others to the Lord by the sheer magnetism of his or her personality, looks, or even testimony. But the thing is, God doesn't need superstars and leaders, as Jeremiah found out. *God* is the leader—and the only thing he needs and wants are people who, regardless of age or talent, are willing to go when he says, "Follow me!"

If you choose to follow the Lord (and make no mistake about it, it is *your* choice), you needn't worry about any limitations you think you have. His promise in Matthew 28:20 stands: "I'll be with you as you do this, day after day after day, right up to the end of the age" (*The Message*).

See also: Proverbs 3:5–6; Romans 8:31–32; Ephesians 4:10–16

■■ MAYBE TOMORROW

> ***Devote yourselves to prayer, being watchful and thankful.***
>
> COLOSSIANS 4:2

I keep telling myself I need to pray more. But something always comes up. I suppose it's been weeks since I've talked with God. Maybe months. It's hard to remember.

Last night, I planned to go up to my room after dinner, dig my Bible out of my closet, and read a chapter or two. And later, spend some quality time in prayer. But the Bible was tucked under some magazines, which seemed more interesting. You know how it goes.

Then the phone rang. It was just a friend from work who wanted to switch hours. But we got to talking about that new girl on the job—the one with the California tan and cover-girl smile. When

I hung up and glanced at the clock, I couldn't believe it was already time for my favorite show on TV, a two-hour special.

Before I knew it, the night was shot. I had to take a quick shower and make a sack lunch for work the next day.

It was hard to read my Bible and pray at 11:30 after all that. No energy. I tried, but kept thinking about that new girl and a thousand other things. So I ended up just mumbling a few bless 'ems before drifting off to sleep.

I know I need to pray more. I mean, to *really* pray. Other Christians I know say prayer changes things. So it must be important. But time slips away so easily. You know how it goes.

Maybe things will be different tomorrow. Yeah, maybe.

See also: Psalm 116:1-2; Matthew 7:7; 1 Thessalonians 5:17

██ A FAMILY MATTER

You received the Spirit of sonship. And by him we cry, "Abba, Father." The Spirit himself testifies with our spirit that we are God's children.

ROMANS 8:15-16

One day when I was traveling through England, 7,500 miles from home, I decided to call my parents. I wasn't in trouble. I didn't even need money. I simply wanted to chat.

So I tracked down the nearest phone booth, punched the international access code for direct calling and, within a few moments, heard their familiar voices. I now don't remember anything we talked about, except that at the close of conversation my father said, "Son, it's 3 a.m. here ... but we still love you. It's good just to hear your voice."

The sound of familiar voices can be very comforting. Given the emphasis the Bible places on prayer, I believe God longs just to hear our voices. And not just when we're in trouble—sometimes just to chat.

Yet people make prayer seem so formal. They prescribe everything from stance (on your knees) to timing (preferably before sunrise). Others even use a special language (Thy, Thou, Thine), while some think you can't talk to God directly—you must first go through an "operator" (such as a priest).

There's only one problem with all of this formality: Christ was often very *informal* in the way he prayed. In the Garden of Gethsemane, shortly before his crucifixion, Christ grew deeply distressed. The Bible says he fell on the ground and prayed, beginning, "Abba, Father..." He addressed God not just as Father, but also with the Aramaic word *Abba*, meaning Daddy.

Such familiarity was not reserved solely for Christ, the Pope, and perhaps a few other spiritual Supermen and Wonderwomen. According to this verse from Romans, we are God's own children. That means we have direct access to him, regardless of the time of day or night. Also, we needn't address him as "Sir!" or "Omnipotent Creator!" or "Almighty God!" *Daddy* is good enough. It's very personal—just the way you'd want to address your heavenly Father, who never tires of hearing his children's voices.

See also: Matthew 18:1–4; Mark 14:32–36; Ephesians 6:18

■■ PROBLEMS WITH PRAYER

Pray in the Spirit on all occasions with all kinds of prayers and requests. With this in mind, be alert and always keep on praying for all the saints.

EPHESIANS 6:18

The only time I used to talk to God was when I was stretched out on my mattress, late at night. Whatever prayers I managed were punctuated by snores.

Discouraged, I shifted my prayer time to early mornings. But then, too, my mind was in a half stupor. (I tend to sputter awake in the morning, like an old car on a very cold day.)

So I got desperate. Determined to remain awake when I talked with God about things that were important to me, I started praying when I was most awake: while taking a shower. And I've done much of my praying ever since while bathing.

This developed a whole new interest in God for me. No longer did prayer seem like a chore I grudgingly put off or tried to whip through. To "pray on all occasions with all kinds of prayers ... and keep on praying" was impossible for me when I thought of God like a big shadow floating around space somewhere. It became more feasible when I realized how much prayer was like talking with a best friend—someone I wanted to be with and talk with at all times of day.

So I began to expand my prayer times. Not only did I pray in the shower, but I began to pray while driving, while jogging on the beach, while sitting in math class bored stiff. Whenever someone came to mind during the day, I immediately prayed for that person. If I felt thankful, I'd pause right then and whisper a quick "Thanks!" to God; if desperate, a quick "Help!" The spontaneity kept both my prayers fresh and me awake.

This attitude of staying in touch with God throughout the day is seen in the life of a man who called himself Brother Lawrence. In his book *The Practice of the Presence of God*, he writes that some of his closest moments with God were *not* spent on his knees. He tried to remain in constant communion with God throughout the day—and found he was sometimes most able to do that "in the noise and clatter of my kitchen, while several persons are at the same time calling for different things."

Try practicing the presence of God yourself—amidst the noise and confusion of the world you'll be facing today.

See also: Luke 18:1–8

⊞ POINTS TO PONDER–PRAYER

Pray continually.

1 THESSALONIANS 5:17

Prayer is conversation with God.

CLEMENT OF ALEXANDRIA

Tell God all that is in your heart, as one unloads one's heart to a dear friend. People who have no secrets from each other never want for subjects of conversation; they do not weigh their words, because there is nothing to be kept back. Neither do they seek for something to say; they talk out of the abundance of their hearts, just what they think. Blessed are they who attain to such familiar, unreserved intercourse with God.

FRANÇIS DE LA MOTHE FÉELON

Since the lines have been cleared between the Lord and me, the telephone has never stopped ringing.

BERNARD L. CLARK

What men usually ask for when they pray to God is that two and two may not make four.

RUSSIAN PROVERB

Seven days without prayer make one weak.

FOLK SAYING

Prayer is not an argument with God to persuade him to move things our way, but an exercise by which we are enabled by his Spirit to move ourselves his way.

LEONARD RAVENHILL

Most of us have much trouble praying when we are in little trouble, but we have little trouble praying when we are in much trouble.

RICHARD P. COOK

"Praying for particular things," said I, "always seems to me like advising God how to run the world. Wouldn't it be wiser to assume that He knows best?" "On the same principle," said he, "I suppose you never ask a man next to you to pass the salt, because God knows best whether you ought to have salt or not. And I suppose you never take an umbrella, because God knows best whether you ought to be wet or dry." "That's quite different," I protested. "I don't see why," said he. "The odd thing is that He should let us influence the course of events at all. But since He lets us do it in one way I don't see why He shouldn't let us do it in the other."

C. S. LEWIS

The fewer words the better prayer.

MARTIN LUTHER

There is nothing that makes us love a person so much as praying for him.

WILLIAM LAW

Many a person is praying for rain with his tub the wrong side up.

SAM JONES

Much of our praying is just asking God to bless some folks that are ill, and to keep us plugging along. But prayer is not merely prattle; it is warfare.

ALAN REDPATH

The sweetest side of any fruit or vegetable is the side which grows toward the sun.

J. H. BOMBERGER

You need not cry very loud: he is nearer to us than we think.

BROTHER LAWRENCE

What a person is on his knees before God, that he is—and nothing more.

ROBERT MURRAY MCCHEYNE

See also: Proverbs 15:8; Matthew 7:7–11; Mark 11:24

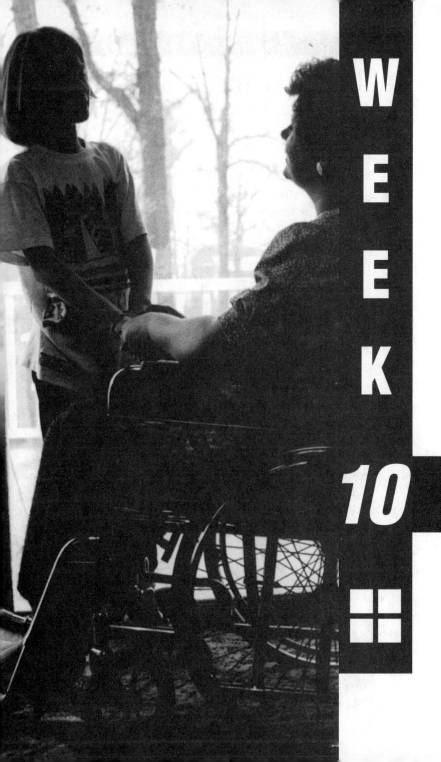

▥ FUTURE FEARS

> *We are hard pressed on every side, but not crushed; perplexed, but not in despair.*
>
> 2 CORINTHIANS 4:8

There was a time your world seemed safe, secure. But you were much younger then. Your primary needs were met by others. Food? Clothes? The future? These were not yet concerns of yours.

But you grew, only to find your boundaries too confining. And now, you're so stifled you can't even breathe. So you thrash harder, fighting for more space—an elbow here, a knee there.

Finally, someone seems to get the message, and you slowly feel yourself being forced from your "nest." Pressures build. Your heart pounds wildly. All of the walls around you seem to collapse. There was no way to anticipate that it would be like *this*. It's all happening too fast. You try to dig in your heels to fight the pressure, but it's no use. You can't even get a fingerhold. You feel crushed by the dark tunnel you're being forced down—so scared you can't even cry.

And then, push turns to pull. Poised at the threshold of your new world, you feel cold fingers grabbing. Eyes stare. People are all smiles, but their strange faces are more like hideous masks. Panic strikes with sledgehammer force and you start to bawl. Your body shakes with each loud, racking sob.

"There, there. Everything will be all right," someone tries to comfort. But you're not so sure . . .

Congratulations! *You have just been born.*

If birth from a baby's perspective seems familiar now, it's because the feelings and sensations are not unlike those you face as you look ahead. You want to pursue your future, but you're scared of the unknown. Everything seemed so familiar, so secure a few years ago. "The Good Old Days," we call those times. Yet we know we must leave them—we must necessarily grow, develop, mature. College? Marriage? Career? These are the unfamiliar worlds toward which we grope.

We want to find God's specific will for our lives, but the process of finding it can be heartrending. There's always pressure, pain, and darkness. Yet just around the corner is a bright, new world full of new faces, challenges, and adventures.

Rest assured. Everything *will* be all right. Not because teachers, parents, pastors, or friends say so, but because *God* says so: "For I know the plans I have for you," declares the Lord, "plans to prosper you and not to harm you, plans to give you hope and a future" (Jeremiah 29:11).

See also: Isaiah 42:16; Hebrews 10:35–36; James 1:2–4

■■ THE OTHER SIDE

Whoever wants to save his life will lose it, but whoever loses his life for me will find it.

MATTHEW 16:25

When I knew Susan, she had everything going for her: good grades, good looks, good job. Then she was in a car accident and was never the same.

I never quite understood what happened, but the drugs the doctors used to save her life apparently caused her to gain a huge amount of weight. She ballooned to two hundred and plenty pounds and lost most of her friends. Those who didn't know her just assumed she was some blimpo who gorged herself on cream pies and doughnuts. Trouble was, Susan gained weight even when she didn't eat.

"Now I know," she once told me, "how it feels to be on the other side of the fence, to feel like you're a nobody because you don't look like the girls in *Glamour*."

I later went away to college and didn't see Susan for about four years. One day after graduation I was in her area and decided to stop by. She was as big as ever, and wore a dress that looked like a Sears pup tent. But she also wore a smile that indicated she wasn't as self-conscious about her weight.

"All my life," she said, "I was programmed to think success. I had it all. And I couldn't understand why other people weren't as together as me, you know? It was like I was the yardstick, and they didn't measure up. And God may have been somewhere out there, but I didn't need him because I was doing fine on my own.

"But now I understand—that I didn't understand anything before. The needs and hurts of others? Didn't see them. Never noticed because I was all that mattered. That all changed when I became the Sumo Lady. You look like this, it's hard to have much pride.

"Now? I'm not so full of myself," she continued. "And when there's less of me, there's more room for God. The amazing thing? It's easier now to help others. To really care. To risk everything for God.

"The ironic thing?" she asked. She paused a moment and looked down. And then she came up smiling. "The irony is, I thank God for the accident. It took the car to lose myself. But that was really nothing. I lost me, but found something more important that can never be taken away."

See also: Mark 8:34–38; Luke 12:15; 1 Corinthians 10:12–13

■■ THE SIGNAL

We have this hope as an anchor for the soul, firm and secure.

HEBREWS 6:19

I feel it coming on again: fear, crawling under my skin.
   That quiet, unspoken, never-admitted feeling ...
   That haunting, ever-nagging, turn-your-back-and-run panic ...
Fear: not of spiders or big dogs or the pull of the ocean,
   But fear of my ability, people's reaction, the future, mistakes.
O Lord, help me to face my fears and turn them around.
   Be my anchor; stand by me until I—
Stop fearing I might lose in love ...
   But fear instead that I might never love at all.
Stop fearing there are others better than me ...
   But fear instead that I will never discover my true potential.
Stop fearing I might not meet others' expectations ...
   But fear instead that I might never know yours.
Stop fearing what lies ahead tomorrow, next week, next month, next year ...
   But fear instead that I might never experience life's drama today.

Stop fearing hurt and sorrow and tears . . .
   But fear instead that I will never know the pains of growth.
Stop fearing I might fail . . .
   But fear instead that I might never try.
Stop fearing others will laugh at me . . .
   But fear instead that I might never learn to laugh at myself.
O Lord, help me to anchor my life on your hope
   Instead of my fear.
O Lord, I know an adventurous life can never be fear-free . . .
   But at least help my fears to be my soul's signal for rallying
   Instead of running.

See also: Psalm 34:4; Romans 8:15; 1 John 4:18

▉ WORKOUT

> **Continue to work out your salvation with fear and trembling.**
>
> Philippians 2:12

When in training for my college rowing team, I couldn't let up. Six days a week my alarm rang at 4:30 a.m. Whether I felt like it or not, I'd drag myself out of bed and into my sweats. Breakfast was two raw eggs smooshed together in a glass of orange juice and guzzled on my way out the door.

Headlights of my old Chevy cut a swath of brightness in the black, predawn day as I headed for the boathouse for a two-hour workout before classes. After each workout, I'd be soaked with sweat, and there were many times when my hands would be raw and bloody from the constant twisting and rubbing of the oar. The salt water of Mission Bay stung my palms—until my eyes welled with tears.

Sometimes I'd sit alone in the locker room after practice and think I was crazy to stick with it. But I didn't quit because I knew it took that kind of work and determination to meet my athletic goals.

I sometimes feel a certain guilt in knowing I have not often set and pursued spiritual goals with the same relentless work and determination. There have been times I've neglected my salvation to the point of becoming spiritually flabby. Those aren't enjoyable times, because I know I've fallen short of God's standards. So I dig in and redouble my efforts to work out my salvation amidst daily battles with sin. It's not easy, but then God never promised it would be.

Being a Christian in a non-Christian world is a sweaty struggle. It's the hardest thing you'll ever do. But huge rewards await those who face the struggle, work diligently, and don't let up.

See also: 1 Corinthians 9:24–27; Hebrews 12:1–13

■■ BUSINESS MATTERS

I have brought you glory on earth by completing the work you gave me to do.

JOHN 17:4

For years, an unfinished overpass leading nowhere arched across Highway 101 outside of San Jose, California. It spanned the freeway at a height of about 70 feet, but stopped abruptly with steel rods poking like spaghetti from either end. All construction equipment had been removed from the site, and the towering mass of concrete and twisted steel served as a sort of monument to "unfinished business."

Whenever I passed beneath that "overpass to nowhere," I thought of the unfinished business lingering in my life: the books half read, thank-you letters never mailed, and paintbrushes never cleaned. Perseverance in such day-to-day projects is important, but there are two areas in which our commitment to completion is even more crucial: *People Projects* and *God Projects.*

People Projects. Is there a friend you have unfinished business with–maybe someone you wronged and need to ask forgiveness from? Perhaps there's a classmate you said you'd pray for, but never did. Is there someone you need to befriend–perhaps that quiet girl who always sits alone at lunch? When did you last tell anyone *sincerely,* "I love you"?

God Projects. Unfinished business here includes secret sins you may still be holding onto–parts of your life you'd like others and especially God not to know about. Perhaps you made a vow to God that you never kept. Have you abandoned any spiritual goals? Are there friends or family members you've neglected to tell about Jesus Christ and salvation?

In the 33 years Christ lived on earth, he fulfilled God's every purpose for his life. He loved the unlovable, healed the sick, rejected temptation . . . and pointed people to God. Toward the end of his life he could rightfully say, "I have brought you glory on earth by completing the work you gave me to do."

But there was one last matter. It was necessary that he die on the cross for our sin. And as he hung there, he cried his final words, "It is finished!"

He had no unfinished business. Do you?

See also: Luke 14:28–33; Hebrews 12:1–3

▓▓ SECOND NATURE

> *Those who hope in the Lord will renew their strength. They will soar on wings like eagles; they will run and not grow weary, they will walk and not be faint.*
>
> ISAIAH 40:31

A simple task like walking is not something you probably give much thought to—unless, of course, you've injured yourself badly enough to require therapy. And then you feel like a squat-legged infant again: wiggly and rubber-kneed as you first learn to balance. Very slowly and very painfully you progress to the step-rock-step-rock pattern that is, for most people, second nature—as simple as breathing.

The same is true of any learned task. As I work now at my computer to compose this paragraph, I do not fret about where to place my fingers, or hunt and peck to find certain letters. Years ago, that keyboard looked impossibly complex. But with a certain amount of training and coaching, typing became second nature.

No one needs to tell you there are times when being a Christian in a non-Christian world feels next to impossible. You face temptations that blitz your mind daily: things like lust and sex, a chance for revenge, use of a credit card, a second helping of cream pie. You feel discouraged, beat, and wonder if there's any hope for you. *Will you ever be spiritual?* You wonder about God. Will he finally just give up on you and stomp off, leaving you to manage on your own?

It's appropriate that Christ referred to the act of becoming a Christian as being "born again." In God's eyes you are a newborn infant—and he wants to train you ... his way. That training process is difficult. At times, very difficult. But God has not left you to blunder your way in darkness like some sadistic father who turns the light out on his wobble-kneed infant and then laughs when the kid smashes into a table.

Rather, "God works in you to will and act according to his good purpose." That's to say he helps you in your Christian walk, and he's there to pick you up again if you fall. It's when you take his outstretched hand and follow him that walking feels like second nature. And it's then that you feel most able to not just *walk*, but to "s*oar* on wings like eagles" and "*run* and not grow weary."

See also: Philippians 2:12–13; 1 John 1:5–7

:: POINTS TO PONDER – INDIVIDUALITY

> *Each one should test his own actions. Then he can take pride in himself, without comparing himself to somebody else, for each one should carry his own load.*
>
> GALATIANS 6:4

We require individualism which does not wall man off from community; we require community which sustains but does not suffocate the individual.

ARTHUR M. SCHLESIGNER

Everything without tells the individual that he is nothing; everything within persuades him that he is everything.

XAVIER DOUDAN

Individuality is either the mark of a genius or the reverse. Mediocrity finds safety in standardization.

FREDERICK E. CRANE

The greatest works are done by the ones. The hundredths do not often do much—the companies never; it is the units—the single individuals, that are the power and the might. Individual effort is, after all, the grand thing.

CHARLES SPURGEON

If the world is ever conquered for Christ, it will be by every one doing their own work, filling their own sphere, holding their own post, and saying to Jesus, Lord, what wilt thou have me to do.

THOMAS GUTHRIE

There is as much difference between us and ourselves as between us and others.

MICHEL DE MONTAIGNE

We forfeit three-fourths of ourselves in order to be like other people.

ARTHUR SCHOPENHAUER

The things that are wrong with the country today are the sum total of all the things that are wrong with us a individuals.

CHARLES W. TOBEY

It is an absolute perfection ... to know how ... to get the very most out of one's own individuality.

MICHEL DE MONTAIGNE

At bottom every man knows well enough that he is a unique being, only once on this earth; and by no extraordinary chance will such a marvelously picturesque piece of diversity in unity as he is, ever be put together a second time.

FREIDRICH NIETZCHE

It is a blessed thing that in every age some one has had the individuality enough and courage enough to stand by his own convictions.

ROBERT INGERSOLL

I am one individual on a small planet in a little solar system in one of the galaxies.

ROBERTO ASSAGIOLI

The race advances only by the extra achievements of the individual. You are the individual.

CHARLES TOWNE

In heaven an angel is nobody in particular.

GEORGE BERNARD SHAW

See also: 1 Corinthians 15:58; Ephesians 4:16; Philippians 2:1–3

W
E
E
K

11

:: HOT UNDER THE COLLAR

> *In your anger do not sin: Do not let the sun go down while you are still angry, and do not give the devil a foothold.*
>
> EPHESIANS 4:26–27

You're already late to class when that big-eared jock on the wrestling team blindsides you and sends your books flying.

"Hey, be careful or you'll drop your books," he laughs and keeps walking.

You scramble to pick up your ego and scattered belongings from the hall floor, feeling that familiar fire of anger creep up your neck. Your nerves go taut and your heart starts twanging away. You feel like jumping the bum and landing a haymaker to his head.

Such feelings are automatic and normal—you shouldn't feel uncomfortable that they exist. God didn't create you like a power-cooled, controlled-temperature Whirlpool fridge. But you do have a choice in how you *respond* to anger and other strong emotions. Paul suggests it's possible to respond in a way that doesn't go against God.

Your first impulse is to get revenge, if only to yell, "You stupid lughead, can't you see where you're going!" You want to stick up for your rights—to save face. But considering the guy's size, you realize you'll probably *lose* face if a fight were to break out.

Regardless of size, James suggests we ought to be "slow to speak and slow to become angry." Mark Twain had a comment on this matter: "When angry, count four; when very angry, swear." Maybe you should instead count to 10 or take a couple of deep breaths. The more time you have to think about your response, the less hurtful it will be.

"A gentle answer turns away wrath," wrote Solomon in Proverbs. In other words, be creative in an explosive situation. Adding fuel to a fire just makes a bigger fire. Dealing with people is much the same. You can often diffuse a potentially explosive situation with a touch of humor. For instance, you might try something like: "Hey, Mack, roller derby practice doesn't start for another week!"

However you respond, Paul suggests you deal with anger within the day. Stewing overnight may be great for a slab of barbecue meat. But with people it's the recipe for an ulcer.

See also: Proverbs 15:1; James 1:19–20

■■ PAPIER-MÂCHÉ FACADE

Through Christ our comfort overflows.

2 CORINTHIANS 1:5

When Christa's parents divorced, she wasn't surprised. There had been plenty of clues—the fights, the drinking, the accusations about unfaithfulness. But she was surprised by the volcanic feelings that erupted within her, especially since she considered herself a "strong" Christian.

Christa knew it was normal for Christians to feel crummy at times—as if their world were caving in. But she was afraid to talk to anyone about the depths of her despair, because she didn't know what they would think. Her friends had always considered her level-headed and emotionally calm. What would they say if they knew she was just hiding her feelings behind a papier-mâché smile that was beginning to crack?

Then one night as she lay crying in bed, she began to talk to God about the problems she faced. If anyone understood, she figured he would. She told God of her anger, bitterness, and confusion. She told him she felt totally crushed by her parents' situation and didn't think she loved her father. She told God there was something inside her that craved a daddy's shoulder to cry on, for a daddy's arms to hold her and give her a sense of confidence. Without that, she told God, she didn't feel like a whole person.

As weeks passed, God became that father she could turn to. That's not to say the going was easy. It was especially hard to cope during the lonely, stare-at-the-ceiling hours before she could fall asleep at night. She was still hurt. But she felt God wanted to help. By opening her heart to him, she gained the security and confidence to face her problems and the support to work them out.

See also: Psalm 5; 23; Matthew 11:28–30; John 14:27

⬛ A MATTER OF THANKS

Give thanks in all circumstances, for this is God's will for you in Christ Jesus.

1 THESSALONIANS 5:18

The day after Christmas was always the same around my house. My mom would start hassling me to write thank-you letters for gifts I'd received. Grandparents, aunts and uncles, cousins I hardly knew—everyone was due a note of thanks. Eventually—at least by March—I'd get the last of the cards mailed.

It's not just people we forget to thank. We often neglect God, too. Take some time to write a letter of thanks to God for the greatest gifts of all: his son, his forgiveness, his love. Perhaps there are other things you'd also like to thank him for.

Dear God,

I'd just like to say thanks for _____

_____

_____

I'd also like to thank you for _____

_____

_____

The gifts you've given me have really made a difference in my life. For example, _____

_____

_____

In closing, I'd just like to say: _____

_____

_____

Love always,

_____

See also: John 3:16; Luke 17:11–19: Romans 6:23; 8:28

■ THE DECIDING VOTE

The high priest asked him, "Are you the Christ, the Son of the Blessed One?" "I am," said Jesus. "And you will see the Son of Man sitting at the right hand of the Mighty One and coming on the clouds of heaven."

MARK 14:61–62

Imagine you're at Rockefeller Plaza in the concrete jungle of New York City, sitting in a black vinyl chair behind a wall of glass marked PERSONNEL. You fidget nervously with the small tear in the armrest as the somber-faced interviewer reviews your job application and then says, "For starters, tell me something about yourself."

To his infinite surprise you blurt, "Well, I'm Rocky's son." He stares at you, and then breaks into a deep, low chuckle. At which you reply, "And someday I'll be his chief aide—his right-hand man." Your interviewer now has a choice to make. Are you a Rockefeller or a fake? Chances are he'd decide the latter and notify security.

A similar situation existed when Christ stood before an elite gathering of chief priests and elders—the religious honchos of his day. In effect, they asked him to recite his résumé. His reply? He claimed to be the Son of God. And if that wasn't crazy enough, he said he would one day sit at God's right hand.

The inquisitors, at that point, had a decision to make: to either bow or give him a knuckle sandwich. Mark, one of Christ's twelve disciples, described what followed: "They all condemned him as worthy of death. Then some began to spit at him; they blindfolded him, struck him with their fists, and said, 'Prophesy!' And the guards took him and beat him." The cross was not far behind.

Jesus' claims of kinship with God led some to reject and eventually kill him. Those same words—and the life that backed them up—motivated others to alter their lives radically, to serve him . . . and even to die for him.

Some 2,000 years later that choice still stands. Is he King of kings or Kook of kooks? His bizarre claims demand a verdict. And you've got the deciding vote.

See also: Matthew 27:41–43; John 10:24–38

∎∎ THE MAYOR IS MOVING!

*For you know the grace of our Lord Jesus Christ,
that though he was rich, yet for your sakes be became
poor, so that you through his poverty might become rich.*

2 CORINTHIANS 8:9

Cabrini Green—if you'd ever want a taste of hell, this sprawling public-housing project in Chicago would be a good place to start. Sharp rat-a-tat bursts of gunfire echo regularly through its 81 highrises and row houses. Mysterious screams split the night, but no one dares to investigate. Gangs exercise total control of the estimated 14,000 people living there—raping, extorting, and murdering those who get in their way.

During the winter when I lived in a nearby suburb, Chicago's mayor made a much-publicized tour of Cabrini Green and told its terrorized residents, "You are going to live in security and safety." It seemed like a typical comment from a typical politician. Didn't the nut realize that even Chicago's police were powerless amidst the guns, gangs, and terror?

The following week, the mayor took things a step further and announced plans to temporarily move to Cabrini Green to see firsthand the problems of that crime-ridden neighborhood. City politicians said they'd never heard anything like it before. "It is a pretty dramatic thing to do," said one. MAYOR MOVING TO CABRINI! headlines screamed.

As I followed the story over the succeeding months, I couldn't help but think how Christ did much the same thing when he vacated heaven to live on earth. I imagine some of the angels thought it too radical and dangerous. They would have been right on both accounts.

But Christ knew he had to visit our planet to make it possible for us to experience life in all its glory—a taste of heaven in the midst of hell.

See also: John 3:16; 14:27; Philippians 2:3–11

■ WITH APOLOGIES TO LUKE

The angel said to them, "Do not be afraid. I bring
you good news of great joy that will be for all the people."
LUKE 2:10

And it came to pass in those days, that there went out a decree from managers of all department stores, large and small, that first payments on all Christmas purchases be delayed until February 1.

And the news met people with gladness, and they all went to their nearest Nordstroms, Saks, and, yea, even to Wal-Mart and Kmart, to freely buy. And they brought forth their packages, wrapped in colored tissues and bright ribbon, and laid them beneath their artificial trees; because that was fitting and proper during the yuletide.

And there were in the same season children abiding beside their bedroom windows, keeping watch over the skies by night. And lo, the glory of Saint Nick shone round about them, and they were sore afraid.

And the rotund little man said unto them, "Fear not. For behold, I bring you good news of great joy that will be for all children of affluent homes. For unto you will be given at dawn, computerized toys and dolls and train sets."

And it came to pass, the morning after the appearance, the children screamed with delight when they saw the gifts, and made known to their elders the message foretold the previous night.

Indeed, the elders knew their children had merely dreamed dreams; at their young ages they were sheltered from the true reality of credit cards, finance charges, and overdrawn accounts. And the children's parents kept all these things, and pondered them heavily within their hearts.

See also: Matthew 6:19–24; 1 Timothy 6:6–10

■ POINTS TO PONDER– THE INCARNATION

Today in the town of David a Savior has been born
to you; he is Christ the Lord.
LUKE 2:11

Since Christ's birth some 2,000 years ago, much has been written about this God/man and those years when he walked in our shoes. Planet Earth never had such a visitor, and writers have never gotten over it:

You can never truly enjoy Christmas until you can look up into the Father's face and tell him you have received his Christmas gift.

JOHN R. RICE

The hinge of history is on the door of a Bethlehem stable.

RALPH W. SOCKMAN

Santa Claus never died for anybody.

CRAIG WILSON

A man who was merely a man and said the sort of things Jesus said wouldn't be a great moral teacher. He'd either be a lunatic—on a level with a man who says he's a poached egg—or else he'd be the devil of hell. You must make your choice. Either this man was, and is, the son of God, or else a madman or something worse.

C. S. LEWIS

Christ is greater than our faith in him.

JAMES HASTINGS

Christmas is not just the birth of a baby; it is the heavenly father saying good-bye to his son.

ANONYMOUS

I sometimes think we expect too much of Christmas Day. We try to crowd into it the long arrears of kindliness and humanity of the whole year. As for me, I like to take my Christmas a little at a time, all through the year.

DAVID GRAYSON

A man may go to heaven without health, without riches, without honors, without learning, without friends; but he can never go there without Christ.

JOHN DYER

Christ is the great central fact in the world's history. To him everything looks forward or backward. All the lines of history converge upon him. All the great purposes of God culminate in him. The greatest and most momentous fact which the history of the world records is the fact of his birth.

CHARLES H. SPURGEON

Christmas is a son away from home.

NORMA ALLOWAY

I wish we could put some of the Christmas spirit in jars and open a jar of it every month.

GERALD STANLEY LEE

It is Christmas in the heart that puts Christmas in the air.

W. T. ELLIS

God and I have this in common—we both love his son, Jesus Christ.

LANCE ZAVITZ

You needn't worry about not feeling brave. Our Lord didn't—see the scene in Gethsemane. How thankful I am that when God became man he did not choose to become a man of iron nerves; that would not have helped weaklings like you and me nearly so much.

C. S. LEWIS

Questions about Christ's identity haven't changed much in 2,000 years. Either he was a full-tilt crazy with the asylum key, or he carried the key to unlock the entire universe. The choice is yours: Kook of kooks or King of kings.

S. RICKLY CHRISTIAN

See also: Luke 1:26–38; 2:1–20

WEEK 12

▪▪ MARKS OF A CHRISTIAN

The fruit of the Spirit is love, joy, peace, patience, kindness, goodness, faithfulness, gentleness and self-control. Against such things there is no law.

GALATIANS 5:22–23

Outwardly, Christians look like any other people you'd pass in the locker hall or mall. They don't wear uniforms and salute, like Scouts and soldiers. They don't all have the same weird kind of hairstyle, like Hare Krishna cultists. They don't wear special jackets or rings or have special handshakes, like members of some club or gang. They don't go to the same church, drive the same car, or listen to the same music.

So you might wonder: What's the big difference between a Christian and a non-Christian?

The Bible is clear that there should be very distinguishing characteristics. "If anyone is in Christ," the apostle Paul wrote, "he is a new creation; the old has gone, the new has come." In other words, when people become Christians, their insides are transformed. They aren't quite the same anymore. New life has begun!

This transformation occurs from the inside out. Christianity is not a fish insignia on your car or a gushy "Praise the Lord!" or hands held high in church. It's a seed of faith planted in the heart. And as that seed is nurtured, it begins to grow and sprout what Paul calls "fruit of the Spirit."

These nine characteristics—love, joy, peace, patience, kindness, goodness, faithfulness, gentleness, and self-control—are the marks of a true Christian. They are an indication that the seed of faith has sprouted and new life has begun. (In the following two-and-a-half weeks, we'll take a closer look at each of these characteristics. And you'll have an opportunity to take a personal inventory to determine how much "fruit of the Spirit" is growing in your life.)

No, you can't spot Christians in a mirror or across a crowded cafeteria. But they *are* somehow different. The next pages will describe a few of the ways *you* should be different.

See also: Matthew 7:15–23; 2 Corinthians 5:17

■ MARKS OF A CHRISTIAN–LOVE

The fruit of the Spirit is love.

GALATIANS 5:22

Of the nine "fruits of the Spirit" mentioned by Paul in the passage you read yesterday, love tops the list. It is not just another mark of a Christian, but the *birthmark* of a Christian–sort of like God's thumbprint in your life.

When asked what the greatest commandment was, Christ replied, "Love the Lord your God with all your heart and with all your soul and with all your mind." The second, he said, was like it: "Love your neighbor as yourself." In other words, your life as a Christian should be marked first by your love for God, and then by your love for others and yourself.

Love for God. If you think of God as a great shadow or force that flits about with the satellites, it will be difficult loving him. The Bible is clear that God is not some nebulous, celestial power, but a person as real as your best friend. That's why Christianity is not a religion, but a *relationship.* Your love for God can be measured by the amount of time you want to spend with him and by how much you allow him to influence your life. Is he a secret friend you're ashamed of, or is he someone you eagerly introduce others to? Have you told God you love him during the past week? He wants to know!

Love for others. Love loves the unlovely, the unloving, the unlovable. It doesn't care if it's loved in return. Said Christ, "Love your enemies and pray for those who persecute you.... If you love those who love you, what reward will you get?" Christian love turns a blind eye toward others' faults and keeps no record of wrong. It's patient, kind, and never fails.

Love for yourself. Many people have trouble with this. They wear many masks and try to appear smooth and controlled. But inside they're full of low self-esteem, perhaps because of their upbringing or because their looks or abilities don't measure up to those around them. Self-love is the recognition that you're a unique creation of God. He made *you* for a reason–with every scar and idiosyncrasy. You can love and accept yourself, because God first loved you!

"All mankind loves a lover," wrote Ralph Waldo Emerson. And as a Spirit-filled Christian, you should be the world's greatest!

See also: Matthew 22:35 – 39; Ephesians 3:14–20

■■ MARKS OF A CHRISTIAN–LOVE

The fruit of the Spirit is love.

GALATIANS 5:22

Shortly before Christ went to the cross, he gave his disciples some final instructions on living as Christians after he was gone.

"I will be with you only a little longer," he began, and then launched into his favorite topic. "A new commandment I give you: Love one another. As I have loved you, so you must love one another." Jesus probably paused at this point before adding the clincher: "All men will know that you are my disciples *if you love one another.*" In this verse, Jesus gives everyone who knows you the right to judge the validity of your Christianity ... based on your love for others.

With this in mind, consider that you've just been arrested for being a Christian. Could the prosecutors build a case (based solely on your observable love toward others) to find you guilty? Take a few minutes to jot down some of the evidence they would present against you in court:

_____

_____

_____

_____

_____

_____

What does the above evidence suggest about your Christianity? Do you have enough "fruit of love" in your life to be convicted?

See also: John 13:33–35; 1 Thessalonians 3:12

■ MARKS OF A CHRISTIAN–JOY

The fruit of the Spirit is . . . joy.

GALATIANS 5:22

If one of the distinguishing marks of a Christian is supposed to be joy, you wonder what went wrong. Why is it that many people view believers as a gloomy bunch of pious poops with personalities like soggy Cream of Wheat? They equate Christianity with suit-and-tie churchiness, nose-in-the-air stuffiness. What was meant to be a relationship that's full of joy has, in many cases, deteriorated to a form of religion full of stiff formality.

Somber Christians daily display the "costs" of following Christ: They've given up drinking, smoking, swearing, fornicating, and fighting. But they've also given up smiling and laughing and having genuine good ol' times every day of the week.

This is not a recent problem. Jesus frequently had confrontations with the stuffy, religious people of his day–people who thought they knew all about God, but didn't know how to live, laugh, or love. On days of fasting, they displayed drawn, hollow-eyed looks so others would recognize their sacrifice. They gushed flowery prayers and stood sad-eyed on street corners to advertise their supposed holiness. Their misery was infectious, because many people have been following their example ever since.

But Christianity isn't for deadheads. At least if you take Christ as the model. He was not so much a "man of sorrows" as a man of joy. We know he didn't stifle his tears–but he also didn't cover up his laughter and joy. He liked parties and fun and swarms of kids–because it was for things like this that the rigid Pharisees most criticized him. The stories he told were often of joyous feasts and celebrations. He likened the kingdom of God not to a convention of bleary-eyed librarians, but to a rollicking banquet and a wedding feast–tremendous times of joy. And some of his most widely reported miracles (turning water into wine and multiplying the fish and loaves) were done for the pleasure of those around him.

Joy was indeed "serious business" with Christ. And if you're filled with his Spirit, you also ought to be filled with his joy!

See also: Psalm 100; Romans 15:13

▦ MARKS OF A CHRISTIAN–JOY

The joy of the Lord is your strength.

NEHEMIAH 8:10

When you think of the word "joy," chances are you equate it with some sort of emotional high or outward jollity. You might think of how you feel when a teacher tells you, "The test is canceled," or the rush you experience when kissed by someone other than your grandma. It might be when your braces come off, you win a big race, or get accepted to college. You might think of smiles and laughter and good times.

But joy is much more than all of these things. It's not a fleeting feeling that's here today, gone tomorrow. You can be down in the dumps and still have joy. Consider the story of Job. His crops, flocks, herds, and home were destroyed, his servants and family were killed, and *he* broke out with excruciating boils "from the soles of his feet to the top of his head." A boil is like a grape-sized pimple. If you've ever had one, you can imagine the torture Job felt with thousands–even in his armpits and between his toes. Yet he still spoke of his "joy in unrelenting pain" (Job 6:10).

As for Jesus, he spoke about joy over a very sad dinner with a group of his best friends. The occasion: his "going away" supper–the last meal he had before the Roman goon squad nailed him to a cross. Jesus was more or less saying his good-byes, and everyone in the room, including him, was probably bawling and sobbing like a baby. But he didn't mention the tears. He talked about joy (John 15:11).

Joy doesn't depend on good times. If it did, many people would be left out. It doesn't depend on good luck or good news–both of which are fleeting and often outweighed by bad luck or bad news. It doesn't depend on smiles, which are skin deep. Joy is soul deep, and should be evidenced in your life when you can find nothing to smile about.

How has your understanding of joy changed? Jot down a few of your new concepts in the space below:

_____

_____

_____

_____

_____

_____

See also: 2 Corinthians 7:4; Hebrews 12:2–3; James 1:2–4

■■ MARKS OF A CHRISTIAN – PEACE

The fruit of the Spirit is ... peace.

GALATIANS 5:22

I once read about two artists who were commissioned to paint a picture signifying their individual concepts of perfect peace.

The first artist pulled on his boots and hiked into the Rockies outside Boulder, Colorado. Several miles beyond the nearest ski lift, he erected his easel beside a secluded lake known only to locals. Poised in this Hallmark-perfect setting, he filled his canvas with the lace-like haze of early morning as it dissolved before the first golden rays of daylight. The brilliant greens of the towering pines were so vivid in the painting that the artist's oils seemed to smell of the forest. A hawk floated lazily across the sky, its image reflected in the mirror of the lake's still surface. It was the kind of picture you'd expect to see on a greeting card or on the cover of your grandpa's *Reader's Digest*.

The second artist applied for press credentials, hopped a red-eye flight for war-torn Lebanon, and set his easel near the gutted building which then served as headquarters of the terrorist Palestine Liberation Organization. Shielded by a heap of bricks and twisted girders, the artist filled his canvas with a fiery maelstrom as violent as that which fell from the bombers overhead. Rockets cut a swath of destruction across the painting—so lifelike that explosions and screams seemed to roar with each stroke of his brush. But there, just outside the ruins in the crook of a bent little tree, was a bird resting atop a nest of eggs. Seemingly insulated from the chaos all about, it sat with its tiny head tucked serenely beneath its wing.

The second artist was the one who captured the essence of genuine peace—the kind of peace Christ offers those who heed his call, "Come to me, all you who are weary and burdened, and I will give you rest." His rest doesn't come in an isolated setting where you are immune from people and problems. It comes when you need it most. Being a Christian doesn't guarantee you freedom from hardships and confusion. For many, it seems to *ensure* them. But in the middle of difficulties you face at home, work, or school, God will help develop the "fruit of peace" in your life. That is, peace amidst your biggest wars.

See also: Psalm 4:8; Matthew 11:28–30

:: POINTS TO PONDER – CREATION

"To whom will you compare me? Or who is my equal?" says the Holy One. Lift your eyes and look to the heavens: Who created all these? He who brings out the starry host one by one, and calls them each by name. Because of his great power and mighty strength, not one of them is missing. Why do you say, O Jacob, and complain, O Israel, "My way is hidden from the Lord; my cause is disregarded by my God"? Do you not know? Have you not heard? The Lord is the everlasting God, the Creator of the ends of the earth. He will not grow tired or weary, and his understanding no one can fathom.

ISAIAH 40:25–28

No philosophical theory which I have yet come across is a radical improvement on the words of *Genesis,* that "in the beginning God made Heaven and Earth."

C. S. LEWIS

Nature is beautiful, always beautiful! Every little flake of snow is a perfect crystal, and they fall together as gracefully as if fairies of the air caught water-drops and made them into artificial flowers to garland the wings of the wind!

LYDIA M. CHILD

It's easier to suppose that the universe has existed from all eternity than to conceive a Being beyond its limits capable of creating it.

PERCY BYSSHE SHELLEY

One summer night, out on a flat headland, all but surrounded by the waters of the bay, the horizons were remote and distant rims on the edge of space. Millions of stars blazed in darkness, and on the far shore a few lights burned in cottages. Otherwise there was no reminder of human life. My companion and I were alone with the stars: the misty river of the Milky Way flowing across the sky, the patterns of the constellations standing out bright and close, a blazing planet low on the horizon. It occurred to me that if this were a sight that could be seen only once a century, this little headland would be thronged with spectators. But it can be seem many scores of nights in any year, and so the lights burned in the cottages and the inhabitants probably gave not a thought to the beauty overhead; and because they could see it almost any night, perhaps they never will.

RACHEL CARSON

There is no more reason to believe that man descended from some inferior animal than there is to believe that a stately mansion has descended from a small cottage.

W. J. BRYAN

That man is the richest whose pleasures are the cheapest.

HENRY DAVID THOREAU

Grant that, this day and every day, we may keep our shock of wonder at each new beauty that comes upon us as we walk down the paths of life.

UNKNOWN

Thunder is that great artillery of God Almighty.

WILLIAM TEMPLE

There are joys which long to be ours. God sends ten thousand truths, which come about us like birds seeking inlet; but we are shut up to them, and so they bring us nothing, but sit and sing awhile upon the roof, and then fly away.

HENRY WARD BEECHER

Flowers are the sweetest things that God ever made and forgot to put a soul into.

' H.W. BEECHER

I think that I shall never scan a tree as lovely as a man. A tree depicts divinest plan, but God himself lives as a man.

UNKNOWN

There is a signature of wisdom and power impressed on the works of God, which evidently distinguishes them from the feeble imitations of men. Not only the splendor of the sun, but the glimmering lights of the glowworm, proclaims his glory.

JOHN NEWTON

What a pity flowers can utter no sound—a singing rose, a whispering violet, a murmuring honeysuckle—oh, what a rare and exquisite miracle would these be!

H. W. BEECHER

Nature is the living, visible garment of God.

JONATHAN WOLFGANG VON GOETHE

How singular, and yet how simple, the philosophy of rain! Who but Omniscient one could have devised such an admirable arrangement for watering the earth!

ANDREW URE

See also: Genesis 1; Psalm 104; Romans 1:18–20

WEEK

13

:: MARKS OF A CHRISTIAN–PEACE

Peace I leave with you; my peace I give you. I do not give to you as the world gives. Do not let your hearts be troubled and do not be afraid.

JOHN 14:27

Peace for some people means a six-pack of beer or a couple of joints. Others try to overcome hassles by going on an eating binge and downing a carton of Ding Dongs. Some play mental gymnastics with their problems and wind up with ulcers from worrying. Others try to vent their frustrations by screaming a lot or going on a spending spree. There are as many ways to find peace as there are people seeking it.

But Christ said that only one way works. His way. The peace he gives is different from what the world gives. Take some time today to write down what some of those differences are. Use the space below. The verses on the next page can help give you some ideas.

The World Says PEACE Is:	The Bible Says PEACE Is:
A wild party on Friday night	_____
Enough drugs	_____
The latest issue of *Penthouse*	_____
_____	_____
_____	_____

Honestly evaluate your own life. Which side of the line most accurately describes your response to stress and hassles? Begin working with God to make his "Peace Plan" more evident within you.

See also: Psalm 23; Matthew 6:25–34; Philippians 4:6–7

:: MARKS OF A CHRISTIAN– PATIENCE

The fruit of the Spirit is . . . patience.

GALATIANS 5:22

Patience: It's an odd word in this "aspirin age" where relief from pain and problems is just two pills and a swallow of water away. In a society that pioneered "presto living" through such everyday commodities as microwaves, frozen gourmet dinners, and minute rice, patience seems like some concept from a time warp—as outdated as typewriters and phonograph records.

Yet the Bible's standards haven't changed. Patience is the trademark stamp of God's Holy Spirit in your life. As with love, joy, peace, and the other fruit of the Spirit, God wants to grow more patience in your life: patience to persist when you fail the first time; patience to endure hardship and personal struggles without griping, knowing you'll somehow be stronger in the end; patience to listen when your parents ramble about "back when I was your age ..."

Patience is not honking when stuck on the freeway behind the little old lady from Pasadena; it's not kicking a hole in the door when locked out by your kid sister. Patience is waiting for God's absolute best in your life, whether a marriage partner or a job. This kind of patience will not sprout overnight. The making of a Christian who is Christlike is a timely process that God does not rush.

The book of James talks a lot about patience. James launches the first chapter with the words: "Consider it a sheer gift, friends, when tests and challenges come at you from all sides. You know that under pressure, your faith-life is forced into the open and shows its true colors" (James 1:2–4, *The Message*). It's important that we let pressure do its work, he adds, "so you become mature and well-developed, not deficient in any way." In other words, the hardships you'd prefer to sidestep are the very things you should patiently and joyfully endure.

Grit your teeth, but don't forget to smile! Don't let your daily problems at home, work, or school drive you to panic—let them drive you joyfully to patience ... and to a closer relationship with Christ. As a Christian, you are to be what Amy Carmichael calls "the Lord's diehards, to whom can be committed any kind of trial of endurance, and who can be counted upon to stand firm whatever happens."

James closes his book on the same topic: "You see farmers do this all the time, waiting for their valuable crops to mature, patiently letting the rain do its slow but sure work. Be patient like that. Stay steady and strong" (James 5:7–8, *The Message*). Don't give up or give in—the fruit of patience is well worth the wait.

See also: Romans 12:12; Hebrews 12:1–12

:: MARKS OF A CHRISTIAN– PATIENCE

Be patient, bearing with one another in love.

EPHESIANS 4:2

Perhaps you've seen those lapel buttons that read: "PBPGIN-FWMY." *Please be patient—God is not finished with me yet.* You are God's special project—he is at work in your life, but he's not done.

Just as God hasn't given up on you, so you shouldn't give up on others who also are God's workmanship. Each person (Christian or not) is of infinite value to the Lord—created in God's image—and in each, his "construction project" is at a different stage of completion. Knowing how patient God has been with you should help you demonstrate patience toward others and enable you to "bear with one another in love," as Paul writes.

Take a few minutes to think about ways in which God has shown patience toward you. Your life has undoubtedly changed since you became a Christian, but what areas still need work? List some of these "hot spots" below:

_____

_____

_____

_____

God works patiently. He doesn't spot something negative in your life and then twist your arm or beat you with a stick until you make it right. He loves you until you, of your own free will, decide you want what he wants. God's patience toward you is not unique—it's how he responds to everyone because patience is part of his character. And he wants it to be part of yours, too.

Think of people who most try your patience: the motor-mouth in English, your slob brother, your nice but overbearing Aunt Anita. With their names in mind, jot down a few ideas about how you might be more patient with them:

_____

_____

_____

_____

In the days to come, ask God to help you practice patience—to be the "Lord's diehard" toward these people.

See also: Ephesians 2:10; Philippians 1:4–6; 2 Peter 3:9–15

:: MARKS OF A CHRISTIAN—KINDNESS

The fruit of the Spirit is ... kindness.

GALATIANS 5:22

Kindness doesn't take a lot of time or ingenuity. It is such a little, seemingly inconsequential, thing. Yet this mark of a Christian in your life will help make life for others seem consequential. That's because little things matter to most people—things like a warm smile, encouraging word, or squeeze of the hand. Without such gestures, their lives become a blur of uninterrupted days; with them, moments punctuated by exclamation points.

Kindness is an offer to help clean up after the dog, a "thank-you" note, a whispered "I love you." Kindness is listening to someone who hasn't brushed his teeth in days, a handful of flowers given "just because," a careful compliment, a word of praise. Kindness is taking your kid sister and her giggly-faced friends to the bowling alley and staying to laugh with them later over Cokes, consoling the new kid who just moved from Indiana, talking computers with the geek who walks like an old man with tight shoes.

Kindness is refraining from saying something you have every right to say, dropping "you always" and "you never" from your vocabulary, letting your dad be right. Kindness is letting someone else go first, ignoring a fault, holding no grudge. Kindness is allowing Christ to work through you to touch lives and show compassion in very ordinary ways.

In the back of my Bible is a yellowed sheet of paper containing a somewhat musty poem by an unknown author. Though the style is dated, the words never will be:

Is anybody happier because you passed his way?
   Does anyone remember that you spoke to him today?
This day is almost over, and its toiling time is through.
   Is there anyone to utter now a friendly word for you?
Can you say tonight in passing with the days that slipped so fast,
   That you helped a single person, of the many that you passed?
Is a single heart rejoicing over what you did or said?
   Does one whose hopes were fading now with courage look ahead?
Did you waste the day, or lose it? Was it well or poorly spent?
   Did you leave a trail of kindness or a scar of discontent?

See also: Hebrews 13:2

:: MARKS OF A CHRISTIAN–
KINDNESS

> *If anyone gives even a cup of cold water to one of these little ones because he is my disciple, I tell you the truth, he will certainly not lose his reward.*
>
> **MATTHEW 10:42**

Small acts of kindness seem so inconsequential. In the verse above, a cup of cold water is such a little thing. Yet Christ indicates that it pays big dividends. Later on (Matthew 25:34–46), Christ explains that kindness to others is an act of love toward God:

"The King will say ..., 'I was hungry and you gave me something to eat, I was thirsty and you gave me something to drink, I was a stranger and you invited me in, I needed clothes and you clothed me, I was sick and you looked after me, I was in prison and you came to visit me.'

"Then the righteous will answer him, 'Lord, when did we see you hungry and feed you, or thirsty and give you something to drink? When did we see you a stranger and invite you in, or needing clothes and clothe you? When did we see you sick or in prison and go to visit you?'

"The King will reply, 'I tell you the truth, whatever you did for one of the least of these brothers of mine, you did for me.'"

Such simple things are the very things that matter to God ... and make a Christian stand apart from the crowd. Feeding the hungry, giving your jacket to someone shivering, sharing your room with someone homeless, visiting the sick or imprisoned—such acts reap great rewards. Your trail of kindness leads straight to God.

In the coming week, experiment with kindness to see what a difference it really makes to other people, and how good it feels to you. Your project? Demonstrate small acts of kindness *anonymously* to: (1) each member of your family, (2) a neighbor, (3) someone you don't like, and (4) a stranger.

If they find out that it was you, it doesn't count—you'll have to be kind to them all over again!

See also: Proverbs 25:21–22

■■ MARKS OF A CHRISTIAN– GOODNESS

The fruit of the Spirit is ... goodness.

GALATIANS 5:22

The news report went something like this: "John Wayne Gacy was arrested this morning on charges stemming from the recent murders of several young Cook County boys." Police eventually pinned Gacy with the brutal slayings of nine youths, but they unearthed 27 bodies from shallow graves in the crawl space beneath his home and linked him with the murders of five others. Long paragraphs related the details of the grisly crimes, followed by quotes from surprised neighbors, such as: "He *seemed* like such a good man. He even helped out with the neighborhood carnival." Perhaps John Gacy had also once helped a neighbor fix her car, given a child a cookie, or taken a group of Scouts on an outing. Based on a few isolated acts of goodness, neighbors assumed the best and were horrified when his inner character bubbled to the surface.

Trouble is, there's a big difference between doing some particular good thing and being a good person. Goodness can't be measured by the outward things we do, but by the inward thing we are.

On this matter, C. S. Lewis wrote: "Someone who is not a good tennis player may now and then make a good shot. What you mean by a good player is the man whose eye and muscles and nerves have been so trained by making innumerable good shots that they can now be relied on. They have a certain tone or quality which is there even when he is not playing, just as a mathematician's mind has a certain habit and outlook which is there even when he is not doing mathematics. In the same way a man who perseveres in doing just actions gets in the end a certain quality of character."

It is that inner quality rather than a particular set of actions that Paul refers to in Galatians 5:22 as "goodness," and about which Hugh Latimer noted, "We must first be made good before we can do good."

See also: Romans 7:15–25; Galatians 6:7–10

:: POINTS TO PONDER – SATAN

> *There was a war in heaven. Michael and his angels fought against the dragon, and the dragon and his angels fought back. But he was not strong enough, and they lost their place in heaven. The great dragon was hurled down – that ancient serpent called the devil or Satan, who leads the whole world astray. He was hurled to the earth, and his angels with him.*

> REVELATION 12:7–9

The devil can cite Scripture for his purpose.

WILLIAM SHAKESPEARE

The devil is no idle spirit, but a vagrant, runagate walker, that never rests in one place. The motive, cause, and main intention of his walking is to ruin man.

T. ADAMS

There are two equal and opposite errors into which our race can fall about the devils. One is to disbelieve in their existence. The other is to believe, and to feel an excessive and unhealthy interest in them. They themselves are equally pleased by both errors, and hail a materialist or a magician with the same delight.

C. S. LEWIS

The devil and me, we don't agree; I hate him, and he hates me.

SALVATION ARMY HYMN

If there is no hell, then a good many preachers are obtaining money under false pretense.

WILLIAM A. SUNDAY

He who would fight the devil with his own weapons, must not wonder if he finds him an overmatch.

ROBERT SOUTH

To admire Satan, then, is to give one's vote not only for a world of misery, but also for a world of lies and propaganda, of wishful thinking, of incessant autobiography. Yet the choice is possible ...

C. S. LEWIS

The devil has at least one good quality. That he will flee if we resist him. Though cowardly in him, it is safety for us.

TRYON EDWARDS

Talk of devils being confined to hell, or hidden by invisibility! We have them by shoals in the crowded towns and cities of the world. Talk of raising the devil! What a need for that, when he is constantly walking to and fro in our streets, seeking whom he may devour.

UNKNOWN

The road to hell is paved with good intentions.

SAMUEL JOHNSON

The devil's best ruse is to persuade us that he does not exist.

CHARLES BAUDELAIRE

The devil is a gentleman who never goes where he is not welcome.

JOHN A. LINCOLN

Temptation is a fearful word. It indicates the beginning of a possible series of infinite evils. It is the ringing of an alarm bell, whose melancholy sounds may reverberate through eternity. Like the sudden, sharp cry of "Fire!" under our windows by night, it should rouse us to instantaneous action, and rouse every muscle to its highest tension.

HORACE MANN

When the flesh presents thee with delights, then present thyself with dangers; where the world possesses thee with vain hopes, there possess thyself with true fear; when the devil brings thee oil, bring thou vinegar. The way to be safe is to never be secure.

FRANCIS QUARLES

As no good is done, or spoken, or thought by any man without the assistance of God, working in and with those that believe in him, so there is no evil done, or spoken, or thought without assistance of the devil, who worketh with strong though secret power in the children of unbelief. All the works of our evil nature are the work of the devil.

J. WESLEY

See also: Romans 16:20; 2 Corinthians 11:14–15; 1 Peter 5:8–9

Religion 101

WEEK

14

■ ■ MARKS OF A CHRISTIAN– GOODNESS

He has showed you, O man, what is good. And what does the Lord require of you? To act justly and to love mercy and to walk humbly with your God.

MICAH 6:8

My first job out of college was working on a small-town newspaper. Every morning I started my day by compiling obituaries for people who had died the night before.

Death notices in little towns are among the most widely read newspaper columns. So I had to do more than call the mortuary to compile a list of survivors and the cause of death. I'd call associates and relatives and friends–they'd often tell me things about the deceased that the mortician didn't know, such as their interests in life, the clubs they had joined, and the good things they had done for the community. In some cases there was little good to be said.

One of the hot movies of the '70s was "Oh, God!" The star, John Denver, received a house call from God, portrayed by the late George Burns. Denver was understandably startled, as you would be, too, if God suddenly popped into your home. Once you calmed your jitters and the squeak left your voice, what would you tell God about your life?

Is "goodness" a characteristic you would mention? In the space below, jot down some items you are proudest of about your-self–a list that you'd not want God to leave your home without:

_____

_____

_____

_____

Of course, Christianity is based on grace, not works. There is nothing you can do, no matter how good or great, to talk your way into heaven. However, the values you live by now are the values others will remember you by later. In the end, true goodness never dies.

See also: Romans 2:6–7; Ephesians 2:8–10; 2 Thessalonians 1:11

■■ MARKS OF A CHRISTIAN– FAITHFULNESS

The fruit of the Spirit is ... faithfulness.

GALATIANS 5:22

I have been to many weddings where the bride and groom have pledged to remain faithful to each other "until death do us part." Yet within a few short years their relationship is marred by faithlessness.

The change is never a sudden thing. It begins gradually— perhaps when one partner discovers the other gargles wrong, coughs too loud, or squeezes a tube of toothpaste from the top—and then escalates until love is just a memory. This is especially true of couples who think love and faith are things you feel, rather than things you do. When their rosy glow fades, their marriage soon flickers.

If you talk to a husband and wife who have been married a long time, they'll admit they've faced a roller coaster of feelings toward each other—from exuberant highs to gut-wrenching lows. They'll talk about the problems, hardships, and hurts they have experienced together. And then they'll probably smile and say something like: "But it's been worth it."

What do they mean? Simply that the end result of faithfulness outweighs any short-term gain they could have found by ditching love partway. The rewards of long-term love are worth the perseverance and endurance it takes to develop them.

These words *perseverance* and *endurance* appear frequently throughout the Bible where faithfulness is mentioned. Like marriage, your relationship with God will be marked by hardship and heartache. There will be low times when you wake up and don't feel like a Christian ... and there will be temptations that will sort of blitz your belief.

If your love for God is based on warm feelings, a mere change in mood will destroy the relationship. But where the fruit of faithfulness exists, you'll have your eyes set on the long-term reward and, as C. S. Lewis wrote, "hold onto things your reason once accepted, in spite of your changing moods."

"We'd better get on with it," the writer of Hebrews says (Hebrews 12:1–2 *The Message*). "Strip down, start running—and never quit! No extra spiritual fat, no parasitic sins. Keep your eyes on *Jesus*, who both began and finished this race we're in."

The fruit of faithfulness enables you to complete this difficult race and capture the extravagant rewards God has promised. Get on with it. Just do it.

See also: Proverbs 14:14; Matthew 16:27; 2 John 8–9

⣿ MARKS OF A CHRISTIAN– FAITHFULNESS

Do you not know that in a race all the runners run, but only one gets the prize? Run in such a way as to get the prize. Everyone who competes in the games goes into strict training. They do it to get a crown that will not last; but we do it to get a crown that will last forever. Therefore I do not run like a man running aimlessly; I do not fight like a man beating the air. No, I beat my body and make it my slave so that after I have preached to others, I myself will not be disqualified for the prize.

1 CORINTHIANS 9:24–27

Paul never heard of Nikes or Adidas; he probably wasn't even a jogger. Chances are the only exercise he got was running from those who wanted to lynch him. The way he describes his calamities (see 2 Corinthians 11:24–33), people were fairly standing in line to do him in.

But he knew enough about track and field to realize that winning was a goal few attained. The rest in the pack have all sorts of reasons for not having won: "It was an off day," "My ankle was sore," "I didn't get enough sleep," "I was slow out of the blocks," "My shoes were bad," "I drank too much water before the race," "My legs just didn't respond."

There are also many reasons Christians give for quitting the race (giving up on God) or slackening their pace (backsliding). Few are faithful to the end. The things that hinder you and hold you back from living the kind of life God wants for you may be many and varied. Your obstacles might be a wrong attitude or bad habit, perhaps a fear of the future, a tendency to lie or lust, or a poor relationship with another person.

Take some time to develop a list of your Big Ten—the ten biggest obstacles that hold you back from running a fast race and being completely faithful to God. Write them down below, using a short phrase or word:

1. _____   6. _____

2. _____   7. _____

3. _____   8. _____

4. _____   9. _____

5. _____   10. _____

If the fruit of faithfulness is missing in your life, your Big Ten is the likely culprit. Talk to God about these regularly, asking him to help you whittle the list down. He's on your side, rooting for you to finish your race.

See also: Galatians 5:7–10; Hebrews 10:36–39, 12:1–3

■■ MARKS OF A CHRISTIAN— GENTLENESS

The fruit of the Spirit is ... gentleness.

GALATIANS 5:22–23

Gentleness is not something shameful
*   Or subordinate*
*   Or second-best.*
It is supreme strength of character—
*   Minus the muscle.*
Gentleness is being vulnerable and honest—
*   Removing your masks and forgetting everything you ever heard*
*   About "macho" men and Marlboro "manliness."*

It says: "Can I help you?"
  And "I'm sorry"
    And "Thanks a million."
Gentleness is admitting you have
  Needs and hurts and fears–
    And is willing to ask for help.
It stands up for the rights of others
  And not for your own.
Gentleness is the unfading beauty of a quiet spirit,
  Or an encouraging word
    Or a kind smile
      Or a good cry.
It is being able to talk openly
  With a member of the opposite sex
    Or to play with a child
      Or to laugh with an adult.
Gentleness soothes the broiling edge of anger
  And hate
    And prejudice
      And pride.
It is strength that grows
  From the inside out.
Gentleness is a velvet-wrapped brick.

See also: Proverbs 15:1–2; 25:15; 1 Peter 3:3–4

⠿ MARKS OF A CHRISTIAN– GENTLENESS

Let your gentleness be evident to all.

PHILIPPIANS 4:5

The Bible verses below all describe specific incidents in Christ's life on earth. They present three quick flashes of his character. After each entry, jot down a few notes about what the incident suggests about gentleness, based on Christ's example.

Pass the Kleenex—John 11:32–44

_____

_____

_____

Kid Stuff—Mark 10:13–16

_____

_____

_____

Velvet-Wrapped Brick—John 2:13–16

_____

_____

_____

Some people equate gentleness with weakness. They always have and always will. There were those who probably cringed when Jesus started blubbering at the tomb of Lazarus, and again later when he got choked up about how people in Jerusalem turned their backs on him. Nor did they think it was becoming when he cuddled a bunch of goober-nosed kids. It was only when Jesus raised a little holy hell in the temple that their doubts about his weakness were laid to rest.

Yet even then they mistook the quiet strength of his gentleness for something else.

See also: Ephesians 4:2; 1 Peter 3:13–16

■■ MARKS OF A CHRISTIAN— SELF-CONTROL

The fruit of the Spirit is ... self-control.

GALATIANS 5:22–23

It took more than good intentions and ability for Nancy Swider to make the U.S. Olympic speed skating team and win a world record. Lots of skaters had both and did neither.

It primarily took self-control—the desire to focus every thought on her biggest and best goal and say no to lesser wants. So, late at night when her friends were partying, Nancy would shovel snow from the school track to get in one last set of wind sprints. The next day she would rise with the milkmen for predawn workouts. That's no way to live if you don't care about the Olympics. It's the only way to live if you do.

"To be in good moral condition," wrote Nehru, "requires at least as much training as to be in good physical condition." When you became a Christian, you in effect said yes to God. That's sort of like saying "I do" when you get married. To love your spouse completely, you must forsake all other loves. That means getting rid of certain old pictures in your wallet, scrapping dated love letters, and tossing your little black book.

The same is true of your relationship with God. To love him completely, you must wrench your affections from all that hinders your relationship. To desire his fruit of the Spirit in your life, you must say no to the weeds of the flesh, including such things Paul lists in Galatians 5:19–21: impure thoughts, eagerness for lustful pleasure, hatred and fighting, jealousy and anger, constant effort to get the best for yourself, complaints and criticisms, and the feeling that everyone else is wrong except those in your own little group.

The fruit of self-control is the desire to focus your thoughts on attaining God's biggest and best plans for your life. And once you've made a habit of saying yes to God, saying no to lesser desires is easier. That doesn't mean giving up anything, for "giving up" implies a loss. As Fulton Sheen wrote, "Our Lord did not ask us to give up the things of earth, but to exchange them for better things."

A self-controlled life means you are living an "exchanged" life. Even then, it's no way to live if you don't particularly care what happens on the other side of death. It's the only way to live if you do.

See also: Mark 8:34–38; 1 Thessalonians 5:1–11

■■ POINTS TO PONDER –
PREJUDICE

Here there is no Greek or Jew, circumcised or uncircumcised, barbarian, Scythian, slave or free, but Christ is all, and is in all.

COLOSSIANS 3:11

One may no more live in the world without picking up the moral prejudices of the world than one will be able to go to hell without perspiring.

H. L. MENCKEN

He hears but half when he hears only one party.

AESCHYLUS

Prejudice is a child of ignorance.

WILLIAM HAZLITT

We hold these truths to be self-evident: that all men are created equal; that they are endowed by their Creator with certain inalienable Rights; that among these are Life, Liberty and the pursuit of Happiness.

THE DECLARATION OF INDEPENDENCE

Opinions founded on prejudice are always sustained with the greatest violence.

FRANCIS JEFFREY

It is as hard to do your duty when men are sneering at you as when they are shooting at you.

WOODROW WILSON

If we were to wake up some morning and find that everyone was the same race, creed and color, we would find some other causes for prejudice by noon.

GEORGE AIKEN

There are only two ways to be quite unprejudiced and impartial. One is to be completely ignorant. The other is to be completely indifferent. Bias and prejudice are attitudes to be kept in hand, not attitudes to be avoided.

CHARLES CURTIS

There is a great difference between rejecting something you have known from the inside and rejecting something (as uneducated people tend to do) simply because it happens to be out of fashion in your own time.

C. S. LEWIS

Most men, when they think they are thinking, are merely rearranging their prejudices.

KNUTE ROCKNE

The people who are the most bigoted are the people who have no convictions at all.

G. K. CHESTERTON

Prejudice is a mist, which, in our journey through the world, often dims the brightest, and obscures the best of all the good and glorious objects that meet us on our way.

TALES OF PASSIONS

Beware of prejudices. They are like rats, and men's minds are like traps; prejudices get in easily, but it is doubtful if they will ever get out.

FRANCIS JEFFREY

Everyone is a prisoner of his own experiences. No one can eliminate prejudices—just recognize them.

EDWARD MURROW

Prejudice squints when it looks, and lies when it talks.

DUCHESS DE ABRANTES

See also: Matthew 22:39; 2 Corinthians 5:17–21

WEEK

15

◼◼ MARKS OF A CHRISTIAN–
SELF-CONTROL

The highway of the upright avoids evil; he who guards his way guards his soul.

PROVERBS 16:17

I once read a newspaper story about a man from the South whose wife sued him for divorce. The reason? She discovered he was secretly married to two other women, maintained three separate households, three separate families, and three separate jobs in three different states. A salesman, the man would visit one of his families, stay a couple of weeks, and then move on to the next—a pattern he kept up for many years.

Sometimes Christians maintain secret loves. They have pledged their love to God, but in reality they split their affection. They want to be a Christian, but not too Christian. They desire God's will . . . as long as it conforms to their own. They shut the door on sin, but spend the rest of their lives peeking through the keyhole and trying to pick the lock.

As discussed yesterday, the presence of self-control in your life is simply a desire to cultivate God's fruit of the Spirit and to hack away at the roots of the weeds of the flesh. It means not giving in to every desire, whim, and temptation.

The ability to say *No!* to temptation is not some special, mystical, mumbo-jumbo power that belongs solely to those who have memorized Leviticus and can read the Gospels in Greek. It belongs to *you.* Self-control can be evidenced in your life in very practical ways. It means passing up the joint or bottle that is offered you at a party. It means not checking the answers of a friend's test against your own, even when you know they're probably better. It means walking a block out of your way to avoid a magazine rack that tempts you. It means not saying something you have every right to say. And it means waging hand-to-hand combat with the Big Ten you listed earlier this week. Not because you want to appear righteous, but because you realize God's best for your life is better than second, third, or ninth best.

See also: Proverbs 25:28; Titus 2:11–14

:: LET'S PRETEND

*The Lord does not look at the things man looks at.
Man looks at the outward appearance, but the Lord looks
at the heart.*

1 SAMUEL 16:7

The magazine advertisement featured a pretty blonde with a Palm Springs tan and Maybelline looks. Her face was used to hype a leading school of modeling. Beneath the picture was a bold caption: "Be a model ... or just look like one."

Wouldn't it be strange if that same principle were applied to other things, say Christianity: "Be a Christian ... or just look like one." What if Jesus had *really* said things such as: "Truly I say to you, if you do not have a fish insignia on your car you cannot be my disciple;" or "Be careful to appear righteous before men, to be seen by them. If you do, you will have a reward from your father in heaven;" or "Whoever wants to become great among you must always wear a pious smile and often say, 'I'll pray for you;'" or "I tell you the truth, unless you act like you're born again, you cannot see the kingdom of God."

Trouble is, we often live as if that's exactly what the Lord did say. We know all the rules of "religiosity" and "churchianity." We know what not to do, or at least what not to get caught doing around certain people. We speak Christianese fluently ("PraiseGawdI'llpray-aboutitLordblessyou!"), and go through the outward motions of *looking* like we think a Christian should and disregard the hard, daily, dirty struggle of *being* a Christian. We woof the woof, but we don't walk the walk.

Though some people might be fooled, God never is. He sees through counterfeit Christianity and knows when we're living by dual standards, with one set of rules for outward behavior and another for our hearts and minds. He knows the #@!*&% stab-in-the-back thoughts we harbor and the jealous, lustful feelings that flood our minds. He knows when we're just pretending to love, pretending to care. He sees straight to the heart. "Before a word is on my tongue you know it completely," David wrote in one of his psalms.

Being a Christian means being concerned about the disparity between how we live and how we look, between what we do and what we say. It helps to know God doesn't just care what we do on Sundays—that we have learned to go to church often enough to be labeled "active" and "faithful." He cares how we live and act the other six days as well. He cares that our Christianity is evidenced in every part of our lives: the mental, social, physical ... as well as the spiritual.

God wants out of the closet. He wants the freedom to affect every part of our lives. And he wants us to discover the difference between a Sunday school faith and a living, gutsy belief that is more than skin deep.

See also: Psalm 139:4; Romans 12:9–21; 2 Timothy 3:1–5

:: ONE SOLITARY LIFE

The stone the builders rejected has become the capstone.

MATTHEW 21:42

The name of the writer is unknown, but prior to his death he wrote these words about another solitary life:

> Here is a young man who was born in an obscure village, the child of a peasant woman. He grew up in another village. He worked in a carpenter shop until he was thirty, and then for three years he was an itinerant preacher. He never wrote a book. He never held an office. He never owned a home. He never had a family....
>
> He never went to college. He never put his foot inside a big city. He never traveled 200 miles from the place where he was born. He never did one of the things that usually accompany greatness. He had no credentials but himself....
>
> While he was still a young man the tide of public opinion turned against him. His friends ran away. He was turned over to his enemies. He went through the mockery of a trial.
>
> He was nailed to the cross between two thieves. While he was dying, his executioners gambled for the only piece of property he had on earth, and that was his coat. When he was dead he was laid in a borrowed grave through the pity of a friend.
>
> Nineteen centuries wide have come and gone, and today he is the central figure of the human race and the leader of the column of progress....

All the armies that ever marched and all the navies that ever sailed, and all the parliaments that ever sat, and all the kings that ever reigned, put together, have not affected the life of man upon this earth as has that one solitary life.

This man, of course, is Jesus Christ . . . who is not just some great, dead leader, but the cornerstone of God's mission of love to earth. "For God so loved the world that he gave his one and only Son, that whoever believes in him shall not perish but have eternal life" (John 3:16).

See also: Philippians 2:5–11

■ JESUS OF CHINA

I have set you an example that you should do as I have done for you.

JOHN 13:15

One of the United States' earliest missionaries to China, Henry Poppen, made an extended trek to a remote village. Though he'd lived in that country for some forty years, he knew of no Christian who had ever visited the secluded little town with its unadorned huts and simple people.

Upon his arrival, the villagers listened patiently as he tried to explain who Jesus was. He talked about Christ's gentleness, his truthfulness, his all-encompassing love. The villagers nodded their heads and smiled. Some had moist eyes.

He described how Jesus bore no grudges when wronged, how he lived for what he could give rather than get. He spoke about how Christ was selfless to the point of death.

The grizzled old villagers glanced back and forth with knowing eyes. Finally, one of them spoke. "We know this man. Your 'Jesus' lived here."

Dr. Poppen smiled, but shook his head. Feeling there was some misunderstanding, he explained that Christ had actually lived many thousands of miles away.

"No, no. He lived and died right here," the old, wrinkled villager insisted. Rising to his feet, he pointed off in the distance down a rutted dirt path. "Follow me, I'll show you his grave."

Dr. Poppen shrugged his shoulders and followed. He trudged behind the pack of men and women as they guided him away from the huts to a Chinese cemetery. There they stopped at a headstone carved with the name of a Christian medical missionary— a man who felt God had led him to that secluded corner of the world. He had lived and died there—his existence unknown even to other missionaries. Yet he was so Christlike that Jesus of Nazareth was mistaken for "Jesus" of China.

Every Christian is a missionary—God's representative—in his or her own corner of the world. In *your* school, *your* home, *your* job, you'll meet people no other Christian can.

That's why Christ said his life is an example for you. By following it and being faithful to the pattern, others are bound to see Christ in you ... and perhaps to even mistake you for the real thing.

See also: 2 Corinthians 5:20; Philippians 2:5–8; 1 Timothy 1:15–16

:: THE SIXTH MAN

Greater love has no one than this, that he lay down his life for his friends.

JOHN 15:13

Flight 90 began like any other flight: the dash down the runway, the gentle lurch skyward, the stewardess saying something about the location of exits. Sitting quietly in the rear, a balding man in his 50s fingered his extravagant mustache and stared out the 737's window at the bite of winter. The heavy snowfall obscured vision of the frozen Washington, D.C., landscape below.

Suddenly, tragedy struck. The Florida-bound plane with 74 passengers skidded across a traffic-clogged bridge. Cars were sheared in half. Then the jet quickly sank beneath the ice-clogged Potomac River.

When a rescue helicopter arrived, only six passengers were visible. As they floundered in the icy water, losing their grip on life, the helicopter dangled a life preserver to the man with the mustache. But each time the ring was lowered, the man passed it to someone else who was then shuttled safely to shore. He waved the ring off five times. When the helicopter finally returned for him, the man had disappeared to his death ... anonymously and selflessly, known only as "the sixth man."

A hero? Yes. A Christian? No one knows. But in his last minutes of life he faced death with charity and gave his life so others might live.

I sometimes wonder if I would have done the same. Probably not. And then I think, Is there anyone I'd die for, *really*, if the choice was set before me? My parents? Well, they're kind of old and ... My brother or sister? We've never really been too close ... My best friend? Too flippant....

In the end, I'd want to be absolutely sure the person I swapped my life for was *worth* it — I might consider giving up my life if the individual was some kind of cross between Einstein and Billy Graham, but even then....

Compared to the Bible's standards (and to "the sixth man's"), my love and selflessness are pretty puny. And then I stop and think about how Christ gave his life for me. By my standards I wouldn't be *worth* dying for. But by God's standards, everyone was worth dying for.

His evaluation was a radical valuation. The world still hasn't gotten over it.

See also: Mark 8:34–38; Romans 5:6–8

■■ HOMEWARD BOUND

Even to your old age and gray hairs I am he, I am he who will sustain you. I have made you and I will carry you.

ISAIAH 46:4

The first Saturday of each month, I'd meet Grandpa on the Ocean Beach pier. We'd each bring a fishing pole, tackle box, and bucket for any fish we might catch. He always razzed me that he'd catch the bigger fish, though we both seldom caught anything but seaweed. So on the way home, we'd stop and buy some fresh bass fillets. Grandma always thought they were fish we'd caught ourselves, which made Grandpa smile and wink.

He was a simple man. He liked the quiet solitude he found while fishing, he liked to walk in the woods, he liked to read his Bible, and he seldom missed church on Sunday. He was at home there, and tried to arrive early so he could shake hands with all of his friends.

Things changed somewhat when Grandpa had a stroke and lost most of his hearing. Sometimes he'd be out walking and have what he'd call a "spell." Something in his head would click, and he'd crumple unconscious to the ground.

After that point, he still made it to church sometimes, and would shake hands all around. He'd turn his hearing aid up until it buzzed, but even then I don't think he heard much of the sermon. Yet he'd sit in his regular spot three pews from the front, his gentle face shining with the joy of one who's made his peace with God.

As years passed, I grew up and moved away. And Grandpa just grew older. I got letters from him often—letters that talked about how he enjoyed watching the birds or fixing breakfast for Grandma, or how the Lord was as natural to him as his next breath. But his handwriting got shaky, and he began having more "spells." We both knew his home-going was drawing near, and that saddened me. But the thought didn't bother him. He said, smiling, that it would be like getting in an old fishing boat and crossing from one shore to another—and greeting the Lord face-to-face on the other side.

Most people think growing old and dying are life's greatest tragedies. To them, Grandpa would say, "Humbug!" And he would stamp his foot when saying it. And then he'd point out, as did Melville, that life is a voyage that's homeward bound.

See also: John 14:2; 1 Thessalonians 4:13–18

■■ POINTS TO PONDER–
LIFE AND DEATH

Whoever finds his life will lose it, and whoever loses his life for my sake will find it.

MATTHEW 10:39

Life is not lost by dying; life is lost minute by minute, day by dragging day, in all the thousand small uncaring ways.

STEPHEN VINCENT BENÉT

It matters not how long you live, but how well.

PUBLILIUS SYRUS

Not, how did he die? But, how did he live?
Not, what did he gain? But, what did he give?
These are the merits to measure the worth
Of a man as man, regardless of birth.
Not, what was his station? But, had he a heart?
And how did he play his God-given part?
Was he ever ready with word or good cheer
To bring a smile, to banish a tear?
Not, what was his church? Nor, what was his creed?
But, had he befriended those really in need?
Not, what did the sketch in the newspaper say?
But, how many were sorry when he passed away?

UNKNOWN

We go to the grave of a friend, saying, "A man is dead." But angels throng about him, saying, "A man is born."

GOTTHOLD

Creative life is always on the yonder side of convention.

C. G. JUNG

I believe in life after birth.

UNKNOWN

Have you wept at anything during the past year? Has your heart beat faster at the sight of young beauty? Have you thought seriously about the fact that someday you are going to die? More often than not do you really listen when people are speaking to you instead of just waiting for your turn to speak? Is there anybody you know in whose place, if one of you had to suffer great pain, you would volunteer yourself? If your answer to all or most of these questions is No, the chances are that you're dead.

FREDERICK BUECHNER

To fear love is to fear life, and those who fear life are already three parts dead.

BERTRAND RUSSELL

Take care of your life; and the Lord will take care of your death.

GEORGE WHITEFIELD

The waters are rising but I am not sinking.

CATHERINE BOOTH (LAST WORDS)

Death: to stop sinning suddenly.

ELBERT HUBBARD

[Some say] that death ought not to be final, that there ought to be a second chance. I believe that if a million chances were likely to do good, they would be given. But a master often knows, when boys and parents do not, that it is really useless to send a boy in for a certain examination again. Finality must come sometime, and it does not require a very robust faith to believe that omniscience knows when.

C. S. LEWIS

Life can only be understood backward; it must be lived forward.

SÖREN KIERKEGAARD

See also: Job 1:21; Matthew 7:13–14; John 10:10

❖ TRUE LOVE

The commandments, "Do not commit adultery,"
"Do not murder," "Do not steal," "Do not covet," and
whatever other commandment there may be, are summed
up in this one rule: "Love your neighbor as yourself."

ROMANS 13:9

One of the nonfiction bestsellers a few years ago was a book called *Looking Out for Number One*. I didn't buy it because, rightly or wrongly, I've always been *very* good at looking out for myself and figured I didn't need additional help. For example:

I pamper myself. My favorite way to pamper myself is to do what I most enjoy—like running barefoot through mud, making faces in the mirror, and swishing Jell-O in my teeth. I also pamper myself by guzzling root beer on a hot day, going to a movie when I'm bored, and changing my socks when they smell.

I protect myself. When I head to the beach, I grease up with sun block. I also play it safe by wearing gloves in the snow, carrying a spare tire in my trunk, and by staying away from those who sneeze. Friends, books, and a portable CD player protect me from loneliness.

I challenge myself. I challenge myself by always trying to run a faster mile, by looking at stars through a telescope, or a drop of puddle water through a microscope. Perhaps my biggest challenge is just trying to be myself.

I honor myself. When I've done something well, I honor myself by broadcasting my accomplishment. "Hey, I just sold another magazine article!" I'll shout to a friend across the grocery store aisle. And when the check comes in the mail, the first dollar is spent on myself to celebrate my success.

I accept myself. I don't like the way I sound on a tape recorder and I don't like my knobby bird legs. But I've learned to accept what I cannot change. I know I will never be a good spellur or the life of a party. But that's okay—I wouldn't be *me* otherwise.

If it sounds like I think of myself a lot, it's because I do. I pamper, protect, challenge, honor, and accept myself for one reason:

I love myself. There's nothing wrong with that. God doesn't want me to love myself any less. He just wants me to love others the same way.

See also: Luke 10:25–37; John 13:34–35; 1 John 3:11–18

∷ LASTING MEMORIES

Whatever you do, whether in word or deed, do it all in the name of the Lord Jesus.

Colossians 3:17

I was visiting a town I'd never been in before and stopped for a pizza. Suddenly I heard someone calling my name from the far side of the restaurant. It was Tony, a high school friend whom I'd not seen in years. I joined him for dinner, and for the next couple of hours we talked of "the good old days."

"Remember Harry?" Tony said late in the evening. I nodded with a smile. Everyone always used to make fun of Harry. Then, laughing hard, he described an impersonation of Harry I'd done one day in speech class when the teacher stepped out. I tried hard, but couldn't remember the incident.

"I'll never forget it," said Tony, nearly in hysterics by that time. "I remember it every time I think of you."

Later that night I pondered what Tony had said. A scene I couldn't even recall was printed indelibly in his mind. He remembered it as being funny. But the laughs were all at Harry's expense.

I would like to have been remembered in other, kinder ways: the weekends I spent working with Mexican orphans, the day I took a retarded girl on a wheelchair stroll to the 7–11 store, the time I tutored a friend all night in English. But it was my mimicry of Harry's duck walk and stutter that Tony best remembered.

The role I play in the memories of others is bothersome, because their minds, like security cameras, record everything. What they remember about me is something I cannot control. *Or can I?*

Thinking of this incident with Tony, I've often stopped myself just as I'm getting ready to lash out at somebody in anger. I've caught myself on the verge of making a crude comment, excusing my behavior to my family, or telling a lie. Knowing that my every action and comment can be recorded in the mind's camera of others, I try harder to guard my words and behavior.

When the camera clicks on, I want only my best side to show.

See also: Proverbs 29:11; James 3:3–12

:: THE QUICK FIX

Consider it pure joy, my brothers, whenever you face trials of many kinds, because you know that the testing of your faith develops perseverance. Perseverance must finish its work so that you may be mature and complete, not lacking anything.

JAMES 1:2–4

When you grow up in a society that pioneered such things as instant pudding, Minute Rice, freeways, one-step cameras, and fast-food restaurants, waiting does not come easy. If you must wait longer than 30 seconds for a Big Mac, you start glancing at your watch, wondering if the zit-faced cook isn't missing half his brain. And when you later develop indigestion, you grab an instant solution from the nearest medicine chest.

In this "aspirin age" of ours, we've also come to expect instant solutions to our personal pressures and daily trials. We don't want a timely struggle with our problems—we'd prefer to catapult over them. We want to smile and feel happy and say "Praise the Lord!" a lot. So we attend all kinds of Bible studies, victory rallies, youth camps, super Sunday seminars, and revival meetings to discover the spiritual key and that hidden verse that will help us combat "what's wrong" in our lives.

Yet, what's wrong is that we want answers—NOW! And if our youth pastor or minister can't provide them, we'll hop to another church to get the spiritual "fix" that hopefully—for another hour, day, or week—will numb the panic and pressure we feel about school, work, a personal relationship, our future, or our families.

The daily frustrations we want off our backs are the very things James says we not only ought to endure but endure *joyfully*. The joy comes from knowing the difficulties we face help us grow up spiritually. In other words, negative experiences can produce positive results. The lives of Joseph, Sarah, Job, Daniel, and Paul all attest to this.

I like to think of these experiences as pearls. Pearls don't just happen. To begin with, a grain of sand imbeds itself in the soft inner folds of an oyster, which in turn soothes the irritant with a rich body fluid. In time, and plenty of it, that fluid forms a smooth, hard surface—a pearl.

And so it is with us: God is at work in our lives, turning our biggest irritants into priceless, one-of-a-kind gems. It's a timely process that can't be rushed.

See also: Romans 5:3-5; Philippians 1:4-6

:: GO THE DISTANCE

Pursue righteousness, godliness, faith, love, endurance and gentleness. Fight the good fight of the faith.
1 TIMOTHY 6:11-12

One of the most successful movies of all time was the original *Rocky*—the roaches-to-riches story of an untested Philadelphia brawler who was given a chance to box the world champion. It was all a public-relations gimmick hatched by the champ hitman, Apollo Creed.

A cute idea, Rocky's friends agreed. But they also agreed the odds against their "Italian Stallion" were overwhelming. The Creed would make hamburger of him. Rocky didn't doubt it would be a tough fight—he simply wanted to complete the 15 grueling rounds, to remain standing at the final bell. In his words, he wanted to "go the distance."

In a fight of another sort—a bout without satin trunks and Everlast gloves—the apostle Paul faced similar staggering odds. His was a spiritual battle, yet he maintained the same goal of "going the distance." If you think Rocky had it tough, read 2 Corinthians 11:24-33. It's Paul's account of the beatings, whippings, stonings, shipwrecks, imprisonments, and threats he faced in his "fight of the faith." Yet he endured and persevered through every trial, temptation, discouragement, and despair.

At the end of his life he could write: "I'm about to die, my life an offering on God's altar. This is the only race worth running. I've run hard right to the finish, believed all the way. All that's left now is the shouting—God's applause! Depend on it, he's an honest judge. He'll do right not only by me, but by everyone eager for his coming" (2 Timothy 4:6–8, *The Message*).

In the "fight of the faith," the odds sometimes seem staggering. You face temptations daily that blitz your belief. You face moral decisions that others never have to consider. Yet the Bible indicates an eternal prize awaits those who remain faithful to the final bell.

It's one thing to join the fight for a time, and then quit. It's quite another to go the distance and finish it.

See also: 1 Corinthians 9:24–27; 1 Timothy 4:7–8; 2 John 8–9

:: FAITH IS A VERB

Faith by itself, if it is not accompanied by action, is dead.

JAMES 2:17

Charles Blondin is credited with having crossed Niagara Falls several times—on a 1,100-foot tightrope, 160 dizzying feet above the thundering water. His high-wire feats often included theatrical variations, such as walking on stilts or pushing a wheelbarrow. He'd even pause to stand on his head, turn a backward somersault, balance atop a chair, or cook an omelette!

One day in 1860, Blondin was again preparing to cross the famous falls. He turned to the huge crowd and asked if they believed he could cross without falling. They shouted their assent. He asked if they believed he could do it carrying another person on his back. Again the crowd roared. But when Blondin asked a man standing nearby to volunteer, the man refused.

Had the man believed, I mean *really* believed, his faith would have prompted him to climb atop Blondin's back. True faith is more than just mental assent or verbal agreement. It involves action.

The same is true, James writes, of those who profess to believe in Christ. Faith is dead if it's not accompanied by action.

Put your faith to the test by getting involved in people's lives. Don't just pray for others; roll up your sleeves and help them. Anyone can say they believe. But how many are willing, for example, to spend time with the unpopular kid at school whom others ignore?

Your faith and love for God ought to motivate you to love others— actively and practically. Faith like that speaks louder than words.

See also: Genesis 15:1–6; Mark 9:14–24

■■ HOLDING OUT

We live by faith, not by sight.

2 CORINTHIANS 5:7

Those who like baseball will never forget the 1994 season. It was the year players went on strike. TV sets were quiet. There was no World Series. Stadiums were as still as a small-town street after midnight. Season tickets had all been sold, but games were canceled because the players were holding out. They wanted more money, more benefits, more guarantees.

When it comes to holding out on God, most of us are pros. We want to play by our rules come hell or high water. Back in high school when I first sensed a need for God, I did a lot of bargaining. It was June, during the three-month summer siesta. I more or less told God I wanted to wait until September to become a Christian. Summers were too much fun to be wrecked by going to church, reading a Bible, and worrying about things like drinking and going to the wrong parties. Trouble is, God *waited.* And I had my most miserable summer ever.

People hold out on God in other, different ways. They want guarantees. They'll do what God wants, *if* . . . You know, *if* God gets them the job they want, *if* God heals their mom's cancer, *if* God allows them to fall in love, *if* God gets them accepted to the right college, *if* God lets them be a cheerleader or baseball team all-star. The list is a mile long.

But we've got it all wrong. God doesn't promise us fail-safe, risk-free Christianity. He doesn't assure us things will work out like in the movies, with everyone living happily ever after. He doesn't guarantee us immunity from hurt and hardship. There are no guarantees other than the fact that he'll be our God if we'll be his people.

We want promises, but God wants faith. Sure, there are risks. But faith takes the risks, without knowing where it is being led. That's because faith loves and follows—no strings attached—the one who leads: Jesus Christ.

You can think of it as taking a trip without maps. Or you can think of it as a true and absolute adventure.

See also: Hebrews 11

:: POINTS TO PONDER—FAITH

Faith is being sure of what we hope for and certain of what we do not see.

HEBREWS 11:1

I believe in the sun, even when it is not shining; I believe in love even when I feel it not; I believe in God, even when he is silent.

ANONYMOUS

I prayed for faith and thought that some day faith would come down and strike me like lightning. But faith did not seem to come. One day I read in the 10th chapter of Romans, "Faith cometh by hearing, and hearing by the Word of God." I had up to this time closed my Bible and prayed for faith. I now opened my Bible and began to study, and faith has been growing ever since.

D. L. MOODY

I always prefer to believe the best of everybody—it saves so much trouble.

RUDYARD KIPLING

God made the moon as well as the sun: and when he does not see fit to grant us the sunlight, he means us to guide our steps as well as we can by moonlight.

RICHARD WHATELY

The life of faith is not a life of mounting up with wings, but a life of walking and not fainting.... Faith never knows where it is being led, but it loves and knows the one who is leading.

OSWALD CHAMBERS

Never put a question mark where God has put a period.

JOHN R. RICE

I back the scent of life
Against its stink.
That's what faith works out at
Finally.

G. A. STUDDERT KENNEDY

Never, never pin your whole faith on any human being: not if he is the best and wisest in the whole world. There are lots of nice things you can do with sand; but do not try building a house on it.

C. S. LEWIS

Faith is not being sure where you're going but going anyway. A journey without maps.

FREDERICK BUECHNER

Faith is not believing that God *can*, but that God *will!*

ABRAHAM LINCOLN

Don't be afraid to take a big step if one is indicated. You can't cross a chasm in two small jumps.

DAVID LLOYD GEORGE

Faith is not an effort, a striving, a ceaseless seeking, as so many earnest souls suppose, but rather a letting go, an abandonment, an abiding rest in God that nothing, not even the soul's short-comings, can disturb.

ANONYMOUS

See also: Matthew 17:20; Romans 10:17; Ephesians 2:8; Hebrews 11

**W
E
E
K**

17

:: WHO IS HE?

A very large crowd spread their cloaks on the road, while others cut branches from the trees and spread them on the road. The crowds that went ahead of him and those that followed shouted, "Hosanna to the Son of David!" "Blessed is he who comes in the name of the Lord!" "Hosanna in the highest!"

When Jesus entered Jerusalem, the whole city was stirred and asked, "Who is this?"

MATTHEW 21:8–10

I was at New York's Kennedy airport one evening when a crowd of people swarmed the gate of an approaching 747. Most had their cameras cocked and were bouncing nervously on their feet.

Suddenly, a popular rock musician stepped through the door. Pandemonium broke loose. Flashes exploded. Girls elbowed closer. And everyone battled for autographs.

I was standing near an elderly lady, who had stopped out of curiosity. She wore a puzzled look and tapped me on the shoulder. "Excuse me," she said, "but who is that?"

A similar thing happened when Jesus entered Jerusalem on Palm Sunday, just five days before his death. A huge crowd had gathered, ensuring his arrival into the grand capital city would never be forgotten. There was much commotion and shouting among those who knew about Jesus, his miracles and claims. The fuss was so great, Matthew wrote, that the whole city was stirred into frenzy. Yet there were many, he noted, who scratched their heads and asked those standing nearby, "Pardon me, but who's the guy on the donkey?"

They were puzzled about Jesus of Nazareth. Could he possibly be the one and only Son of God as he claimed? Had God actually stepped out of the shadows, so to speak, and shown his face? The Old Testament forecast it. And everyone knew if you read it there, it *had* to be true. But still, how could it be? It didn't make sense that the homeless, jobless son of two hick Jews could be who he claimed.

As C. S. Lewis wrote on this matter: "A man who was merely a man and said the sort of things Jesus said wouldn't be a great moral teacher. He's either be a lunatic—on a level with a man who says he's a poached egg—or else he'd be the devil of hell. You must make your choice. Either this man was, and is, the son of God, or else a madman or something worse."

Questions about Christ's identity haven't changed much in 2,000 years. Either he was a full-tilt crazy with the asylum key, or he carried the key to unlock the entire universe. The choice is yours: Kook of kooks or King of kings.

See also: Joshua 24:14–18; Matthew 16:13–16

■■ OLD CHARLIE

I am just like you before God; I too have been taken from clay.

JOB 33:6

As I walked past Old Charlie's house on the way home from school, I spotted him on the porch swing, just staring away his time. Normally I wouldn't have bothered with him. After all, we had nothing in common; sixty years separated us. He'd always seemed like a leftover relic from some long-ago age.

But my grandma had died just a few weeks before, and I got to thinking that he probably wasn't too many steps from the grave himself. So I threw my hand in the air and waved. "How ya doing, Charlie?" I shouted.

He grunted something I couldn't hear. I had time to kill, so I crossed his lawn and stepped up on the porch. I stood around for a few minutes, wondering how you talk to an old man. Finally, not knowing what else to say, I asked if he was married.

"Naw. The wife's been gone now twenty years." He started tugging on his collar and looking into the sky as if he were trying to spot Jupiter. "But I'm thinking of getting hitched again," he said, looking as nervous to me as I probably looked to him.

"Got a girlfriend, eh, Charlie?"

"Aw, it's hardly worth talking about. Every time I bring the subject up, my family makes a big deal about my age. You'd think I'm old enough to make my own decisions, but they treat me like a kid."

"Things aren't much better around my place," I joked, relaxing a bit. Somehow we got talking about other things: my studies, my job hunt (my age was always a problem), football, and how it looked like the Chargers would finally make the Super Bowl.

"I'd of bought me a season pass if I had the money," he said. "But I'd of needed a job, and nobody wants someone *my* age."

Suddenly it struck me. "You know, the thing about you, Charlie, is ... well, you're just like me."

That night as I lay in bed, I wondered how many other people I'd shut out of my life—simply because they didn't look, talk, or dress like me. How many other *Charlies* had I excluded?

See also: Isaiah 35:3–4; Matthew 5:46–47; Romans 12:16

▪▪ PRESERVE AND SEASON

You are the salt of the earth.

MATTHEW 5:13

If Christ were speaking today to a contemporary audience, he might not have used salt as a metaphor to describe the intended relationship between Christians and the rest of the world. Instead, he might have said, "You are the Kenmore refrigerator of the world."

Two thousand years ago, salt served the same basic purpose as refrigeration does today. It was a preservative—a means to maintain freshness and hinder decay. Meats, fish, and poultry were either rubbed carefully with salt or allowed to soak in a brine solution to ward off the natural rotting process.

Our purpose as Christians should be to penetrate the non-Christian community with the message of God's love and saving power, and thereby ward off spiritual decay. We shouldn't stand apart from the world and piously exclaim, "Things sure are a mess these days. The divorce rate is up, the crime rate is up, the suicide rate is up." What's so surprising about that, anyway? After all, Christ indicates that people without God are like meat without salt. There is a natural rotting process. So let's please pass the salt ... quickly!

Christ goes on to warn that salt that's lost its saltiness is good for nothing, except to be thrown out and trampled. Tough words, and rightly so. God is a jealous God. He paid an immeasurable price for our salvation by sending his only Son to the cross. If we habitually and purposefully sin, we ignore God's sacrifice. We also deny him the opportunity to use our lives to penetrate, preserve, and season the lives of non-Christians with whom we have daily contact.

If we're truly salt, we need to be about God's business. We need to get out of the salt shaker.

See also: Matthew 5:14–16; 28:18–20; Colossians 3:1–17

■■ AGE-OLD CONCERNS

Don't let anyone look down on you because you are young, but set an example for the believers in speech, in life, in love, in faith and in purity.

1 TIMOTHY 4:12

You haven't seen the fat cousin of your mom's in many years. "Last time I saw you," she grins, "you could run under the breadboard. And now look at my Little Chrissy," she says, giving your cheek a playful pinch.

Your coach glares down at you. "You call that a push-up?" he barks. "I want to see your chest BOUNCE. Do it again! ONE ... TWO ... Faster! ... THREE ... FOUR ... Work off that baby fat! ... FIVE ... SIX ..."

You approach your dad cautiously. All you want is to borrow a few bucks for your first razor. Admittedly, you're a "late bloomer." But you're not prepared for his response. "Stand in the light," he says, trying to stifle a laugh. "I'll get that whisker with the tweezers."

Adults probably don't mean much by such comments, but their remarks can eat at your insides for days and reinforce the myriad anxieties and insecurities you already have. At a time when you feel very grown-up and are having to make sweeping decisions about your future (College? Career? Marriage?), you're constantly belittled and reminded of your youth.

Timothy was in a similar position. It's not known how old he was when Paul told him, "Don't let anyone look down on you because you are young," but he was young enough that Paul elsewhere refers to him as "son." And he was young enough to be chastised about his age—otherwise Paul wouldn't have brought the subject up. Perhaps Timothy had somehow communicated that he felt young and inexperienced—that he'd be more effective for the Lord if he was a little older.

Whatever the situation was, Paul told him that his actions, his quality of life, and everyday, practical godliness would speak louder than his age. In other words, he was saying Timothy's *spiritual* maturity mattered more than his *physical* maturity.

That's the same message God conveyed to Jeremiah when the young prophet complained of being too young to do what God had in mind for him. "Do not say, 'I am only a child' ... for I am with you," the Lord said. And his message is the same today.

If you feel hindered by your age or limited talents, remember that these are not concerns of God's. He can use your life in very big, extraordinary ways if you're willing to trust him in very ordinary ways each and every day of your life ... *for he is with you.*

See also: Jeremiah 1:4–10; Romans 8:31; Ephesians 4:10–16

▪▪ LIFE IN THE FAST LANE

Come near to God and he will come near to you. Wash your hands, you sinners, and purify your hearts, you double-minded.

JAMES 4:8

Gregg had been active in church—one of the leader types. But after graduation he started working for his father in a lucrative family business, and I seldom saw him again. I don't know what he made, but it was big bucks. He paid cash for a fire-truck-red Mustang and drove it off the lot one Saturday.

On Friday nights he party-hopped until 3:00 a.m. and once confided, "Mike, that was some par-tee! Two girls for every guy, and enough booze to float a boat in!" At one of the parties he met a flight attendant, and a few months later she moved into his park-front condo.

I bumped into him once at the mall and asked how things were. "Hey, great! Got a new girl, and just bought a new ski boat."

"You sound pretty happy."

The comment stopped him cold. He shifted on his feet and looked down. "Yeah, I suppose." For some reason he started talking, and eventually got around to saying he wanted to get back with God and how he felt *old* at twenty-two. "Everyone thinks I've got it great, but they don't really know . . ."

As Gregg talked, I got to thinking about a story I once heard about how some hunters in South America catch monkeys. They drill a small hole in a coconut, drain the milk, and scrape out the meat. Then they drop in a piece of candy and chain it to a tree.

A monkey, I was told, is curious enough that it will stick its hand through the hole and grab the candy. But its clenched fist is too big for the hole. The only way to release its hand is to let go of the candy. Trouble is, a monkey is too greedy for that. It'll scream all day trying to bash the coconut. It's doomed because it won't make the choice to give up the sweet. Eventually a hunter will wander by, brain the monkey, and take it home to barbecue.

Gregg had the potential to do something decent with his life and to find true contentment. But there were some things he needed to let go of first.

See also: Isaiah 1:18; 2 Corinthians 7:1; Ephesians 4:17–24

▪▪ BE PREPARED

Why do you stand here looking into the sky? This same Jesus, who has been taken from you into heaven, will come back in the same way you have seen him go into heaven.

ACTS 1:11

From the time I became a Christian in high school and heard someone pray, "Come soon, Lord Jesus," I've always been excited about the Second Coming. The very thought is staggering: a person who died some 2,000 years ago is still alive . . . and will return to earth!

When will it happen? Tomorrow? Next month? In five years? There are some honest disagreements among sincere Bible scholars about the timing of Christ's homecoming. Some very popular books have been written on the subject, complete with charts, diagrams, and predictions to make everything seem precise. Other authors interpret biblical prophecy differently. The dates they've circled in red are not the same.

But the Bible is clear about one thing: "No one knows about that day or hour, not even the angels in heaven, nor the Son, but only the Father.... Therefore keep watch, because you do not know on what day your Lord will come (Matthew 24:36 – 42).

Why will it happen? There are two basic reasons why the return trip will be made. First, Christ will come to judge sin and to honor faithfulness. Some people think they can get away with anything, but we are all accountable for our sin. When Christ returns, "All the nations will be gathered before him, and he will separate the people one from another as a shepherd separates the sheep from the goats.... Then they will go away to eternal punishment, but the righteous to eternal life" (Matthew 25:32 – 46). In other words, the choices we make on earth are binding in eternity.

Second, Christ will come to rule. The world is currently in rebellion against God, with the rebel leader being Satan himself. But that will all change when Christ returns! As promised in Revelation 11:15, "The kingdom of the world has become the kingdom of our Lord and of his Christ, and he will reign for ever and ever."

All of this talk about judging and reigning is, of course, very true. But it sounds rather formal and stiff. I'm sure that much of the reasoning behind Christ's Second Coming is simply his desire to return to his old stomping grounds to be with old friends and loved ones. It's a homecoming you won't want to miss!

See also: 1 Thessalonians 4:13 – 5:11

:: POINTS TO PONDER–HEAVEN

Our citizenship is in heaven.

PHILIPPIANS 3:20

To believe in heaven is not to run away from life; it is to run toward it.

JOSEPH D. BLINCO

Heaven will be the perfection we have always longed for. All the things that made earth unlovely and tragic will be absent in heaven. There will be no night, no death, no disease, no sorrow, no tears, no ignorance, no disappointment, no war. It will be filled with health, vigor, virility, knowledge, happiness, worship, love and perfection.

BILLY GRAHAM

A man's reach should exceed his grasp,
Or what's a heaven for?

ROBERT BROWNING

If I find in myself a desire which no experience in this world can satisfy, the most probable explanation is that I was made for another world.

C. S. LEWIS

What a pity the only way to heaven is in a hearse.

STANISLAW J. LEC

To be in hell is to drift; to be in heaven is to steer.

GEORGE BERNARD SHAW

A continual looking forward to the eternal world is not a form of escapism or wishful thinking, but one of the things a Christian is meant to do. It does not mean that we are to leave the present world as it is. If you read history, you will find that the Christians who did the most for the present world were just those who thought most of the next.

C. S. LEWIS

Religion can offer a person a burial service, but Christ offers every person new, abundant and everlasting life.

WILMA REED

Life's a voyage that's homeward bound.

HERMAN MELVILLE

There is nothing in the world of which I feel so certain. I have no idea what it will be like, and I am glad that I have not, as I am sure it would be wrong. I do not want it for myself as mere continuance, but I want it for my understanding of life. And moreover "God is love" appears to me nonsense in view of the world he has made, if there is no other.

WILLIAM TEMPLE

Faith is the Christian's foundation, hope is his anchor, death is his harbor, Christ is his pilot and heaven is his country.

JEREMY TAYLOR

When you speak of heaven let your face light up. When you speak of hell—well, then your everyday face will do.

CHARLES H. SPURGEON

A good many people will see little heaven hereafter if they do not begin to look for more of heaven now.

RICHARD MONTAGUE

See also: Isaiah 65:17–25; John 14:1–6

WEEK

18

██ ONE DAY AT A TIME

This is the day the Lord has made; let us rejoice and be glad in it.

PSALM 118:24

Just for today I will try not to fret about yesterday's "F" in math or worry about tomorrow's Spanish test. I will banish anxiety and forget past mistakes. I will discover God's will for my life one day at a time.

Just for today I will not try to appear perfectly packaged. I will feel free to cry, to doubt, to express my fears, to laugh till I hurt. I will think less about the mirror and about pleasing people and more about pleasing God.

Just for today I will be a good listener—no strings attached. I will comfort others . . . and keep my mouth shut. I will love others for *who* they are (unique creations of God) rather than for *what* they are (good-looking, funny, rich). I will do something nice for my parents.

Just for today I will take time to create a memory. I will *make* someone a birthday card instead of buying a Hallmark. I will take a walk at sunset. I will pick a flower, talk to a child, read an entire book in the Bible, smile at a teacher, take a bubble bath, greet a stranger. I will take off my watch.

Just for today I will try to be scrupulously honest. I will be literal about right and wrong. I won't sneak into the store express lane with twelve items when the sign says "ten items or less." I will drive *under* the speed limit.

Just for today I will trust God for the "impossible": a friendship healed, a bad memory erased, a sin forgiven, a family reconciled. I will stop just *telling* people I'm a Christian and start *showing* them.

Just for today I will quit a bad habit and replace it with one that is good. I will finish a project. I will not minimize or justify my wrong—even my speeding ticket. I will say, "It's my fault," and take the heat for my behavior.

Just for today I will thank God that sometimes "the race is not to the swift or the battle to the strong." For Christ's sake I will delight in my weakness, knowing that "God chose the weak things of the world to shame the strong."

Just for today I will try to live out my faith in very everyday, ordinary ways . . . and trust God in very extraordinary ways. Tomorrow will take care of itself.

See also: Ecclesiastes 9:11; Matthew 6:25–34

GOOD COMPANY

If we claim to be without sin, we deceive ourselves and the truth is not in us. If we confess our sins, he is faithful and just and will forgive us our sins and purify us from all unrighteousness.

1 JOHN 1:8–9

From time to time I experiment to see how long I can go without consciously sinning. I don't advertise it like some kind of Guinness contest. It's just a quiet little competition, the results of which are just between me and God.

I remember the time I tried to stop lusting. I wanted to treat girls like people, not as beautiful objects to undress with my eyes. The first day went relatively smoothly. Whenever I saw a girl I felt tempted to ogle, I thanked God for making such an attractive creation. Seriously. I simply whispered a quick, "Boy, God, you sure know how to grow 'em, if you know what I mean." I might smile and say hi, but my eyes never lost contact with hers. On the second day, my eyes and will wandered a bit. And I generally blew it the third day by taking second and third glances.

Knowing I can't even last a week without consciously sinning is a spiritual disappointment, because it reminds me how far short of God's standards I fall. Yet I'm not alone. The Bible is full of stories of the "great" men and women of God who fumbled badly themselves. Righteous Noah liked his booze. Abraham sacrificed his wife's chastity for his own safety. Moses frequently blew his stack and one day sent an Egyptian to the morgue. Rahab ran the best little whorehouse in Jericho. David had a fling with the next-door lady, and then murdered her husband to cover up his sin. Jeremiah drowned his courage in self-pity. John the Baptist doubted Christ's true identity. And that's to say nothing of half the apostles and most of the bit players in the Bible.

It's encouraging to know that I'm in good company: Even those who were most used by God fell short of his holy expectations. They frequently missed his goals by a country mile. I feel a certain kinship with them because they were real people with real weaknesses. Yet God used their lives in mighty ways ... because they knew they were spiritually bankrupt and sought his forgiveness. And I know God can and *will* do the same for me. His arms are open wide to those who draw near with confession.

As the prophet Isaiah wrote, "Though your sins are like scarlet, they shall be as white as snow; though they are red as crimson, they shall be like wool" (Isaiah 1:18). It's the greatest story ever told.

See also: Isaiah 55:7; Luke 15:11–32

■■ THE MOTORMOUTH

In humility consider others better than yourselves.
Each of you should look not only to your own interests, but
also to the interests of others.

PHILIPPIANS 2:3–4

Janna was home sick one day, and I made the mistake of dropping her assignments by her home after school. She met me at the door with a smile. And from then on she thought of me as a best friend.

A week later she cornered me on the bus ride home after seventh period. She said she just wanted to talk. I kind of shrugged and said, "Sure. I mean, fine." What else could I have said? Then she launched into a rambling, giggling monologue about her sister's new kid, her crazy history teacher, and her appointment to have her wisdom teeth pulled.

"I'll probably be all swelled up like, you know, a pregnant squirrel or something," she said, laughing like she'd told some sort of joke. And all I could think was, *Lord, when is this nut going to shut up and leave?*

Just before stepping off the bus, Janna looked me straight in the eye, flashed a toothy smile and said, "Thanks." I raised my eyebrows and gave her a funny look.

"You know, just for listening. For being, well, a good friend." And then she gave my arm a little grandma pat.

Right out of the blue, just like that.

No kidding, Lord, people never fail to surprise me. Here I do a stupid little thing like drop off her algebra book, and then spend the next few weeks trying to avoid her in the halls and on the bus. This girl—her motormouth bothers me, and I can't understand why she clutches at me almost in desperation, why she thanks me for being a friend. With friends like me, who needs enemies?

Help me, Lord, to understand this odd girl. Help me disregard my pride so I can truly reach out and befriend her ... like a *real* friend would. And thank you for blinding her to my insensitivity. Just help me to care ... like you would, Lord.

See also: Romans 12:9–16; Philippians 2:5–8

■■ WINNERS AND LOSERS

You will know that I am the Lord, for you have not followed my decrees or kept my laws but have conformed to the standards of the nations around you.

EZEKIEL 11:12

When you're a kid, you believe in the impossible: reindeer that fly, a fat man that slides down chimneys, rabbits that lay eggs. You also believe you'll grow up to be a winner, like maybe a tennis champ or TV reporter. Perhaps even the President.

But when you actually *do* grow up, you realize you've been duped. All that talk about Rudolph and Santa and the Easter Bunny was fairy tale. And the hope you had of being a winner began to seem equally absurd. Along with high school you discover you'll never be as successful as those around you. You flunk a French test. You get chosen last in P.E. You sit home Friday nights. Meanwhile, everyone else seems to be getting the awards, the lead roles, the friends, the scholarships, the dates, the attention.

You feel like a loser, but don't want to let on. You just try all the harder to be a winner. Maybe you'll be OK if you keep trying to fit in, gain acceptance somehow, and stop the familiar fog of depression and frustration from creeping behind your eyes.

It's easy, you think. Maybe things will come together . . . if you just try a new fad diet . . . if you just get some decent clothes . . . if you just use cologne . . . if you just listen to different music . . . if you just act a little more together and try some new things.

Pretty soon you've got yourself convinced: What harm can really come if I experiment a little and "go all the way" or smoke a couple of funny cigarettes or get smashed once or twice? I mean, what harm can it *really* do?

Before long, you're listening not to the "still small voice of God" but to Hollywood celebrities and hot-talking DJs and rock 'n' roll raunchies and semiliterate athletes who rake in $3 million a year. And by their standards, if you dare call them that, we all fall short. Success will always be one rung higher.

Because we are Christians, our success ought to be gauged by our changed lives. Period. But no lives will ever change if we're living by the world's standards and trying to win at all costs.

It's not that God has such a huge grudge against winning. It's just that most of us spend too much time trying to win the wrong contests.

See also: Romans 12:2; 1 Corinthians 1:18–31

:: LEARNING TO TRUST

Trust in the Lord with all your heart and lean not on your own understanding; in all your ways acknowledge him, and he will make your paths straight.

PROVERBS 3:5–6

When I was a kid learning to swim, I gripped the pool's edge until my knuckles turned white. But my instructor thought I could learn faster if I let go. Since she was also my mother, I thought I could trust her. So I took a deep breath, loosened my fingers . . . and just about drowned. I thrashed the water into a whirlpool, trying to stay afloat. And the harder I kicked and splashed, the quicker I sank.

"Don't fight the water," my mother said, slipping her hand beneath my back. "Trust it to hold you up, and use your strength to propel you." She slowly removed her hand, leaving me buoyed flat on my back. "I'm floating, I'm actually floating!" I said with a huge smile. Over the next few months, I learned I could not only trust the water to support me but also swim the distance of the pool.

I find that learning to trust God is like learning to swim. The hardest part is simply letting go and trusting God for such things as finding a job, coping with the death of a close friend or relative, working out hassles at home or school, dealing with the pressures of temptation. You may agonize over your uncertainties and insecurities. But God is there to support those who trust in his certainty and security. To you he promises a future and a hope.

As Isaiah writes, "Those who hope in the Lord will renew their strength. They will soar on wings like eagles; they will run and not grow weary, they will walk and not be faint."

The verbs he uses are all action words. The action begins when you make your first move.

See also: Psalm 37:3–4; 139:1–2; Isaiah 40:31; Jeremiah 29:11

▪▪ ON THE ROAD

> *In all your ways acknowledge him, and he will make your paths straight.*
>
> PROVERBS 3:6

From the observation deck atop Chicago's 100-story John Hancock Building, bits of clouds rush by within arm's reach, and sailboats dot Lake Michigan some 1,000 feet below like kids' toys in a backyard pool. Eight lanes of traffic snake along Lake Shore Drive. They carve a path between million-dollar condos and the waterfront, fueling a spaghetti-like network of expressways that lead to the outskirts of Chicago and suburbs beyond.

Sharing the observation deck with sightseers is a traffic control center, manned by a radio technician who uses a powerful telescope to monitor the maze of autos during rush peaks. But he doesn't just watch—he broadcasts things like: "There's a twenty-five-minute delay on the inbound Eisenhower Expressway due to a jack-knifed semi. Detour at Ogden." He points out the stalled cars, the accidents, the construction delays—the paths that should generally be avoided—and guides drivers along the route he feels is best, according to his broader perspective.

Not all drivers tune in to his station. Those who don't must necessarily choose their own route, based on a ground-level perspective. They may dodge and dart from lane to lane, thinking they are gaining time. But for all they know, the highway may be blocked just up ahead. The problem: they can't see much beyond their own front bumper.

In our day-to-day lives, we're much like these misguided drivers. We rely on our own limited perspective as we face our futures and the road up ahead. "There is a way that *seems* right to a man," the Bible says, "but in the end it leads to death." *The road is blocked,* but you can know that only if you're in tune with God, who views the world like a traffic controller scoping the roadways that stretch from horizon to horizon. He sees the roads you roam—where you've been and where you're headed. He knows where the detours are.

But God doesn't just watch—he *directs.* You're not just another somebody lost in the honky-honk rush of life. You're a unique creation of his that he will lovingly guide along the route he feels is best for you, according to his broader perspective.

Tune in today. Allow the one who is above all to "make your paths straight."

See also: Proverbs 14:12; Isaiah 42:16; 46:10

■■ POINTS TO PONDER –
CLOTHES AND FASHION

Why do you worry about clothes? See how the lilies of the field grow. They do not labor or spin. Yet I tell you that not even Solomon in all his splendor was dressed like one of these. If that is how God clothes the grass of the

*field, which is here today and tomorrow is thrown into the
fire, will he not much more clothe you, O you of little faith?*
MATTHEW 6:28–30

That which is striking and beautiful is not always good, but that
which is good is always beautiful.

NINO DE L'ENCLOS

Do not conceive that fine clothes make fine men, any more than
fine feathers make fine birds.

GEORGE WASHINGTON

Remember that the most beautiful things in the world are the
most useless; peacocks and lilies, for instance.

JOHN RUSKIN

What is really beautiful needs no adorning. We do not grind down
the pearl upon a polishing stone.

SATAKA

A fashionable woman is always in love—with herself.

FRANÇIOS DE LA ROCHEFOUCAULD

To get into the best society nowadays, one has either to feed
people, amuse people, or shock people.

OSCAR WILDE

Fashion is the science of appearances, and it inspires one with the
desire to seem rather than to be.

E. H. CHAPIN

Every generation laughs at the old fashions but follows religiously
the new.

HENRY DAVID THOREAU

Change of fashion is the tax which industry imposes on the vanity
of the rich.

SEBASTIAN ROCH CHAMFORT

Fashion is a tyrant from which nothing frees us. We must suit ourselves to its fantastic tastes. But being compelled to live under its foolish laws, the wise man is never the first to follow, not the last to keep them.

BLAISE PASCAL

Fashion is a form of ugliness so intolerable that we have to alter it every six months.

OSCAR WILDE

It is absurd to suppose that everything fashionable is bad, as it would be to suppose that everything unfashionable is good.

ALFRED W. MOMÉRIE

Fashion is the great governor of the world. It presides not only in matters of dress and amusement, but in law, physic, politics, religion, and all other things of the gravest kinds. Indeed, the wisest men would be puzzled to give any better reason why particular forms in all these have been at certain times received, and at other times universally rejected, than that they were in, or out of fashion.

JAMES THOMAS FIELDING

The perfection of dress is in the union of three requisites—in its being comfortable, cheap, and tasteful.

CHRISTIAN NESTELL BOVEE

The vanity of loving fine clothes and new fashions, and valuing ourselves by them, is one of the most childish pieces of folly.

SIR M . HALE

See also: Isaiah 61:10; Galatians 2:6; Colossians 3:12–14

WEEK

19

■■ A WORD OF THANKS

Enter his gates with thanksgiving and his courts with praise; give thanks to him and praise his name. For the Lord is good and his love endures forever; his faithfulness continues through all generations.

PSALM 100:4–5

I could talk about problems. There are plenty of those. But today, Lord, I want to say thanks . . . for friends and freckles and footrests and Frisbees; for footballs, fireflies, flamingos, and fathers. For cartoons and Christmas and cash (when I've got it); for campfires, cashews, Coke and . . . ahem, commodes, I thank you this day.

My creator, I thank you for graham crackers, grandparents, graduation, good grades. Not to forget hamburgers, heartthrobs, home and homecoming, the four-minute mile, and coaches that smile.

Ever-loving God, I offer thanks for Jell-O, jukeboxes, June, and July, for jeans that fade and dreams that don't. In addition, for small mistakes and big erasers, for music that's good, librarians that laugh, chairs that swivel, and hiccups that stop, I voice my praise.

God of glory, I'm grateful for breath mints and beaches, popcorn and pizza, dreams and drive-throughs, weekends and winks, as well as a mother's hugs, stingerless bugs and chocolate taste . . . without the chocolate waist. And my sincerest thanks for "You've never looked better!" "Welcome home!" "The exam's been canceled!" "Take a day off!" and "Keep the change!"

And most of all, dear Father, I thank you for yourself: the King of all kings, author of love, giver of life beyond life and hope in despair.

For these things and easily a hundred thousand others, I offer this prayer.

See also: Ephesians 5:19–20; Philippians 4:4,8

▪▪ FOLLOW THE LEADER

The Lord himself goes before you and will be with you; he will never leave you nor forsake you. Do not be afraid; do not be discouraged.

DEUTERONOMY 31:8

Our school football coach was like a member of the CIA—a super sleuth of sorts, who often sneaked into pregame practices of the opposing team.

Sitting in the stands undetected, he'd scout their biggest and best players, analyze their plays, determine their weaknesses, and log notes about the condition of the playing field. If there was a gouge in the turf on the 40-yard line or a puddle in the corner of the end zone, he knew about it. And based on all of this foreknowledge, he'd compile a game plan—a strategy of attack that he then communicated to our team.

Come game time, his advance work paid off. Every play was engineered to pit our strengths against the opponent's weaknesses. Naturally, he could not play the game for us—*we* had to carry the ball. But we carried it best when we followed his instructions. And we could always count on him to stand behind the team, directing, rooting, encouraging, challenging.

The same is true of your relationship with God. You don't know what kinds of challenges you'll face next week, next month, next year. You don't know where your future will lead. But God does, because he's scouted ahead.

"The Lord himself goes before you," the Bible says. God has seen what lies up the road. He has scouted the opposition, and he knows every obstacle, every rut and puddle that stands between you and ultimate victory.

But God doesn't just go before you and then recline in the stands, quiet and smug, as you blunder along. He goes the next step and "will be with you." Yes, God knows all about whom you'll marry, where you'll go to school, where you'll work. He knows in detail the struggles you'll face. And he's right at your side, directing, rooting, encouraging, and challenging.

The Bible offers the ultimate assurance that God "will never leave you nor forsake you." *Never.* He's with you from now through eternity. You needn't be afraid, nor discouraged. You need only follow the Leader.

See also: Isaiah 42:16; 49:10

■■ ON YOUR MARK...

Since we are surrounded by such a great cloud of witnesses, let us throw off everything that hinders and the sin that so easily entangles, and let us run with perseverance the race marked out for us.

HEBREWS 12:1

Sports analogies are frequently used in the Bible to describe hard-to-understand spiritual concepts. Swimming, wrestling, and boxing are among the sports mentioned. In the passage above, the writer of Hebrews uses running to explain "faithfulness." Maintaining a long-term relationship with God, he says, is like preparing for a difficult race: say, for example, the Boston Marathon.

Lacing up your first pair of Nikes can be deceiving. You feel like you can outrun Flo Jo or sprint faster than Carl Lewis. It's just your imagination.

After jogging a few blocks, you wheeze like an old smoker with emphysema. Stripping off your sweats helps. But after struggling another couple of blocks, you duck behind a tree and glance around quickly. Then you barf the Three Musketeers and Doritos you had for breakfast, wipe your mouth, and head for home.

Only after months of long, hard workouts do things come easier. Your endurance and speed pick up. You drop some weight. Your muscles are toned. After a year or so, you think more seriously about Boston. It seems like an attainable goal.

But ... you can't help noticing that when you run, you run alone. Your friends, who used to invite you out on Friday nights, no longer bother. Some think you're crazy. It crosses your mind that maybe they're right. Perhaps you *are* overdoing it.

So you take some time off. You revert to junk food and late-night parties. You sleep in. But fitness, unlike body fat, cannot be stored, and soon you're out of shape again. The entry deadline for the race passes unnoticed. And you end up watching ESPN reports about the marathon from your dad's easy chair.

The author of Hebrews wasn't a letterman in track. But he knew enough about marathons and enough about being a Christian to know neither is a cakewalk. Both require all-out effort. You can't worry about others, or you'll lose your focus. Persistence and endurance are musts. Certain things you must do without. Attitude is essential.

And then after all the training and preparation, you've got to hit the track and run like the wind if you want to receive the prize. No race—not even a figurative one—can be won by sitting on your laurels. You just can't get far in an easy chair.

See also: 1 Corinthians 9:24–27; Hebrews 10:36–39

KING OF HEARTS

After the people saw the miraculous sign that Jesus did, they began to say, "Surely this is the Prophet who is to come into the world." Jesus, knowing that they intended to come and make him king by force, withdrew again into the hills by himself.

JOHN 6:14–16

Jesus could have had a cushy job in politics for the asking. He had the charisma and magnetism campaign managers drool about. Barely 30, his political future seemed bright. But he had a hard time convincing people he didn't want his name on the ballot.

Take, for example, the day he retreated with his apostles to a remote shore of the Sea of Galilee. It was a favorite spot where they could be alone to pray, swim, fish, or just lie out and get some sun. However, a crowd of thousands tracked him to their hideaway. Some simply wanted to shake his hand and perhaps get an autograph. But most came because they were sick and tired of being sick and tired.

One look at the diseased multitudes, and the apostles voted to send them away. Half were probably contagious. But Jesus rolled up his sleeves and spent the rest of his day healing everyone he could get his hands on. And then toward nightfall he took a few loaves and fishes and whipped together a picnic feast that more than fed everyone—even those wanting seconds and thirds.

After supper, the crowd got a bit rowdy. The fast-food miracle convinced many that Jesus was the Messiah who was to come and rule his people. They believed his kingdom would be a strong-arm political force that would drive out their enemies and provide peace and independence. You can almost hear the people starting to chant: "JEE-ZUSSS! JEE-ZUSSS!" You can almost see the campaign buttons: *Jesus, King of the Jews.* But their candidate didn't hang around for speeches. He pulled up his toga and hightailed it for the hills.

Christ didn't usually run from confrontation, even when people conspired against him. But now they conspired *for* him. He insisted his kingdom was not of the earthly sort—of marble halls and golden thrones. Nevertheless, "King of the Jews" was a tag that stuck with him until death.

Christ probably would have preferred something more along the line of "King of Hearts," a tag that has stuck now some 2,000 years.

See also: Luke 17:20–21; Revelation 3:20

▓ REVERSED AMERICAN STANDARDS

> *Blessed are the poor in spirit, ... those who mourn, ... the meek, ... those who hunger and thirst for righteousness, ... the merciful, ... the pure in heart, ... the peacemakers, ... those who are persecuted because of righteousness, for theirs is the kingdom of heaven.*
>
> **MATTHEW 5:3–10**

When the final class was finished and the locker halls quiet ... when the stereos had been clicked off and the glossy magazines closed ... when the sun had set and day was done ... the people snuggled under covers with these thoughts numbing their minds to sleep:

Blessed are the wealthy, for theirs is the kingdom on earth. They will have no needs and will charge the desires of their hearts at Nordstroms and Saks.

Blessed are the merrymakers, for they will get invited to the best parties and never be lonely or sit by themselves at lunch.

Blessed are the arrogant, for they can stomp without being stomped in return. Their way through life will be paved by the weak and the meek.

Blessed are those who change with the times, for they will never be caught by surprise. They will know what's in and what's out, who's hot and who's not. They'll never wear the wrong label or tell old jokes.

Blessed are the steel-hearted, for they are masters of their emotions. Their mascara will never run.

Blessed are those whose morals are flexible, for they will never feel awkward. Nor will they be haunted by a nagging conscience.

Blessed are the troublemakers, for they will never wait in line.

Blessed are those who are chastised for their craftiness and unyielding ambition, for they will rise above their critics.

Blessed are you when people pat you on the back, praise you, and admit you into their inner circle. Rejoice and be glad, because great is your reward on earth, for in the same way they honored the winners who came before you.

Yes, blessed are you winners, for you will always feel secure in yourself. And when you snuggle under the covers, close your eyes, and drift deep into sleep, don't be surprised if your hellish nightmare is not a nightmare at all.

See also: Proverbs 16:18; Luke 12:15–21; 1 Corinthians 10:12

■■ THE LIST MAKER

> *Man is destined to die once, and after that to face judgment.*

> **HEBREWS 9:27**

Bonnie was the most organized person I ever knew. Her life was regulated by a daily schedule, which included everything from *shower—6:20 a.m.* to *remove makeup—8:40 p.m.* She was always referring to one list or another: *Things to Do-Wah-Diddy Today, Things to Remember, Things to Buy,* and *People to Call.* She planned for everything, and was never surprised.

We were talking once when the subject of God came up. A relative had died, and I happened to mention how glad I was this person was a Christian. Bonnie looked at me funny. "God's a cop-out," she finally said. "People have to face reality and take charge of their own lives." And then she pulled a small binder out of her purse and showed me her *Goals List,* which was divided into weekly goals, monthly goals, and future goals. On the list was everything from the books she would read in the coming months, offices she would run for in student-body elections, the type of guy she would eventually marry, etc. She placed a red check-mark next to goals she had already attained.

Well, Bonnie was so disciplined that she met every one of her goals in years to come. She earned her varsity letter in volleyball and read *War and Peace* her junior year; was elected class president her senior year; attended a prestigious university; worked for a big newspaper back East; married a doctor; drove an antique Triumph; and lived in a two-story colonial—just as she had planned.

Everything was perfect … until she had a fatal traffic accident and woke up in hell. It was the one thing she hadn't planned on.

See also: Luke 16:19–31; Romans 6:23

▪▪ POINTS TO PONDER—HELL

When the Son of Man comes in his glory, and all the angels with him, he will sit on his throne in heavenly glory. All the nations will be gathered before him, and he will separate the people one from another as a shepherd separates the sheep from the goats. He will put the sheep on his right and the goats on his left. Then the King will say to those on his right, "Come, you who are blessed by my Father; take your inheritance, the kingdom prepared for you since the creation of the world." Then he will say

to those on his left, "Depart from me, you who are cursed,
into the eternal fire prepared for the devil and his angels."
MATTHEW 25:31–34, 41

Hell was not prepared for man. God never meant that man would ever go to hell. Hell was prepared for the devil and his angels, but man rebelled against God and followed the devil. Hell is essentially and basically banishment from the presence of God for deliberately rejecting Jesus Christ as Lord and Savior.

BILLY GRAHAM

The one principle of hell is "I am on my own."

GEORGE MACDONALD

All hope abandon, ye who enter here.

DANTE (INSCRIPTION OVER GATEWAY TO HELL)

The road to hell is thick with taxicabs.

DON HEROLD

To be in hell is to drift; to be in heaven is to steer.

GEORGE BERNARD SHAW

In all discussions of hell we should keep steadily before our eyes the possible damnation, not of our enemies nor our friends ... but of ourselves.

C. S. LEWIS

Fear not that your life shall come to an end, but rather that it shall never have a beginning.

JOHN HENRY NEWMAN

The choices of time are binding in eternity.

JACK MACARTHUR

I willingly believe that the damned are, in one sense, successful, rebels to the end; that the doors of hell are locked on the *inside*. I do not mean that the ghosts may not *wish* to come out of hell, in the vague fashion wherein an envious man "wishes" to be happy: but ... they enjoy forever the horrible freedom they have demanded, and are therefore self-enslaved just as the blessed, forever submitting to obedience, become through all eternity more and more free.

C. S. LEWIS

The mission of Jesus cannot be defined without speaking of man being lost.

HENRI BLOCHER

The wicked work harder to reach hell than the righteous to reach heaven.

JOSH BILLINGS

See also: Isaiah 14:12–15; Luke 12:5

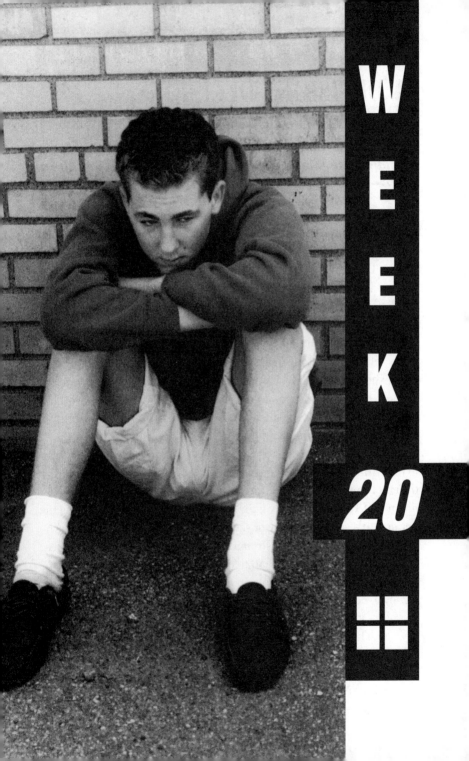

WEEEK

20

■■ DECISIONS, DECISIONS, DECISIONS

*If anyone comes to me and does not hate his father
and mother, his wife and children, his brothers and sisters—yes, even his own life—he cannot be my disciple.*

LUKE 14:26

Making decisions has never come easy to me. I'm at my worst in a restaurant. The waiter will come to the table with his pencil and pad, and I'll say something like, "How is the chili tonight?"

As he begins to tell me, another item catches my eye. "I think, maybe, I'll order a BLT instead, with fries ... except I always have that. What's the Chef's Special?"

When I contemplated faith in Christ, the decision was especially difficult. My conversion wasn't a euphoric fireworks-and-tears type experience. It was a painful, anguishing process of counting the costs: What would it mean to my goals and ambitions? How would it affect my family and friends? Was being a Christian really worth it? It was the biggest choice I'd ever make.

I knew that by saying yes to God I had to *comparatively* say no to everything else; by loving God I had to *comparatively* hate all other things. In using the word "hate" in the verse above, Christ doesn't mean that I treat my family like Nazi henchmen who have gassed my pet dog. It's simply his way of saying that my love for him should be infinitely deeper, infinitely stronger than any other love I might have.

Because of that, I had to *comparatively* relinquish my devotion to my desires and dreams, to my family, and even to my own life. I knew God demanded my complete devotion. Not a part—not even the biggest part. All of it.

That's what Moses meant when he told the Israelites: "The LORD our God, the LORD is one. Love the LORD your God with all your heart and with all your soul and with all your strength." If they loved God as directed—with their full emotional, mental, and physical capabilities—that didn't leave room for them to *really* love anything

else. But then, God has no peers, no partners. If he's truly L[
throne cannot be shared.

I once saw a bumper sticker that read, "Things go better
with Christ." It was a takeoff on the old Coca-Cola commercials. But
God never intended things to "Go better with Christ," as though he
were the Coke that perfectly complements a burger and fries. No, he
is the meal. And when we choose him, we must necessarily forsake
all other loves.

It's certainly not an easy choice. But it is a choice God
demands we make.

See also: Deuteronomy 6:4 – 5, 13; Mark 8:34–38

:: ONE OF THE GANG

*Let us purify ourselves from everything that
contaminates body and spirit, perfecting holiness out of
reverence for God.*

2 CORINTHIANS 7:1

When it comes right down to it, most people are probably
uncomfortable with the word "holy." It makes you think of nuns and
angels and retired ministers. It's definitely not the label I wanted to
be known by. In my school yearbooks, my friends used a lot of different words to describe me. They scribbled little notes, saying I was
... oh, "a great friend" ... "fun-loving" ... "a great guy to hang
around with" ... "funny, in a different kind of way"—things like that.

No one said I was "holy." Holiness just wasn't the goal I
aspired to.

Maybe that's because my first concern was seldom God—it
was *myself.* My self-worth was often defined by how well I was
accepted by others. I wanted to fit in. Sure, I was a Christian, I just
didn't want to be *too* Christian. As a result, I often compromised my
innermost beliefs about what I knew was right and wrong. With a
crowd of Christians I could act very Christian. But change my surroundings and I'd turn color like a chameleon to blend right in. I'd
do whatever it took to be "one of the gang."

After times like that, God always seemed distant. Maybe it was because I hadn't "acted like a Christian should." I knew God wasn't fooled with an act or outward appearance. He searched my heart—and we both knew I had compromised myself. To gain the respect of others, I had lost respect for myself. And the greater need behind self-respect is the inner assurance of feeling accepted by God.

By God's standards for our lives, we all fall short. We conform to the pattern of the world when the Bible warns against it. We mimic the lives of unbelievers when we should mirror Christ. In effect, we've turned holiness into a bad word.

"Be holy, because I am holy," the Lord said.

On your own that's as impossible to attain as growing another foot in height. But we're assured in Philippians 2:13 that we're not struggling alone. God is at work in us to *help* us desire and attain his standard and purpose for our lives. It's just a matter of allowing him enough elbow room to do the job.

See also: Romans 12:2; 2 Corinthians 6:14; 1 Thessalonians 4:3–8

▪ NO ORDINARY PEOPLE

> *The LORD said to [Moses], "What is that in your hand?" "A staff," he replied. The LORD said, "Throw it on the ground."*
>
> EXODUS 4:2–3

When you become a Christian, the thought of being used by God to "make a difference" in people's lives can paralyze you with insecurity. Your brain is gripped by the thought that you have such plain talents. You feel so ordinary, so insignificant. But God's outlook is different. With him there are no ordinary people.

When I wrestle with insecurity, I like to review the first chapters of Exodus where God tells an "ordinary" jelly-willed shepherd named Moses that he'll be used by God to confront the Egyptians, the most powerful nation on earth. But the withering, self-doubting Moses promptly stutters several reasons why he *can't* do what God says he *can* do.

Finally, God directs his attention to the plainest prop in the vicinity: the dead, dirty staff of wood Moses carried. When he obeys God's command to throw it on the ground, the walking stick becomes a slithering, hissing snake. When Moses picks it up again, it reverts to wood.

A celestial magic show? No, just God demonstrating that he can use what is ordinary to us in extraordinary ways. The key is Exodus 4:20: The staff of Moses had become the "staff of God."

More importantly, Moses had become the "Moses of God." He finally realized that what he felt *incapable* to do, God was *able* to do. And in the succeeding chapters of Exodus, you'll read the story of how God used this "ordinary" shepherd and "ordinary" rod to perform numerous miracles and alter the course of human history.

The same thing happened with the twelve disciples chosen by Christ to convey his message to the world. They were a ragtag group Christ selected from wharves and back alleys, not from marble palaces or judicial chambers. But they were willing to follow the Lord—to become "men of God."

In a sense, God's in the business of making "somebodies" out of "nobodies." And in his eyes, there are no ordinary people— just people either willing or unwilling to follow him. This is the challenge we must each face individually: Am I *really* the "Bradley of God," the "Andrea of God," the "Tyler of God," the "_____ of God" that the Lord wants me to be? Nobody can answer that but *you*.

See also: Proverbs 3:5–6; Luke 9:23–26

■■ OPINION POLL

"Who do you say I am?" Simon Peter answered, "You are the Christ, the Son of the living God."

MATTHEW 16:15–16

George Gallup has made millions by asking people questions. His biggest business comes during election years when would-be congressmen, senators, and presidents seek his help conducting random surveys to determine where they stand in the public eye. Is anything they say getting through? They want to know.

Jesus had a similar concern during the three years he spent traveling about the Palestine countryside some 2,000 years ago. Wherever he went, he attracted massive crowds of people. They sometimes followed him night and day, even when they had no food. Never before had someone performed the kinds of miracles he did: healing the sick, raising the dead, calming the storm-tossed seas, multiplying a sack lunch into a lavish picnic for thousands. And never before had anyone made the kinds of claims he did: to be the one and only Son of God, the bread of life, the forgiver of sin, the only way by which people might know God the Father.

But did the public believe him? Was anything he said getting through? Christ wanted to know.

He didn't have the benefit of a sophisticated polling service. Taking a random survey was unheard of. So he relied heavily on his disciples for feedback. One day he asked them, "Who do people say the Son of Man is?" Their reply: "Some say John the Baptist; others say Elijah; and still others, Jeremiah or one of the prophets."

This public confusion probably stung Christ. People knew *about* him, but they didn't know him as he wanted to be known. He was fixed in the public's eye. But he was not yet firmly implanted in their hearts as Lord.

Suddenly Christ fired another question: "But what about you? Who do you say I am?" he asked The Twelve, his closest companions.

"You are the Christ," Simon Peter said firmly, "the Son of the living God."

Peter hit the proverbial nail smack dab on the head. Jesus' message was *finally* getting through. And if Jesus ever felt like dashing into Peter's arms and giving him a rib-crushing hug, I'm sure he did at that moment.

See also: Matthew 10:32; Acts 2:36

:: MATTERS OF CONSCIENCE

I strive always to keep my conscience clear before God and man.

ACTS **24:16**

I had some time to kill before my next class, so I stopped by the library. Flipping through a dog-eared magazine, I discovered a humorous story about the government's "Conscience Fund."

Guilt has a way of nagging at some people—people such as the man who sent a buck to Washington to pay for the bottle of typewriter oil he stole while serving in the Air Force years before ... or the former federal employee who mailed $157 to the fund to make up for the nights he had left work early ... or the New Yorker who bought an air-mail stamp to return a penny he said belonged to the government.

I chuckled through most of the story. But then I began to wonder *why* I was laughing. After all, what was *really* so funny about people who simply wanted to be able to look at themselves in the mirror while brushing their teeth? Was it humorous that their code of ethics was stronger than my own as a Christian?

The "small wrongs" they couldn't live with were not that different from the ones I regularly ignored or rationalized. That struck me—just as I was about to rip the story out of the magazine for future reference. *Who's going to miss an article they wouldn't read anyway?* I excused myself.

It was reinforced the next day when I wrote a letter to a friend but didn't have any postage. So I began peeling an uncanceled stamp from another letter to use again. *No big deal—it's just a stamp,* I thought.

Later that day I was nearly to the post office when I noticed I was driving 10 mph over the speed limit. *But everyone is going that fast,* I rationalized.

And I kept the extra dime the postal clerk mistakenly gave me. *It's just small change,* I reasoned.

These were all little wrongs—things that really didn't hurt anyone else. Still, I was amazed how often and easily I minimized them. I had been living as if only the "big" stuff—the *real grossies*—mattered, and had developed a callousness toward small infractions. I had fooled myself into thinking that living as a Christian involved more than just following Christ's righteous pattern of life in very ordinary, everyday ways.

I can't say my life has changed drastically since that realization hit. And yet I find myself being a little more literal about right and wrong. I weigh my small decisions more carefully, knowing that will help me with big decisions.

Each day has become an experiment in which I, like Paul, strive to keep my conscience clear before God and man. It can be a very radical way of living.

See also: 1 Peter 1:15–16

:: EVERYONE LIKES BABIES

The time came for the baby to be born, and she gave birth to her firstborn, a son. She wrapped him in strips of cloth and placed him in a manger, because there was no room for them in the inn.

LUKE 2:6–7

Everyone likes babies. There is something inherently cute about them, regardless of looks—something that brings out the child in normally mature, reserved adults. Just watch their reactions outside any hospital nursery.

I suppose people thought Jesus was kind of cute, too, as he lay in the feed trough with bits of rolled oats and hay clinging to his bunting. If you could just get over the smell of cow dung that hung in the air, you could watch for hours as he drooled and bubbled and cooed. But baby Jesus grew up fast—and as he did, people's reactions changed dramatically.

As a man, Christ presented the sternest challenge ever made to mankind. He was vocal—some thought belligerent—about his beliefs, and a contract was put out on his life to shut him up. Everywhere he went he was trailed by a hit squad. People got riled when he claimed he was visiting earth on a special mission from God. All of a sudden, it was not good enough to be a mind-your-own-business Jew, to go to synagogue, clean up after your dog, and not spit in the marketplace. Christ changed the rules of the game overnight by saying he was the way to God—the only way—and that no one could come to God except through him. It was the worst news some people had received in years.

More than that, Jesus demanded people's total allegiance, and frequently reminded them that such loyalty would separate entire families and set father against son, mother against daughter. He never promised that his followers would win friends and influence people. He said they would be scorned.

Had Christ been a little more moderate in his statements, he would have been left alone. But he stuck to his guns and the Jewish mafia finally caught up with him. In the centuries that have come and gone since, it's odd how many people forget how truly radical Christ was. At Christmas, churches fill to capacity with people who come to hear the story of a baby born to two hick Jews in a stinky barn.

Everyone likes babies—especially baby saviors. They forget, however, that the baby grew up.

See also: Matthew 10:34–39; Luke 14:28–33; 16:13

■■ POINTS TO PONDER– CONSCIENCE

> *I strive always to keep my conscience clear before God and man.*
>
> ACTS 24:16

There is no witness so terrible—no accuser so powerful—as conscience which dwells within us.

SOPHOCLES

Conscience is a sacred sanctuary where God alone may enter as judge.

ABBÉ HUGO FELICITE DE LAMENNAIS

There is no pillow so soft as a clear conscience.

FRENCH PROVERB

Faces we see, hearts we know not.

SPANISH PROVERB

The more faithfully you listen to the voice within you, the better you will hear what is sounding outside. And only he who listens can speak.

DAG HAMMARSKJÖLD

As long as your conscience is your friend, never mind about your enemies.

ANONYMOUS

Sometimes a man with a clear conscience only has a poor memory.

NEAL O'HARA

There is a difference between him who does no misdeed because of his own conscience and him who is kept from wrongdoing because of the presence of others.

THE TALMUD

We were talking about cats and dogs the other day and decided that both have consciences but the dog, being an honest, humble person, always has a bad one, but the cat is a Pharisee and always has a good one. When he sits and stares you out of countenance he is thanking God that he is not as these dogs, or these humans, or even as these other cats!

C. S. LEWIS

It's what makes a boy tell his mother before his sister does.

FRANKLIN P. JONES

Conscience is merely your own judgment of the right and wrong of our actions, and so can never be a safe guide unless enlightened by the work of God.

TRYON EDWARDS

It is astonishing how soon the whole conscience begins to unravel if a single stitch drops. One single sin indulged in makes a hole you could put your head through.

C. BUXTON

See also: Acts 23:1; Romans 9:1; 1 Corinthians 4:4; Titus 1:15-16

:: TEAM SPIRIT

> *Let us not give up meeting together, as some are in
> the habit of doing, but let us encourage one another – and
> all the more as you see the Day approaching.*

HEBREWS 10:25

Why bother with church? Why can't I just worship God
alone on the bank of a river, in a pine forest, or better yet, in bed
with the covers pulled tight around my shoulders? I can meditate
about the Lord as easily in the hammock out back as in a hard pew.
I can sing hymns in the shower as well as I can in a sanctuary.

Today, and for the rest of the week, we'll address these concerns and try to dredge up some answers to the question: Do I really
need church? Why?

I need church because I'm a member of the team.

Imagine my excitement if, after weeks of grueling tryouts, I
wandered by the gym after school and saw my name posted on the
final football team roster. Just as I'm about ready to whoop it up, the
head coach rounds the corner and slaps me on the back, saying,
"Way to go, Bruiser! You made the cut. I'll see you at the first team
meeting – Tuesday at six."

But what if my response was, "Hey, Coach, terrific! I can't
tell you how much it means to make the team. But one question:
What's this about a team meeting? They're kind of a drag, if you
know what I mean. Besides, Tuesday nights are sort of bad for me –
my favorite TV show is on. How about letting me know if anything
important happens. Or, tell you what, how about just stopping by the
house afterward? I'll put on some popcorn, and you can relay the
highlights of what you told the team ..."

This scenario is understandably absurd. By skipping the
team meeting, I'd miss a big part of what it means to be a team member. Team meetings are called to renew spirits and gather perspective – perhaps after a loss the week before. It's a time to organize
strategy for next week; a time of retreat that provides a temporary
sanctuary from the clamoring crowds. It's a time of encouragement when the coach challenges the team and offers advice. And

being together generates team spirit—a spirit that can't be duplicated on my own.

As head of the church, Jesus Christ has called us to meet together. We're members of his team, and there are some things he'd like to tell us.

See also: Matthew 18:20; Colossians 4:7–9

■ FAMILY MATTERS

Just as each of us has one body with many members, and these members do not all have the same function, so in Christ we who are many form one body, and each member belongs to all the others.

ROMANS 12:4–5

Why bother with church? Attending services on Sunday doesn't make me a Christian any more than climbing a tree makes me a monkey. If my relationship with God began as a personal matter, then why gather with old men in sport coats, gray-haired grandmothers, screaming kids, and hypocrites?

Do I really need church? Why?

I need church because it is a family reunion.

A family reunion is composed not only of people my age, but also of old folks who snooze in the shade, nursing mothers and their whining infants, neat-as-a-pin aunts, raucous uncles, slobber-mouthed cousins, parents, and yapping dogs.

Before the weekend reunion is over, Tyler will break a window with his B.B. gun, Aunt Becki and Uncle Dave will not be speaking to each other, Grandma will finish knitting another afghan, I will be told fifteen times that I have my great-grandfather's eyes, Grandpa will lose his glasses, Uncle Scott will tell the same, dumb joke six times, my brother will get sick behind a tree from too much lime-Jell-O-and-carrot salad, the dog will tree the cat, and most people will be sniffling. Really, there's nothing quite like it.

Reunions are important because they bring together a diversity of people who have not led perfect lives, married saints, and raised kids that don't mash peas on the wall. Each person, myself included, is imperfect—but we remain linked to each other by reason of a common heritage.

Together, we're a melting pot of people who have overlooked our differences to thrive as a family through sickness and health, births and deaths, successes and failures. By holding reunions, we affirm the importance of family and create a sense of unity that spans generations.

As head of the church, Jesus Christ has slated regular family reunions. Every week. As his children, we are privileged to share in these ongoing gatherings that affirm family ties and bridge both years and idiosyncrasies.

See also: Romans 12:6–8; 1 Corinthians 12:12–31

■■ TIME OUT

> *By the seventh day God had finished the work he had been doing; so on the seventh day he rested from all his work. And God blessed the seventh day and made it holy, because on it he rested from all the work of creating that he had done.*

> Genesis 2:2–3

Why bother with church? My life is so hectic already that attending Sunday services is just another item on my pressure-cooker list of things to do. I've got three chapters to read for history, a five-page paper due in English, my dad is on me to clean the garage, the oil in my car needs to be changed, and my friends think I am ignoring them. I don't think my schedule can take any additional strain at this point.

Do I really need church? Why?

I need church because it is a retreat.

When I get so busy that I have no time for church, then I'm simply too busy. It may be just another item on my "Things to Do" list, but it's one of the most important because it gives me time to stop, gather my perspective, reflect on the coming week, and to "be still" and meditate with God.

It's a time to ungarble my mind, restring my nerves, and calm my churning stomach. Church is a place to realign priorities, to worship God, and celebrate Christ's empty tomb. *Celebrate*—yes, that's the word. By no means should church be Dullsville.

In the first chapter of Genesis, the Bible details how, in six days, God created everything from cotton-candy clouds, snails, and monster surf at Sunset Beach ... to the whiskered walrus, Venus fly trap, and lightning bolts. And on the seventh day he took a breather: "God blessed the seventh day and made it holy, because on it he rested from all the work of creating that he had done."

Jesus often did the same by retreating with his disciples to a sanctuary, a hiding place, where they could release their heavy loads of anxiety, strengthen their slender threads of patience and, most of all, *remember* their heavenly Father.

As head of the church, Jesus Christ has called for us to take weekly breathers—to rest up, to celebrate ... and to remember.

See also: Psalm 46:10; Matthew 11:28; John 14:27

■■ HOSPITAL TREATMENT

It is not the healthy who need a doctor, but the sick.
I have not come to call the righteous, but sinners.

MARK 2:17

Why bother with church? I can understand why some Christians go every Sunday—they're basically loser types. But I've got talent and confidence. So why can't I just skip the stained-glass, hard pews, pipe organ, and preacher pep talks ... and study the Bible myself?

Do I really need church? Why?

I need church because it is a hospital.

I may *feel* fine, but if I were diagnosed with an internal tumor I would seek treatment fast. The other option would be to check out a surgery textbook from the nearby medical library, buy some razor blades and a bottle of whiskey ... and operate on myself. The directions would be right there in the book, sort of. But I'd carve myself into hamburger before I made sense out of the medical lingo and references.

Instead, I would place myself in the care of a trained specialist who has studied the textbook extensively—someone who knows a lot more than I about muscle tissue, veins, nerves, organ functions, and suturing. The operation would take place in a hospital, where my surgeon would be helped by assistants, an anesthetist, a scrub nurse, and a circulating nurse. Nearby would be some surgical technicians and aides—all well trained and generally understanding of their patient's needs.

When you're admitted to a hospital, you are surrounded by a strange wonderland of sights, smells, and feelings. They don't serve Big Macs at dinner and the nurses don't wear jeans. Everything is a bit formal, and you can get to feeling uneasy. But a comforting thought is that a hospital is a place where sick people gather for one purpose: to have their health restored. It's a place to be examined and cared for by trained experts; a place to find comfort from those who have faced similar operations and illnesses; and a place where you, too, can comfort others as you recover.

As head of the church and Chief Physician, Jesus Christ has diagnosed us all with a terminal illness called sin. Thankfully, he has established a "hospital for sinners."

See also: Psalm 147:3; Luke 5:27–32

▪▪ IN MEMORIAM

The Lord Jesus, on the night he was betrayed, took bread, and when he had given thanks, he broke it and said, "This is my body, which is for you; do this in remembrance of me." In the same way, after supper he took the cup, saying, "This cup is the new covenant in my blood; do this, whenever you drink it, in remembrance of me." For whenever you eat this bread and drink this cup, you proclaim the Lord's death until he comes.

1 CORINTHIANS 11:23–26

Why bother with church? If worship is a private matter between me and God, then why all the fuss and public pageantry?

Do I really need to cram my body into a crowded pew every Sunday or participate in rituals such as communion?

Do I really need church? Why?

I need church because it is a memorial service.

Imagine that I had been driving down a lazy country road when I lost control of the car and rolled it, end over end, into a ditch. A passerby spotted the wreckage and pulled me free . . . just as the car exploded, killing him instantly. A few days later, a memorial service is held for the man. Would I go? Of course.

The Bible says that Christ was God's sacrifice for me—that Jesus stepped between me and death. And when I attend church, it's a way of remembering that. I could, of course, observe a moment of silence while lying in bed or during a commercial break on TV. I could just sing a hymn in the shower or read a psalm on my way to the store. But I think God deserves more than that.

A memorial service is intended to be a group affair. "Let us not give up meeting together, as some are in the habit of doing," the author of Hebrews wrote to a band of young believers. By drawing together weekly and by taking communion, we share in a common experience and inspire one another to greater enthusiasm toward God.

That spirit of worship cannot be captured in the same way when I'm stretched out in bed with the covers yanked tight around my shoulders.

As head of the church, Jesus Christ has invited us to his memorial service. He died for us, and he doesn't want us to forget that act of love.

See also: 2 Timothy 2:8; Hebrews 10:25

■■ IN TRAINING

Train yourself to be godly.

1 TIMOTHY 4:7

Why bother with church? I don't have much in common with others who attend. Besides, going to church doesn't make me a Christian any more than going to a bank makes me rich. Am I not safe as long as I've invited Christ into my heart and asked his forgiveness for sin?

Do I really need church? Why?

I need church because it is a training camp.

When I rowed for my university crew team, there was a fellow teammate who often ducked practice. "Gee, Coach, I jammed my finger playing volleyball yesterday," he said one morning as the rest of us were suiting up and gathering our oars. The following week he said he'd hurt his leg sliding into second during an intramural softball game. Other times he couldn't work out with the team because he had to work ... or fix his car ... or take someone to the airport.

His well-timed excuses were basically just cover-ups. He wanted the glory of "being on the team." But he wanted it the easy way—without having to train.

Church is like team practice—a training camp where Christians learn how to be better ... well, better *Christians*. I can duck practice, but I'm no good to the team when I do. Like my teammates, I am preparing for a race that will last my entire life—a race that involves following a course established some 2,000 years ago when Christ paved the path that leads to God.

"Train yourself to be godly," Paul wrote to Timothy. When I was born, no one had to train me to be bad. Smearing mustard on the wall and stuffing beans up my nose came naturally. But godliness doesn't "just happen," like an athlete doesn't "just happen" to pole vault eighteen feet or run a four-minute mile. It comes with training—learning the fundamentals and then perfecting them with the help and encouragement of other teammates.

As head of the church, Jesus Christ has called us to join him at training camp. There's a big race ahead, and he wants us to be prepared for it.

See also: Luke 6:39 – 40; 1 Corinthians 9:24–27; 1 Timothy 4:8

■■ POINTS TO PONDER–CHURCH

Be shepherds of the church of God, which he bought with his own blood.

ACTS 20:28

You aren't too bad to come in. You aren't too good to stay out.

CHURCH BULLETIN BOARD

Our great-grandfathers called it the holy Sabbath; our grandfathers, the Sabbath; our fathers, Sunday; but today we call it the weekend.

WESLEYAN METHODIST

God never intended his church to be a refrigerator in which to preserve perishable piety. He intended it to be an incubator in which to hatch converts.

F. LINCICOME

The holiest moment of the church service is the moment when God's people—strengthened by preaching and sacrament—go out of the church door into the world to be *the Church*. We don't *go* to church; we *are* the Church.

ERNEST SOUTHCOTT

When Christian worship is dull and joyless, Jesus Christ has been left outside—that is the only possible explanation.

JAMES S. STEWART

The birth and rapid rise of the Christian Church remain an unsolved enigma for any historian who refuses to take seriously the only explanation offered by the Church itself.

C. F. D. MOULE

Don't stay away from church because there are so many hypocrites. There's always room for one more.

ARTHUR R. ADAMS

Tell me what the young of England are doing on Sunday, and I will tell you what the future of England will be.

WILLIAM E. GLADSTONE

Jesus spoke about the ox in the ditch on the Sabbath. But if your ox gets in the ditch every Sabbath, you should either get rid of the ox or fill up the ditch.

BILLY GRAHAM

You see, God, it's like this: We could attend church more faithfully if your day came at some other time. You have chosen a day that comes at the end of a hard week, and we're all tired out. Not only that, but it's the day following Saturday night, and Saturday night is one time when we feel that we should go out and enjoy ourselves. Often it is after midnight when we reach home, and it is impossible to get up on Sunday morning. We'd like to go to church, and know we should; but you have just chosen the wrong day.

TWENTIETH-CENTURY CHRISTIAN

When I first became a Christian . . . I thought that I could do it on my own, by retiring to my rooms and reading theology, and I wouldn't go to the churches and Gospel Halls; . . . I disliked very much their hymns, which I considered to be fifth-rate poems set to sixth-rate music. But as I went on I saw the great merit of it. I came up against different people of quite different outlooks and different education, and then gradually my conceit just began peeling off. I realized that the hymns (which were just sixth-rate music) were, nevertheless, being sung with devotion and benefit by an old saint in elastic-side boots in the opposite pew, and then you realize that you aren't fit to clean those boots. It gets you out of your solitary conceit.

C. S. LEWIS

See also: Acts 2:42; 1 Corinthians 12:27; Hebrews 10:25

WEEK

22

:: LIMBO

Because you are lukewarm – neither hot nor cold –
I am about to spit you out of my mouth.

REVELATION 3:16

A couple of months after I became a Christian, Rachel invited me to a party at her place. We'd met at a Bible study a few weeks earlier, and she seemed like a fun person to get to know.

By the time I arrived, cars snaked down both sides of her street. I parked at the end of the line, behind a Toyota with a couple necking in the backseat. Not knowing what a "Christian" party was like, I stuck a small Bible in my pocket just in case.

My knock at the door couldn't be heard above the music, so I finally just walked in. When I entered, Rachel staggered toward me through a blue haze of cigarette smoke.

"Well, if it isn't Misser Chrishun!" she said through a crooked, silly smile. She started to tilt and I grabbed her arm. "No, no, I'm *perfely* sober. Now," she said, giving me a little push toward the kitchen, "the Bud's in there. Go get yersef lit and we'll talk s'more." I hesitated. "Go an get yersef happy. There's plenny beer!"

Months earlier, I would have felt perfectly comfortable being there. But the things I enjoyed doing changed when I became a Christian. I thought that happened to *everyone* who claimed to be a Christian. But Rachel seemed to be an exception. As soon as she turned her back, I quietly slipped out.

The following Monday I spotted her in the cafeteria and tried to explain why I'd left. "Don't be such a deadhead," she said nonchalantly. "People were just having a little fun. Besides, being a Christian doesn't mean I can't have a good time."

It was hard to figure Rachel out. She periodically continued to attend Bible studies. But I wondered what difference it made, because she reverted to being her same old self as soon as she left the meeting.

If she blew an easy tennis shot in the class we shared, she'd throw a fit that made John McEnroe seem polite. She wore her blouse open an extra button and flirted with everyone, even the bald math teacher. Whenever I passed her in the halls, she was on the arm of one of the loosest guys at school. I heard talk that she was taking the pill. That may have been rumor, but I somehow doubted it.

The odd thing is that Rachel often wore a necklace with a gold cross. I know the Bible tells us not to judge others, but I always thought it looked out of place dangling from her neck. I think to her it was just a piece of jewelry instead of a symbol of the One who died for our sins.

See also: Matthew 3:10; 7:21–23; Ephesians 4:17–5:21

■■ KNOCK KNOCK...

I am the way.

JOHN 14:6

From inside the large, elegant supper club came the sounds of laughter and fun. It was a bright, clear night—the kind of evening where the millions of stars seem to be within hand's reach, where the sidewalks seem to lead straight to the moon. On this magic night in Los Angeles, scores of couples had come to dine and dance. Music seeped beneath the doors, drifted through the windows, and seemed to enliven all that passed by outside.

Suddenly, the merriment turned to horror. Smoke and flames poured from the lobby. The dining area was enveloped in a dark, choking cloud. The only light came from the flashing orange tongues that licked at the walls and ceiling. Patrons scrambled from their chairs, screaming, and stampeded for the side exits.

A clot of people fought to get to the same doors. Panic ensued. Those felled by the smoke and fire were trampled. People climbed over bodies, pushing and shoving to get outside. But through the din of cries and wails came the horrific scream, "THE DOORS ARE LOCKED!"

Those who saw this story in the newspaper probably just skimmed a few paragraphs, felt a pang of incredulity, and then forgot it. Similar catastrophes happen so frequently that we are desensitized—especially when we don't know any of the dead. But the disaster stuck in my mind, perhaps because it reminded me of another closed-door tragedy that I see happening all around me. The difference is, my friends and family are among the victims.

You see, Jesus Christ is the doorway to God. He left no doubt about it: "No one comes to the Father except through me." On another occasion he added: "If anyone enters through me, he shall be saved." On this matter, Christ was *dead* serious.

To put it quite literally, he went to hell and back to open heaven's door and pave the way for us to forgiveness of sin, closeness with God, and eternal life. And even though people reject that claim and slam the door in his face, yet he stands there patiently knocking. Rather, patiently *pounding.* At stake is a matter of life and death.

See also: Matthew 7:8; Luke 12:35–36; John 6:37; Revelation 3:20

:: POSSIBILITY BELIEVING

Everything is possible for him who believes.

MARK 9:23

Christ made this statement when a man approached him with his son, who was possessed with some kind of an evil spirit. The spirit had turned the boy into a neighborhood freak, a circus sideshow of sorts.

As the boy stood face-to-face with Jesus, surrounded by a large crowd, he flopped on the ground and started writhing about like a fish out of water. Foam from his mouth mingled with dust to form a dark, dirty pool. His rigid legs beat the earth like drumsticks. It must have been some sight; you can imagine the bystanders gawking and whispering to each other.

"If you can do anything, take pity on us and help us," the man said to Christ, ignoring the crush of people.

"'*If* you can'?" replied Jesus. "Everything is possible for him who believes."

Christ didn't say everything is possible if you run with the right crowd, kneel when you pray, and wear designer togas. He didn't say all is possible if you're a premed student at Jerusalem U., tithe your shekels to First Central Synagogue in Nazareth, or know how to win friends and influence people. The only prerequisite was simply that the man *believe* Christ could turn his "impossibility" into a possibility.

"I do believe," the man immediately blurted. "Help me overcome my unbelief!" His lingering doubt vanished quickly when Christ did exactly that and healed his son.

"If you have faith as small as a mustard seed," Christ later told his disciples, "you can say to this mountain, 'Move from here to there' and it will move." Close your eyes a moment and think about the mountains in your life—the impossible and sometimes unbelievable situations facing you—that need to be moved.

Perhaps it's a haunting memory of past sin, a wrong relationship, or a problem at home. Perhaps it's a crippling feeling of inferiority or a nagging worry about your future. These "mountains" are what Charles Swindoll calls "great opportunities brilliantly disguised as impossible situations."

The "opportunity" is to allow God enough elbowroom in your life to do what he's best at: turning your impossibilities into possibilities. Listen to Jeremiah's words: "Ah, Sovereign Lord, you have made the heavens and the earth by your great power and outstretched arm. *Nothing is too hard for you.*"

Moving mountains is not something to tackle on your own. No chance of budging them an inch if you think you can do the job alone. Every chance in the world if you trust God to do it.

See also: Proverbs 3:5–6; Jeremiah 32:17; Luke 1:37; 18:27

■■ THE BOX

> *Be very careful, then, how you live—not as unwise but as wise, making the most of every opportunity, because the days are evil. Therefore do not be foolish, but understand what the Lord's will is.*

Ephesians 5:15–17

Sitting in a sauna is basically a passive experience. Blasts of steam envelop your body, making you sweat as if you've just returned from a long run on a hot summer day. In a sense, a sauna tricks your body: it creates feelings associated with having done something when you really have done nothing.

Watching television works basically on the same principle. It washes your mind with sights and sounds that create the feeling of "being there." A program about whitewater rafting, for example, will make it seem like you're actually in the bucking boat. But when the commercial blinks on, you realize you've been duped. You're actually doing nothing—just sitting in a room staring at a box.

Studies indicate the average American youth spends between twenty and twenty-four hours a week watching a piece of furniture crack jokes, tell stories, relay news, and otherwise entertain. That's about three to four hours a day—one-fifth of your waking hours. In small doses, TV may help you relax and get your mind off hassles at school, home, or work. But after a certain point, you must ask yourself: "What am I *not* doing during the time I spend watching TV?"

Because television is a recent invention, the Bible says nothing about it—just as it doesn't mention Ford Mustangs, Bazooka bubble gum, or McDonald's. But it has much to say about what we fill our minds with and how we use our time. In Ephesians 5:15–17 the apostle Paul indicates that these last days are evil days. The Lord's return is near. Each day is therefore extremely valuable. We shouldn't squander our hours. He says we should live wisely, "making the most of every opportunity" to do good and be about God's business.

Someday soon we will all face God and be asked to give an account for our lives. How about you? Will you have something to show? Or will the story of your life read like pages from *TV Guide?*

See also: Romans 12:2; 14:12; Philippians 3:14–21

:: DAY BY DAY

Give us today our daily bread.

MATTHEW 6:11

One of Thomas Carlyle's most ambitious works, a book on the French Revolution, took two years to write. The day he finished, he gave the only copy of the manuscript to a friend and fellow writer, John Stuart Mill, to read and critique.

Several days later, Mill raced back to Carlyle's home in a frenzy. He pounded on the front door like a crazy man. "I-I don't know what to say or how to apologize," he stammered, and then told how his dim-witted housegirl had used the manuscript as kindling to start a fire.

No answer from Carlyle—just a glazed, empty stare. When the extent of the tragedy sunk in, his face paled. He hung on the door for support. Two full years of his life were lost. The thousands of long, lonely hours spent writing were wasted. It was the worst nightmare he could imagine. How could he possibly write the book again? The thought paralyzed him, and he lapsed into one of the deepest, darkest depressions of his life.

Then one day, as he was walking the streets to gather his mind and seek some direction for his life, he stopped to watch the construction of a massive stone wall. Carlyle was transfixed. That tall, sweeping wall was being raised one stone at a time.

He knew what he had to do. "I'll just write one page at a time. One page today, one page tomorrow—that's all I will think about."

When faced with seemingly impossible situations, we often see the wall and not the individual stones. Perhaps you're overwhelmed by the demands from your teachers, your boss, your parents. As a whole, the load can seemingly break you. But taken day by day, task by task, the load is manageable.

The same is true of spiritual matters. You can feel boggled reading the Bible because God's expectations are a mile long. Take them instead one by one. Worry less about attaining God's plan for your *life* . . . just work on *today*. Godly character is built by laying stone on stone, minute by minute, day by day, in a thousand small, seemingly insignificant ways. Give your entire attention to what God is doing right now.

Let Christ be your example. He prayed for *daily* bread, *daily* sustenance. He knew tomorrow would take care of itself.

See also: Joshua 1:9; Proverbs 27:1; Matthew 6:25–34

⊞ ONE-NIGHT STANDS

*Just as you received Christ Jesus as Lord, continue
to live in him, rooted and built up in him, strengthened in the
faith as you were taught, and overflowing with thankfulness.*

COLOSSIANS 2:6–7

The way some people talk, becoming a Christian is hardly more involved than mixing a bowl of instant oatmeal. They speak of being born again, and can circle dates on calendars. But if you check with many of them after a few months or years, you'll likely find their warm, mushy feelings about God have cooled.

"It just didn't work," they'll say with a shrug, as if the directions on the box were bad.

A recent Gallup Poll showed that some 50 million Americans claim to have had a dramatic, one-time encounter with God. With all of the trouble in the world, I suspect that "being on God's side" somehow made them feel safer. The same Gallup Poll concluded with these shocking words: "Religious experience is on the increase; morality is on the decrease."

That's odd. Shouldn't a confrontation with God cause an upswing in morality? Or is it just that one-night stands with God have no life-changing impact?

Becoming an instant Christian makes as much sense as becoming an instant surgeon. Dr. Christiaan Barnard didn't just pick up a scalpel and suddenly start transplanting hearts. Nor can you arrive overnight as a Christian. In Romans 6, 7, and 8, Paul describes the constant struggles Christians face—it's as if we have civil wars raging in our hearts. Winning those battles takes *time*.

In his letter to the Colossians, Paul speaks about being *rooted, strengthened, built up* in faith. Salvation, like corn, doesn't sprout overnight. If it's true and healthy, it must be nurtured, weeded, watered, fertilized. It is a loving *process* of drawing closer to God.

As you read yesterday, lasting change is built by laying stone on stone. It takes work, risk, dedication, sacrifice ... and especially time. God rushes no one, and expects instant saints of none.

See also: Galatians 6:7–9; Ephesians 3:14–21; Hebrews 3:14

POINTS TO PONDER –
MATERIALISM AND MONEY

No one can serve two masters. Either he will hate the one and love the other, or he will be devoted to the one and despise the other. You cannot serve both God and Money.

MATTHEW 6:24

The safest way to double your money is to fold it over once and put it in your pocket.

FRANK MCKINNEY HUBBARD

Make all you can, save all you can, give all you can.

JOHN WESLEY

We can hardly respect money enough for the blood and toil it represents. Money is frightening. It can serve or destroy man.

MICHEL QUOIST

Silly people think that money commands the bodily goods most worth having.

ST. THOMAS AQUINAS

Wealth is a very dangerous inheritance, unless the inheritor is trained to active benevolence.

C. SIMMONS

Our incomes are like our shoes; if too small, they gall and pinch us; but if too large, they cause us to stumble and to trip.

CALEB C. COLTON

Money spent on myself may be a millstone about my neck; money spent of others may give me wings like angels.

R. D. HITCHCOCK

Money is a bottomless sea, in which honor, conscience, and truth may be drowned.

KOZLAY

If a man runs after money, he's money-mad; if he keeps it, he's a capitalist; if he spends it, he's a playboy; if he doesn't get it, he's a ne'er-do-well; if he doesn't try to get it, he lacks ambition. If he gets it without working for it, he's a parasite; and if he accumulates it after a lifetime of hard work, people call him a fool who never got anything out of life.

VIC OLIVER

A fool and his money are soon parted.

GEORGE BUCHANAN

If you make money your god, it will plague you like the devil.

HENRY FIELDING

That money talks
I'll not deny,
I heard it once:
It said, "Goodbye."

RICHARD ARMOUR

To be clever enough to get a great deal of money, one must be stupid enough to want it.

G. K. CHESTERTON

One of the dangers of having a lot of money is that you may be quite satisfied with the kinds of happiness money can give and so fail to realize your need for God. If everything seems to come simply by signing checks, you may forget that you are at every moment totally dependent on God.

C. S. LEWIS

When money speaks the truth is silent.

RUSSIAN PROVERB

See also: Ecclesiastes 5:8–20; Matthew 25:14–28

WEEK

23

:: GUILT THAT KILLS

Let us then approach the throne of grace with confidence, so that we may receive mercy and find grace to help us in our time of need.

HEBREWS 4:16

It was late summer, during the lull that precedes the start of school. Bobby, 18, and his 16-year-old girlfriend, Joanne, were on their way to visit friends. But before they arrived, Bobby fell asleep at the wheel and smashed into an 18-wheel truck, killing Joanne instantly. Bobby escaped with bruises.

Knowing he was to blame for Joanne's death, Bobby asked God to forgive him. But that seemed too easy. And Bobby wanted others to know how sorry he felt. So a few weeks after Joanne's funeral, he borrowed a gun and shot himself.

Bobby's suicide a few years ago reminded me of the story of the man riding down the road on a donkey, carrying a 200-pound sack of wheat on his shoulders.

"Why don't you take the weight off your shoulders and put it on the donkey?" asked a passerby.

"You don't think," the man responded, "that I'd ask the donkey to carry all that weight, do you?"

Because we're imperfect human beings, we'll never be free from the weight of guilt. It's there to remind us when we fall short of God's standards. Yet God is not some cosmic madman who delights in watching us squirm. He makes it very clear that he wants to remove the burden from our shoulders and give rest to the weary.

But people respond to guilt in different ways. Take Judas and Peter, for example. Both were trusted disciples, yet both turned on Christ. Judas betrayed him to a crowd of thugs and Hebrew zealots, leading to Christ's capture. And then when Christ was on trial for his life, Peter denied three times even knowing him. Both men were overwhelmed with guilt.

Judas wanted to advertise how sorry he felt, so he hanged himself. On the other hand, Peter resolved his guilt before God and went on to become the key disciple in spreading the news of Christ.

Our reactions to guilt may not be as dramatic as were Bobby's, Judas's, or Peter's. But our response can either drive us farther from God or closer to him. The Bible makes it clear that God prefers the latter. He only asks that we admit our need and trust him with the load. And then we can walk in newness of life—precious, free, forgiven life.

See also: Jeremiah 31:25; Matthew 11:28; John 7:37

COACH BILL

It is God who works in you to will and to act according to his good purpose.

PHILIPPIANS 2:13

When I rowed for my college crew team, I awoke six mornings a week to a jangling alarm clock set for 4:30. I was never much of a morning person, but I didn't have much to say about the matter. It was all part of the training regimen set by the coach.

Coach Bill wanted team members up with the street sweepers and on the water by 5:00 for a grueling two-hour workout before classes. He also required that we spend an hour pumping iron and that we run ten miles daily—the last thing I often felt like doing. All of my friends would be having fun, and I'd be out there sweating to death.

Sometimes I'd talk to Coach Bill about the frustrations I felt because of the stiff training schedule or about the searing pain I felt in my legs from shin splints I developed from pounding the pavement each day. Coach Bill never bawled me out for feeling that way. Rather, he'd lace up his running shoes and join me for a jog. You see, he never wanted team members to feel like they were struggling on their own. He wanted us to know he was supporting us and working with us for the same goals.

That same attitude is shared by God. When I get discouraged as a Christian or feel I've fallen short of God's expectations, I take a few minutes to talk it over with him. He doesn't zap me for my shortcomings. Rather, in his ever-loving, ever-compassionate way, he assures me that I am not alone.

Through his Holy Spirit, he's at work in me—helping me to do what he wants. He doesn't set arbitrary goals and then sit back and watch me struggle. He's a hands-on God—always there to help me meet the goals.

See also: Joshua 1:5 – 9; John 14:23–27

⊞ FOLLOWING THE PIPER

Here I am! I stand at the door and knock. If any-one hears my voice and opens the door, I will go in and eat with him, and he with me.

REVELATION 3:20

When I was a kid, we had several cats—adopted, for the most part, by my brother on his way home from school. They'd follow him like the Pied Piper, though I suspect he carried catnip in his hip pocket.

Most of the cats were fat and lazy, with the personality of a pillow. But one tagalong was an alley brawler whose eerie banshee screams kept the neighborhood awake at night. I became fairly used to him dragging home from his back-lot prize fights with a little less fur and a few more holes in his right ear. It's like when you live with someone day after day, you don't notice them gaining or losing weight. The tom was losing parts of his body, but at a slow rate. So I paid little attention until a friend commented, "That cat of yours is sure falling apart."

Our lives as Christians can fall apart like that in ways we hardly notice. God is not first in our lives. He's not even fifth or sixth or thirteenth. He trails the pack of our priorities. We may be vaguely aware that we've taken that slow, downhill slide from God. We may even wake up at night, try to stare down the ceiling, and attempt to determine what went wrong. But "what went wrong" occurred so slowly we thought we were somehow still right. We have lost our joy, happiness, and hope—great hunks of our beings as Christians—yet keep on living as if everything is fine. We don't realize we're in hot water.

Some mad biologist with a penchant for the perverse conducted an experiment in which he put a number of frogs in a pot of water and very, very slowly heated the water to a boil. They could have easily hopped out, but the change in temperature occurred so slowly that none seemed to notice. In the end, every frog died.

We're that way, too. At any time we're free to turn back to God, to seek his help in overcoming the sin and habits and worries that bog us down. "Come unto me," he says, arms open wide. Yet we're slow to embrace his forgiveness and experience healing.

As Christians, we seldom truly wrestle with Satan's powers as we should. We've joined them. We've dropped into line and are following the Piper. Is it too late to stand apart, to renew that fresh joy, to experience the purpose of life you once had? *Never.*

"Here I am! I stand at the door and knock," Christ says. You opened the door once. Go ahead—open it to him again.

See also: Isaiah 1:18; Romans 12:2; Hebrews 10:15–17

:: HIT OR MISS

All Scripture is God-breathed and is useful for teaching, rebuking, correcting and training in right-eousness.

2 TIMOTHY 3:16

Perhaps you've heard the story of the young student who wanted to know God's will for his future. So he took his Bible, opened it at random, closed his eyes, and dropped his finger to the page—assuming that the verse it came to rest on would be God's way of directing his future steps.

To his dismay, his finger fell on Matthew 27:5, which says Judas "went away and hanged himself." The young man tried again, and his finger landed on Luke 10:37: "Go and do likewise." Following the same procedure a third time, his finger pointed to John 13:27: "What you are about to do, do quickly."

The point is clear. You're liable to get the wrong message if you treat Scripture like fortune cookies. But that's what many people do. Instead of reading the Bible in some systematic fashion, they expect good-luck passages to pop out. Or they hunt and peck for God's will in a hit-or-miss manner. And they generally miss more than they hit. Others read only their favorite passages—sticking to the verses they particularly like. But balanced spiritual growth doesn't happen from a milk-and-Twinkies pattern of reading Scripture. Dig into the meat!

Paul says to Timothy that *all* Scripture is God-breathed. In other words, the writers of the Bible didn't just dream up good and challenging thoughts as if writing clever sayings for greeting cards. They penned what the Holy Spirit directed them to write. Because of that, the Bible is like no other book in existence. It is God's owner's manual for the planet Earth. By dissecting it word by word, we can learn how to live life to his full, complete specifications. I think that's sort of what Timothy means when he says *all* of the Bible is *useful*.

It's like the owner's manual for your car. Just reading about how to change the oil won't help you if your carburetor or fuel pump is bad. In the same way, the Bible can help in every area of our lives by *teaching* (educating us about the nature of God, for example), *rebuking* (reprimanding us for wrong behavior), *correcting* (helping us adjust our behavior to God's standards), and *training in righteousness* (instructing us on *how* we can live as God intends).

If all of the Bible is inspired by God, we should read it all. But beyond that, we must let it permeate our lives to the point that we *act* on what we read. "Do not merely listen to the word," writes the apostle James. "Do what it says."

Being a "doer of the word" is not just an idle suggestion. It's the Lord's directive for a truly God-breathed way of living.

See also: Psalm 119:1–16; James 1:21–25

:: OWNER'S MANUAL

> ***Your word is a lamp to my feet and a light for my path.***

PSALM 119:105

Twin borders of white lights stretch the distance of the runway, forming a fluorescent path for planes as they scream down from the darkness and brake for a safe landing. On a clear night, a pilot can see the beacons for miles. They light his way, indicating where he should direct his plane. If he follows the guide lights and stays within their boundaries, all will be well. But if he strays to the right or left, outside the illuminated zone, disaster awaits.

As Christians, we have guiding lights of our own: a best-selling collection of books that mark our boundaries and illumine our path to God. These books, collectively known as the Bible, are God's "Owner's Manual" for the human race. They contain his specs on keeping the human machine tuned correctly and running smoothly.

The Bible is not, however, a technical manual of schematic diagrams and charts, nor a cold, dead, dated document. It's at once a love story, autobiography, biography, self-help text, poetry anthology, compilation of personal letters, songbook, log of genealogy, how-to manual, and collection of prophecy.

It contains testaments from men and women who have trusted God completely—providing guidance and inspiration for you—and details life histories of people who have just as completely disregarded God—giving you fair warning.

Above all, the Bible is God's way of stepping out of the shadows and making himself known. It tells us exactly what he's like, what he expects of us, why things aren't like they ought to be, and what he intends to do about it.

You think it's awful that your father died of a heart attack? So does God: He promises one day to rid the world of death and dry every tear. You think it's unfair that people can cheat and swindle their way to success? So does God: He promises that no sin or sinner will escape his judgment.

Finally, the Bible is God's word—his final word on how to experience a full, rich, abundant life. It guides you out of darkness, and it helps you maneuver through every difficulty of life, whether it's your fears about next year or your tears about a broken relationship. God knows and cares about these matters and more. You've got his word on it.

See also: Psalm 119:1–16; 2 Timothy 3:16

:: EYEWITNESS REPORTS

That which was from the beginning, which we
have heard, which we have seen with our eyes, which we

have looked at and our hands have touched – this we pro-
claim concerning the Word of life.

1 JOHN 1:1

When Pan Am's flight 759 crashed on takeoff from New
Orleans a few years ago, reporters rushed to interview witnesses. "I saw
the belly of it," said one passerby of the doomed 727. "It was spitting
and popping like it couldn't get the motor running." A neighbor added,
"There was a wall of flame all across the street. I thought I was in hell."

Sometimes, when the event that has been experienced is
important or newsworthy enough, the witnesses will write books about
it. Presidents often publish their memoirs of history. And close friends
of famous personalities often write "insider accounts." What was Elvis
or Hitler or Babe Ruth really like? All you have to do is read the book.

If you want to know more about Christ, all you have to do is
open your Bible – a library of books written, for the most part, by his
closest followers. Writing independently, Matthew, Mark, Luke, and
John documented the events of Christ's life scene by scene. Did
Jesus *really* raise Lazarus from death? Did he *really* heal the blind,
rebuke religious leaders, and forgive sinners? Did he *really* say we
are immortal creatures and claim to be the Son of God? You have
the words of four separate writers.

As John wrote in his gospel: "These [things] are written that
you may believe that Jesus is the Christ, the Son of God, and that by
believing you may have life in his name." In his later epistles, John
wanted his readers to know that his words weren't hand-me-down
truths, passed to him from a friend of a friend. As one of the twelve
disciples, John was an eyewitness to all that Christ did and said.
That's why he opened his first epistle by saying, in effect, "I'm writing about what I know personally. I'm not making it up. Believe
me – I was there with Christ!"

Unlike many authors today who ride the talk-show circuit,
John and Jesus' other biographers didn't write for money or fame.
They simply wrote so that others might come to know Christ as well
as they did.

See also: John 20:31; 2 Timothy 1:12; 1 John 1:2–4; 5:13–14

■ POINTS TO PONDER–
THE BIBLE

Don't you know what the Scripture says . . . ?

ROMANS 11:2

Most people are bothered by those passages of Scripture they do not understand, but the passages that bother me are those I do understand.

MARK TWAIN

A man who loves his wife will love her letters and her photographs because they speak to him of her. So if we love the Lord Jesus we shall love the Bible because it speaks to us of him.

JOHN R. W. STOTT

If God is a reality and the soul is a reality and you are an immortal being, what are you doing with your Bible shut?

HERRICK JOHNSON

The Bible was never intended to be a book for scholars and specialists only. From the very beginning it was intended to be everybody's book, and that is what it continues to be.

F. F. BRUCE

I thoroughly believe in a university education for both men and women; but I believe a knowledge of the Bible without a college course is more valuable than a college course without the Bible.

WILLIAM LYON PHELPS

The Bible is a window in this prison of hope, through which we look into eternity.

JOHN SULLIVAN DWIGHT

If you really want some mail, read a letter from Paul.

ANONYMOUS

Warning: This book is habit-forming. Regular use causes loss of anxiety, decreased appetite for lying, cheating, stealing, hating. Symptoms: increased sensations of love, peace, joy, compassion.

ANONYMOUS

I study my Bible as I gather apples. First, I shake the whole tree that the ripest might fall. Then I shake each limb, and when I have shaken each limb, I shake each branch and every twig. Then I look under every leaf.

MARTIN LUTHER

The Christian feels that the tooth of time gnaws all books but the Bible. It has a pertinent relevance to every age. It has worked miracles by itself alone. It has made its way where no missionary had gone and has done the missionary's work. Centuries of experience have tested the book. It has passed through critical fires no other volume has suffered, and its spiritual truth has endured the flames and come out without so much as the *smell* of burning.

W. E. SANGSTER

To read the Bible as literature is like reading *Moby Dick* as a whaling manual or *The Brothers Karamazov* for its punctuation.

FREDERICK BUECHNER

God has given us in written form a volume which spans all the human emotions, the ups, the downs, the diversity of individuals, the good with the bad, the ugly, the beautiful, the sinners, the righteous, the perverted, the saved, the lost, the poetry, the poets, the wisdom, the wise, the human stories, the reality of life, pregnant with meaning, a book in fact of truth, not pale, narrow, religious sayings. The Bible, the Word of God, is solid, human, verifiable, divine indeed.

FRANKY SCHAEFFER

See also: 2 Timothy 3:16–17

WEEK

24

■ ALL HEART

Love must be sincere.

ROMANS 12:9

I'm your basic All-American good guy—as nice as they come. You'd know that if you took the time to get to know me. I get along with *everyone*. Except for those who . . .

Don't wash their gym clothes
Stutter when they talk
  Merge too slowly on freeways
  Look greasy
    Burp in shopping malls
    Have zits on their nose
      Don't listen when I talk
      Walk with a cane
        Don't remember my birthday
        Score higher than me.

And I'm really quite compassionate. All heart, as they say. Except when it comes to . . .

Fat people
Old teachers
  Beer bellies
  People with warts
    Vice principals
    Braggarts
      Abortionists
      And people who shoot abortionists.

We could be very best friends. We'd get along great. I'm as supportive and loving as friends come. Except toward . . .

Prudes
Faggots
  Nerds
  Ditzes
    Skinheads

Druggies
   Holy rollers
   Sluts
     And ... of course, bigots.

See also: Romans 12:3; Philippians 2:3–4

■■ A WANTED MAN

O Lord, please send someone else to do it.

EXODUS 4:13

Few of the characters mentioned in the Bible were truly great men and women. Even the star players suffered from inferiority and doubt. They felt incapable at times of trusting God.

Take Moses, for example. He's often depicted as a tough-minded, bigger-than-life, dashing leader—sort of a cross between Mel Gibson and the Pope. Yet much of his life (see Exodus 2–4) he failed miserably. He botched a murder he tried to commit secretly, fled his country in fear, married a foreigner, and bummed his living off her parents by tending their sheep.

Yet God overlooked his failure, because it was at this rock-bottom time in Moses' life that God appeared to him in the burning bush, calling him to service: "So now, go. I am sending you to Pharaoh to bring my people the Israelites out of Egypt" (Exodus 3:10).

When Moses heard what God wanted, he stuttered with excuses. Feelings of inferiority clawed deep in his brain. All those years scrounging off his in-laws and watching stinky sheep convinced him he was a loser.

"Who am I, that I should go to Pharaoh?" he said (Exodus 3:11). Translation: "You want *me* to do *what?* God, you've gotta be kidding! I'm not capable." Later he blurts, "What shall I tell them? What if they do not believe me?" (Exodus 3:13, 4:1).

God's response was apparently not good enough for Moses, because in desperation he complains, "O Lord, I have never been eloquent ... I am slow of speech and tongue ... O Lord, please send someone else to do it" (Exodus 4:10, 13).

In effect, God hand-picked Moses for a big job. But Moses wanted to run back to the farm. He felt crippled by self-doubt and low self-esteem. Not only didn't he think he was a leader type, he also thought he talked funny.

"I will help you speak and will teach you what to say," the Lord replied.

Can you identify with Moses and his lack of confidence? Perhaps you, too, are ducking God's service or some other task because you're troubled by low self-worth. If so, you've been deceived by the devil. God is able to turn your disabilities into blessings. He's not bound by your self-imposed barriers and inabilities. What you *can't* do, God *can* do. He'll go with you, helping you speak, teaching you what to say—if for no other reason than to keep you trusting him—not yourself—day by day.

If you have any doubts, just read about the rest of Moses' life.

See also: Proverbs 3:5–6

:: GLIMPSES OF GOD

Truly you are a God who hides himself.

ISAIAH 45:15

I have my moments, quite frankly, when it's difficult to worship God—to *connect* with him in some meaningful way. After all, he doesn't exactly maintain a high profile. When was the last time you saw him?

I'd do something about that if I were God. I wouldn't be so shy. I'd come out of hiding every few years just to remind people I was still around and that if it was heaven they were after, they still needed to reckon with me.

Perhaps God could learn from the way they start football games at the Air Force Academy in Colorado Springs. A half dozen or so young cadets bail out of a plane circling overhead and parachute onto the fifty-yard line of the field. The refs, the players, and fans all peer skyward to watch the cadets' descent, and for good reason. The game can't begin until the last parachutist lands, because he carries the game ball. As the ball is passed to the ref, the crowd roars, and then jet fighters scream overhead, slam on their afterburners, and rocket straight up and out of sight. It's enough to make you wet your pants.

I think that's how I'd do it if I were God, except I wouldn't use a parachute and I wouldn't land. I'd free-fall headfirst, and then pull up into a hover just at the top of the stadium. I'd do the jet thing, but would catch them in midair, one in each hand. And then I'd let rip a few lightning bolts just to let people know it was really me, and boom out something like, "I am the Lord your God, and you shall worship me!"

Concerns about God's low visibility are nothing new. Job cried out in desperation, "If only I knew where to find him" (Job 23:3). King David echoed his pleas: "Why, O Lord, do you stand far off?" (Psalm 10:1). Even Philip, one of Christ's disciples, looked him square in the eye and said, "Lord, show us the Father and that will be enough for us" (John 14:8).

The Bible doesn't fully explain why God does not make a bigger deal about being God, but I suspect it's largely out of respect for us. He holds back because he knows we can handle only so much reality at a time. And so he reveals himself in man-sized glimpses: the colorful splash of sunset, the promise of spring, the comfort of his Holy Spirit, the changing expressions of a baby's face, the unity of a family, the miracle of sacrificial love, the melody of rain, the humor of a snail's face, the assurance of forgiveness ...

These glimpses of God are special to me, but I am not content. Deep inside me is the God-given urge to know him more fully, to have regular, audible conversations together. I would eventually like to see him close-up, to worship him face to face.

That opportunity, I believe, will one day be mine.

See also: Romans 1:20; 1 Corinthians 13:12

■ FIREWORKS IN REVERSE

Being found in appearance as a man, he humbled himself and became obedient to death – even death on a cross!

PHILIPPIANS 2:8

Imagine that you are at the fairgrounds, with a video camera cocked to record the Fourth of July fireworks. Comets of color rocket skyward, exploding against the cloud canopy like dye-filled water balloons. The hot summer air is splashed with electric blues, golds, and reds. Giant, iridescent blossoms materialize with a *boom!* out of nothing.

Whoosh-whoosh-rat-a-tat-tat. The noise is louder than World War II bombings. Your whirring camera captures all the razzle-dazzle—right to the stand-up-and-holler finale.

When you later screen your film, you try something different. You switch the projector to reverse. Great, sparkling streamers of light funnel back into their cannon-lobbed canisters. Bursts of shocking greens and radiant oranges are gathered from the horizons to become plain cardboard packages. Nobody oohs and aahs. The razzle-dazzle is gone. It is hard to get too excited about seeing fireworks in reverse.

That phrase, *fireworks in reverse,* is the classic description of Jesus' visit to earth. He could have burst on the scene with a roar and thunder, illuminating the sky with the rainbow radiance of eternity. He could have made the stars twinkle green and red and gold. He could have made a Goodyear blimp of the moon, flashing his message to the huddled masses below.

Instead, God's grandeur was funneled into the plain package of a human being. His Son was born in the stink of a backyard stable and lived in poverty. He sampled the whole of human experience—all the pains, griefs, hardships. And then he died in disgrace. Many thought the razzle-dazzle of God had simply fizzled.

Yet Christ's spark of grandeur was rekindled. On Easter morning the fireworks were lit. Harnessing the heavens, he burst his bounds. He arose from death victorious—to light our lives for eternity.

See also: 2 Corinthians 8:9; Philippians 2:5–11

:: NEW LIGHT

I am the bread of life. He who comes to me will never go hungry.

JOHN 6:35

Yesterday you read about Jesus' visit to earth being like fireworks in reverse. The word *like* is an important word. It is often used to set up an analogy.

For example, I might say I have a hoarse voice. An analogy to describe the same thing might be: My voice sounds *like* the busted gearbox of an old Jeep.

The Bible is full of analogies and figurative speech. Christ often spoke that way himself: "I am the bread of life." He meant he was *like* bread in that he provides spiritual sustenance to believers. Elsewhere he said: "You are the salt of the earth," and "You are the light of the world." He meant that you are *like* salt and light.

Writers of the Bible also frequently used analogies to describe God and their relationship to him. For example, King David wrote that God is *like* a shepherd who "makes me lie down in green pastures" and "leads me beside quiet waters."

Take a few minutes to think of some fresh analogies of your own that describe your feelings about Jesus, God, and his Word—and then write a phrase or two about why that analogy is fitting. For instance, you might say: Christ is *like* a master mechanic, because he has all the right tools to tune my life to his specs. Try a few yourself:

Jesus Christ is like _____

_____

because _____

_____

The Bible is like _____

_____

because _____

_____

God's love for me is like _____

_____

because _____

_____

See also: Psalm 19; Matthew 5:13 – 14; John 10:11

:: THE MISSING BODY

> *On the first day of the week, very early in the morning, the women took the spices they had prepared and went to the tomb. They found the stone rolled away from the tomb, but when they entered, they did not find the body of the Lord Jesus.*

> LUKE 24:1–3

Consider for a moment that Christ did *not* rise from death; that his resurrection story is a fraud. Hoax or not, you must still explain away the empty tomb. Here are the three most probable and popular theories:

The disciples stole the body. This was the explanation first circulated by Christ's opponents. Matthew 28:11–15 records how the chief priests bribed the Roman tomb guards and had them say the disciples stole the body while they were sleeping. The problem here is that all of the disciples (except for Judas and John) later died martyr deaths for their ongoing evangelism. Put yourself in their shoes. You'd face a torturous death willingly only for something you absolutely believed to be true, even if it were actually false. You'd never die for what you knew to be a deliberate lie.

The authorities stole the body. Trouble is, it was the authorities (both Jewish and Roman) who most wanted to snuff out the hysterical claims of Christ and his followers. Killing Jesus was the first step. To drive the last nail in the coffin of Christianity, they could simply have paraded his stinky corpse down Jerusalem Boulevard a week or so after his "Resurrection." That they didn't do this indicates they didn't have the body.

Christ never really died. This theory supposes that Christ entered a coma-like state after the Crucifixion and was mistakenly reported dead. He later revived in the tomb, removed the massive boulder, escaped the guards, and faked resurrection to his disciples and others. Be serious. How would *you* feel after being beaten, whipped, nailed to a cross, stabbed in the side, and entombed for three days without food or water?

Even the German critic David Strauss rejected this idea: "It is impossible that one who had just come forth from the grave, half dead, who crept about weak and ill in need of medical treatment, could ever have given the disciples the impression that he was a conqueror over death; that he was the Prince of Life. Such a resuscitation could by no possibility have changed their sorrow into enthusiasm or elevated their reverence into worship."

There's only one theory that adequately explains the empty tomb: that Christ was truly resurrected from the dead, as recorded in Scripture. You can stake your life on it.

See also: 1 Corinthians 15; 1 Thessalonians 4:13–18

▪▪ POINTS TO PONDER– THE RESURRECTION

He has risen!

LUKE 24:6

Since that Sunday dawn when the tomb of Jesus was first discovered to be empty, much has been written about that day and Jesus' resurrection. Some of those statements are worth pondering: The stone was rolled away from the door, not to permit Christ to come out, but to enable the disciples to go in.

PETER MARSHALL

The biggest fact about Joseph's tomb was that it wasn't a tomb at all—it was a room for a transient. Jesus stopped there a night or two on his way back to glory.

HERBERT BOOTH SMITH

I danced on a Friday
When the sky turned black;
It's hard to dance
With the devil on your back.
They buried my body
And they thought I'd gone;
But I am the dance and I still go on:

Dance, then, wherever you may be;
I am the Lord of the Dance, said he.
And I'll lead you all, wherever you may be,
And I'll lead you all in the dance, said he.

SYDNEY CARTER, SONG

Jesus blew everything apart, and when I saw where the pieces landed I knew I was free.

GEORGE FOSTER

The birth and rapid rise of the Christian Church remain an unsolved enigma for any historian who refuses to take seriously the only explanation offered by the church itself.

C. F. D. MOULE

The Gospels do not explain the resurrection; the resurrection explains the Gospels. Belief in the resurrection is not an appendage to the Christian faith; it *is* the Christian faith.

JOHN S. WHALE

The only shadow on the cloudless Easter day of God's victory is the poverty of my own devotion, the memory of ineffective hours of unbelief, and my own stingy response to God's generosity.

A. E. WHITHAM

The Easter Bunny never rose again.

S. RICKLY CHRISTIAN

Our Lord has written the promise of the resurrection, not in books alone, but in every leaf in springtime.

MARTIN LUTHER

See also: John 20–21; Acts 26:8; 1 Corinthians 15:14–32

WEEK

25

▇▇ INFANT DOE

You created my inmost being; you knit me together in my mother's womb. I praise you because I am fearfully and wonderfully made; your works are wonderful, I know that full well. My frame was not hidden from you when I was made in the secret place. When I was woven together in the depths of the earth, your eyes saw my unformed body. All the days ordained for me were written in your book before one of them came to be.

PSALM 139:13–16

The birth of "Infant Doe" was different than yours or mine. The parents didn't smile. Nor did they want to hold their child. They asked the doctor to take the infant away.

That's because the child wasn't like what they had expected. It would never be an athlete or have a Mensa IQ. Born with a physical handicap, the baby would require surgery to allow food to reach its stomach. But the parents refused to sign the consent form. Instead, they let their child starve to death.

This is no make-believe story. It happened a few years ago in Bloomington, Indiana. Rather than save their child, they chose "treatment to do nothing"—legal gobbledygook allowing them to get rid of their burden by killing it.

For "Infant Doe," being unwanted was a capital offense.

You might think this is an isolated case. It's not. A $350 million abortion industry has developed in this country alone, destroying more than one million babies every year. And in many cases, the killing occurs *after* birth when doctors withhold either needed medical treatment or food—as in the case of the Bloomington baby.

Being unwanted is a dreadful thing. Of course, "Infant Doe" didn't know that, because he was too young to realize the horror of his own death. But each time such a child dies, God surely cringes.

We should, too, because fellow human beings daily declare "unfit to live" those whom God has "fearfully and wonderfully made." It's a lot like what happened in Nazi Germany.

The only reason Nazis got away with their atrocities was because good people did nothing. The same thing is happening here today.

See also: Genesis 1:27; Deuteronomy 5:17

▪▪ EVERY YEAR A NEW LEG

Now we ask you, brothers, to respect those who work hard among you, who are over you in the Lord and who admonish you. Hold them in the highest regard in love because of their work. Live in peace with each other.

1 THESSALONIANS 5:12–13

It was sometimes hard to tell that Pat Vance had a handicap. But there were a few dead giveaways. At the start of every school year he would freak out the new kids by reaching down to adjust his shoe, and then suddenly wrench his leg around backward. Or in gym, he would kick a ball and, on impact, send his leg flying in a dizzy arch. He liked the laughs that got.

Though born with a birth defect that resulted in the amputation of his right leg, Pat says he never felt unusual growing up. He credits his dad for that. In fact, things could have been horrible were it not for his father.

That's because when Pat arrived home after his amputation, his dad quit his job as a space engineer and worked without pay for a year with a maker of artificial limbs. Why? So his son wouldn't have to walk on a crude factory-made prosthesis.

Year after year he tooled and tinkered, experimented with fiberglass and resins, and baked the finished designs in the kitchen oven, filling the house with terrible fumes. He built an entire workshop, just to craft improved legs for Pat. And many nights he worked around the clock to perfect a new model—or a bigger model when his son outgrew the old.

Like most teens, Pat was never really close with his father. His dad was 52 when Pat was born, and always seemed reserved. They had the typical hassles, and sometimes Pat took his dad's absence of emotion for a lack of love. But then one day he got to thinking about how easy it is to get hung up on the "warm fuzzies" side of love and forget that parents show their love in many, very different ways.

"Sometimes it's through cleaning up after their kids have vomited," he said. "Sometimes it's through letting their kids go out with people they really don't approve of or through paying for college when they really want you to go to another school. In my case it's obvious how Dad showed his love to me. I can see the proof in file drawers full of designs and blueprints of my legs. He's in his '70s now, still working, hoping to come up with an improved version next year."

As Pat discovered, a parent's loving actions *do* speak louder than words.

See also: 1 Corinthians 13:1; Colossians 3:20; 1 John 3:18

:: GOODNESS, ME?

At just the right time, when we were still powerless, Christ died for the ungodly. Very rarely will anyone die for a righteous man, though for a good man someone might possibly dare to die. But God demonstrates his own love for us in this: While we were still sinners, Christ died for us.

ROMANS 5:6–8

If asked to list ten of your negative traits, you would probably just take a couple of minutes. To a degree, every person suffers insecurity and harbors a low self-esteem. No matter how talented or smooth people may appear on the outside, they, too, have their shortcomings riveted to their brains. For many Christians, that problem is enhanced because we're so often reminded how far short of God's standards we fall.

But how quick are you at recognizing your genuinely good points and those areas of your life where you come close to God's standards? These special qualities might include something nice you did recently for a member of your family or a talent that you've excelled in at school. Also included might be your godly attitude that always tries to see the best in other people, a giving spirit, self-control, or a sense of humor.

Think *honestly* and *positively* about yourself, and then list ten of those traits in the space below. As you compile the list, remember that your value in God's eyes is so great that he paid a high price (by giving up his Son) — just so you might live together forever in heaven.

1. _____
2. _____
3. _____
4. _____
5. _____
6. _____
7. _____
8. _____
9. _____
10. _____

In the coming week, pursue, practice, and perfect these traits!

See also: John 3:16; 1 Corinthians 6:20; 1 Timothy 6:11–14

▪ OUT OF DARKNESS

My God turns my darkness into light.

PSALM 18:28

Whenever I land at an airport at night, I think of the story told by James C. Dobson about a friend who piloted his single-engine airplane toward a small country airport as the sun dipped behind the mountains.

Dusk settled quickly and quietly, and as lights blinked on in houses below, the man could barely make out the airstrip in the distance. By the time he maneuvered his craft closer for a landing, the black pavement was indistinguishable from the black of night.

His little plane was not equipped with lights, and the airport employees had left for the day. There was no one he could even radio for help. Circling the dark airport again and again, he stared hard below in hopes of spotting the runway. But he saw nothing.

For two hours he droned back and forth above the deserted airport, hoping against hope that his gas wouldn't run out. Yet as the needle of the fuel gauge nosed to empty, he knew that at any moment he could plummet from the sky to a certain death. His heart beat loudly and he wondered what death would feel like.

As his panic clenched tighter, a miracle happened. Someone on the ground had heard the plane circling aimlessly in the dark and had guessed the pilot's predicament. Hopping into his car, the man flashed on his brights and raced back and forth to illuminate the airstrip. And then he parked his vehicle at the far end of the runway and let his beams of light guide the pilot down for a safe landing.

There have been many times when darkness has crept into my life and I have been enveloped in the kind of panic that gripped the errant pilot. Perhaps you know the feeling, too. You face a hopeless tangle of problems at home, school, and work. Your future seems clouded. Favorite sins and bad habits nag at your mind. Maybe someone close to you has died or been divorced, throwing more shadows across your life. Everything seems black.

I've found it's at the blackest moments that God wants to light my path. That light may simply be the assurance that he's in control and will eventually work bad circumstances into positive results. While things may not always improve immediately, he enables us to see the light at the end of the tunnel.

See also: Deuteronomy 31:6–8; Psalm 112:4; Romans 8:28

:: SECOND CHANCE

You are a forgiving God, gracious and compassionate, slow to anger and abounding in love.

NEHEMIAH 9:17

Sitting in a corner of the locker room during halftime of the 1929 Rose Bowl game, a University of California football player named Roy Riegels clutched a blanket tightly around his shoulders and wept.

Moments earlier, in front of a standing-room-only crowd, he had recovered a fumble and sprinted toward the end zone. He thought it was his moment of glory. Everyone shouted his name as he galloped down the open field toward pay dirt. He was alone, except for a teammate who raced wildly after him. And just yards short of an apparent touchdown, his fellow team member made a lunging dive and tackled him.

"You've run the wrong way!" he shouted hysterically.

No one said much during the half-time break in the locker room—not even the coach who normally had a lot to say. About the only sounds were Riegels' sobs. He felt ruined, and could only imagine what the newspaper headlines would say, not to mention his friends and family.

Finally, just before the team again took the field for the second half, the coach simply said, "The same men who played the first half will start the second." Everyone but Riegels filed out. The coach repeated himself.

"But I could never face the crowd again," Riegels said, looking up from his corner hideaway. "I've humiliated the team; I've humiliated myself."

The coach wouldn't listen. Putting his arm across Riegels' shoulder, he said, "Go on out there now. The game is only half over."

Whenever I blow it badly—specifically, at those times when I feel that I have made the world's biggest mistake and feel ruined as a Christian—I think of Roy Riegels, his wrong-way run, and his tremendous coach. And I'm reminded that God's message to me is much the same.

No matter what happens in my life, God is always there, able and willing to give me a second chance, a third chance, a hundredth chance. The game isn't over yet.

See also: 2 Chronicles 7:14; Romans 8:1–2; Ephesians 1:7–8

SPONTANEOUS PRAISE

Since the creation of the world God's invisible qualities—his eternal power and divine nature—have been

clearly seen, being understood from what has been made,
so that men are without excuse.

ROMANS 1:20

To think you find God only in church is as absurd as think-ing you can find art only in a gallery. Bricks and mortar can't hold him. He isn't confined to a building any more than drama is to the stage, music to the radio, or monkeys to the zoo.

Open your eyes and there he is! Right outside your bedroom window. You catch glimpses of heaven in flower petals, a child's smile, the light of the sun, puddle reflections, or a lover's embrace.

As Paul writes, "By taking a long and thoughtful look at what God has created, people have always been able to see what their eyes as such can't see: eternal power, for instance, and the mystery of his divine being" (Romans 1:20, *The Message*). His point: you don't need a church pew to experience God.

"If you have never heard the mountains singing, or seen the trees of the field clapping their hands, do not think because of that they don't," wrote McCandlish Phillips. "Ask God to open your ears so you may hear it, and your eyes so you may see it, because, though few men ever know it, they do, my friend, they do."

Spontaneous worship can erupt any time, any place ... as it did one bright summer day to a young East Coast musician. Walking along the Mohawk Trail in the Berkshire Mountains, he climbed a tower overlooking Connecticut, New York, and Massachusetts. The soft-edged mist of morning had burned off, and the sun cut a golden swath across the sky. Spread before him from horizon to horizon were sparkling lakes, tall trees, and the scent of little things growing.

He was so awestruck that he rushed down to his car, grabbed his cornet, and climbed back into the tower. Suddenly he began playing the instrument with all his heart—for his own plea-sure, the enjoyment of passing hikers, and for the glory of God. He'd heard the mountains singing and wanted to join in accompaniment.

Some people will one day stand before God and try to excuse their lack of belief by saying, "I never knew you because I never darkened the doorway of a church."

"Nonsense!" God will probably snort. "Did you never take a walk, look into the star-spangled sky, hear a clap of thunder, or watch a tree catch fire at sunset? I surrounded you twenty-four hours a day with evidence of my love and glory. You were just too busy to notice."

See also: Psalms 96; 150; Isaiah 6:3

▪▪ POINTS TO PONDER–GOD

Holy, holy, holy is the Lord Almighty; the whole earth is full of his glory.

ISAIAH 6:3

The remarkable thing about the way in which people talk about God or about their relation to God is that it seems to escape them completely that God hears what they are saying.

SÖREN KIERKEGAARD

We see God all around us: the mountains are God's thoughts upheaved, the rivers are God's thoughts in motion, the oceans are God's thoughts imbedded, the dewdrops are God's thoughts in pearls.

SAM JONES

All-wise. All-powerful. All-loving. All-knowing. We bore to death both God and ourselves with our chatter. God cannot be expressed but only experienced. In the last analysis, you cannot pontificate but only point. A Christian is one who points at Christ and says, "I can't prove a thing, but there's something about his eyes and his voice. There's something about the way he carries his head, his hands, the way he carries his cross—the way he carries me."

FREDERICK BUECHNER

The universe is centered on neither the earth nor the sun. It is centered on God.

ALFRED NOYES

The public has a deep respect for the amazing scientific advances made within our lifetime. There is admiration for the scientific process of observation, experimentation of testing every concept to measure its validity. But it still bothers some people that we cannot prove scientifically that God exists. Must we lift a candle to see the sun?

WERNHER VON BRAUN

Does God seem far away? Guess who moved?

ANONYMOUS

We must wait for God long, meekly, in the wind and wet, in the thunder and lightning, in the cold and the dark. Wait, and he will come. He never comes to those who do not wait. He does not go their road. When he comes, go with him, but go slowly, fall a little behind; when he quickens his pace, be sure of it before you quicken yours. But when he slackens, slacken at once; and do not be slow only, but silent, very silent, for he is God.

FREDERICK W. FABER

A God who did not regard this [our own worst sins] with unappeasable distaste would not be a good being. We cannot even wish for such a God—it is like wishing that every nose in the universe were abolished, that smell of hay or roses or the sea should never again delight any creature, because our own breath happens to stink.

C. S. Lewis

See also: Isaiah 64:8; Luke 1:37; Romans 8:31; 2 Peter 3:9–14

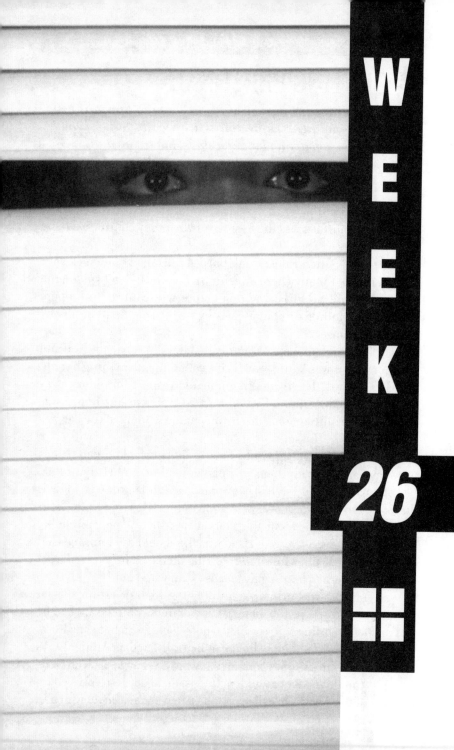

▪▪ GETTING PERSONAL

Because you are sons, God sent the Spirit of his Son into our hearts, the Spirit who calls out, "Abba, Father." So you are no longer a slave, but a son; and since you are a son, God has made you also an heir.

GALATIANS 4:6–7

Like most parents, mine laid down a few basic rules for our house. The short list was the essence of what they considered to be good manners.

Among their rules: Don't burp at the table; don't pick your nose in public (or anywhere else, for that matter); don't spit on the sidewalk; don't hit girls; and don't chew with your mouth open. There was another rule, in a class by itself: Don't call adults by their first names.

No problem if my parents called their best friends Ken and Eleanor. But it was World War III if I called them anything but *Mr.* and *Mrs.* Elbert. The formality indicated respect for elders, they said. So the man who delivered bottled water to our house was always *Mr.* Griffith to me, and the mechanic who fixed the car was nothing but *Mr.* Russell.

The only adults I could address like normal human beings were my parents. With them, just plain old Mom and Dad was fine.

When Moses was first confronted face-to-face by God in Exodus 3, he wasn't quite sure how to address him. He realized the holiness of God demanded something formal, but *Mr. God* probably didn't sound quite right. So he asked God what he should call him, and God suggested he use the name *Yahweh*. That divine name, derived from the Hebrew verb *to be*, roughly means "I am who I am."

Yahweh was primarily used by the high priest on special occasions, because people believed it was too holy to be spoken by just anybody. Ordinary Joes called God *Adonai*, which means Lord, and *Sabaoth* or *Shaddai*, which can be translated as Almighty. As names go, they're still quite formal. But what do you expect with God?

And then, all of a sudden, things changed. Jesus arrived on the face of the earth. He called God by a new name: *Abba*, which in

Aramaic means Daddy. It shook some people up, because God was supposed to be distant, untouchable, unapproachable. "Daddy" was just too personal—a name that sons and daughters called their very own fathers!

They missed the point by a country mile. It was for that very reason that "Daddy" was just fine.

See also: Exodus 3:11–14; Mark 14:36; Romans 8:15–17

■■ NICKNAMES

> *He appointed twelve—designating them apostles— that they might be with him and that he might send them out to preach and to have authority to drive out demons. These are the twelve he appointed: Simon (to whom he gave the name Peter); James son of Zebedee, and his brother John (to them he gave the name Boanerges, which means Sons of Thunder); Andrew, Philip, Bartholomew, Matthew, Thomas, James son of Alphaeus, Thaddaeus, Simon the Zealot and Judas Iscariot, who betrayed him.*
>
> MARK 3:14–19

Close friends often have nicknames for each other. They call each other strange names that otherwise might prompt a fistfight. Silly though they are, names like Noodles, Scooter, Thumper, Flash, or Tiny are actually indicative of extreme affection. One of my best friends, who has a dime-sized mole on his cheek, goes by Nathan to most people. I sometimes call him Spot.

The use of such abbreviated names was common in Bible days. Take, for example, James and John, two of Jesus' closest companions. When these hotheaded brothers once suggested they'd like to nuke a lousy welcoming committee in Samaria (Luke 9:51–56), Jesus nicknamed them Sons of Thunder. They probably smiled every time they heard him calling them.

Then there were the two Simons. Jesus referred to one as The Zealot and affectionately rechristened the other one Peter, a nickname that, humorously enough, means "The Rock." Peter was, after all, somewhat stone-brained on occasion. And a rock is pretty basic; there's nothing too fancy or pretty about it. But in God's creation, barring an earthquake, a rock is about as solid as anything you can find. And when the going got tough, Peter was rock solid.

There's something both touching and very ... well, *human* about this aspect of Jesus' life as reflected in this simple listing of his friends' nicknames. You get the idea that personal relationships really meant something special to him.

In that regard, things really haven't changed much in two thousand years.

See also: John 15:9–17; Romans 5:7–11

:: NAME CALLING

> *Today, if you hear his voice, do not harden your hearts.*
>
> HEBREWS 4:7

Moving through the crowded locker hall, your mind is already on the weekend. Oblivious to oncoming traffic, you're thinking Saturday night even though you're smack in the middle of another ordinary week.

Suddenly you hear your name. Your brain whirs back to the present. You stop, turn, and expectantly scan the nearby faces. And then you spot a good friend, beckoning from across the hallway, and feel a smile starting to spread.

It's a simple pleasure, hearing your name called out in a crowd. It creates a sense of expectancy, of anticipation. Suddenly, you're not just another anonymous, milling face. You have been noticed.

Zacchaeus probably felt that way the day Jesus passed through Jericho. A near-anonymous man whose name is mentioned just once in the New Testament (Luke 19:1–10), he was, in blunt terms, a crook—a legman for the Roman IRS who, if living today, would wear his shirt open to his navel and have three pounds of gold chains dangling from his neck. In addition to being a shyster, Zacchaeus was vertically challenged—something of a legal dwarf. So when the crowd began milling around Jesus, Zacchaeus shinnied up a tree for a better view.

That's when he got the surprise of his life. Through the roar of the crowd, he suddenly heard his name being called. When he turned around in the branches and saw it was Jesus beckoning him, Zacchaeus probably fell out of the tree in astonishment. It's a wonder he didn't suffer a coronary too, because in the next breath Jesus said, "I *must* stay at your house today!"

What could he make of it? What can anybody make of it other than the fact that, for reasons known only to him, God seems to have similar plans for every last peculiar one of us. "I must stay with *you!*"

The only hitch is that you must first cock an ear toward heaven and, above the drone of the humdrum, listen for his still small voice calling your name.

See also: Psalm 46:10; 2 Thessalonians 1:11; Revelation 3:20

■■ A NAME YOU CAN COUNT ON

He who overcomes will . . . be dressed in white. I will never erase his name from the book of life, but will acknowledge his name before my Father and his angels.

REVELATION 3:5

I've become used to being identified by long strings of numbers.

To the feds, I am known by a nine-digit Social Security number. By dialing another number, an eleven-digit sequence (including the prefix 1), anybody in the world can talk directly with me. The bank computer recognizes me by a personal access code, which I can use to withdraw cash from my account at 3 A.M. if I'm so inclined. Since the code is secret, my kid brother is prevented from doing the same if he's likewise so inclined.

I've also got a license plate number that the Department of Motor Vehicles uses to identify me. And to *Time* magazine, I am not Rick Christian, but a file number of twenty-seven letters and digits, CRIMU603S94T591107JUL87CA51. With *Campus Life* magazine, I am 000100769299CLJUL873937.

There are, of course, good reasons why numeric codes are used. They enable you to single out a particular John Smith from all the other billions of funny-looking, two-legged creatures sharing this planet. This is important, say, if you want to send him a parking ticket, or telephone him to whisper sweet nothings in his ear.

Nevertheless, I rather like it when I'm waiting for a haircut or a table at a restaurant, and I hear my *name* being called. And when Luke writes, "Rejoice that your names are written in heaven," I am overcome by one of those stand-up-and-holler kind of feelings.

It reminds me that I'm not just an insignificant blip or a twenty-seven-digit code in some dusty memory bank of the universe. Rather, my name (*my* name!) is carved into the Book of Life. Pure and simple, my salvation is guaranteed in writing.

And on that day when I join my Lord in heaven, I expect he'll be waiting for me at the gates with his arms open wide and my name on his lips.

See also: Psalm 69:27–28; Daniel 12:1–2; Luke 10:20

■■ TOO CLOSE FOR COMFORT

You will receive power when the Holy Spirit comes on you; and you will be my witnesses in Jerusalem, and in all Judea and Samaria, and to the ends of the earth.

Acts 1:8

In the Bible, God put a premium on developing close personal relationships. We're told he walked through the Garden with Adam and Eve. He appeared before Moses and revealed his name. Housed in the temple, he dwelt among the Israelites.

But not even that was personal enough. He wanted to establish a closer relationship. And so, for reasons best known only to himself, he became one of us for thirty-three years.

For some people, his visit was thirty-three years too long. Many just felt too uncomfortable with him around. Jesus challenged what they said and how they lived. Friday nights weren't the same with the Son of God liable to walk around the corner at any moment.

So they took matters into their own hands and nailed him to a cross. God's first-degree love prompted first-degree punishment. And when Christ breathed his last, his executioners thought they could get back to business as usual. They had, of course, underestimated the depth of God's love—and the power of it. His love simply wouldn't die that Friday at Calvary. It was like trying to blow out a trick candle. They huffed and puffed and did everything they were supposed to do, but then a tiny spark suddenly flashed through the smoke, a flame sputtered, and before they knew it some crazy women were saying the king of the Jews had risen. Imagine! The age-old dictum, "Where there's smoke, there's fire," proved to be true.

The flame, fanned by whatever happens to people when they see somebody rise from the dead, spread from house to house. It whipped through the docks, the synagogues, the prisons. The whole city and beyond was engulfed by the wildfire.

Even now, all these years later, if you step outside and sniff ever so gently, you can still smell the smoke. Take a deep breath. Something's burning. It's a thing called love.

See also: Psalm 104:4; John 20:1–18; Acts 2:1–4

■■ THE DEEPEST FRIENDS

The thief comes only to steal and kill and destroy;
I have come that they may have life, and have it to the full.
I am the good shepherd. The good shepherd lays down his
life for the sheep.

JOHN 10:10–11

Some of my most cherished possessions are my school year-books. If my house ever caught fire, they'd be among the first things I'd grab as I ran outside. Penned in various colors of ink throughout the annuals are entries such as this:

Dear Rick, Your friendship means the world to me, and I'll never forget you or the times we shared. Love, Diana.

On adjacent pages are dozens of other entries, signed by other good friends: Helen, Sam, Donna, Jerry, Anita, Mark, Cyndee, and many others. Just seeing my friends' names is enough to flood my mind with endless memories of first loves, broken romances, cruddy jobs, smelly gym clothes, and Friday night football games. Their names conjure to my mind a unique blend of hilarity and agony, accomplishments and embarrassments, bravado and desperado.

Though most of us went our separate ways after graduation, I'll never forget the bunch of them.

Take a minute and think about those people who have had the biggest impact on your life. What are their names, and what do you think of when you think of them? Go ahead, forget about everything else going on around you. Filter out distractions and just drift mentally for a few minutes. Take five, slip your brain into neutral, and focus on two or three of their names.

If you're anything like me, it's impossible to think of anybody's name without also picturing that person's face. And once a person's face is on my mental screen, I am barraged by movie-like sequences. It's as if all during our friendship a little hidden camera had been shooting video to be stored in my head for later playback.

Certain names and faces make you laugh out loud as you recall some hilariously nonsensical moment you shared. Remember the dumb jokes? The sound of that friend's giggle? How another friend's eyes crinkled up at the corners? The video is perfectly intact in your mind.

Of course, not all memories are happy. A broken friendship is among the worst tragedies in the world. And if a good friend has died or moved away, the thought of his or her name can bring tears. That's exactly what happened when Jesus was told his good friend Lazarus had died. No little sniffle; he wept (John 11:35). His buddy was dead, and Jesus felt the loss clear to his bones. That's true of all good friends. The more you care, the more it can hurt in the end.

Friendship was serious business with Christ. When his friends were hurting, he healed them. When they were hungry, he fed them. When they were discouraged, he prayed with them. And when they were dying, he cried for them.

Of course, it wasn't enough that he shed tears. He knew it would take blood. And so he said, "Greater love has no one than this, that one lay down his life for his friends." Shortly thereafter, at a place called Calvary, he put his life on the line for his friends.

The world hasn't gotten over it yet.

See also: John 15:13; Romans 5:7–8; Philippians 2:5–11

■ POINTS TO PONDER – FRIENDSHIP

I have called you friends, for everything that I learned from my Father I have made known to you.

JOHN 15:15

Not many sounds in life, and I include all urban and all rural sounds, exceed in interest a knock at the door.

CHARLES LAMB

Fellowship is heaven, and lack of fellowship is hell.

WILLIAM MORRIS

Bad company is the devil's net.

ANONYMOUS

The only way to have a friend is to be one.

RALPH WALDO EMERSON

Alas, my God, that we should be
Such strangers to each other!
O that as friends we might agree,
And walk and talk together.

THOMAS SHEPHERD

Thy friendship oft has made my heart to ache; do be my enemy— for friendship's sake.

WILLIAM BLAKE

I never found the companion that was so companionable as solitude.

HENRY DAVID THOREAU

Friendship without self-interest is one of the rare and beautiful things of life.

JAMES FRANCIS BYRNES

You can make more friends in two months by becoming really interested in other people than you can make in two years by trying to get people interested in you.

DALE CARNEGIE

The firmest friendships have been formed in mutual adversity, as iron is most strongly united by the fiercest flame.

CHARLES C. COLTON

Friendship is something that raised us almost above humanity. This love, free from instinct, free from all duties but those which love has freely assumed, almost wholly free from jealousy, and free without qualification from the need to be needed, is eminently spiritual. It is the sort of love one can imagine between angels.

C. S. LEWIS

Promises may get friends, but it is performance that keeps them.

OWEN FELTHAM

Jesus' home was the road along which he walked with his friends in search of new friends.

GIOVANNI PAPINI

After the friendship of God, a friend's affection is the greatest treasure here below.

ANONYMOUS

How can I lift a struggling soul and guide him if I never take his arm?

VIOLA JACOBSON BERG

In misery it is great comfort to have a companion.

JOHN LYLY

See also: Proverbs 18:24; Luke 7:34; James 2:21–23; 4:4

■ A TWO-LETTER ANSWER

How long, O Lord, must I call for help, but you do not listen?

HABAKKUK 1:2

Dear God, she's beautiful. We met last week in history, and I knew at first glance we'd hit it off. I could tell the match was made in heaven. After all, she was a strong Christian and had the best legs on campus. So why did she say no when I asked her out? I'd prayed about it and everything. . . .

Dear God, it's only my future. From day one, everybody's called me Shakespeare and acted as if everything I write is Pulitzer material. With that kind of encouragement, I was naturally thinking I'd get a journalism degree and then hitch up with a large metro daily or maybe even write a book. All the details were in place, and I even got a job to cover j-school tuition. So why was my application rejected? I'd prayed about it and everything. . . .

Like it or not, prayers often don't get answered the way we'd like. God doesn't always say *yes*. Sometimes his answer is *wait*. Quite often it is *no*.

King David once prayed nonstop for a week that his son's life would be spared. On the seventh day, the child died. Another time, the prophet Elijah asked God to end his life. But when he opened his eyes, he was still very much alive. Then there's the apostle Paul, who desperately wanted to take a missionary journey to Asia. God sent him to Europe instead. And three times he asked God to remove his thorn in the flesh. Three times he heard God's answer: "No. No. NO!"

Not to forget the time when, shortly before his crucifixion, Jesus prayed, "Father, if you are willing, take this cup from me." His Father wasn't willing; Plan B wasn't good enough. It would take the cross to save the world.

In cases where we get something other than what we want, we tend to become moody. Sometimes we cry and carry on. However, if we were smart enough to know better, we'd turn cartwheels when God responds to our prayers with a short, two-letter answer.

    No is a sign that God has something far better in mind for us than we, from our limited perspective, could have possibly imagined. *No* should be good news. It's when we continually get what we want that we ought to be concerned.

See also: 2 Samuel 12:15–19; 1 Kings 19:3–18; Luke 22:39–44

■ A YOUNG GIRL STILL DWELLS

> *The King will say ... "I was hungry and you gave me something to eat, I was thirsty and you gave me something to drink, I was a stranger and you invited me in, I needed clothes and you clothed me, I was sick and you looked after me, I was in prison and you came to visit me."*
>
> *Then the righteous will answer him, "Lord, when did we see you hungry and feed you, or thirsty and give you something to drink? When did we see you a stranger and invite you in, or needing clothes and clothe you? When did we see you sick or in prison and go to visit you?" The King will reply, "I tell you the truth, whatever you did for one of the least of these brothers of mine, you did for me."*
>
> MATTHEW 25:34–40

    The following poem was written by a woman who died in the old folks' ward of Ashludie Hospital near Dundee, England. It was found among her possessions and so impressed the staff that copies were widely distributed throughout the hospital and beyond:

What do you see, nurse, what do you see?
Are you thinking when you look at me—
A crabbed old woman, not very wise,
Uncertain of habit with faraway eyes?
Who dribbles her food and makes no reply
When you say in a loud voice, "I do wish you'd try"
Who seems not to notice the things that you do,
And forever is losing a stocking or shoe?
Who resisting or not, lets you do as you will
With bathing and feeding, the long day to fill?

Is that what you're thinking, is that what you see?
Then open your eyes, nurse, you're looking at me.
I'll tell you who I am as I sit here so still,
As I move at your bidding, eat at your will ...
I'm a small child of ten with a father and mother,
Brothers and sisters who love one another;
A young girl of sixteen with wings on her feet,
Dreaming that soon a love she'll meet;
A bride at twenty my heart gives a leap,
Remembering the vows that I promised to keep;
At twenty-five now I have young of my own
Who need me to build a secure, happy home;
A woman of thirty, my young now grow fast,
Bound together with ties that should last;
At forty, my young sons have grown up and gone,
But my man's beside me to see I don't mourn;
At fifty, once more babies play round my knee,
Again we know children my loved ones and me.
Dark days are upon me; my husband is dead,
I look at the future, I shudder with dread.
For my young are all rearing young of their own,
And I think of the years and the love that I've known.
I'm an old woman now and nature is cruel;
'Tis her jest to make old age look like a fool.
The body it crumbles, grace and vigor depart;
There is a stone where I once had a heart.
But inside this old carcass a young girl still dwells,
And now, again, my embittered heart swells.
I remember the joys, I remember the pain,
And I'm loving and living life over again.
I think of the years, all too few, gone too fast,
And accept the stark fact that nothing can last.
So open your eyes, nurse, open and see
Not a crabbed old woman,
Look closer—see me!

This poem was intended for those who surrounded the woman in her last days. But there's something about it that reminds me about my own grandparents ... about some of the old people at church that I breeze past without looking them in the eye ... about the old bag lady who paws through our garbage cans on trash days ... about everybody who is somehow different from me, who talks different, looks different or acts different ... and about how Jesus in Matthew 25:35–40 really seems to be saying:

So open your eyes, children, open and see
Not faceless people around you,
Look closer—see me!

See also: Job 31:32; Hebrews 13:1–3; Revelation 20:11–15

■■ TRIVIAL PURSUIT

Do not store up for yourselves treasures on earth,
where moth and rust destroy, and where thieves break in
and steal. But store up for yourselves treasures in heaven,
where moth and rust do not destroy, and where thieves do
not break in and steal. For where your treasure is, there
your heart will be also.

MATTHEW 6:19–21

Stuck away in a deep, very dark corner of my closet is a board game that I'm not very good at and for which I spent too much money. It's called Trivial Pursuit. I generally lose when I play because it's hard for me to remember relatively insignificant information that I never learned in the first place.

To win at Trivial Pursuit, you've got to know answers to such questions as: What's the only mammal that can't jump? Or, What fruit is packed with the most calories? Or, What finger boasts the fastest-growing nail?*

When I draw especially tough questions, which I could never answer in a million years, I often punctuate the silence with

*ANSWERS: The elephant, the avocado, and the middle finger.

loud groans, exasperated sighs, and comments such as: "Wait a sec, the answer is *right* on the tip of my tongue!" When my opponent draws the head-scratchers, I make the exact same noises but substitute comments such as: "*You* get all the easy questions!" In other words, I'm all bluff.

Exasperating as it is, Trivial Pursuit is an entertaining way to kill a couple of hours. But it's more than just a board game. For many people the name describes the way they live their lives: *trivial pursuit.* We play it whenever we spend our time, our energy, our thoughts in pursuit of trivial matters; whenever we ignore what's really important; whenever we are distracted by things of little consequence.

As such, trivial pursuit is a *Playboy* magazine, the backseat of a parked car, or a snort of coke (even just to *try* it). Trivial pursuit is stumbling along with C's when you know you can get A's, running with the wrong crowd, gossiping behind somebody's back, or eating a second doughnut when you know you shouldn't have eaten the first.

Trivial pursuit says, "I'll love you *if* you'll let me borrow the car; *if* you will go to bed with me" ... or, "*because* you were MVP in last week's game; *because* you have a great body and blonde hair."

Trivial pursuit is a game which many people play every single day of their lives. It's a pursuit after goals and ambitions and things that aren't eternal. And because of that, it's a game nobody ever wins.

See also: Proverbs 21:21; John 12:25; Philippians 3:17–21

⠶ ALMOST ... BUT NOT QUITE

You are not far from the kingdom of God.

MARK 12:34

Almost. It's a sad-sounding, six-letter word that implies a fumbled opportunity, near-miss effort, fizzled dream, close-call decision, botched attempt, missed chance. The word means nearly, just about, not quite.

Almost is the pop fly that would have been caught had the sun not flashed in your eyes; the test that would have been passed had you taken more time to study; the relationship that would have been salvaged had you not lost your temper; the appointment that would have been kept had you not run out of gas.

Almost is the fish that got away; the race lost on a technicality; the election defeat by a single vote.

Almost is the near-win attempt, the second-place finish, the runner-up effort, the foul tip, the misfire.

Almost is college basketball star Len Bias, who captured national headlines when he became the top draft pick by the Boston Celtics and then died days later at his University of Maryland dormitory after he OD'd on cocaine.

Almost is the rich young man (see Mark 10:17–22) who'd kept all the commandments since he was a little boy. But by refusing to sell his possessions and follow Jesus, he made it clear that he was unwilling to put Christ first in his life.

Almost is the teacher of the law (see Mark 12:28–34) who could speak fluent Christianese, went to church often enough to be labeled religious, had all the right answers . . . but, as far as we know, never made a personal commitment to Jesus Christ. "You are not far from the kingdom of God," Christ told him in the classic understatement of all time.

What the teacher of the law didn't realize was that with Jesus, there's no middle ground. If you're not hot, you're cold. If you're not a saved sinner, you're a damned sinner. *Almost* may count for something in horseshoes and hand grenades. But with Christ, *almost* is a sure ticket to hell.

See also: Lamentations 3:40; Matthew 7:13–14

■ SWITCHING TAGS

For although they knew God, they neither glorified him as God nor gave thanks to him, but their thinking became futile and their foolish hearts were darkened. Although they claimed to be wise, they became fools and exchanged the glory of the immortal God for images made to look like mortal man and birds and animals and reptiles.

ROMANS 1:21–23

I don't know how stores determine the prices of things they sell, but I generally believe they're all too high. Jeans, swimsuits, perfume, candy bars, shoes, automobile tires—each costs more than double what I think it's worth.

To strike back, I once devised a secret plan whereby I'd hang out at one of the big stores at the mall, and when they announced the store would be closing in five minutes, I'd disappear into a quiet corner. My goal was to be locked in the store overnight. Once the employees had gone home, I'd begin my mischief. I'd switch all the price tags.

As I envisioned it, the store would open the next day as usual. Everything would be the same except for the prices. Nike shoes would cost what handkerchiefs cost the previous day. Tags for CDs would be switched with those for batteries; leather coats with those for electric toothbrushes; tennis rackets with those for ice tongs. A new computer could be had for the price of a set of gym clothes, but paper clips would cost a fortune.

I thought my plan was unique, original, one-of-a-kind. But in one respect, Satan beat me to it. He's confounded us with a false sense of values, whereby we spend staggering sums (of money, time, energy, and emotion) for things that have no lasting value. In this topsy-turvy world, "me first" egoism is more highly esteemed than "you first" altruism, sex has the jump on love, good looks are valued more than a good name, titles rate higher than testimonies, and cheap thrills on Saturday night keep us out of church Sunday morning.

Everywhere you look, price tags have been swapped. The devil's tried to dupe us. Fortunately, the value Christ places on our lives isn't based on appearance or performance. It doesn't matter to him whether we can slam-dunk a basketball, squeeze into a bikini, or memorize Leviticus. He accepts us as we are, without qualification. And just to make sure we don't fall for Satan's bargain basement valuation of ourselves, Jesus put his very life on the line.

The price tag said *Calvary*, and he willingly paid it.

See also: Mark 10:45; Romans 1:25–32; 1 Corinthians 6:19–20; Ephesians 1:7–8; 1 Peter 1:18–21

TROUBLE AHEAD

Blessed are you when people insult you, persecute you and falsely say all kinds of evil against you because of me. Rejoice and be glad, because great is your reward in heaven, for in the same way they persecuted the prophets who were before you.

MATTHEW 5:11–12

Right from the start he was unwelcome. He was born in a barn because the Bethlehem innkeeper wouldn't give his parents the time of day, let alone a set of clean sheets and a room.

If that wasn't bad enough, as a baby he had a contract placed on his life. Disturbed by Micah's prophecy that a "ruler over Israel" would be born in Bethlehem, King Herod envisioned an overthrow of his kingdom by some thumb-sucking monarch. Though Herod may not have personally believed any of that "religious malarkey," everybody knows it is better to be safe than sorry. So he ordered the slaughter of every boy aged two or under throughout the Bethlehem area.

Christ was, of course, pirated out of the country. And for the rest of his life he was on the run. To those who wanted to follow in his footsteps, he curtly said, "Are you ready to rough it? We're not staying in the best inns, you know" (Luke 9:58 *The Message*). He was jeered at, beat up, ridiculed, spat upon, mocked, and finally killed. He knew it was coming, and he forecast the final curtain to his disciples.

He also warned them not to expect any better treatment themselves. Presumably that includes us, too. "You're blessed when your commitment to God provokes persecution," he said at one point (Matthew 5:10 *The Message*). There's a high cost to be paid if you engage in this bitter match against sin. There are no loopholes; every Christian is at risk. As Paul wrote to Timothy: "Anyone who wants to live all out for Christ is in for a lot of trouble; there's no getting around it" (2 Timothy 3:12 *The Message*).

As a general rule, people aren't harmed for acts of kindness. But let that kindness be done in the name of Jesus, and sparks will fly. In some countries, even today, Christians languish in prison.

Some are tortured; others have their brains blown out. But in the Western world, persecution merely means being laughed at or having doors closed in your face. You may lose a friend or two. Perhaps your parents will prevent you from going to church or weeknight Bible studies. If you live in places such as San Diego or Omaha or London or Frankfurt, chances are it won't get any tougher.

But if persecution *did* involve more than that, and if you *could* be arrested for being a Christian, it would be nice to think the district attorney could file charges that would stick: *He was overheard talking to another student about Christ*, or *She was observed making regular visits to the old folks' home.*

What about it? Would there be enough evidence to convict *you?*

See also: John 15:18–21; 16:1–4; Hebrews 10:32–39; 12:1–11

▪▪ POINTS TO PONDER – ADVERSITY

> *Blessed is the man who perseveres under trial, because when he has stood the test, he will receive the crown of life that God has promised to those who love him.*
>
> **JAMES 1:12**

I don't envy those who have never known any pain, physical or spiritual, because I strongly suspect that the capacity for pain and the capacity for joy are equal. Only those who have suffered great pain are able to know equally great joy.

MADELEINE L'ENGLE

Pain is life—the sharper, the more evidence of life.

CHARLES LAMB

When you're up to your waist in alligators, it's difficult to remember that your main objective was to drain the swamp.

ANONYMOUS

Suffering is the seed from which compassion grows.

DOLORES E. MCGUIRE

Our lives have become so antiseptic that we honestly believe we've suffered adversity and experienced affliction if our shoes pinch our toes, if our car is in the shop and we must take the bus, or if we find a bug in our water glass. Meanwhile, much of the world's population can't afford shoes, travel only where they can get by foot, and often die for lack of food and water.

S. RICKLY CHRISTIAN

I have suffered too much in this world not to hope for another.

JEAN JACQUES ROUSSEAU

He knows not his own strength that hath not met adversity. Heaven prepares good men with crosses.

BEN JONSON

Pain adds rest unto pleasure, and teaches the luxury of health.

MARTIN F. TUPPER

Shut out suffering, and you see only one side of this strange and fearful thing, the life of man. Brightness and happiness and rest— It is only one side of life. Christ saw both sides.

F. W. ROBERTSON

No person is more unhappy than the one who is never in adversity; the greatest affliction of life is never to be afflicted.

ANONYMOUS

Prosperity is a great teacher; adversity is a greater. Possession pampers the mind; privation trains and strengthens it.

WILLIAM HAZLITT

I thank God for my handicaps, for through them, I have found myself, my work and my God.

HELEN KELLER

Affliction comes to us not to make us sad but sober; not to make us sorry but wise.

HENRY WARD BEECHER

It is remarkable with what Christian fortitude and resignation we can bear the suffering of other folks.

JONATHAN SWIFT

Though all afflictions are evils in themselves, yet they are good for us, because they discover to us our disease and tend to our cure.

JOHN TILLOTSON

See also: 2 Corinthians 1:3–11; James 1:2–4; 1 Peter 1:3–7; 4:12–19

WEEK

28

▪▪ BETWEEN YOU AND GOD

If your hand causes you to sin, cut it off. It is better for you to enter life maimed than with two hands to go into hell, where the fire never goes out. And if your foot causes you to sin, cut it off. It is better for you to enter life crippled than to have two feet and be thrown into hell. And if your eye causes you to sin, pluck it out. It is better for you to enter the kingdom of God with one eye than to have two eyes and be thrown into hell.

MARK 9:43–47

In some parts of Iran today, crime busting is serious business. Convicted thieves don't just go to jail. They get a finger cut off. If you don't want to spend the rest of your life counting with your toes, you learn to keep your hands off other people's property.

In the verses above, Jesus is not teaching Iran-like self-mutilation, because even a blind man can lust. Rather, he uses hyperbole, an exaggerated figure of speech, to emphasize the need for no-holds-barred action. The Bible clearly states: The wages of sin are death. And so he gives fair warning that if anything stands between you and God, you'd better get rid of it pronto, because otherwise you could spend the rest of eternity in the hothouse.

In the gospels, the story is told of a rich young man who approached Christ with the question: "What must I do to inherit eternal life?" (Mark 10:17). Jesus began reeling off the Ten Commandments, but the man interrupted and said he'd kept the commandments since he was a child. "One thing you lack," Christ replied. "Go, sell everything you have ... then come, follow me." The man's face fell. His bank account stood between him and salvation.

With Pontius Pilate, pride stood in the way. He had the unique opportunity to pardon Christ, but the crowd bellowed for crucifixion. Like many politicians in the public eye, Pilate didn't want people thinking he was a wimp. So he allowed Christ to be killed to spare his own reputation.

Any number of things can stand between you and God. It may be a love relationship, a six-pack of Bud, a flashy car. Perhaps it's ambition, your bedroom mirror, a carton of Marlboro Lights. Maybe it's a hot temper, a ravenous appetite, a lustful thought.

Whatever it is, get rid of it. For God's sake, amputate. Yes, *for God's sake*. Heaven can't wait.

See also: Romans 6:23; 7:14–25; Hebrews 12:1–3; 1 John 1:9

■■ PASSING GRADE

> *Enter through the narrow gate. For wide is the gate and broad is the road that leads to destruction, and many enter through it. But small is the gate and narrow the road that leads to life, and only a few find it.*
>
> MATTHEW 7:13–14

Nestled amidst rolling green farmland in the northwestern corner of West Virginia, Parkersburg's Blennerhassett High was embroiled with controversy a few years ago. Not about gangs or drugs or sex or any of the usual things. The problem was that the earth science teacher gave Ds and Fs to sixty percent of his students, and the principal wanted him to inflate the grades, to be more "fair."

But the teacher, one of the district's best, wouldn't budge. He wasn't about to boost grades merely to get the principal and certain parents off his back. He comprehended what they didn't— students have to work fairly hard *not* to pass.

"One student didn't understand how he could go from a C to an F in three weeks," the teacher told one reporter. "Well, he didn't turn in his exercise book with all his class paperwork for the six-week period. That's a zero. That pulls the average down."

Other students wouldn't take their book home even if told they'd be tested the next day on specific pages. They'd score fourteen out of fifty points, and then ask why they were getting a D.

People's feelings about heaven and hell are, in some regards, similar to the Blennerhassett High controversy. They act as if God were Scrooge, handing out bushels of passes to Death Valley when he could just as easily distribute tickets to Tahiti. They suspect God of being unfair, of setting standards too high. After all, you can't just set the high-jump bar at ten feet and expect miracles.

God's standards are, of course, extremely high. But he's not looking for miracles, because heaven cannot be attained by heroics. In fact, it takes more effort for the wicked to reach hell than it does for the righteous to reach heaven. Credit Jesus for that. When it comes right down to it, Romans 6:23 says it best: "The wages of sin is death, but the gift of God is eternal life in Christ Jesus our Lord." In other words, you work your way to hell. Heaven is a handout, delivered by Jesus.

That's the good news. The bad news is that most people are too proud to accept it.

See also: Romans 3:20–28; Ephesians 2:8–10; Philippians 2:13

:: DEVILISH SCHEMES

Put on the full armor of God so that you can take your stand against the devil's schemes. For our struggle is not against flesh and blood, but against the rulers, against the authorities, against the powers of this dark world and against the spiritual forces of evil in the heavenly realms.

EPHESIANS 6:11–12

Many people grow up thinking of the devil as a Saturday morning cartoon character, dressed in red long johns, with a pair of threatening-but-cute horns protruding from his head. He's as scary as Mickey Mouse with a pitchfork, as frightening as a rubber snake. As might be expected, this Hanna-Barbera image resembles the real thing about as much as Yogi Bear resembles a marauding grizzly.

In his book *The Screwtape Letters*, C. S. Lewis creates fictional correspondence between a wise old devil, Screwtape, and his young protégé Wormwood. Screwtape's letters to the young apprentice help teach him the ropes, and at the same time, reveal a behind-the-scenes look at Satan's true character and schemes:

You will say that these are very small sins; and doubtless, like all young tempters, you are anxious to be able to report spectacular wickedness. But do remember, the only thing that matters is the extent to which you separate the man from the Enemy [God]. It does not matter how small the sins are, provided that their cumulative effect is to edge the man away from the Light and out into the Nothing. Murder is no better than cards if cards can do the trick. Indeed, the safest road to Hell is the gradual one—the gentle slope, soft underfoot, without sudden turnings, without milestones, without signposts.

If you take God seriously, you also ought to take Satan seriously. He's a cunning strategist, both ruthless and relentless. That's why the apostle Peter gives this strong warning in 1 Peter 5:8–9: "Keep a cool head. Stay alert. The Devil is poised to pounce, and would like nothing better than to catch you napping. Keep your guard up" (*The Message*).

Heed the warning. One reason Satan flourishes is that he's treated like a pussycat instead of a roaring lion. Beware of the disguise.

See also: Matthew 4:1–11; 2 Corinthians 11:14–15

■■ GOOD MORNING, AMERICA

My people come to you, as they usually do, and sit before you to listen to your words, but they do not put them into practice. With their mouths they express devotion, but their hearts are greedy for unjust gain. Indeed, to them you are nothing more than one who sings love songs with a beautiful voice and plays an instrument well, for they hear your words but do not put them into practice.

EZEKIEL 33:31–32

From one day to the next, the news doesn't change much. On a research trip to the library, I scanned newspaper articles from a few years ago. They might as well have been written today.

On that particular morning as America woke up, the early front-runner for the White House ended his campaign prematurely in the doghouse—amidst accusations that he'd gone "under cover" with somebody other than his wife ... The *Wall Street Journal* read like the *National Enquirer*, littered with reports that New York's brightest financial wizards were but pin-striped outlaws who traded inside tips to supplement their million-dollar incomes ... A leading recording artist was slapped with a $90 million lawsuit by a young woman who claimed he gave her genital herpes and then told her the disease was "God's way of giving your sex life a rest" ... A popular faith healer pleaded for several million dollars from his TV faithful lest God make good an alleged threat to "call me home" ... The Marines guarding our Moscow embassy faced spy charges after trading secrets for sex ... A defense contractor with $11 billion in annual sales billed the government $1,118.26 for the plastic cap on a stool leg ... The House and Senate Select Committees found that the president permitted overzealous aides to conduct illegal operations right under his nose ... A leading televangelist, who spent his $1.6 million annual salary on such things as gold-plated bathroom faucets, Rolls Royce autos, chandelier-lit closets, and air-conditioned doghouses, fell on hard times after admitting he'd paid $265,000 in hush money to cover up an afternoon of adultery with a 21-year-old church secretary—a tryst arranged by another popular evangelist ... and on and on and onand onandonandon.

On that particular morning as America woke up, the womanizing presidential hopeful blamed the media for the mess he was in ... The president blasted the press for stirring up unnecessary news and refused to admit responsibility for the chaos around him ... The philandering and fast-living televangelist insisted his troubles were part of a "diabolical plot" by rival preachers ... and on and on andonandonandon.

On that particular morning as America woke up, and on *this* particular morning as you crawl out of bed, Satan was and *is* on the prowl—looking for those of us to whom ethical behavior does not become important until the roof caves in, searching for those of us to whom Christian principles and morality are maintained not as guideposts of conduct but as props to make us look as if we were the good folks.

See also: Malachi 4:1–2; Matthew 25:31–46; Titus 1:16

:: TROUBLE IN THE FOREST

Each one should test his own actions. Then he can take pride in himself, without comparing himself to somebody else.

GALATIANS 6:4

Reprinted below is an article from the Springfield, Oregon, Public Schools newsletter. It's a parable that packs a big punch:

Once upon a time, the animals decided they should do something meaningful to meet the problems of the new world. So they organized a school.

They adopted an activity curriculum of running, climbing, swimming, and flying. To make it easier to administer the curriculum, all the animals took all the subjects.

The duck was excellent in swimming; in fact, better than his instructor. But he made only passing grades in flying, and was very poor in running. Since he was slow in running, he had to drop swimming and stay after school to practice running. This caused his webbed feet to be badly worn, so that he was only average in swimming. But average was quite acceptable, so nobody worried about that—except the duck.

The rabbit started at the top of his class in running but developed a nervous twitch in his leg muscles because of so much make-up work in swimming.

The squirrel was excellent in climbing, but he encountered constant frustration in flying class because his teacher made him start from the ground up instead of from the treetop down. He developed "charley horses" from overexertion, and so only got a C in climbing and a D in running.

The eagle was a problem child and was severely disciplined for being a nonconformist. In climbing classes he beat all the others to the top of the tree but insisted on using his own way to get there....

The point of the story is obvious: God has given each of us a very special set of abilities and capabilities. They are ours alone. When we try to be like others, we're like a rabbit that tries to swim or a squirrel that tries to fly. It's frustrating and phony trying to be anybody but yourself. And it is not much fun. True satisfaction comes when you realize you are a unique creation of God—freckles, flat feet, bony knees, long nose, big ears, and all.

So stop comparing yourself to others. Just for today, enjoy being you!

See also: Romans 12:2–8; 1 Corinthians 12:12–26

■■ WANNA BE'S

From him [Christ] the whole body, joined and held together by every supporting ligament, grows and builds itself up in love, as each part does its work.

EPHESIANS 4:16

All around are people who seem "better" than you. They get better grades, have better looks, drive better cars, work better jobs, tell better jokes. If only you had their clothes, their abilities, their brains, their boyfriend; if only you could switch lives and homes and friends and families. Wouldn't it be nice just to be *them?*

Yesterday you read a whimsical article about a bunch of frustrated animals. Their problems were simple enough: By trying so hard to be like others, they lost their own sense of identity. Their successes turned to failures; excellence degenerated to mediocrity. The incredible satisfaction that came from being a web-footed, hard-swimming duck was lost when the duck tried to race around the running track. In the same manner, the rabbit was a failure on the swim team. As a flyer, the squirrel simply proved the law of gravity was still intact. And the eagle was no more successful than a bowling ball as a climber.

If you're a duck, stick to water and thank God you have funny-looking feet. You'll be successful—as long as you paddle with all of your might and quit worrying about running and climbing. So what if you waddle when you walk? That's the way God made ducks.

If you're a rabbit, you'll experience burnout if you continually try to make it on the swim team.

And beware of challenging the territory of the eagle, for the eagle may decide it likes you better for breakfast than for competition.

In the end, you'll do much better (and the body of Christ will work more smoothly) if you concentrate exclusively on being *yourself* and allow others to be *themselves.* Don't try to be like those around you, and don't expect them to be like you. Relax. Get comfortable with your own style, looks, and surroundings. Learn to enjoy your own, very special, unique corner of the forest.

Most of all, realize that when God made you, he was pleased. He could do no better.

See also: Genesis 1:26–31; 2 Corinthians 10:12–18; Galatians 6:4

⊞ POINTS TO PONDER – IDENTITY

If anyone would come after me, he must deny himself and take up his cross and follow me. For whoever wants to save his life will lose it, but whoever loses his life for me will find it.

MATTHEW 16:24–25

When a man is all wrapped up in himself he makes a pretty small package.

JOHN RUSKIN

Man's problem rises from the fact that he has not only lost the way, but he has lost the address.

NICOLAS BERDYAEV

Jesus Christ never met an unimportant person. That is why God sent his Son to die for us. If someone dies for you, you must be important.

M. C. CLEVELAND

If you have anything really valuable to contribute to the world it will come through the expression of your own personality, that single spark of divinity that sets you off and makes you different from every other living creature.

BRUCE BARTON

Men are not against you; they are merely for themselves.

GENE FOWLER

Have confidence that if you have done a little thing well, you can do a bigger thing well, too.

VIOLET ALLEYN STOREY

Here is Christian identity: I know my past, where I came from. I came from God. I know what went wrong. I tried to play God instead of being satisfied to be a real man. I know my future. My destiny is Christ. And I know the present. I can face myself now—

my problems, my hang-ups, my assets, my faults—because I have turned myself over to God.

LEIGHTON FORD

The world is a looking glass and gives back to every man the reflection of his own face.

WILLIAM MAKEPEACE THACKERAY

Do not attempt to do a thing unless you are sure of yourself; but do not relinquish it simply because someone else is not sure of you.

STEWART E. WHITE

The greatest burden we have to carry in life is self; the most difficult thing we have to manage is self.

HANNAH WHITALL SMITH

Modern youth alternates between abysmal hang-ups and fanatical commitments. Psychologists call their malady an "identity crisis." Its chief symptom is the cry: "Who am I?" To them I say, "Have a confrontation with yourself. Then have a confrontation with Jesus Christ."

BILLY GRAHAM

Everybody thinks of changing humanity and nobody thinks of changing himself.

LEO TOLSTOY

He who falls in love with himself will have few rivals.

BENJAMIN FRANKLIN

You can always tell when a man is a great way from God: when he is always talking about himself, how good he is.

DWIGHT L. MOODY

Many could forego heavy meals, a full wardrobe, a fine house; it is the ego that they cannot forego.

MOHANDAS K. GANDHI

See also: John 12:43; Romans 2:7–8; 5:7–8; Philippians 2:1–8

WEEK

29

■■ HANGING TOUGH

Is any one of you in trouble? He should pray.

JAMES 5:13

Some days are tougher than others. You wake up late, with only ten minutes before you must be out the front door. You race for the bathroom, only to find your kid sister hogging it for keeps. You jerk on the handle, which pulls off in your hand.

At school, your history teacher adorns the top of your midterm with a big red F, your boyfriend is flirting with the new girl from Minnesota, and you forget your locker combination. And then at lunch, you spill a carton of yogurt in your lap. You want to scream, but when you accidentally bite your tongue you start to cry instead.

On days like this, I recall the story of the four guys who decided to go mountain climbing one weekend. Approaching the peak, one of the climbers slipped over a cliff, tumbled about sixty feet, and crash-landed on a small ledge.

"Bob, are you okay?" his three friends shouted from above.

"I'm alive . . . but I think I busted both my arms!" a weak voice responded.

"Well, hang in there," yelled his friends. "We'll toss a rope down and pull you up. Just lie still!"

"Fine," answered Bob.

Shortly after lowering one end of the rope, they started tugging and grunting together, working feverishly to pull their wounded companion to safety. When they had him about three-fourths of the way up, they suddenly remembered he said he'd broken *both* of his arms.

"Bob! If you broke both your arms, how in the world are you hanging on?"

"With my TEEEEEEEEEEEEEETH . . ."

On days when all you can do is hold on by your teeth, not even friends are company. Chances are, they're bringing bad news anyway. Remember Job and his friends? They had all kinds of inane advice on how he could improve things.

In times of trouble, you need to avoid bum advice from well-meaning people. You need to act quickly and decisively. There's no time for Plan B. Your lifeline is Jesus Christ. Grab on tight. And then pray like crazy, if only through your teeth.

See also: Proverbs 19:23; John 16:33; Romans 8:38–39

■ YES OR NO

Simply let your "Yes" be "Yes," and your "No," "No."

MATTHEW 5:37

At the heart of life's every decision, even the most difficult ones, are some fairly simple yes-or-no questions. Each situation we encounter, every alternative we face, can be reduced to either a *yes* or a *no.*

Should I get up when the alarm rings? Should I go to school? Should I eat breakfast? Should I talk to my dad? Should I light up in the rest room? Should I kick the habit once and for all? Should I go to the party? Should I have a beer? *Yes* or *no?*

Throughout the day we make thousands of such decisions. Should I ask Becky out? Should I stay home and save my money? Should I order an all-you-can-eat platter of shrimp? Should I stick to my diet? Should I wear black shoes? Should I get married next year? Should I wait? *Yes* or *no?*

The necessity of making yes-or-no decisions is inescapable. All of the great historical decisions have been made, in the end, by a simple *yes* or *no* response. Should the colonies fight Mother England for their independence? Should the North declare war on the South? Should the United States respond to Japan's sneak attack? Should we drop The Bomb?

The most important decision you will ever have to make in your life—the one that determines your destiny for all of eternity—also comes down to *yes* or *no.* Do you believe Jesus is the Christ, the Son of God? Do you think he was just some nut with delusions of grandeur? Do you believe he died for you on the cross? Was he just an ideologue in a bathrobe and sandals who was killed for stirring up controversy? Do you believe he loves you? Well, do you? Answer the question: *Yes or no?*

Eternal life is a simple decision. But it's so important that the angels of heaven have their ears cocked to hear your response. What will it be? Just say *yes* or *no.*

See also: Joshua 24:15; Luke 15:8–10

■■ MY FAVORITE WORD

This day I call heaven and earth as witnesses against you that I have set before you life and death, blessings and curses. Now choose life, so that you and your children may live and that you may love the Lord your God, listen to his voice, and hold fast to him.

DEUTERONOMY 30:19–20

Of all the words in the English language, my favorite is *yes.* What other word makes people more happy or offers more hope? What other word can bring a bigger or faster smile?

"Yes, the exam's been canceled."

"Yes, the X-rays are clear."

"Yes, you're hired."

"Yes, I will marry you."

Yes brings the good news. It seals the commitment. It gets rockets launched and new cars designed and shopping malls built. *Yes* is affirmation that you're on the right track, that you're doing a good job. If I knew I were going deaf and could choose the last word I'd ever hear, that word would be *yes.*

Yes is at least as old as the words of Moses in Deuteronomy: "This day ... I have set before you life and death, blessings and curses. Now choose life."

The first day of the rest of your life began when you said *yes* to God. That may have happened ten years ago; it may have occurred yesterday. On that day, whenever it was, you "chose life." Eternal life.

Pause a few minutes right now. Think back to that special day and to the events leading to your decision. As you recollect, jot down a few of the details that come to mind. In addition, make note of any changes in your life that you've noticed since then.

I became a Christian on or about _____

because I felt _____

_____ ,

and because I needed _____

_____ .

Since becoming a Christian, I've noticed several changes, including

_____

_____ .

     Now, are there areas of your life that still need work? Think about things you've held back from God, attitudes that keep him at arm's length. What decisions have you made where you've said no to him, whether consciously or unconsciously? Work this week at turning a no into a yes.

     It's only a word, but it makes all the difference in the world.

See also: Matthew 9:28; John 11:27; 21:16; 2 Corinthians 1:19–20

■■ JUST SAY NO

> *So I find this law at work: When I want to do good, evil is right there with me. For in my inner being I delight in God's law; but I see another law at work in the members of my body, waging war against the law of my mind and making me a prisoner of the law of sin at work within my members. What a wretched man I am! Who will rescue me from this body of death? Thanks be to God–through Jesus Christ our Lord!*

> ROMANS 7:21–25

     As you read yesterday, the word *yes* is full of optimism and hope. It signals new life and causes smiles to blossom. It may be everybody's favorite word, but beware.

Though *yes* brings happiness, it also brings much heartache. In fact, *yes* can get you in more trouble than you ever thought possible. The wisdom of the hour is, "Just say *no*."

There are times when *no* is the absolute best, most positive response you can make:

"My parents are going away for the weekend. How about spending the night?"

Just say *no*. Virtue is too precious to lose in one night.

"Hey dude, got me some good dope. Wanna get blitzed Friday night?"

Just say *no*. "Good dope" is a contradiction in terms.

"What's your problem? Everybody's doing it. Say *yes* and quit worrying."

Just say *no*. Your worries will start if you say *yes*.

Unfortunately, it's not often easy to say *no*. Take a few minutes right now, and think about those times you said *yes* when you know you should have said *no*. Wrong decisions can keep you awake all night. They can haunt you for months and may even impact the rest of your life.

If you went to bed last night with a weight of guilt on your shoulders, you can be out from under the burden by bedtime tonight. When you're at the end of your rope, who will rescue you? Is there anyone who can do anything to help? Isn't that the real question?

As the apostle Paul said in the verse above (with a slightly different emphasis provided from another version of the Bible): "The answer, thank God, is that Jesus Christ can and does" (*The Message*). He acted to set things right, to make sense of this life of contradictions, to pull you back from the influence of sin.

It is Jesus Christ, and *only* Jesus Christ, who gives you the power to say no, and to serve God with all your heart and mind.

See also: 2 Corinthians 2:14–15; 2 Timothy 2:22

▪▪ SLIP SLIDING AWAY

Each one is tempted when, by his own evil desire,
he is dragged away and enticed. Then, after desire has

conceived, it gives birth to sin; and sin, when it is full-grown, gives birth to death.

JAMES 1:14–15

A lot of hormones were flying whenever Danny and Dawn were together. Both were Christians and both thought they could control their relationship. But they were far past the holding-hands-and-kissing stage, and even when they sat in a crowded cafeteria they couldn't seem to get close enough to each other.

The harder they tried to keep things under control, the more frustrated they both became. Before long, their relationship with Christ was on the rocks. And this wonderful couple that everybody thought would last forever was breaking apart—fast. Finally, they called it quits as a couple to salvage their love for God before it was too late.

However, Danny couldn't stay away from the phone. *No big deal,* he thought, *it's just a phone call.*

Dawn was thrilled to hear his familiar voice on the line, and when he asked her out, she was quick to say yes. *There's nothing wrong with just seeing him,* she reasoned.

After the movie, the night was still young. So Danny drove around for a little while, feeling comfort in Dawn's presence beside him. *So far, so good,* he said to himself. *So what if we get home just a little late?*

When Danny eventually pulled off the road and parked beneath a stand of trees, they both had an uneasy feeling. They'd been down this same path before, and knew exactly where it led: straight to the backseat.

Nearly two hours later when they pulled back onto the road, neither said a word. They were both deep in thought, trying to recollect how an innocent evening together could end in the same old way in the same old place, with both feeling so empty and so desperately guilty.

It was a sad, quiet thought that haunted them for nine long months—right up until the birth of their unexpected baby.

See also: Proverbs 26:27; 1 Thessalonians 4:3–8

▓▓ TOUGH DECISIONS

Love the Lord your God with all your heart and with all your soul and with all your strength.

DEUTERONOMY 6:5

Making decisions has never been particularly easy for me. Girls whom I dated wanted me to be more decisive. I drove them crazy because I had no idea what I wanted to do when I asked them out. I just wanted to be together. Where we ended up wasn't important to me.

"Well, what do you want to do?" I'd ask once we were in the car.

If it was a new relationship, the girl would generally shrug and smile. "Whatever you want."

I'd smile right back. "I don't really care. Where would *you* like to go?"

"It doesn't matter. *You* decide."

We'd go back and forth like that, as if playing verbal ping-pong. Only after an extended volley would we settle on a movie or restaurant or some other place where we could spend the evening and all of my money. And then I would promptly get lost trying to get there.

Perhaps that's why it was so tough when I had to decide what I was going to do about Jesus Christ. I couldn't just ignore him. His claims and promises were too insistent. But I knew that if I followed in his footsteps, if I said yes to him, I must *comparatively* say no to everything else. I had to *comparatively* relinquish my devotion to my desires and dreams, to my family, and even to my own life. I knew God demanded my complete devotion. Not a part. Not even the biggest part. But all of it.

That's the way it is with Christ. If we love him with all our heart and with all our soul and with all our strength, there's really no room for competing loves. If we follow Moses' advice to the Israelites and love God with our full emotional, mental, and physical capabilities, all other loves and desires pale by comparison. If he is truly Lord, his throne cannot be shared.

A tough decision? Yes. We must necessarily forsake all other loves. It's certainly not an easy decision. But it's a decision he demands we make. And like it or not, we must make it daily.

See also: 1 Samuel 12:24; Psalm 1; Mark 8:34–38; Luke 14:26

■■ POINTS TO PONDER – CHOICE

Choose for yourselves this day whom you will serve. . . . But as for me and my household, we will serve the Lord.

JOSHUA 24:15

God has no need of marionettes. He pays men the compliment of allowing them to live without him if they choose. But if they live without him in this life, they must also live without him in the next.

LEON MORRIS

I hate to see things done by halves. If it be right, do it boldly; if it be wrong leave it undone.

BERNARD BILPIN

God's love shouts for our salvation; Satan's enticements whisper for our damnation. The one is like a bullhorn; the other as light as a tickle. We must decide which voice we hear, and at what volume. The choice is wholly ours to make; our destiny, solely ours to determine. If the choice is not consciously taken, the choice has nonetheless been unconsciously made.

S. RICKLY CHRISTIAN

Between two evils, choose neither; between two goods, choose both.

TRYON EDWARDS

It is possible for a man to run against the wrong object and bend his lance for good.

A. W. TOZER

Father, make of me a crisis man. Bring those I contact to decision. Let me not be a milepost on a single road; make me a fork, that men must turn one way or another on facing Christ in me.

JIM ELLIOT

When a Christian is in the wrong place, his right place is empty.

T. J. BACH

As sure as I lived, I knew that I possessed a will, and that when I willed to do something or willed not to do something, nobody else was making the decision.

AUGUSTINE OF HIPPO

Perhaps no mightier conflict of mind occurs ever again in a lifetime than that first decision to unseat one's own tooth.

GENE FOWLER

To be a Christian, or not to be, is not a matter of being a somewhat better man, or a man perhaps not quite so good. It is a matter of life or death.

JAMES DENNEY

He who chooses the beginning of a road chooses the place it leads to. It is the means that determine the end.

HARRY EMERSON FOSDICK

A man is too apt to forget that in this world he cannot have everything. A choice is all that is left him.

H. MATTHEWS

In darkness there is no choice. It is light that enables us to see the differences between things; and it is Christ who gives us light.

A. W. HARE

Let it be known on whose side you are. If there is any doubt about it, something is wrong.

ANONYMOUS

We make our decisions, and then our decisions turn around and make us.

F. W. BOREHAM

The block of granite which was an obstacle in the pathway of the weak becomes a stepping-stone in the pathway of the strong.

THOMAS CARLYLE

See also: Deuteronomy 30:19–20; Proverbs 1:28–29

▪▪ SERIOUS TROUBLE

> *I am convinced that neither death nor life, neither angels nor demons, neither the present nor the future, nor any powers, neither height nor depth, nor anything else in all creation, will be able to separate us from the love of God that is in Christ Jesus our Lord.*

> ROMANS 8:38–39

Some days you feel like you should have stayed in bed. Things start out bad and progressively get worse. If you've got it bad today, consider the plight of this young construction worker as detailed on his company's accident form:

When I got to the building, I found that the hurricane had knocked off some bricks around the top. So I rigged up a beam with a pulley at the top of the building and hoisted up a couple barrels full of bricks.

When I had fixed the damaged area, there were a lot of bricks left over. Then I went to the bottom and began releasing the line. Unfortunately, the barrel of bricks was much heavier than I was—and before I knew what was happening, the barrel started coming down, jerking me up.

I decided to hang on since I was too far off the ground by then to jump, and halfway up I met the barrel of bricks coming down fast. I received a hard blow on my shoulder. I then continued to the top, banging my head against the beam, and getting my fingers pinched and jammed in the pulley. When the barrel hit the ground hard, it burst its bottom, allowing the bricks to spill out.

I was now heavier than the barrel. So I started down again at high speed. Halfway down I met the barrel coming up fast, and received severe injuries to my shins. When I hit the ground, I landed on the pile of spilled bricks, getting several painful cuts and deep bruises.

At this point, I must have lost my presence of mind because I let go of my grip on the line. The barrel came down fast—giving me another blow on my head and putting me in the hospital.

I respectfully request sick leave.

When you've got it *that* bad, you need help. You don't want somebody to say, "Cheer up." You want somebody to be with you, to share your pain. You want somebody who understands, not somebody who just got off the turnip truck or crawled out of the ivory tower. Experience helps. If somebody has known pain personally, chances are good they can help alleviate yours. You want somebody who won't run when the going gets tough, somebody who will never leave you or forsake you ...

That "somebody" sounds an awful lot like Jesus.

See also: Proverbs 19:23; John 16:33; Hebrews 12:2–3

WOODLAND HILLS TRAGEDY

You shall not murder.

EXODUS 20:13

A few years ago, workmen repossessed a boxcar-sized dumpster from the yard of Malvin R. Weisberg of Woodland Hills, California. When the padlocked doors were opened, workers faced a wall of wet boxes and a stench that was as thick as fog.

As the cartons were unloaded, the bottom of one suddenly tore, and clear plastic containers tumbled to the floor. Out of one pint-sized tub spilled something wrapped in cotton gauze. When the workers gathered around to examine the contents, they were horrified. Several threw up on the spot.

"It was human flesh, pure and simple," said the yard supervisor. "What I saw was two hands, two feet, and a mutilated body."

Eventually, 16,433 bodies were retrieved from the storage container—the smaller ones in cottage cheese tubs, the larger in gallon buckets. Each was a baby who died before birth. The cause of death: abortion.

The real tragedy is not that one man collected nearly 17,000 dead babies in his backyard over a four-year period. The real tragedy is that there are that many children aborted nationwide every three to four days. In the next twelve months, nearly 1.5 million unborn babies will lose their lives in the United States; millions more in other countries. To compound the tragedy, millions of adoption requests will remain unmet because there aren't enough babies to go around.

Some people believe we should look the other way when it comes to abortion, if only because of civil rights. It's a free country, and nobody's supposed to have the right to impose religious beliefs on another person. That's true, but we also live in a country wherein nobody is granted the right to deprive another person of life and liberty. To do so is not imposing a religious belief but violating a principle that's basic to every culture in the world: Thou shalt not kill.

Nevertheless, the killing continues. It doesn't make the newspapers because abortion is a quiet death. But someday ... someday, the tragedy and injustice of this silent holocaust will be as obvious as is our hindsight today of slavery or the mass exterminations in Nazi Germany.

See also: Deuteronomy 30:19; Psalm 139:13–16; Matthew 19:14

■■ A LANGUAGE BARRIER

Who is wise and understanding among you? Let him show it by his good life, by deeds done in the humility that comes from wisdom.

JAMES 3:13

When I graduated a few years ago with a communications degree from Stanford, I considered myself fluent in English. Upon graduation, I was hired as an obituary writer.

Among my first newspaper stories was something like: *Joe McGee, 81, died yesterday after being gored by a runaway forklift. An area native, he was a member of the Forklift Operators Society of America and the Plentiful Harvest Baptist Church. McGee is survived by his mother, Ella Mae, 102.* Three sentences; each short and understandable.

I still do okay with the language, but I understand less and less. If you ask me, most politicians and economists don't speak English. Astronomers, with their talk of anagalactic goings-on, are just as bad. And I was left scratching my head when I read a movie review the other day. The film was criticized because its "dim-witted sanctity begs to be beaten into lean meat." I'd much rather somebody just say the movie was a dog.

I wish Christians spoke more plainly as well. Too many times we shield our experiences and feelings in a kind of Christian lingo. I ooze pity for the uninitiated when they are "witnessed to" about being "born again." Huh? It sounds like some court case involving a strange birthing procedure. Talk about "being saved by the blood" sounds like the plot of the next Stephen King thriller, while "soul winning" could be a new release from Motown Records.

Such talk may sound rather spiritual. But *sounding* spiritual has never been the same as *being* spiritual. That's what Christ found with the Pharisees. These religious honchos talked godly and prayed loudly. But they lived pretty godless lives, and their prayers just bounced off the wall.

In the end, actions speak louder than words. They always have and they always will. You might consider that the next time you *tell* somebody you're a Christian. Try *showing* them as well.

See also: James 1:26; 1 Peter 3:1–2

■■ FISHLESS FISHERMEN

> *"Come, follow me," Jesus said, "and I will make you fishers of men."*
>
> MATTHEW 4:19

A few people I know became Christians just by reading the Bible. But the vast majority, myself included, would never have established a personal relationship with Jesus Christ unless somebody first talked to them about his love, his forgiveness, his death and resurrection. With that in mind, I pass along the following parable by John M. Drescher:

Now it came to pass that a group existed who called themselves fishermen. And lo, there were many fish in the waters all around. Week after week, those who called themselves fishermen met and talked about the abundance of fish and searched for better methods of fishing.

*They loved slogans such as "Every fisherman is a fisher,"
sponsored special "Fishermen's Campaigns," convened nationwide
congresses to promote fishing, constructed beautiful "Fishing Headquarters," and built large printing houses to publish fishing guides.
One thing they didn't do, however. They didn't fish.*

*In addition to meeting regularly, they organized a board of
those with great vision to send fishermen to faraway streams and
lakes. The board, in turn, hired staffs and appointed committees, but
they did not fish.*

*Expensive training centers were built to teach fishermen how
to fish, the nature of fish, and where to fish. Those who taught had
doctorates in fishology, but they did not fish. Many were graduated,
given fishing licenses, and sent to do full-time fishing. But they spent
their time building power plants to pump water for fish, plowing new
waterways, supplying fishing equipment, and visiting fish hatcheries.
They didn't fish.*

*One day after a stirring meeting on "The Necessity of Fishing,"
one young fellow actually went fishing. The next day he reported he
had caught two outstanding fish. He was honored for his excellent
catch and scheduled to speak everywhere. To have the time for that,
he had to quit fishing.*

*Now it's true that many fishermen sacrificed and put up with
many difficulties. Some lived near the water and bore the smell of fish
every day. They were ridiculed about their fishermen's clubs. So
imagine how hurt some were when one day a person suggested they
were really not fishermen. It made them stop and think.*

*But after all, are you really a fisherman if year after year you
never fish?*

See also: Isaiah 6:5–8; James 1:22–25

▪▪ SHOW OR TELL

**Dear friends, I urge you, as aliens and strangers in
the world, to abstain from sinful desires, which war
against your soul. Live such good lives among the pagans**

*that, though they accuse you of doing wrong, they may see
your good deeds and glorify God on the day he visits us.*

1 PETER 2:11–12

When Christ talked about God to everyday people he met
on the street, he tried to be as understandable as possible. He used
a lot of parables, or word pictures, and told many stories. But he
knew it took more than words to communicate. It took action. He
didn't just *tell* people about God's love, he *showed* them love.

What would you do if you woke up mute one morning—you
couldn't say a word? What if others could discover Jesus based only
on your actions instead of your words? Take a few minutes to jot
down a few ideas below about how you might visibly display Jesus
in various areas of your life.

At school, my friends would be able to see Jesus in my life
if I would: _____

_____ .

At home, my family would be able to see Jesus in my life if
I would: _____

_____ .

At work, my boss and fellow employees would be able to see
Jesus in my life if I would: _____

_____ .

See also: James 2:14–26

■■ LOOK WHO'S TALKING

*No one lights a lamp and puts it in a place where
it will be hidden, or under a bowl. Instead he puts it on its
stand, so that those who come in may see the light.*

LUKE 11:33

When I first became a Christian, I got a rash just thinking about talking to somebody else about God. It was worse than the mental gymnastics I'd go through before calling a girl for the first time. When the topic of God came up, I developed a sudden shy attack. My mind turned to Jell-O and my mouth felt like a sweater.

At the heart of these feelings was my desire not to offend people. My friendships were important to me, as was my reputation. And so, not wanting others to think of me as a shallow-minded religious weirdo, I mostly kept quiet about my faith. Witnessing became nothing more than smiling a lot, occasionally inviting somebody to church, being nice, and hoping others would somehow "catch on."

But it wasn't long before I noticed an amazing thing happening: *nothing*. Nobody caught on to anything. Though I saw the needs and emptiness in my non-Christian friends, I was paralyzed to help. The reason was simple. I cared more about how *they* saw me than how God saw me.

About that time, I discussed my feelings with an older Christian whom I respected. He wasn't exactly gushy about his faith, but he'd look you in the eye when he talked about Jesus. And he'd tell you openly that his prime goal in life was to take as many people with him into heaven as possible. I've never forgotten his words to me.

"Rick, your life will never save anyone," he said. "Being a nice guy is fine, but people aren't won to God because of nice guys. They're won to God because of Jesus' life and death. And how will anybody know about Jesus' life and death unless you tell them?"

My feelings about evangelism didn't change overnight. In fact, my mouth sometimes still feels like a sweater when I talk to others about Jesus. But at least now I'm talking. When it comes to being the "light of the world," I may not be as powerful as a lightning bolt. Some days I feel no brighter than a lightning bug.

But as the saying goes, it only takes a spark to get a fire going.

See also: Matthew 5:13–16; John 1:6–9; 8:12

POINTS TO PONDER – EVANGELISM

> Then Jesus came to them and said, "All authority in heaven and on earth has been given to me. Therefore go and make disciples of all nations, baptizing them in the name of the Father and of the Son and of the Holy Spirit, and teaching them to obey everything I have commanded you."

MATTHEW 28:18–20

Evangelism applies a supernatural remedy for the need of the world.

FARIS WHITESELL

Lighthouses don't fire guns or ring bells to call attention to their light; they just shine.

ANONYMOUS

The real witnessing Christian does not talk about people he has "converted." Witnessing is hard work unless it is done in the Spirit, and then we can't brag about it.

WILLIAM R. BRIGHT

If a man has a soul—and he has—and if that soul can be won or lost for eternity—and it can—then the most important thing in the world is to bring that man to Jesus Christ.

ANONYMOUS

When a Christian is winning souls, he isn't messing around with sin.

GEORGE L. SMITH

The trouble with some of us is that we have been inoculated with small doses of Christianity which keep us from catching the real thing.

LESLIE DIXON WEATHERHEAD

Our business is to get people to close with Christ. Again and again they come up to the point of decision, but we don't push them over—we hardly try. We work their minds into thorough agreement that this and that must be done, but we don't clinch things on the spot. And so the metal cools again and nothing happens.

ARTHUR JOHN GOSSIP

When you need God, religion won't do.

S. RICKLY CHRISTIAN

Evangelism is the proclamation of the Gospel of the crucified and risen Christ, the only Redeemer of men, according to the Scriptures, with the purpose of persuading condemned and lost sinners to put their trust in God by receiving and accepting Christ as Savior through the power of the Holy Spirit, and to serve Christ as Lord in every calling of life and in the fellowship of his church, looking toward the day of his coming in glory.

WORLD CONGRESS ON EVANGELISM, BERLIN, 1966

Evangelism is a sharing of gladness.

ANONYMOUS

Something must really change in the world, and this can come only through men who themselves are changed. But when a man is changed under the influence of grace, then not only the state of his soul, but also his whole comportment, is changed. He is suddenly free from the old habits which kept him imprisoned, free from the rancor and remorse that consumed him. [He has] become whole in a broken world.

PAUL TOURNIER

When it comes to loving the unlovable, easy *doesn't* do it.

S. RICKLY CHRISTIAN

My feeling about people in whose conversion I have been allowed to play a part is always mixed with awe and even fear: such as a boy might feel on first being allowed to fire a rifle. The disproportion between his puny finger on the trigger and the thunder and lightning which follow is alarming.

C. S. LEWIS

See also: John 1:12–13; 3:1–21; Romans 3:23; 6:23

WEEK

31

:: LIFE ON THE HILL

Whoever is kind to the needy honors God.

PROVERBS 14:31

Most of us take our fast lives and fast food for granted. We seldom take a break from our stereos, schedules, and Big Macs to think about how much we really have . . . or, for that matter, how much the rest of the world does *not* have. That's because "the world," with its billions of people and problems, seems too big and far away to really worry about.

As suggested by World Vision, a Christian world-relief agency, maybe we'd all be better off to think smaller. That is, we could imagine our planet of people represented by a small town of one thousand.

In our community, 180 of us live high on a hill, called the developed world, overlooking everything else. The other 820 live on the rocky bottom land, called the rest of the world. The fortunate 180 have more than 80 percent of the wealth of the town and more than half of all rooms, with two rooms per person. The 820 people down below have less than half of all the rooms, with five persons to a room.

According to the best estimates, those of us on the hill have 85 percent of all automobiles; 80 percent of all TV sets; 93 percent of all the telephones; and an average income per person of $5,000 per year. The rest of the town gets by on an average of about $700 per person, though many exist on $200 or less.

How does the fortunate group on the hill use its incredible wealth? As a group, these people spend less than one percent of their wealth to aid the bottom land. In the United States, for example, of every $100 earned $18.03 goes for food; $6.60 is spent on recreation and amusement; $5.80 is used for clothes; $2.40 is paid for alcohol; $1.50 buys tobacco; $1.30 is given for religious and charitable uses, and only a very small fraction of that goes to share the hill peoples' knowledge of Jesus Christ with the rest of the town.

Meanwhile, the town is unable to house, clothe, or feed 350 of its residents, 125 never get enough to eat, and 250 of the townspeople eat the wrong kinds of food. They have something called malnutrition, but they don't know it.

Jesus offered us a model and challenge when he instructed his followers to feed the hungry, give water to the thirsty, house strangers, clothe the naked, aid the sick, and visit the imprisoned. You see, as far as Christ is concerned there's no distinction between the hill people and the flatlanders.

He keeps hoping the people with the view will realize that. But many of them appear to spend a good part of their waking hours *asleep*—another luxury not shared by the rest of the town.

See also: Matthew 25:31–46; Hebrews 13:1–2; James 2:14–17

■■ MISSING PART

Jesus said, "Let the little children come to me, and do not hinder them, for the kingdom of heaven belongs to such as these."

MATTHEW 19:14

By the time Lori was eighteen, she'd already had two children and was pregnant with a third. Under pressure from all sides to "put an end to this pregnancy nonsense," Lori consented to an abortion. At the time, her baby was twelve weeks old.

"The nurse assured me I'd feel no pain and that everything would be fine the next day," Lori told me in the course of research I was doing. "But the doctor dilated me with a series of metal rods that ripped up my cervix. I kept screaming and grabbing my tummy every time he scraped the suction tool around inside, but the nurse pinned me down, and the doctor told me to quit being so hysterical about something that was just a 'blob of jelly.' As if to prove his point, he kept smearing bloody bits of the child and placenta on the sheet beside me. 'See, there is no baby,' he said. 'Of course not,' I yelled. 'You just ground it to hamburger before my eyes!'"

After the abortion, Lori hemorrhaged terribly and had constant cramps. Finally, two weeks after the abortion, she went into labor. The contractions were horrible. "I staggered into the bathroom, and there I delivered a part of my baby the doctor had missed," she told me. "It was only about the size of a quarter, but there was no mistaking what it was. It was the head of my baby."

The horror of holding her child's head in her hands, coupled with incredible guilt, brought Lori to the verge of suicide. But in her darkest moment, she remembered the stories she'd heard as a child about God's forgiveness. And in the quietness of her room, she prayed for God to come into her heart and forgive her. But forgiveness was one thing; forgetting, something entirely different.

"Sometimes I still set the dinner table for three children instead of two," Lori said. "And I still have nightmares in which I am forced to watch my baby being ripped apart in front of me. But the most difficult aspect is that I simply miss my baby. I often wake up wanting to nurse my child, to hold my child. The doctor never told me I'd experience any of this. He said the only feeling I'd have would be relief. But I call it emptiness."

See also: 2 Chronicles 7:14; Psalm 139:13–16; Matthew 11:28

▪▪ LIFE SENTENCE

Do not be misled: "Bad company corrupts good character." Come back to your senses as you ought, and stop sinning; for there are some who are ignorant of God – I say this to your shame.

1 CORINTHIANS 15:33–34

"Welcome to the State Penitentiary." The sign attempted a warm greeting. From a tower, a guard armed with a high-powered rifle watched as my friend stopped and took one final look at the door of the prison. With two life sentences, he had every reason to expect he'd never be free again.

At one point, my friend's future had been star bright. Though not the world's best student, he was a hometown athletic legend. The boy could *play.* His senior year in high school, he captained the basketball, baseball, and football teams. College scholarship offers rolled in, and scouts courted him at school.

But the future always seemed far away and my friend was attracted to the present. *Now* was all that mattered. He started running with a fast crowd, passing time with alcohol and colored pills. After one particular blur of parties that lasted an entire week, he drove two buddies to the home of some girls. He waited in the car. Minutes later they sprinted back shouting, "Drive! Drive! We shot a man!"

The scare sobered my friend and he broke off his relationship with the two others. But a year later, FBI detectives burst through his door and arrested him. Scared for their own futures, the pair fingered my friend for the crime. Justice was fickle and he was convicted of the murder.

"Ordinary people can sometimes get into extraordinary trouble," he says now, looking back on the incident. Their lives don't end up the way they're "supposed to." Little wrongs lead to bigger wrongs, and soon they're in over their head.

Maybe you know the feeling. Perhaps, like my friend, you've made some wrong choices along the way. Maybe time has gotten away from you, and you find yourself slip-sliding away—away from where you know God wants you to be. Perhaps you know what it's like to lie awake at 3 A.M. because of overwhelming guilt or to cry yourself to sleep night after night because of some past sin.

Thankfully, wrong choices, actions, and thoughts are forgivable. Kneeling in his roach-infested cell, my friend eventually found the transforming power and love of Jesus Christ. And years later, he received a full parole and pardon.

Though the closest brush most people have with the law is to spot a flashing red light in their rearview mirror, they can still be walled in by a prison of sin. If you're in that position, Jesus Christ can open the door and give you a full pardon. As the psalmist says, "The Lord sets prisoners free." That includes you and me, too.

See also: Psalm 51:1–12; Isaiah 1:18; Romans 6:23

■ EXTRAVAGANT TIME

I awoke and looked around. My sleep had been pleasant to me.

JEREMIAH 31:26

You push the little button down—a simple effort that guarantees your alarm will not ring. With no obnoxious buzz to jolt you awake, a dreamlike smile sweeps your mind and you stretch once, twice. Feeling like an heir to some latter-day throne, you pull your blanket up over your shoulders and doze off into never-never land …

Turning off an alarm is an extravagant pleasure—on par with walking barefoot in the mud. Actions like these keep the cobwebs out. Without them, we close our eyes at seventeen and open them at sixty-five.

So loosen up today. If you need some ideas on how to go about it, lavish yourself with some of the following:

Smile at a child. Smile at the child's parents, too. Tell them they've got a good-looking kid—even if he looks like a lizard. Or round up a couple of friends, dig out a jump rope, and have an old-fashioned aerobic workout. If you want to make a friend for life, invite your mom to jump in.

Laugh out loud. Climb a tree. Take a bubble bath. Count your teeth with your tongue. Chew a wad of gum and pop the bubble on your face. Smell a freshly mowed lawn. Better yet, visit the biggest library in town, stand in the center, and take a long, slow whiff. Inhale the fragrance of thoughts and wisdom. Breaths of library air should cost a quarter each. So get what you can now—free—while the supply lasts.

Walk on a brick wall and sing "Amazing Grace." Sit on your roof and watch the sun set. After it's down, make some popcorn and return for the second show: fireflies at dusk. They're more magical than anything Steven Spielberg or Disneyland can produce.

You want extravagance? I'll give you extravagance. Before you go to bed tonight, talk to God. Don't just mumble a few bless 'ems. Really pray. While you're at it, thank God for sunsets and fireflies and bubble baths. Not to forget babies and popcorn … and alarms that don't ring.

See also: Psalm 69:32; 118:24; Luke 10:38–42; Romans 5:17

▣ MORE EXTRAVAGANCE

I commend the enjoyment of life.

ECCLESIASTES 8:15

So you think you can handle two straight days of extravagant pleasure? Aren't you getting a bit carried away? This much pleasure is only for those who are mature. No kids allowed. If you can handle it, cut loose again:

Spend an hour reading French poetry—especially if you can't read French. Pretend you're a taco. Skip down the street backward. Write a letter to your grandparents. Change your bedsheets. Pound a nail with a banana.

Volunteer—it doesn't matter what for. Burp as loud as possible. Fly a kite. In the absence of a strong wind, lie flat on your back and watch the clouds. Pick out faces of people you know in the cottony billows and pray for them before they turn into sheep.

Go to a baseball game. If it's not the season, just buy some peanuts and Cracker Jack. Toss an occasional piece in the air, and catch it in your mouth. Chalk your initials (together with those of a special friend) inside a heart on the sidewalk. If your friend is with you, chalk up a hopscotch game and have a go at it. Try to catch a butterfly. Try to catch each other.

Suck a lemon. It may not strike you as pleasure, but it'll put you in touch with your senses and remind you that you're *alive*. Putting an ice cube down your pants will do the same thing.

Fill up a birdbath. Feed your dog a cookie. If you've never seen a dog smile, feed it another and wait five seconds. Change into your shorts and wash someone else's car. Don't be particular—any old car on the block will do.

Before going to sleep, get your Bible down off your shelf. Dust it off and lay it beside your bed, within reach. Turn off the alarm. When you wake up, thank God for time—and for enabling you to enjoy it. And then ask him for a special day. Ask him to begin by leading you to a special verse in the Bible.

See also: Psalm 16:11; 100; Ecclesiastes 2:26; John 10:10

▓ HOW MUCH LONGER?

No one knows about that day or hour, not even the angels in heaven, nor the Son, but only the Father. As it was

*in the days of Noah, so it will be at the coming of the Son of
Man. For in the days before the flood, people were eating
and drinking, marrying and giving in marriage, up to the
day Noah entered the ark; and they knew nothing about
what would happen until the flood came and took them all
away. That is how it will be at the coming of the Son of Man.*

                                      MATTHEW 24:36–39

When I was a kid, time seemed to drag in slow motion. On
long car trips, my parents tried to quiet me by playing stupid license-
plate games or seeing who could spot the next Holiday Inn billboard.
But I would have none of it. "How much longer?" I'd whine. The
response I wanted was, "Soon, very soon."

I'm still time conscious, except now I have my own watch. It
tells me when to get up, go to meetings, and when to head home. It
indicates how much time is left in class and when the minister will
finish his sermon. "How much longer?" A glance at my watch will
tell me.

However, watches are useless when it comes to distant events.
In determining how much longer till, say, my birthday or Christmas,
I consult the calendar.

But neither a watch nor a calendar will help when it comes
to determining how much longer till the most momentous event to
occur since Jesus visited earth: his second coming. The Bible
stresses repeatedly that Christ will return. But you're wasting time if
you check a watch or calendar. The Bible just says to be ready.

On our family car trips, we often left in the middle of the
night. So when I went to bed, I slept in my clothes. I didn't want to
fumble around in my pj's for a half hour. I wanted to be *ready*.

That same level of preparedness also ought to mark our attitude toward Christ's long-heralded second coming. We ought to live
in anticipation that it could happen tomorrow. Or, for that matter,
today. Our hearts should be ready; our lives in order.

"How much longer?" If Christ were to answer that question,
I like to think he'd respond, "Soon, my child, very soon."

See also: Acts 1:7–11; 1 Thessalonians 4:13–5:11

■■ POINTS TO PONDER – TIME

Dear friends, now we are children of God, and what we will be has not yet been made known. But we know that when he appears, we shall be like him, for we shall see him as he is. Everyone who has this hope in him purifies himself, just as he is pure.

1 JOHN 3:2–3

Every experience God gives us, every person he puts in our lives, is the perfect preparation for the future that only he can see.

CORRIE TEN BOOM

Each of us has a capacity for God and an ability to relate to him in a personal way. When we do, he brings to us pardon for the past, peace for the present, and a promise for the future.

RALPH S. BELL

Enjoy the little things, for one day you may look back and realize they were the big things.

ROBERT BRAULT

No man ever sank under the burden of the day. It is when tomorrow's burden is added to the burden of today that the weight is more than a man can bear. Never load yourself so. If you find yourself so loaded, at least remember this: it is your own doing, not God's. He begs you to leave the future to him, and mind the present.

GEORGE MACDONALD

What we are is God's gift to us. What we become is our gift to God.

ELEANOR POWEL

The future has a habit of suddenly and dramatically becoming the present.

ROGER W. BABSON

Lost, yesterday, somewhere between sunrise and sunset, two golden hours, each set with sixty diamond minutes. No reward is offered, for they are gone forever.

HORACE MANN

Those who make the worst use of their time are the first to complain of its shortness.

JEAN DE LA BRUYERE

It is said that sheep may get lost simply by nibbling away at the grass and never looking up. That can be true for any of us. We can focus so much on what is immediately before us that we fail to see life in larger perspective.

REV. DONALD BITSBERGER

If you can spend a perfectly useless afternoon in a perfectly useless manner, you have learned how to live.

LIN YUTANG

We all find time to do what we really want to do.

WILLIAM FEATHER

Throughout the whole [New Testament] there runs the conviction that the time looked forward to by the prophets has in fact arrived in history with the advent of Jesus Christ . . . The time of Jesus is *kairos*—a time of opportunity. To embrace the opportunity means salvation; to neglect it, disaster. There is no third course.

JOHN MARSH

Does thou love life? Then do not squander time, for that is the stuff life is made of.

BENJAMIN FRANKLIN

We are so little reconciled to time that we are even astonished at it. "How he's grown!" we exclaim, "How time flies!" as though the universal form of our experience were again and again a novelty. It is as strange as if a fish were repeatedly surprised at the wetness of water. And that would be strange indeed; unless of course the fish were destined to become, one day, a land animal.

C. S. LEWIS

See also: Ecclesiastes 3:1–8; Jeremiah 29:11; Matthew 6:25–34

WEEK

32

:: DOUBLESPEAK

If you live according to the sinful nature, you will die; but if by the Spirit you put to death the misdeeds of the body, you will live, because those who are led by the Spirit of God are sons of God.

ROMANS 8:13–14

I once interviewed a TV personality who was often described in the press as being "outspoken" and "ruddy-faced." I didn't know exactly what to expect, but I soon found out. It was a nice way of saying the man was an abusive drunk.

A nice way of saying negative things is what I call *fuzzifying*. For example, the Pentagon fuzzifies when it uses the term *sunshine units* as a measure of nuclear radiation; it's when the president institutes *revenue enhancements* instead of raising taxes. Fuzzifying is what happens when we call war *pacification*, or name the MX missile *Peacekeeper*. That makes as much sense as calling the guillotine a headache remedy.

This linguistic camouflage is seen in the recent slaughter of eight million chickens that were spreading an influenza virus throughout Pennsylvania. The Feds stepped in and gassed them all. When they finally announced what happened, they fuzzified. They said they *depopulated* the birds.

We often fuzzify what the Bible calls s-i-n. The little word sounds too offensive, too harsh, too judgmental. So instead we talk about our "weaknesses," the "things we can't help," our "shortcomings," our "natural inclinations." And so sin flourishes because we treat it like a head cold instead of a cancer.

A rose by any other name may smell just as sweet. And so it is with rattlesnakes and sin. By any other name they're just as lethal. Even in this age of fuzzifying, the wages of "things we can't help" haven't changed a dime.

See also: Ezekiel 18:5–32; Romans 5:17; 6:23; Galatians 6:7–8

EQUAL TREATMENT

Love your neighbor as yourself.

MARK 12:31

Loving other people is practically the hardest thing you can ever do. It's right up there in difficulty with trying to stop lusting, kicking the tobacco habit, not making fun of beach geeks, or eating all of your brussels sprouts.

Loving others is hard because we're all basically "me-oriented." That's why Jesus gave us a tip on how to love people more effectively. He said to love 'em like you love yourself. In other words:

Are you as interested in them as you are in the menu at Wendy's when you're starved?

Do you give them the attention you give your nose upon discovering a zit the day before a big date?

Do you feel the same glow for them as you feel when the cop gives you a warning instead of a ticket?

Do you share with them the joy you reserve for a night out with friends?

Do you have the same compassion for their pain as you do for yourself when your finger is slammed in the car door?

Are you as enthusiastic about them as you are about getting paid?

Do you fuss over them as much as you fuss over your hair before heading for the mall?

Do you feel the same pride in their achievements as you do when you receive a good grade in a tough class?

Do you guard their secrets as jealously as you do your measurements?

Do you have the same level of honesty with them as you do when you look square into the bathroom mirror?

Do you pray for them as much as you pray when you're in BIG trouble?

When it comes right down to it, we're all pretty lousy at loving others. Perhaps that's mostly due to the fact that we love ourselves so much. God doesn't want you to love yourself any less. He just wants you to love others to the same degree.

See also: Romans 13:9; 1 Corinthians 13; 1 John 4:7–21

▪▪ THE TRUTH ABOUT PHONIES

The heart is deceitful above all things.

JEREMIAH 17:9

In rummaging through the garage recently, I found a box filled with old school newspapers. One of them contained my picture, coupled with a brief interview. What struck me most was my response when asked about my greatest dislike. My answer was brief and to the point: "I can't stand phonies."

How profoundly original. I might just as well have said I couldn't stand warm Coke or dents in my car door. *Everybody* dislikes fakes. Though there's fraud and deceit in all of us, it's just a lot easier to spot in other people. But who's fooling whom?

You misjudge a fly ball and it drops safely at your side. For the next half hour you cover yourself by telling everybody you lost it in the sun.

You're in a grocery store and somebody waves. You wave back and smile ... until you realize you've never seen the person before in your life. At that point you just pretend to be scratching your head.

Ten minutes after you arrive home from an evening out, your mother stops by your bedroom to ask how things went. You don't feel like rehashing the night, so you pretend you've fallen asleep.

A friend who's been sick asks you how church was on Sunday. You say it was OK—even though you slept in and watched a football game instead.

These are all little wrongs that don't really hurt anybody. That's probably what Ananias and Sapphira thought when they sold some of their property for the church. They reported a smaller selling price and kept some of the money for themselves. Nobody else really knew the difference. But God knew their hypocrisy and struck them dead on the spot.

In others we call such double-dealing hypocrisy. We call them fakes. In ourselves, well ... it pretty much goes overlooked. We seldom face up to the fact that, apart from God, we're all as phony as three-dollar bills.

See also: Psalm 119:29; Acts 5:1–11; James 1:26

■■ THIEF IN THE NIGHT

> *Now, brothers, about times and dates we do not need to write to you, for you know very well that the day of the Lord will come like a thief in the night. While people are saying, "Peace and safety," destruction will come on them suddenly, as labor pains on a pregnant woman, and they will not escape. But you, brothers, are not in darkness so that this day should surprise you like a thief.*
>
> 1 THESSALONIANS 5:1–4

A lot of our neighbors are spooked these days. There's been a rash of break-ins and burglaries, and everybody's skittish because the thief hasn't been caught. He moves quickly and is out before you know he's in. But when you look around the next morning, your VCR, stereo, and most of your valuables are gone.

I don't like surprises, so we keep a dog. I've never been a particular animal lover—in part because a cat I once had always delivered her litters in my desk drawer, and I got tired of wiping slime off my geometry textbook. But I put up with our dog because it barks at people who do suspicious things near our house at night.

In the Bible, Christ's second coming is described as something that will happen like a thief in the night. That's an odd word picture; it brings to mind missing stereos. But if something disappears, it won't be your CD player and speakers. Christ will only take his children. Christians will go to sleep on one side of eternity and wake up face-to-face with Jesus. It will be that quick—"in a flash, in the twinkling of an eye," the Bible says in 1 Corinthians 15:52.

In other words, it's not something you can prepare for at the last minute. And if you're not ready, don't think a guard dog will alert you.

See also: Matthew 24; 2 Peter 3:3–18

■■ TIME OF ARRIVAL

> *In my Father's house are many rooms; if it were not so, I would have told you. I am going there to prepare a place for you. And if I go and prepare a place for you, I will come back and take you to be with me that you also may be where I am.*

JOHN 14:2–3

You read yesterday of Christ's return to earth—an event that will occur as suddenly and unexpectedly as "a thief in the night." That day, known as the Second Coming, is something Christ promised during his last days on earth. He wanted people to know he wasn't ditching them. He would return to take them home. The promise bears his stamp of approval, so you can stake your life on it. In fact, if you *don't* stake your life on it, you are, quite literally, a damned fool.

Nearly two thousand years have passed since Christ talked about coming back and snatching us away to spend the rest of eternity together in heaven. He didn't say when that date would be; he just urged us to live in anticipation of it at all times.

When I first became a Christian, I thought the Second Coming would occur within the next couple of years. But I secretly hoped Christ would at least wait until after I got my driver's license. Then I fell in love, and began to hope he'd hold off until after the wedding night ... and then until after I had children ... and then until I had some money in the bank.

Now, however, I hope Christ returns sometime very soon. I still have a lot of goals and ambitions, dreams, and desires. Nothing has changed in that department. What has changed is my intense desire to meet Christ face-to-face. There's also another reason: I am tired.

I am tired of the struggle of the Christian life, of the daily battle with lust and pride and jealousy and nagging habits. I've grown weary of looking out for myself, making excuses when I hurt other people, and apologizing when I blurt unkind words. I am tired of Satan's whispers. Most of all, I'm tired of asking forgiveness from the one I love most.

That is why, when I wake in the morning, the first thought on my still-sleepy mind is, "Come soon, Lord Jesus." For all these years he's been preparing a place for us, and I imagine it's getting to be quite a mansion.

I know the homecoming date is near—and that any day now we'll hear the trumpets blow.

See also: Acts 1:10–11; 1 Thessalonians 4:13–18

■ A DEATH EXPERIENCE

> *Do not be deceived: God cannot be mocked. A man reaps what he sows. The one who sows to please his sinful nature, from that nature will reap destruction; the one who sows to please the Spirit, from the Spirit will reap eternal life.*

> GALATIANS 6:7–8

Buried in the shadows of Paul's closet is a large box brimming with cards and letters. Each contains some variable of "I love you" expressed a hundred different ways by his girlfriend Denise. Their love seemed Hallmark perfect . . . until she got pregnant and, against his wishes, had an abortion. And now, the letters have stopped coming.

"The abortion was like a death experience," Paul told me, "and I'm still trying to recover. I still think about what it would have been like to have a son—teaching him to ride a bike or play ball. Or I wonder about having a daughter—taking her to ballet lessons, buying her pretty dresses, kissing her good night.

"Most people probably think that when a guy finds out his girlfriend is pregnant, all he wants to do is pay a few hundred bucks for an abortion and never think about it again," Paul continued. "But some days I can think of nothing else. I wanted the child. I wanted to get married. I told Denise I'd do whatever it took to make a home for her and the baby.

"But the people at the clinic had an easier solution. They told her abortion was really no big deal—it was just like removing a 'little glob of tissue.' Maybe it's easier to kill something if you think of it like that," Paul said. "But that 'little glob of tissue' had a heartbeat. It was my child. And my child would have been three on October eleventh..."

It was difficult listening to Paul because I knew the roots of pain went clear to his bones. I also knew, as did Paul, that the baby never would have been conceived had Paul maintained his relationship with God. But he scrapped his beliefs when Denise entered the picture.

At any point God's forgiveness could be extended to him for the asking. "Though your sins are like scarlet, they shall be as white as snow," says Isaiah. Paul's sins (and Denise's, too) could be erased easily, as they can with any of us. But God's forgiveness doesn't always erase the consequences of sin. Paul's lonely, very painful thoughts about his child are proof of that.

See also: Psalm 139:13–16; Isaiah 1:18; Romans 6:11–13

:: POINTS TO PONDER – GUILT

> *Let us draw near to God with a sincere heart in full assurance of faith, having our hearts sprinkled to cleanse us from a guilty conscience and having our bodies washed with pure water.*

HEBREWS 10:22

Every man is guilty of all the good he didn't do.

VOLTAIRE

The one thing that doesn't abide by majority rule is a person's conscience.

HARPER LEE

Remorse: beholding heaven and feeling hell.

GEORGE MOORE

Humanity is never so beautiful as when praying for forgiveness, or else forgiving another.

JEAN PAUL RICHTER

It is about as hard to absolve yourself of your own guilt as it is to sit in your own lap. Wrongdoing sparks guilt sparks wrongdoing ad nauseam, and we all try to disguise the grim process from both ourselves and everybody else. In order to break the circuit we need somebody before whom we can put aside the disguise, trusting that when he sees us for what we fully are, he won't run away screaming with, if nothing worse, laughter.

FREDERICK BUECHNER

If his conditions are met, God is bound by his Word to forgive any man or any woman of any sin because of Christ.

BILLY GRAHAM

Conscience—the only incorruptible thing about us.

HENRY FIELDING

The only tyrant I accept in this world is the still voice within.

MAHATMA GANDHI

If we are sinners forgiven, we ought to behave as forgiven, welcomed home, crowned with wonderful love in Christ, and so cheer and encourage all about us, who often go heavily because we reflect our gloom upon them instead of our grateful love, hope, confidence.

FATHER CONGREVE

Remorse is the pain of sin.

THEODORE PARKER

There is no better feeling than to wake up on Sunday morning and be able to face yourself in the mirror. The ability to sleep soundly and then look yourself square in the eye after a Saturday night is life's truest reward.

S. RICKLY CHRISTIAN

See also: John 9:39–41; Romans 7:15–25; James 2:8–10

WEEK

33

■■ A REASON TO LIVE

As he went along, he saw a man blind from birth. His disciples asked him, "Rabbi, who sinned, this man or his parents, that he was born blind?"

"Neither this man nor his parents sinned," said Jesus, "but this happened so that the work of God might be displayed in his life."

JOHN 9:1–3

Harold's bed was surrounded by get-well wishes, but he was so weak from cancer treatments that he left the envelopes untouched. Finally, on a good day, he opened a letter from a young woman in New Jersey. "I am praying for you," she said. It was signed, Crystal Lavelle.

After exchanging several more letters, she wrote, "If you send me your picture, I'll send you mine." He complied, and then waited expectantly for her next envelope. He pictured her as having long blonde hair and blue eyes, but when her picture arrived he got the surprise of his life. Crystal was in a wheelchair, her body and legs twisted by cerebral palsy.

In an accompanying note, she explained that she'd been born with the disease. Eventually, Harold learned that her parents, who had become wealthy through business, had given her up at birth and she'd spent her life in institutions. But God replaced her bitterness toward them with love. He also gave her a reason to live: she wanted to see her parents meet her Savior.

Toward that goal, Crystal spends six hours every day at work—screwing nuts and bolts together. All year she saves her nickels and dimes for a plane ticket to visit her parents and tell them Jesus loves them. She also visits local high schools, telling young people how God transformed her life.

One night Crystal called Harold late at night. His cancer was in remission and he was feeling better. But Crystal said she wasn't doing well and asked him to pray for her. And so he did, right there on the phone, asking God to free her from the wheelchair. But she promptly cut him off.

"No, Harold," she said. "The wheelchair is my pulpit, my ministry. I am freer in this chair than most people who have complete use of their bodies. I don't have legs, but I've got Jesus. And he's all I need."

That night Harold witnessed genuine faith, which helped him cope with his own serious problems. In Crystal he saw a woman who had never climbed a tree, pedaled a bike, or experienced the love of her parents. But she knew the love of God clear to her bones.

She also knew God could heal her with a snap of his fingers. But she didn't want that for one reason: Were she to be healed, her pulpit would be empty.

See also: Hebrews 11; James 5:13–16

■■ SUBSTITUTE MOM

If anyone wants to be first, he must be the very last, and the servant of all.

MARK 9:35

As the saying goes, behind all great people there is a woman. Yesterday you read about Crystal, who radiates greatness if only because she believes in a great God. But is there a woman who stands behind Crystal? Yes. Her name is Mary Sue.

Most people would not look twice at Mary Sue. Her clothes are worn, she is elderly, she is black. On her tired hands and feet are calluses and bunions of Rocky Mountain proportions. They mark her lifetime of service.

One of fifteen children, Mary Sue mothered seven of her younger brothers and sisters when her own mother died. Then came a bad marriage, the birth of a handicapped son, nonstop work, and sleepless nights. She supports her family and extended family by doing what she does at home: caring for people. For more than twenty years, she has been the mother Crystal never had, and has loved her day by day as she grew from a child to an adult.

Mary Sue arrives at Crystal's institution about the same time as the first light of dawn, and spends most of her time in the kitchen making all the meals for Crystal and the other fifteen residents.

When Mary Sue isn't mixing and frying and scrubbing and sweeping, she sits in a corner beside Crystal, talking gently and stroking her hair. Her eyes fairly glow.

In the evening, she returns home to her grandchildren and severely handicapped son to draw baths and chase everybody off to bed while she tends house long into the night.

Mary Sue doesn't do what she does for a material reward; there is none. She is driven solely by love and a desire to serve. If there is a bonus, it is the chance to hear Crystal sing in her twisted but happy voice, "Jesuh, I 'ove 'ou. I 'ove 'ou with all my 'eart. Jesuh, I 'ove 'ou. I give 'ou my all!"

Mary Sue's love is the love of Christ, displayed in very ordinary, everyday ways. And though most people wouldn't notice her on the street, I know there is a special corner in heaven waiting for her ... and for those among us who would follow Christ by following her example.

See also: Mark 10:35–45; Philippians 2:3–8

∷ THE ARRANGEMENT

Children, obey your parents in the Lord, for this is
right. "Honor your father and mother"–which is the first
commandment with a promise– "that it may go well with
you and that you may enjoy long life on the earth."

EPHESIANS 6:1–3

Imagine the scenario. You've just returned home from school, and all you want to do is plop down on the bed, crank up the stereo, and think about your close encounter with Blue Eyes. But there's a car in the driveway, and you swallow hard. Forget the dreams–your parents are interviewing to find you a spouse.

For the past several months, they have scoured their social circles for potential match-ups. And now they've finally settled on Chris, who's not exactly *ugly* but is not in the same league as Blue Eyes. Not that anybody's asked your opinion, but ... the kid's got braces and Snow White legs! Not to mention that you don't even go to the same school and have only seen each other once before at that stupid Parent/Kid club your parents joined when they were hunting for a wife for your big brother.

Over the next eight years, you and Chris see each other only twice, and when you finally get married and move in together, you are virtual strangers. But you have no choice, so you force yourself to make the best of things.

This scenario may seem pretty absurd, although over half of all marriages in the world today are still arranged. But every day you have to deal with a situation that's not all that different. You've got to share living quarters with a group of people you did not personally select: your family.

Generally speaking, you didn't pick your parents; they didn't pick you. The same is true of any siblings you may have. And if you're like most families, the mix of personalities, individual needs, and daily demands can be both interesting and explosive.

Chances are, your parents don't understand some pretty basic things about you. Nevertheless, God asks that you honor and obey them—in essence, *love* them. Why? Perhaps because "getting along" is such a tremendous need in the world. Maybe if we'd all practice more at home, our own little corner of the world would improve. That's not an easy task. But with dogged effort—and a great deal of grace—it can be done.

See also: Proverbs 6:20–22; Colossians 3:20; 2 Timothy 3:1–2

■ BRIDGING THE GAP

> *Listen, my son, to your father's instruction and do not forsake your mother's teaching.*
>
> PROVERBS 1:8

Do you sometimes feel your parents are aliens? That your mother is from Mars and your father is from Pluto? That they don't understand a thing about you? But how much do *you* really know about *them*, other than that they're old and wear funny swimsuits?

In spite of all of your differences, ask God to help you better understand your parents. Toward that goal, sit your parents (one will do) down tonight, and get them to respond to the following mini-questionnaire. Their answers may surprise you and also may open up some new lines of communication.

1. Tell me one funny thing that happened to you growing up.
2. Tell me one thing you did wrong as a kid for which you never got caught. Honesty counts ten points.
3. What's your favorite ice cream flavor?
4. Describe a typical day for you when I'm at school—what do you actually do?
5. Tell me about when you met Mom (or Dad). How old were you when you got married? Why did you get married?
6. Who was the first person you ever kissed? Describe the scene, with all of the juicy details. Who initiated it?
7. Describe your two closest friends when you were my age.
8. Which do you like better, sunrise or sunset? Why?
9. What did you always want to be when you grew up?
10. Did you ever have a boss you didn't particularly like?
11. What really bugs you?
12. Tell me about something you've done that really makes you proud.
13. Which do you like better, Saturdays or Sundays? Why?
14. Which emotion is the hardest for you to express? Why?
15. If you knew you were going to die tomorrow, what would you want to say to me today?

If you want to really do this interview right, tape the conversation, or better yet, shoot it on video. Messing with all the equipment may be a hassle, and you can probably think of fifteen reasons *not* to do it. But do it anyway. And for once, forget that your parents are your parents. Think of them as real, live people who possibly, just maybe, might have something interesting to say.

Oh, and hang on to the tape. Tuck it away someplace safe. Ten years from now it will be worth its weight in gold.

See also: Ecclesiastes 7:25; Luke 2:41–52

■■ TIME TRAVELS

> *Show me, O Lord, my life's end and the number of*
> *my days; let me know how fleeting is my life. You have*
> *made my days a mere handbreadth; the span of my years*
> *is as nothing before you. Each man's life is but a breath.*

PSALM 39:4–5

Mrs. Simone once loved life. But that was before her last slip in the tub when something clicked in her brain; before she started spending all day in bed, refusing to look out the window; before she began her time travels.

"Where's Daddy?" she demanded when I walked in the room. "He should be home by now."

"He's dead," I said as calmly as possible. "Remember?"

She didn't, of course. Daddy was her husband, who'd passed away ten years earlier. It was only in the past couple of months that she'd forgotten he was gone. We used to talk about him on Sundays when I'd visit her and other nursing home residents after church.

I was at the home once when her only son stopped by. He walked over to her side and kissed her on the cheek. She drew back, as if he had a horrible, infectious disease.

"Who are you?" she asked.

"Robert," he said quietly.

She shook her head. "Robert's this big," she said, holding her veiny hand about three feet from the floor.

"I'm Robert, Mom," he tried again, combing his fingers through his hair, which was gray at the sides. The pain of having a mother who did not recognize him showed on his face.

"Did I tell you what Libby Briggs said today at the parlor?" she asked this stranger-son standing beside her.

"Libby died fifteen years ago, Mom," he replied.

"Close the door, you're letting the flies in," she said abruptly.

I don't know what he was thinking as he stood there carrying on this sad and silly conversation. But I imagine his brain was racing—thinking back on all the good times they shared; the times when he actually *was* three feet high and needed his mother like he needed his next breath; the times when his mother was young and vivacious and caring; the times when getting out of the tub was as easy for her as brushing her teeth; the times before her time travels.

That all probably seemed like yesterday to him as he searched his mother's porcelain face for any sign of recognition. But there was none, not even a glimmer. Though her body was still alive, the woman he'd grown up calling Mom and who'd made all those special memories possible was gone. She'd disappeared, as if her life was but a breath of air, which is exactly what life is.

Unable to do anything else but love this poor shell of a mother that used to be, he leaned over and kissed her lightly. When he turned to leave, he had tears in his eyes.

See also: Job 14:2; Ecclesiastes 3:1-2; 12:1

▪▪ A PLACE CALLED HOME

Above all, love each other deeply, because love covers over a multitude of sins.

1 PETER 4:8

When I think of family, I think a lot about the home I grew up in. It was situated on a sleepy cul-de-sac in San Diego, just around the corner from a huge canyon where we caught lizards and built forts, and a short block from the elementary school where I learned the true meaning of the words *vice principal.* On a map it was located at 8891 Armorss Avenue.

Of course, home was more than an address or the material used to build it. Home was *family*, without which it would have been just another house. And oh, what a family we were!

We were a pretty diverse bunch, consisting of a Mr. Goodwrench father, who could fix just about anything but broken dreams; a Betty Crocker mother who made sense of stock market tables as easily as she made good meals; a goody-goody sister who befriended teachers as easily as boys; and a daredevil brother who wasn't happy unless he was breaking his bones.

We all generally got along, except when we didn't. That is, we had our share of differences which sometimes erupted into top-of-the-lungs fights. One or the other of us may have even threatened on occasion to pull the other's tongue out. But we all survived, even prospered, because the words "I love you" were expressed daily in our home and because it was always very clear that my dad loved my mother, my mother loved my dad, and together they loved each of us kids. That love enabled us to overlook our differences and thrive as a family—through sickness and health, births and deaths, successes and failures.

In recent years, we've all gone our separate ways, and the old home was finally sold. But each of us remains linked to the others by our common heritage and bond of love, together with all of the memories and good times and joys we shared at that place called home.

As John Henry Jowett points out, "The Bible does not say very much about homes; it says a great deal about the things that make them. It speaks about life and love and joy and peace and rest. If we get a house and put these into it, we shall have secured a home."

And that's what I had: a home *secured* by all that God intended. It was, truly, a foretaste of heaven, an interpretation of what will one day be our Home of homes.

See also: Proverbs 3:33; 10:12; Ephesians 6:1–3

▪▪ POINTS TO PONDER – FAMILY AND HOME

> *Honor your father and your mother, so that you may live long in the land the Lord your God is giving you.*
>
> EXODUS 20:12

All happy families resemble one another; every unhappy family is unhappy in its own way.

LEO TOLSTOY

Children aren't happy with nothing to ignore, And that's what parents were created for.

OGDEN NASH

My parents taught me how to put one foot before the other, how to balance on a bike, and how to work the gear shift of an automobile. But when they gave me my first Bible, I discovered I had wings.

S. RICKLY CHRISTIAN

The most important thing a father can do for his children is to love their mother.

THEODORE M. HESBURGH

Home is where the heart is.

PLINY THE ELDER

The words that a father speaks to his children in the privacy of home are not heard by the world, but, as in whispering-galleries, they are clearly heard at the end of posterity.

JEAN PAUL RICHTER

A family is a unit composed not only of children but of men, women, an occasional animal, and the common cold.

OGDEN NASH

A happy family is but an earlier heaven.

JOHN BOWRING

Home interprets heaven. Home is heaven for beginners.

CHARLES H. PARKHURST

Everybody believes divorce breaks up families. This is not so. The broken family is not the result of divorce; divorce is the result of the broken family.

PAUL W. ALEXANDER

Heaven will be the perfection we have always longed for. All the things that made earth unlovely and tragic will be absent in heaven. There will be no night, no death, no disease, no sorrow, no tears, no ignorance, no disappointment, no war. It will be filled with health, vigor, virility, knowledge, happiness, worship, love, and perfection.

BILLY GRAHAM

Every father expects his boy to do the things he wouldn't do when he was young.

KIM HUBBARD

The first half of our lives is ruined by our parents and the second half by our children.

CLARENCE DARROW

It is dangerous to confuse children with angels.

DAVID FYFE

Domestic happiness depends upon the ability to overlook.

ROY L. SMITH

See also: Proverbs 1:7–8; Acts 16:31–34

WEEK

34

▪▪ QUIET ME, LORD

The Lord your God is with you, he is mighty to save. He will take great delight in you, he will quiet you with his love.

ZEPHANIAH 3:17

Quiet me, Lord,
From the crash-boom-bam noise of life
That overpowers my ears like the slamming of locker doors,
The blare of stereos,
The honk of traffic,
The scream of revenge.

Slow me, Lord,
From the hit-and-run pace of life
That overwhelms my peace like the breathlessness of time,
The blur of yesterday,
The rush of today,
The press of tomorrow.

Relax me, Lord,
From the knot-in-the-gut tension of life,
That stews my insides like the strain of broken friendship,
The grind of ambition,
The ulcer of bad habits,
The gnaw of hormones.

Shelter me, Lord,
From the haymaker-to-the-head blows of life
That assault my strength like the slap of old memories,
The sting of sharp words,
The clash of competing motives,
The dig of gossip.

Quiet me with your love, Lord,
Slow me with your patience,
Relax me with your peace,
Shelter me with your Spirit.

But most of all, Lord,
Overwhelm
me
with
you.

See also: Psalm 46:10; John 14:27; Galatians 5:22

:: RESOLUTIONS

> *Strengthen your feeble arms and weak knees. "Make level paths for your feet," so that the lame may not be disabled, but rather healed. Make every effort to live in peace with all men and to be holy; without holiness no one will see the Lord. See to it that no one misses the grace of God and that no bitter root grows up to cause trouble and defile many. See that no one is sexually immoral, or is godless.*
>
> HEBREWS 12:12–16

At the start of every year I retreat from the rush of everyday concerns and think about what might have been and what might yet be. Sometimes I even write out resolutions.

Consider adopting the following list. It works just as well in the middle of the year as on January 1. If you faithfully adhere to it week after week, you will end up with the year of your life.

1. I will gain no more than 2.3 percent of my body weight in pimples, unless I give up Big Macs and fries, which is obviously something I won't do ... even if I could.
2. Once and for all, no matter what, by the grace of God, I will kick the _____ habit. (Fill in the blank, unless your parents snoop.)
3. I won't write run-on sentences they are hard to read.
4. I will surprise my parents and thank each of them for something, *anything*, once a week for at least five weeks, even if they snoop and deserve hard labor in upper Siberia.
5. I will never admit that I swish Jell-O between my teeth, unless in confidence to fellow swishers.

6. I will make every effort to smile at somebody I'd rather not smile at—for at least the next seven times I see them.

7. I will volunteer for no more than two extracurricular assignments per week that I have no intention of doing.

8. I will remind myself overandoverandover again that God loves me—even if I still haven't kicked the _____ habit, which I'll do, doggone it, if it's the *last* thing I do.

9. I will not spend money frivolously, except for cherry Jell-O.

10. I will read the Bible verse at the beginning of each day's reading in this book (Does the one above sound like a New Year's list of sorts?) and also look up and read the verses at the end of every day.

See also: Romans 6:4–7; 2 Corinthians 5:17

■■ MORE RESOLUTIONS

> *You were taught, with regard to your former way of life, to put off your old self, which is being corrupted by its deceitful desires; to be made new in the attitude of your minds; and to put on the new self, created to be like God in true righteousness and holiness.*

EPHESIANS 4:22–24

Yesterday I mentioned that I start out most new years with the idea of doing things differently. No matter if things are going poorly; every January offers a fresh start. If things are going well, I expect them to get even better. But why wait for January? As the saying goes, today is the first day of the rest of your life.

Review yesterday's list of resolutions, then incorporate the following additions. Tomorrow you can personalize the list by writing some of your own.

1. I will not eat anything fried or containing white flour before 2 P.M., unless I'm absolutely sure I can take a one-hour nap in the library before the end of the school day.

2. I will try for a personal record and see how long I can go without consciously sinning. When I fail, I will immediately 'fess up to God, who honestly cares about these things.

3. I will never again use Lysol as a substitute deodorant.
4. Did I say I'll do everything I can to kick the habit?
5. Even when my teeth feel like a sweater, I will never ever floss in the company or sight of any living creature.
6. I will be more kind, especially to nerds and geeks and gorps and other alien creatures.
7. I won't use no double negatives, or, commas, which aren't necessary.
8. I will eat fewer beans and more frozen yogurt.
9. I will keep my distance from the television, unless it happens to be on. But under no circumstances will I watch anything dealing with dwarf throwing or the mating habits of South American sea slugs.
10. Today, at this very moment, I will claim the power that is mine as a believer. I will actually start living like a Christian and quit just sounding like one.

See also: Isaiah 1:18; Romans 8:18–23

■■ A PERSONAL LIST

> ***What is impossible with men is possible with God.***
> LUKE 18:27

For the past couple of days we've been looking at implementing changes in our lives. Thankfully, for a Christian, every day can bring a fresh start. As A. W. Criswell said, "Christianity is the land of beginning again."

Now it's your turn to personalize the list. (Ten points for honesty!) When you're done, refer to these combined lists often. And remember, the hardest things to change are the very things God is most eager to help you with. As the verse above indicates, his business is turning your impossibilities into possibilities.

1. I've been putting it off for months (years, if the truth were known), but the time is finally right to try to

_____ .

2. When it comes to my relationships with the opposite sex, I will, with God's help, do my best to _____ .

3. I'm going to quit battling with myself and finally turn

    _____ over to the Lord, knowing
    that *nobody* cares as much about the situation as he does.
4. With regard to my family, I will honestly try to

    _____ .
5. The one area of my personality I'd like to work on in the next

    few weeks is _____ .
6. I always seem to open my big mouth at the wrong time and
    embarrass myself. Lord, help me to zip my lip, especially when

    _____ .
7. I will spend at least _____ minutes alone daily, reading
    God's Word and honestly talking to him about my concerns.
8. My life would be a whole lot easier if I could just quit

    _____ , which I can do, because "What
    is impossible with men is possible with God."
9. I'm not asking for body alterations, but I can improve my

    looks in little ways by _____ .
10. Yeoowww! Cowabunga! To get truly excited about my life I will

    start _____ *today.* Awoooo!

See also: Matthew 19:26; Romans 12:9–21; Hebrews 12:1

■■ I KNOW THE FEELING

All have sinned and fall short of the glory of God.
ROMANS 3:23

    Turgenev. Maybe you've heard of him, maybe not. He didn't
figure skate or play hockey or sing in a gypsy band. He was a famous
Russian novelist. And like most Russians, his first name was Ivan.
    Based on something he wrote way back when, I feel a sort
of kinship with him. You see, he penned two sentences that I've not
been able to get out of my mind: "I don't know what the heart of a

bad man is like. But I know what the heart of a good man is like, and it's terrible."

What he was getting at is the same thought the apostle Paul had in mind in the verse above from Romans: failure. It's as if God set a big target on a tree, and we all shoot wide. Not only do we not hit the bull's-eye, we often miss the entire target. Our arrows end up in the dirt, the branches, the bushes—everywhere but where we aim. Simply put, we fail. Not every minute of every day, but often enough to understand failure better than anything else we do.

Failure is the feeling of saying something you regret, of compromising your virtue, of giving in to the same old sin. Failure is the feeling of being overrun by lurid thoughts. It's the feeling of brushing God aside—again.

I know the feeling. So did Turgenev. So did the apostle Paul, as you can tell from his very personal remarks in Romans 7:15–25 (*The Message*):

"What I don't understand about myself is that I decide one way, but then I act another, doing things I absolutely despise. So if I can't be trusted to figure out what is best for myself and then do it, it becomes obvious that God's command is necessary.

"But I need something *more*! For if I know the law but still can't keep it, and if the power of sin within me keeps sabotaging my best intentions, I obviously need help! I realize that I don't have what it takes. I can will it, but I can't *do* it. I decide to do good, but I don't *really* do it; I decide not to do bad, but then I do it anyway. My decisions, such as they are, don't result in actions. Something has gone wrong deep within me and gets the better of me every time.

"It happens so regularly that it's predictable. The moment I decide to do good, sin is there to trip me up. I truly delight in God's commands, but it's pretty obvious that not all of me joins in that delight. Parts of me covertly rebel, and just when I least expect it, they take charge.

"I've tried everything and nothing helps. I'm at the end of my rope. Is there no one who can do anything for me? Isn't that the real question?"

Good question. The poor guy, he sounds just like me. But his answer was even better: "The answer, thank God, is that Jesus Christ can and does. He acted to set things right in this life of contradictions where I want to serve God with all my heart and mind, but am pulled by the influence of sin to do something totally different."

Things haven't changed much in these two thousand years. On our own, we're trapped. Only Jesus Christ can free us from sin's prison. He stands with his hands outstretched, ready to help us off of failure's merry-go-round. Ready to help us start over, to rebuild, to begin again. All we have to do is ask.

See also: Hebrews 4:14–16; Revelation 21:1–4

:: HEROIC FAILURES

Whatever your hand finds to do, do it with all your might.

ECCLESIASTES 9:10

If you've ever felt you're continually crashing against closed doors and that your dreams are routinely dismissed, don't give up. The following examples, courtesy of Norman Chalfin of the Jet Propulsion Laboratory's Office of Patent Control, indicate that you're in distinguished company:

- When Samuel F. B. Morse asked Congress for a grant to build a telegraph line between Washington, D. C., and Baltimore, he was greeted with derision and suggestions that instead he build "a railroad to the moon."
- Asked by Parliament whether the telephone would be of any use in Britain, the chief engineer of the British Post Office answered, "No, sir. The Americans have need of the telephone, but we do not. We have plenty of messenger boys."
- H. G. Wells, the visionary British writer, did not think it likely that aeronautics would ever be important in transportation. "Man is not an albatross," he said.

- In 1903, a year before the Wright brothers flew at Kitty Hawk, Prof. Simon Newcomb, a distinguished astronomer, said that flying without a gas bag was impossible, or at least would require the discovery of a new law of nature.
- A week before the Wright brothers' flight, the *New York Times* editorialized on the rival efforts of Samuel Pierpont Langley, who had just achieved flight by an unmanned heavier-than-air craft: "We hope that Prof. Langley will not put his substantial greatness as a scientist in further peril by continuing to waste his time and the money involved in further airship experiments. Life is short and he is capable of services to humanity incomparably greater than trying to fly."

Within three years, the Wrights had an airplane that could fly forty miles an hour for one hundred miles. They offered it to the British navy. The Admiralty declined, explaining that the aeroplane would be of no practical use in the naval service.

If it's mediocrity you're after, it can be had easily. But if you are to attain excellence, no matter what the field, you must work with all of your might. You can't be allergic to sweat. You must also, on occasion at least, thumb your nose at the skeptics around you. They've been wrong before and they'll be wrong again.

See also: Ecclesiastes 11:6; Colossians 3:23

■■ POINTS TO PONDER – FAILURE

> *Because of the Lord's great love we are not consumed, for his compassions never fail. They are new every morning; great is your faithfulness.*

LAMENTATIONS 3:22–23

When I was young I observed that nine out of every ten things I did were failures, so I did ten times more work.

GEORGE BERNARD SHAW

Show me a thoroughly satisfied man and I will show you a failure.

THOMAS EDISON

Failures are divided into two classes—those who thought and never did, and those who did and never thought.

JOHN CHARLES SALAK

There is no failure so great that a Christian cannot rise from it.

HELEN C. WHITE

It is not a disgrace to fail. Failing is one of the greatest arts in the world.

CHARLES KETTERING

The only time you don't fail is the last time you try anything—and it works.

WILLIAM STRONG

I never knew any man in my life who could not bear another's misfortunes perfectly like a Christian.

ALEXANDER POPE

A failure is a man who has blundered but is not able to cash in the experience.

ELBERT HUBBARD

Not failure, but low aim, is crime.

JAMES RUSSELL LOWELL

A man can fail many times, but he isn't a failure until he begins to blame somebody else.

JOHN BURROUGHS

Ninety-nine percent of the failures come from people who have the habit of making excuses.

GEORGE WASHINGTON CARVER

I cannot give you the formula for success, but I can give you the formula for failure: Try to please everybody.

HERBERT BAYARD SWOPE

A law of nature rules that energy cannot be destroyed. You change its form from coal to steam, from steam to power in the turbine, but you do not destroy energy. In the same way, another law governs human activity and rules that honest effort cannot be lost, but that some day the proper benefits will be forthcoming.

PAUL SPEICHER

A man should never be ashamed to own he has been in the wrong, which is but saying, in other words, that he is wiser today than he was yesterday.

JONATHAN SWIFT

Fail forward.

S. RICKLY CHRISTIAN

See also: Proverbs 15:22; 2 Corinthians 6:3–10; 12:9–10; 13:5–7

WEEK

35

▪ GETTING EVEN

Do not take revenge, my friends, but leave room for God's wrath, for it is written: "It is mine to avenge; I will repay," says the Lord. On the contrary: "If your enemy is hungry, feed him; if he is thirsty, give him something to drink. In doing this, you will heap burning coals on his head."

ROMANS 12:19–20

To be quite blunt, I struggle with being warm and loving toward those who have done me wrong. Take for instance the four-wheeling jerk who splashed mud all over my car at the corner of Allegheny and Delmonico in April 1994 when I simply honked at him for parking at a green light. *You know who you are, even after all this time, and if you're that jerk, I hope your radiator blows up!*

See? I'm not quite there yet.

Confession time: I also gloat sometimes when misfortune visits somebody who "deserves it." I once had a boss with major-league arrogance who was a direct descendant of Hitler. His chief ambition was to make me miserable, and in that regard, he was very good at his job. The thing is, he mistreated everybody. And when a whole group of us "crybabies" complained to *his* boss, Hitler Jr. was quietly transferred to an obscure area of the company.

The day I heard the news, I whooped it up like New Year's. A few months later I spotted him across a room. His arm was in a cast. I didn't know how he busted it, nor did I care. All I could think of was that it couldn't have happened to a more deserving guy.

OK, I am aware of the huge disparity between my reaction when wronged and that of Jesus, whose sole response to those who shamed him, flogged him, beat him, and crucified him was: "Father, forgive them, for they do not know what they are doing." He could have wasted the bunch of them. Instead, he died for them, with a prayer for them on his lips.

I don't come close to his standard. I gloat. I bear grudges. I seek revenge. I hate. And that's why he died for me, as well.

See also: Leviticus 19:18; 1 Peter 2:23

■ TOUGH BREAK, CHUMP

You should not look down on your brother in the day of his misfortune.

OBADIAH 12

Yesterday I gave you a glimpse into my sometimes dirty, withered soul. However, I wasn't completely honest. I didn't go far enough in the tour of my parched heart of hearts.

To continue, sometimes those I've begrudged may not have actually done me wrong. They may have, say, won a scholarship that I thought I really deserved, or slammed a lucky home run when everybody *knows* the guy couldn't hit the side of a barn if he were standing right in front of it. For that matter, maybe they just have a nicer car or get better grades.

Related to all of the above is the pleasure I derive when somebody's misfortune benefits me. This happened once when the father of a kid who was getting too friendly with *my* girlfriend got transferred two thousand miles away. My reaction? Tough break, chump.

There's also the quiet rush I feel when those who live in ivory towers get a taste of real life. For example, I had no trouble sleeping when that goofy televangelist with the big hair got jailed, or on hearing the homecoming queen blimped out after graduation and gained fifty pounds, all in her thighs.

I don't want you to get the wrong idea. I'm actually a terrific guy, whom my mother would describe as warm and sensitive. But deep down I know I fall light years short of the glory of God; so do we all. I am well aware, even if others aren't, that I don't often represent humanity at its best.

My lapses give me a clear picture of my desperate, daily need for a Savior. They also provide an inkling of how certain individuals may feel toward me the next time I fall flat on my face.

See also: Exodus 23:4–5; Matthew 5:44–47; 7:1–5

■■ TRUE LOVE

This is how we know what love is: Jesus Christ laid down his life for us.

1 JOHN 3:16

Boy meets girl, they fall in love. It's the oldest plot around, but it still sells movies, records, and books, along with cosmetics, cars, health club memberships, and most everything else you can imagine except Preparation-H.

However, with all the talk about love in our culture, it's amazingly difficult to define. You can *love* the smell of Opium perfume. You can *love* your main squeeze. You can *love* Julia Roberts' hair. And then, you can *love* God.

You may be unable to easily define love, but chances are you know it when you *feel* it. That's why I found it so difficult as a young Christian to get really excited about God. I expected to *feel* more. When I invited Christ into my heart, I was actually a little disappointed. The way some people talked about their conversion experiences, I expected a major rush. But when the Big Moment arrived, I experienced no celestial surges, no Fourth-of-July fireworks in my toes. I couldn't even raise a goose bump.

Did the absence of stand-up-and-holler emotion mean I wasn't a Christian? It crossed my mind. But over time, I began to understand that my love for God—that is, deeply-rooted, unconditional love—was nothing like the love that's portrayed by Madison Avenue. It was and is a love based not on feelings but on historical *fact*: that Christ died for my sins, that he was buried, and that three days later he was resurrected. Therein lie the roots of true love.

There are days I don't *feel* very Christian; my prayers just seem to bounce off the ceiling. At such times, God feels distant. But the *fact* remains: Because of the cross I can know true love that will last through all eternity. Without the cross, I would get exactly what I deserve: a non-refundable one-way ticket straight to hell.

See also: 1 Corinthians 13; 15:3–5; 1 John 4:19

■■ LOOSE LIPS

Whoever would love life and see good days must keep his tongue from evil and his lips from deceitful speech.

1 PETER 3:10

It didn't seem like such a big deal at first. A young woman casually mentioned that she'd heard somebody had been bitten by a snake when trying on a K-mart coat imported from the Far East. As preposterous as the tale was, it spread crazily throughout the entire Detroit area—and beyond.

Similar nightmarish rumors have circulated often in recent years. False worms-in-the-burgers stories were first directed at Wendy's in Chattanooga, but then latched onto McDonald's as the rumors spread and mutated across the country. Other recent bogus scares included charges that fried chicken companies used batter that caused sterility and served fried rats; that Proctor & Gamble's moon-and-stars logo betrayed a link to devil worship, that Corona Extra was contaminated with urine; that the Moonies controlled Entenmann's Bakery; that major oil companies were dumping gas in the Nevada desert to create a shortage and thereby hike pump prices; and that a Brazilian worker fell into a vat of Coca-Cola and was never retrieved.

Unfortunately, these rumors did not quietly go away. The above-mentioned companies were forced to spend millions of dollars to regain their reputations. But what happens if you're not a corporation? What happens if the rumors are just as preposterous, but are directed toward you, a flesh-and-blood human being? As Joseph Hall said, "A reputation once broken may possibly be repaired, but the world will always keep their eyes on the spot where the crack was."

And so it was with Cindy. One weekend she went to the mall with her cousin Bob, who was several years older. Somebody saw them, and on Monday her friends were oohhing and ahhhing about the hunk they'd heard she was with. A couple of days later people were talking about her new *college boyfriend*. Before long Cindy and her mystery friend were said to be intimate and, well, the stories deteriorated from there. Though she explained over and over what the true story was, every denial was met with smiles and winks.

In the months that followed, Cindy was a wreck. It's fair to say I saw her die emotionally before my eyes. I felt like the witness of a homicide. The murder weapon was a tongue.

See also: Psalm 140:1–3; James 3:5–6

▪▪ FIRST IMPORTANCE

> *For what I received I passed on to you as of first importance; that Christ died for our sins according to the Scriptures, that he was buried, that he was raised on the third day according to the Scriptures, and that he appeared to Peter, and then to the Twelve.*

1 CORINTHIANS 15:3–5

The Bible is the product of various writers conveying important truths about God, man, life, and the afterlife over several thousand years. Each of the writers had a different message to convey.

Moses brought us the Ten Commandments—an official rule book of morality. King David delivered the Psalms—an intimate songbook that mirrors God's personal relationship with man. King Solomon wrote Ecclesiastes—a despairing look at the meaninglessness of life apart from God. Matthew, Mark, Luke, and John penned the gospels—dramatic narrations of Jesus' life on earth. The apostle Paul gave us much of the New Testament—summaries of the Christian faith for the new church.

In view of the sheer bulk of the Bible, have you ever asked yourself what it all comes down to? What is God really trying to communicate anyway? Can his agenda be condensed to a single verse? Genesis 1:1, maybe? Or perhaps Romans 3:23? The final showdown between God and Satan? What is *most* important?

That was something Paul wrestled with in his letter to the young church at Corinth. What do you tell a group of believers who are struggling to make sense of God amidst all the immorality and materialism around them? Paul's response: "For what I received I passed on to you as of first importance; that Christ died for our sins ..."

There you have it: *first importance.* In all God's dealings with man, from Genesis onward, nothing matters more than the cross. Why? Because the very Son of the very Creator of the universe hung there. Nowhere else did God so vividly display his love. Nowhere else did he put it all on the line.

The cross. It was where love mastered evil, where time intersected eternity, where God bridged heaven and earth. The cross. The closer we live to it, the more we truly live.

See also: John 3:16; 1 Corinthians 1:18; 2:2

■■ GOD! LET ME PRAISE YOU

Through Jesus, therefore, let us continually offer to God a sacrifice of praise—the fruit of lips that confess his name. And do not forget to do good and to share with others, for with such sacrifices God is pleased.

HEBREWS 13:15–16

God! Let me praise you
By taking an active role in my corner of your creation,
And filling the area in which I live with
Your light, warmth, love, and happiness.
God! Let me praise you
By brightening the lives of those around me,
And encouraging them with such words as
"I love you," "Thanks," and "I forgive you."
God! Let me praise you
By sharing with others everything you've given me,
And being the first in a group to offer
A smile, hug, condolence, and helping hand.
God! Let me praise you
By fighting back gloom when it surrounds me,
And not being contagious whenever I'm feeling
Discouraged, upset, lonely, and disappointed.
God! Let me praise you
By turning to you at every moment of every day,

And acknowledging your love for me with
My words, actions, thoughts, and prayers.

See also: 2 Corinthians 1:3–4; Ephesians 1:3–14; James 3:9–12

:: POINTS TO PONDER – PRAISE

> *Enter his gates with thanksgiving and his courts with praise; give thanks to him and praise his name. For the Lord is good and his love endures forever; his faithfulness continues through all generations.*
>
> Psalm 100:4–5

What else can I do, a lame old man, but sing hymns to God? If I were a nightingale, I would do the nightingale's part; if I were a swan, I would do as a swan. But now I am a rational creature, and I ought to praise God: this is my work; I do it, nor will I desert my post, so long as I am allowed to keep it. And I exhort you to join me in this same song.

Epictetus

It is a sure sign of mediocrity to be niggardly with praise.

Marquis de Vauvenargues

I can live for two months on a good compliment.

Mark Twain

Praise God, from whom all blessings flow; Praise Him, all creatures here below; Praise Him above, ye heavenly host; Praise Father, Son, and Holy Ghost.

Thomas Ken

One thing scientists have discovered is that often-praised children become more intelligent than often-blamed ones. There's a creative element in praise.

Thomas Dreier

The trouble with most of us is that we would rather be ruined by praise than saved by criticism.

Norman Vincent Peale

Praise makes good men better and bad men worse.

THOMAS FULLER

If you have never heard the mountains singing, or seen the trees of the field clapping their hands, do not think because of that they don't. Ask God to open your ears so you may hear it, and your eyes so you may see it, because, though few men ever know it, they do, my friend, they do.

MCCANDLISH PHILLIPS

After silence, that which comes nearest to expressing the inexpressible is music.

ALDOUS HUXLEY

Praise is warming and desirable. But it is an earned thing. It has to be deserved, like a hug from a child.

PHYLLIS MCGINLEY

The continual offering of praise requires stamina; we ought to praise God even when we do not feel like it. Praising him takes away the blues and restores us to normal.

HAROLD LINDSELL

Don't pat yourself on the back and boast and crow like a bloated rooster. People think you're a puffed up gas bag if you blow your own horn. Save your breath and your reputation. If praise is to be given, let it come from other people. Let them exalt and honor and say nice things about you if they're so inclined. Let them pour on the commendations and dish out the praise. It's amazing how far applause is heard if it's not the sound of a single hand clapping.

S. RICKLY CHRISTIAN

Praise is like a plow set to go deep into the soil of believers' hearts. It lets the glory of God into the details of daily living.

C. M. HANSON

We should be thankful for our tears; they prepare our eyes for a clearer vision of God.

WILLIAM A. WARD

There are three kinds of giving: grudge giving, duty giving, and thanksgiving.

ROBERT N. RODENMAYER

See also: Proverbs 27:2; John 12:43; Philippians 1:3; James 3:7–12

WEEK

36

■ THE BIRTHDAY REQUEST

What good will it be for a man if he gains the whole world, yet forfeits his soul?

MATTHEW 16:26

It was a lavish birthday party fit for a king, complete with ice swans, music, neon lights, and fountains spouting pink champagne. And just when the everybody-who-is-anybody crowd was wondering if life could get any better, Salome took the stage in her sequined leotard with the plunging neckline clear down to here, and danced till King Herod's skin tingled. When she was done, the birthday boy whooped it up and told her to name her price—up to and including half his kingdom.

Since Salome was already a member of the royal brat pack and had everything a future teen queen could want, she asked her mother to make a wish. When she relayed her mother's message to the king, Salome leaned clear over, and her words were barely audible over the sound of Herod's pulse.

"I want you to give me right now the head of John the Baptist on a platter," she cooed, as eager as her mother to be rid of the Baptist party pooper who constantly harped about loose living.

As intoxicated as he was by Salome's eighty-proof perfume, Herod turned stone-cold sober when he heard her request. He was "greatly distressed," the Bible says, because he "knew [John] to be a righteous and holy man." He *knew* it. But in the end, "because of his oaths and his dinner guests, he did not want to refuse her." And so, figuring he had everything to gain and little of consequence to lose, he summoned the goon squad.

This tragedy, recounted in great detail by both Matthew and Mark, is one of the clearest pictures of the ultimate consequence of compromise. Aside from the fact that John lost his head in the deal, Herod was basically right in the short term. He won the approval of his party guests, and maybe even had a little fun with Salome on the side. In effect, he gained the world.

In the long run, however, he lost big. He lost his soul.

See also: Mark 6:17–25; Galatians 6:7

■■ THE WHYS OF LIFE

*The secret things belong to the Lord our God, but
the things revealed belong to us and to our children forever,
that we may follow all the words of this law.*

DEUTERONOMY 29:29

Yesterday you read of the murder of John the Baptist, the man of whom Jesus once said, "Among those born of women there has not risen anyone greater" (Matthew 11:11).

I'm sure many people wondered why God allowed such a senseless tragedy to occur. After all, John wasn't just anybody. He was hand-picked by God to pave the way for Jesus' arrival. He was a good man, who didn't live high on the hog. He lived under the stars, ate bugs and honey, and wore a flea-bitten camel skin for clothing.

Questions regarding the whys of John's murder are met by silence in the Bible. There are no clues, no answers. What we do know is that Jesus didn't console his disciples by saying great good would come of John's death, or explain cheerily that they would someday understand God's purpose. He offered no platitudes like you hear these days. All the Bible says is that Jesus slipped away to mourn privately and pray.

Jesus, I believe, understood better than anyone else that sickness, pain, suffering, and death are realities of mortal life. He also understood clearly that nobody, himself included, was immune to it. If there was any big, ultimate purpose for John's life being snuffed out on a whim, I'm sure Jesus would have given a full, point-by-point explanation. But he didn't. He withdrew to be alone with God.

Because of the evil that exists in the world, we must all face and experience the hurts of life. But only for a little while longer. Soon now, very soon, there will be a new heaven and a new earth—without a trace of death or mourning or crying or pain. God will dwell among his people. Every tear will be wiped dry, and we will discover life as it was meant to be lived.

Until then, however, we must accept what we cannot change and content ourselves with knowing: "The secret things belong to the

Lord our God, but the things revealed belong to us and to our children forever, that we may follow all the words of this law."

In other words, God has provided us a big enough peek into the goings-on of his universe to occupy us until he returns. The secret things, including answers to the *whys* of life, must be left to God.

See also: Acts 1:7; Revelation 21:4

▪▪ THE UNTHINKABLE

> *I have chosen you and have not rejected you. So do not fear, for I am with you; do not be dismayed, for I am your God.*
>
> Isaiah 41:9–10

Debbi considered herself to be a good Christian. She didn't smoke, swear, or do drugs. And she drank only occasionally. For nearly three years she'd dated Rob, a wonderful Christian boy. Though they had numerous opportunities to make love, Debbie and Rob chose to maintain their virginity. They were proud about their determination to remain pure, though they sometimes joked about being added to the endangered species list.

Midway through her senior year, the unthinkable happened. Debbi spent the night at a friend's house, got really drunk, and had sex with her friend's older brother. Almost immediately she knew she was pregnant, and her Hallmark world fell apart.

What could she do? An abortion, which she considered to be murder, was out of the question. And she'd probably get killed herself if she talked to her parents. As for Rob, if he found out their relationship would be over. The only way out, she figured, was to trap Rob into having sex so he'd think the baby was his. A quiet marriage could then be arranged.

But deep down, Debbi knew the solution she was toying with would end in disaster. King David was lesson enough. When he'd tried to hush up his shenanigans with Bathsheba by having her husband killed, he didn't get rid of his problem. He merely compounded it. And it wasn't long before he was a miserable, broken man. Sure, Rob could be seduced. He'd probably even marry her. But what would happen later, when he discovered he'd been duped?

In the end, Debbi risked everything and did what she knew was right. She came clean. It was the hardest, bravest thing she ever did, but she felt the Lord assuring her with the words from Isaiah 41:9-10: "I have ... not rejected you. So do not fear, for I am with you; do not be dismayed, for I am your God."

Though Rob called it quits, her friends and family rallied to help her through the crisis. And when Debbi's baby girl arrived, a loving Christian couple adopted her with open arms. Seeing their tears of joy didn't exactly make it all worthwhile, but they did help Debbi know she'd made the right decision.

When I think of Debbi, old-fashioned words like *intestinal fortitude*, and *guts*, and *strength of character* come to mind. Yes, she'd made a big, stupid mistake. But I think our mistakes, in God's eyes, are less important than our response to them. Debbi didn't run; she stood firm. And the Lord stood beside her. Together, they made quite a pair!

See also: 2 Samuel 11-12; Isaiah 40:28-31; Romans 8:31

■■ LITTLE THINGS

> *Whatever is true, whatever is noble, whatever is right, whatever is pure, whatever is lovely, whatever is admirable—if anything is excellent or praiseworthy—think about such things.*
>
> PHILIPPIANS 4:8

In the Rodgers and Hammerstein musical "The Sound of Music," there's a catchy little song in which Maria, the lead character, sings of the wonder of raindrops on roses, whiskers on kittens, bright copper kettles, warm woolen mittens, and brown paper packages tied up with strings. "These," she sings, "are a few of my favorite things."

Though pumped full of NutraSweet, the song is a reminder to take pleasure in the little things. Unfortunately, we generally take such things for granted—all because we spend so much time worrying and grumbling and fretting and stewing and grousing and complaining about *equally* little things.

Chunks of entire days can be ruined because "*DAADDD!*" used your razor; somebody (*For the billionth time, Dorkface, I've gotta GO!*) is hogging the bathroom; somebody (*Mom, I TOLD you tonight was a big deal!*) forgot to pick up your blouse from the cleaners; somebody (*STUPID LADY DRIVERS!!*) is moving slow when you're in a stage-ten rush.

When we're not focusing on somebody else, we're often kicking ourselves unnecessarily for everything from missing an easy shot (*What a total jerk! I shoulda had it!*) to saying the wrong thing (*Try sounding intelligent for a change, Bimbo!*) to blowing an obvious exam question (*Such a DUMBO!*).

All too often we notice the minor problems, the glitches. We harbor petty grievances. Most of the annoyances are hardly worth complaining about, yet dwelling on them has a cumulative negative effect. That's why the apostle Paul encourages us to dwell instead on the positives — on things that are true, noble, right, pure, lovely, admirable, excellent, and praiseworthy.

Positive thinking sometimes sounds a little sappy. But once you get the hang of it, it's really not a bad way to spend the day.

See also: Romans 12:2; Colossians 3:2; 1 Peter 4:7–8

:: WHAT IFS

We know that in all things God works for the good of those who love him, who have been called according to his purpose.

ROMANS 8:28

On any given day when the sun is sitting just right and my feet are propped up and there isn't anything too terribly important going on, I drift off into never-never land and ponder "What if …" questions.

What if I'd not gone to college? What if I'd married some-body else? What if I'd accepted that job in Hollywood? What if I'd decided *not* to become a Christian?

"What if" questions concern what might have been — the path not taken. When faced with a fork in the road, you've got to decide which way to go. Right or left? And once you head one direction, the life that awaited you along the other quietly disappears. The big mystery is never knowing what the other fork would have brought. Had I gone another direction, would my life be totally different? Would I be rich and famous? Would I be happier?

And what about our mistakes—the forks we gleefully head down expecting Disneyland, only to find something resembling a bad dream? I've made what I mostly consider smart decisions. I've got my wife to show for one of them. But I've made a few of the other kind along the way. Nevertheless, God has used those bad decisions in a positive way in my life. In all things God has worked for the good—even in the negatives. In *all* things.

In the verse above, God promises to do that. But it's conditional. That is, the promise is yours *if* you love him and are called according to his purpose. Today, at this very moment, can you say you truly love the Lord? As you're reading now, can you say you are exactly where God wants you to be?

God can't make your decisions for you. They are yours alone to make; the consequences, yours alone to live with. But once you've made the decision, he'll be at your side every step of the way.

See also: Genesis 50:15–20; Romans 8:31–32; Ephesians 2:10

■ QUIET TIMES

The Spirit helps us in our weakness. We do not know what we ought to pray, but the Spirit himself intercedes for us with groans that words cannot express. And he who searches our hearts knows the mind of the Spirit, because the Spirit intercedes for the saints in accordance with God's will.

ROMANS 8:26–27

In my lonely keep-to-myself times,
Hear my sighs, Lord,
For I am tired of going unnoticed and unloved.
In my fearful I've-been-hurt-before times,
Hear my anxiety, Lord,
For I'm scared to stick my neck out again.

In my grieving words-can't-express-the-hurt times,
Hear my tears, Lord,
For I don't know if I can face tomorrow.
In my angry leave-me-alone times,
Hear my grinding teeth, Lord,
For I'm so blasted mad I could scream!
In my worried knot-in-the-gut times,
Hear my wrinkled brow, Lord,
For I'm burdened today by yesterday and tomorrow.
In my hectic hit-and-run times,
Hear my pounding feet, Lord,
For I'm running late instead of running to you.
In my searching I-don't-understand times,
Hear my shrugging shoulders, Lord,
For I struggle with the whys and hows of life.
In my troubled I've-done-it-now times,
Hear my beating heart, Lord,
For I feel the weight of having failed—again.
In my anxious I-need-action-now times,
Hear my tension, Lord,
For I get tired of smashing into closed doors.

See also: Joshua 1:5; Psalm 23

:: POINTS TO PONDER – WORRY

Who of you by worrying can add a single hour to his life? Since you cannot do this very little thing, why do you worry about the rest?

LUKE 12:25–26

We would worry less about what others think of us if we realized how seldom they do.

ETHEL BARRETT

If a care is too small to be turned into a prayer, it is too small to be made into a burden.

ANONYMOUS

There are two days in the week about which I never worry. Two carefree days, kept sacredly free from fear and apprehension. One of these days is yesterday—and the other is tomorrow.

ROBERT BURDETTE

The thinner the ice, the more anxious is everyone to see whether it will bear.

JOSH BILLINGS

It is distrust of God to be troubled about what is to come; impatience against God to be troubled with what is present; and anger at God to be troubled for what is past.

SIMON PATRICK

Never trouble trouble till trouble troubles you.

ANONYMOUS

You can't change the past, but you can ruin a perfectly good present by worrying about the future.

ANONYMOUS

The first thing, when one is being worried as to whether one will have to have an operation or whether one is a literary failure, is to assume absolutely mercilessly that the worst is true, and to ask What then? If it turns out in the end that the worst is not true, so much the better: but for the meantime the question must be resolutely put out of mind. Otherwise your thoughts merely go round and round a wearisome circle, now hopeful, now despondent, then hopeful again—that way madness lies. Having settled then that the worst is true, one can proceed to consider the situation.

C. S. LEWIS

Worry is rust upon the blade.

HENRY WARD BEECHER

Worry and trust cannot live in the same house. When worry is allowed to come in one door, trust walks out the other door; and worry stays until trust is invited in again, whereupon worry walks out.

ROBERT G. LETOURNEAU

Borrow trouble for yourself, if that's your nature, but don't lend it to your neighbors.

RUDYARD KIPLING

Anxiety does not empty tomorrow of its sorrows, but only empties today of its strength.

CHARLES H. SPURGEON

Ulcers are something you get from mountain-climbing over molehills.

ANONYMOUS

It ain't no use putting up your umbrella till it rains.

ALICE CALDWELL RICE

Anxiety is the natural result when our hopes are centered in anything short of God and his will for us.

BILLY GRAHAM

Don't tell me that worry doesn't do any good. I know better. The things I worry about don't happen.

ANONYMOUS

See also: Psalm 37:7–11; 46:1; Luke 10:38–42; Revelation 3:8

WEEK

37

▪▪ GRAYBAR HOTEL

> *Do not get drunk on wine, which leads to debauchery. Instead, be filled with the Spirit.*
>
> EPHESIANS 5:18

Jerry did not want to go to the Graybar Hotel, but that's where he ended up on his eighteenth birthday after being arrested for drunk driving. He tried to explain that he'd only had two beers, but the officer said drunk was drunk.

Jerry's stay at the Graybar Hotel began with a breath test, followed by the gathering of his possessions, including his billfold and watch. They also took his belt, just in case his thoughts turned suicidal. An arrest report was typed, he was given a booking number, and was then led to a holding tank with eight other people (including a male prostitute who kept winking at him). An officer pointed out the phone on the wall and told Jerry he could make one call. He swallowed hard, then called home. When his mother heard where he was, she wept.

After being fingerprinted and photographed, he was issued a mattress cover and cheap blanket, and then ushered to a dormitory cell with twenty-three other men, most of whom smelled like ripe gym clothes. Before the night was over, two cell mates propositioned him and another shoved him up against the wall and threatened to beat his brains out for having sat on his bed. Jerry didn't dare go to sleep.

Rest room facilities consisted of a bank of sinks and toilets on the wall, in full view of everybody, including passersby in the hall. Since Jerry was the newcomer, his bunk was nearest to the toilets.

As for food, breakfast was scrambled eggs and toast washed down with a cup of water. After eating, Jerry returned to his cell where he whiled away the hours on his bunk, keeping a wary eye on his cell mates.

Due to the banks being closed, Jerry's father was unable to raise bail, so Jerry's stay was extended to Monday. Consequently, he had plenty of time to think about how easily he could have avoided his stay at the Graybar. He could have said no when the six-pack was passed.

As bad as the Graybar Hotel was, Jerry could have had it worse. He might have been taken to another facility for drunks across town. It's known as the morgue.

See also: Romans 13:11–14; 1 Corinthians 6:19–20

▪▪ EXCUSES, EXCUSES

> *Mary took about a pint of pure nard, an expensive perfume; she poured it on Jesus' feet and wiped his feet with her hair. And the house was filled with the fragrance of the perfume. But one of his disciples, Judas Iscariot, who was later to betray him, objected, "Why wasn't this perfume sold and the money given to the poor? It was worth a year's wages." He did not say this because he cared about the poor but because he was a thief; as keeper of the money bag, he used to help himself to what was put into it.*
>
> JOHN 12:3–6

As one of the Twelve, Judas Iscariot was like a brother to Christ. For about three years they traveled the dusty roads side by side, shared the same food, and slept together beneath the stars. Despite his Judean roots (the others were from Galilee), Judas was treated like one of the boys. He was even entrusted with the group's money bag, which was a big mistake because he began skimming from the kitty.

I'm sure he excused his wrong as being no big deal. After all, he'd left a good job to follow Christ and wasn't compensated for what he was worth to begin with. Not to mention the long hours and extra responsibility—that had to be worth *something*. And as treasurer, wasn't it really within his job description to determine how the money was paid out? Call it stealing or embezzlement if you will; in his mind he was just getting what he was due.

The Bible is clear that the consequence of unconfessed sin is death. However, that doesn't happen overnight. Judas didn't suddenly palm a quarter from the cookie jar and then find himself in hell. It was a long gradual slope with a downward grade so slight that he probably didn't even notice it. But each time he excused or minimized his petty thievery, he took another step down that slippery path. For Judas, the path took a downward plunge when the money purloined from the cookie jar was no longer enough. Judas wanted more.

Judas eventually got what he wanted—a little side job with a tidy payoff. However, the side job happened to involve betraying the Son of God. Later, after he'd done his dirty work, he felt tremendous remorse. In fact, he got so worked up when he thought about the nice guy he used to be and the devil he'd become that he returned the money. And then he promptly went out and tied a noose around his neck.

He was sorry—all the way to hell.

See also: Matthew 26:14–16; 27:3–5; Romans 6:23

:: THE MONSTER

While [Christ] was still speaking, Judas, one of the Twelve, arrived. With him was a large crowd armed with swords and clubs, sent from the chief priests and the elders of the people. Now the betrayer had arranged a signal with them: "The one I kiss is the man; arrest him." Going at once to Jesus, Judas said, "Greetings, Rabbi!" and kissed him.

MATTHEW 26:47–49

I don't like to think too long about Judas because my mind always swells with disgust. What kind of man could share three solid years of both good and bad times—of holy, supernatural times—with Jesus, witness all of the miracles, hear all of the teaching . . . and then betray him with a kiss of death? What was the traitor really like? How is it possible for a fellow human being to act as Judas acted? Was he a madman? A monster?

Those same questions were posed of Adolf Eichmann, a principal architect of the German Holocaust. The executioner of millions of Jews, Eichmann stood trial in 1961. People expected to see a cunning man full of malice and sadistic savagery. What they found, instead, was that evil doesn't always look monstrous.

This was most apparent when Yehiel Dinur, a concentration camp survivor, entered the courtroom to testify against Eichmann.

As he strode down the aisle to mount the witness stand, he suddenly stopped and wheeled around to face Eichmann. The courtroom hushed silent. And then Dinur did something strange: he began to weep. Moments later, he crumpled unconscious to the floor.

Was Dinur overcome by hatred? Fear? Horrid memories? No, he was simply overcome to discover that evil looks like what you see when you look in the mirror. As he later told reporters, he realized all at once that Eichmann, who'd turned killing into a science, was not some animal, but just an ordinary human being. And in that moment of understanding, "I was afraid about myself," he said. "I saw that I am exactly like he."

The same can be said of Judas. Like Eichmann or any of our latter-day madmen, the man who betrayed Christ was *normal*. A more scary thought is hard to imagine.

See also: Isaiah 64:6; Romans 3:10–18, 23; 7:24

■■ GROWING UP

Since you already know this, be on your guard so that you may not be carried away by the error of lawless men and fall from your secure position. But grow in the grace and knowledge of our Lord and Savior Jesus Christ.

2 PETER 3:17–18

If you've been a Christian for any length of time, it is easy to become comfortable in your relationship with Christ. You're on a first-name basis now, and things seem to be going fairly smoothly. The most obvious sins have already been dealt with, and the little nuisance sins that remain behind don't really seem all that harmful. So is it too much to ask that Christ just settle in, put his feet up and his tools away, and quit poking around?

The question, however, is not how comfortable you are with the relationship, but how comfortable Christ is in your heart. C. S. Lewis addressed this very topic in his book *Mere Christianity:*

Imagine yourself as a living house. God comes in to rebuild that house. At first, perhaps, you can understand what he is doing. He is getting the drains right and stopping the leaks in the roof and so on: you knew that those jobs needed doing and so you are not surprised.

But presently he starts knocking the house about in a way that hurts abominably and does not seem to make sense. What on earth is he up to? The explanation is that he is building quite a different house from the one you thought of—throwing out a new wing here, putting on an extra floor there, running up towers, making courtyards.

You thought you were going to be made into a decent little cottage: but he is building a palace. He intends to come and live in it himself.

See also: Ephesians 4:15; Philippians 2:12–13; Revelation 3:20

▪▪ THE MOMENT OF TRUTH

Consider him who endured such opposition from sinful men, so that you will not grow weary and lose heart. In your struggle against sin, you have not yet resisted to the point of shedding your blood.

HEBREWS 12:3–4

I considered her a casual friend, but she thought we were an item made in heaven. When she pushed the relationship, however, I explained I didn't want to get serious; I just wanted to be friends. That's when she started to cry.

Not knowing what to say or do, I put my arm around her and told her not to cry. She didn't say anything for a while. But then she finally looked up and, with a vulnerable but inviting tone in her voice, said, "I'd do anything to stay close."

I looked at her to see if I was hearing her correctly.

"Anything?"

She blushed a little, and then nodded.

"You mean . . ."

"My parents won't be home Saturday."

In the next several moments, a full-scale war broke out in my heart as I toyed with temptation. I told myself the idea was wrong, and then teased myself into believing it was really no big deal. Who would know? Who would care? I halfheartedly asked God's help to resist . . . and then the moment of truth came, and I had to say something.

Our eyes caught and I forced a smile. And then weakly, grudgingly, I shook my head no. "God has something better for both of us," I said quietly.

During subsequent weeks, I replayed the conversation over and over in my mind. What I felt was not a sense of victory or virtue for having withstood temptation, but a dull, worn-out, exhausted feeling. And in those tired moments, I was again reminded just how hard it is to live the Christian life, because if it's lived right, it's lived in direct opposition to Satan.

Of course, God never promised that the Christian life would be easy. It's warfare, pure and simple. And there are days when you can feel the battle clear to your bones.

See also: James 4:7; 1 Peter 2:11

■■ BIG FIVE

For the grace of God that brings salvation has appeared to all men. It teaches us to say "No" to ungodliness and worldly passions, and to live self-controlled, upright and godly lives in this present age, while we wait for the blessed hope—the glorious appearing of our great God and Savior, Jesus Christ, who gave himself for us to redeem us from all wickedness and to purify for himself a people that are his very own, eager to do what is good.

TITUS 2:11–14

Sitting in the darkened room, team members stare at the flickering images on the screen before them. The movie, shot at the preceding week's game, is without sound. But the room is abuzz with conversation. Out of the darkness, the coach barks comments to the players, identifying weaknesses that can be attacked in the coming week's practices.

"Number 42, you gotta stay with your man! A little head fake, and he moved right past you ... You call that blocking? Come on, girls, gotta dig in and stay low ... Number 16, keep your eyes on the game, not the cheerleaders!"

Identifying specific problem areas can be valuable for us as Christians, too. To live victorious, faithful lives, it takes more than praying that God help us become better Christians.

Better in what areas? Getting better control of your tongue? Improving your thought life? Eating less? Kicking a certain bad habit? Mending a certain relationship?

Take a few minutes and jot down five specific areas you'd like to work on in the days ahead, using a short phrase or word:

The Big Five

1. _____

2. _____

3. _____

4. _____

5. _____

If you can't honestly say you are drawing closer to God, the Big Five is probably the reason why. Talk to God about helping you overcome these specific obstacles, and thereby shorten the list. And don't forget, it's not your problem exclusively. God has a lot at stake in the outcome. He's on your side, rooting for you to succeed.

See also: Ephesians 2:10; Philippians 2:12–13; 3:14

▪▪ POINTS TO PONDER – TEMPTATION

When tempted, no one should say, "God is tempting me." For God cannot be tempted by evil, nor does he tempt anyone; but each one is tempted when, by his own evil desire, he is dragged away and enticed. Then, after desire has conceived, it gives birth to sin; and sin, when it is full-grown, gives birth to death.

JAMES 1:13–15

Most people want to be delivered from temptation but would like to keep in touch.

ROBERT ORBEN

Lord, often have I thought to myself, *I will sin but this one sin more, and then I will repent of it, and of all the rest of my sins together.* So foolish was I and ignorant. As if I should be more able to pay my debts when I owe more; or as if I should say, "I will wound my friend once again, and then I will lovingly shake hands with him." But what if my friend will not shake hands with me?

THOMAS FULLER

Change your thoughts and you change your world.

NORMAN VINCENT PEALE

It is much easier to suppress a first desire than to satisfy those that follow.

FRANÇOIS DE LA ROCHEFOUCAULD

The things that I can't have I want, and what I have
  seems second-rate;
The things I want to do I can't, and what I have to do I hate.

DON MARQUIS

Inflation hasn't affected the wages of sin. It's still death.

BUMPER STICKER

God's plan made a hopeful beginning,
But man spoiled his chances by sinning.
We trust that the story will end in God's glory.
But, at present, the other side's winning.

ANONYMOUS

Only those who try to resist temptation know how strong it is.... A man who gives in to temptation after five minutes simply does not know what it would have been like an hour later. That is why bad people, in one sense, know very little about badness. They have lived a sheltered life by always giving in. We never find out the strength of the evil impulse inside us until we try to fight it:

and Christ, because he was the only man who never yielded to temptation, is also the only man who knows to the full what temptation means—the only complete realist.

C. S. LEWIS

Virtue consists, not in abstaining from vice, but in not desiring it.

GEORGE BERNARD SHAW

As the Sandwich-Islander believes that the strength and valor of the enemy he kills passes into himself, so we gain the strength of the temptations we resist.

RALPH WALDO EMERSON

I can resist anything except temptation.

OSCAR WILDE

Better to shun the bait than struggle in the snare.

JOHN DRYDEN

See also: Matthew 26:41; 1 Corinthians 10:13; Hebrews 2:14–18; 4:15

WEEK

38

■ BULL'S-EYE

> *All kinds of animals, birds, reptiles and creatures of the sea are being tamed and have been tamed by man, but no man can tame the tongue. It is a restless evil, full of deadly poison. With the tongue we praise our Lord and Father, and with it we curse men, who have been made in God's likeness. Out of the same mouth come praise and cursing. My brothers, this should not be.*
>
> JAMES 3:7–10

The words came out of my mouth like the blast of a shotgun. Released in a moment of anger, they were sharp and biting. I'd been hurt and wanted to maim in return.

I could tell I hit the target because my words brought immediate tears. It was a bull's-eye blast, and I turned away feeling good inside.

The good feeling, however, barely lasted ten minutes. After that I felt awful. I'd gone too far. Instead of turning the other cheek, I'd retaliated. Not only that, but I'd retaliated at a level grossly out of proportion to my own private hurt. I'd merely had my ego bruised. It was as if I'd been grazed by a BB. In return, I'd pulled the trigger of a double-barreled Winchester at point-blank range, leaving a gaping wound.

A few days later I went back and said I was sorry, that I didn't really mean what I'd said. But even as I mouthed the words, I felt "sorry" was so inadequate. If I didn't mean it, then why did I say it? *Why?* It was like I was trying to patch up a bloody mess with a Band-Aid.

I know that the person I hurt could, to this day, repeat verbatim what I said when I lashed out years ago. Terrible pain goes deep, and hers went clear to the bone. She was probably not much different from a young woman I once read about. Before committing suicide, she left a note that simply read, "They said ..."

The note was never finished. Something "they said" killed her.

See also: Matthew 5:21–24; 1 Peter 3:8–12

■■ LOW (VERBAL) BLOWS

Everyone should be quick to listen, slow to speak and slow to become angry, for man's anger does not bring about the righteous life that God desires.

JAMES 1:19–20

Most of the troubles and heartache I've caused other people have been smoothed over with a "sorry." It works better than Bactine on minor hurts. If I say the wrong thing, I merely need to mutter an apology and everything will be all right.

However, as the incident mentioned yesterday helped me realize, things aren't always that simple. Contrary to the kid's rhyme about sticks and stones breaking bones but words never hurting, low verbal blows can cause lasting damage. And the wounds they inflict can't always be bandaged over with apologies.

Imagine if every snub were that serious. Imagine if every time you lashed out, laughed at another's expense, ignored a lonely person or stood by while somebody was taunted by others—you couldn't patch things up with a "sorry." And what if you were held permanently responsible for even "minor" slights?

In actuality, that's the way things are. We can minimize our wrongs, but God can't. In the end, "he will say to those on his left, 'Depart from me ... For I was hungry and you gave me nothing to eat, I was thirsty and you gave me nothing to drink, I was a stranger and you did not invite me in, I needed clothes and you did not clothe me, I was sick and in prison and you did not look after me.... Whatever you did not do for one of the least of these, you did not do for me'" (Matthew 25:41–43, 45). In other words, when we hurt other people, even *indirectly*, it's the same as hurting Christ *directly*.

I sometimes wish God could shrug off these little things and not be so literal about right and wrong. But sin is serious business with him—to the extent that he demanded a drastic solution. Somebody had to pay the consequences. In the end, Christ stepped forward—to be ridiculed, laughed at, beaten, and finally killed—*on my behalf.*

Knowing that my sin prompted such a sacrifice and that Christ feels the pain when I hurt others, I am trying to adopt a less belligerent, more benevolent attitude toward others. And when I do blow it, "sorry" may work some of the time, but the only lasting relief is repentance.

See also: Romans 12:17–21; 1 Thessalonians 5:15; James 1:26

▪▪ MEASURING UP

Do not love the world or anything in the world. If anyone loves the world, the love of the Father is not in him. For everything in the world – the cravings of sinful man, the lust of his eyes and the boasting of what he has and does – comes not from the Father but from the world. The world and its desires pass away, but the man who does the will of God lives forever.

1 JOHN 2:15–17

I sometimes wondered what it would be like to play on the varsity football team. With just a few more muscles in the right places, I could have strutted through the locker halls like I owned them, smiled and flirted with the cheerleaders, listened to my name boom over the loudspeakers, and watched as people jumped and hollered when I scored a touchdown.

I sometimes wondered what it would be like to be confined to a wheelchair. With just a little different body position on any number of accidents and "close calls," I could have been crippled for life. I could have rolled through the locker halls and been stared at, learned to eat without use of my hands, taught myself to write and paint by using my mouth, and had a special license plate so I could park near the front door of any store.

I sometimes wondered what it would be like to live in the really nice part of town. With a lot more money, I could have worn all of the right clothes, invited kids over to swim in a backyard pool, driven a really fast car, eaten out for lunch instead of always bringing brown bags, and not counted pennies every time I wanted to turn around.

I sometimes wondered what it would be like to be dirt poor and live on the other side of the tracks. With a lot less money, I could have slept on something besides a mattress, never washed with hot water because it takes money to heat water, never taken an aspirin or used deodorant because it takes money for that, too, and quit school at fifteen because the nice kids from good homes would make fun of my clothes and my smell.

I sometimes wondered about the tremendous disparity in life between the haves and have nots, the rich and the poor, the healthy and the sickly, the beautiful and the ugly, the wise and the foolish. I just thank God that each of us, regardless of the world's standards, stands equal before God. And someday soon, very soon, we will all be asked to give an account for our lives.

The only thing that will matter then is how we measure up to God's standards.

See also: Ecclesiastes 2:14–15; Luke 14:13–23; James 2:1–13

■■ AS THE WORLD TURNS

God "will give to each person according to what he has done." To those who by persistence in doing good seek glory, honor and immortality, he will give eternal life. But for those who are self-seeking and who reject the truth and follow evil, there will be wrath and anger.

ROMANS 2:6–8

Every morning in our local paper, one of the TV reporters writes about what happened the previous day on the various soaps. If there were not hundreds of people who wanted that information, the reporter would write instead about beached whales, sewage spills, or other community concerns. But he doesn't; he outlines the worst programs Hollywood has ever created.

Following is his verbatim report for one of the leading daytime soap operas, a show which reflects human nature more accurately than anybody cares to acknowledge:

Margo had Tom served with divorce papers after catching him in a clinch with Barbara. Meg kept mum that she saw Holden kissing Lily. Marsha told her lawyer, Jennings, that she, not Doug, had kidnapped Frannie and Kim. Steve was livid to learn that Tad had outbid Steve on several construction jobs. Feeling snubbed by Lucinda, Lily decided to remain at Emma's farm. Lucinda is plotting to reunite Sierra and Craig. Sierra agreed to help Craig find out the identity of the mystery woman, who Craig believes is Shannon.

There's no tremendously deep or theological point to be made from this, other than to point out that if you want a quick glimpse of the vast disparity between God's standards and the world's standards, all you need to do is flip on the TV some afternoon when you happen to be home.

But if you have the faintest doubt as to where it all leads and what happens to those who side with the world instead of God, you won't find it on TV or in the newspaper.

For that you need your Bible.

See also: Romans 6:23; 2 Timothy 3:1–9; 1 John 2:17

:: THE JUNGLE

Be self-controlled and alert. Your enemy the devil prowls around like a roaring lion looking for someone to devour. Resist him, standing firm in the faith.

1 PETER 5:8–9

The South American village had its good side of town and its bad side. The bad side was close to the jungle where the Beni River began to pick up a little speed. The good side occupied a section surrounding a modern hotel. I happened to stay on the good side, so I remember the village as both clean and friendly. In fact, by Bolivian standards it was paradise.

So I was surprised recently to read that that same sleepy town was the scene of a brutal ambush that took the lives of many innocent people. I had been there just a short time before, and it didn't seem possible that such a heinous crime could occur in such a nice locale. But paradise or not, there was one thing I was forgetting: The jungle was not that far away.

Call it the "jungle of the heart," if you will—it is never that far away. Remember that the next time somebody leaves you in the wake of their turbo-charged ambition; the next time you forget your bearings and lash out at somebody in anger; the next time you see somebody making fun of a severely handicapped person. The jungle is not that far away.

Remember that the next time somebody you greatly respect shatters every perception of what you thought a good Christian was like; the next time you take a good look at the dark side of your soul; the next time you see a blatant display of hypocrisy in your church. The jungle is not that far away.

Remember it, too, the next time you are at the mall and find yourself lusting after the world's standards; the next time you think that to be truly successful you've got to have a high-paying job, a fast car, and a big house; the next time you take a good look in the mirror.

The jungle, my friend, is not that far away.

See also: Luke 12:15; James 4:4–10

▪▪ SHIFTING SAND

Everyone who hears these words of mine and puts them into practice is like a wise man who built his house on the rock. The rain came down, the streams rose, and the winds blew and beat against that house; yet it did not fall, because it had its foundation on the rock. But everyone who hears these words of mine and does not put them into practice is like a foolish man who built his house on sand. The rain came down, the streams rose, and the winds blew and beat against that house, and it fell with a great crash.

MATTHEW 7:24–27

When the O'Malleys bought their dream home on the sands of Long Island's Westhampton Beach, there was a sprawling dune and glistening beach separating them from the Atlantic. But gale-force winds kicked up the surf, and before long they were looking down the barrel of nature's gun.

They lost the dune their first winter, and the beach disappeared beneath their feet soon after. Two years later their roof and top floor were blown away. Rebuilding was a joke. Before long, their steps were gone, the homes on both sides of them toppled, and water lapped at their foundation. It was just a matter of time before their home was reduced to driftwood.

Like the O'Malleys, the Alfords bought a sea-view home. Theirs was atop a 160-foot cliff in Bolinas, California, and on a clear day they could see San Francisco. But when storms brewed, the churning water carved out great chunks of the cliff. One day there was a deep-rooted tree in their backyard; the next day it was gone, along with a fifteen-foot slice of their yard. Soon there was nothing but air between their deck and the raging surf below.

Foolish as it is to build on sand, it must be dreadful to watch your property reduced to driftwood. That's what Jesus was getting at in the verses above, except that he wasn't talking about real estate.

He was talking about those for whom the Word of God merely goes in one ear and out the other; those who go to church often enough to be considered religious, but nothing they hear ever really soaks in. Before long, their lives are eroded and splintered by the concerns of the world.

If you find yourself in that category today, you need to start, I mean *really* start, taking your Christianity seriously. You need to get solid rock beneath you, and fast. The water is rising.

See also: Matthew 7:21; James 1:22–25

■■ POINTS TO PONDER – OUR WORLD

My soul yearns for you in the night; in the morning my spirit longs for you. When your judgments come upon

the earth, the people of the world learn righteousness.
Though grace is shown to the wicked, they do not learn
righteousness; even in a land of uprightness they go on
doing evil and regard not the majesty of the LORD. O
LORD, your hand is lifted high, but they do not see it. Let
them see your zeal for your people and be put to shame;
let the fire reserved for your enemies consume them.

ISAIAH 26:9–11

The world has a lot of glitter, but it doesn't have the glow.

BILL FRYE

It is five minutes to twelve on the clock of the world's history.

ADOLPH KELLER

The ship's place is in the sea, but God pity the ship when the sea gets into it. The Christian's place is in the world, but God pity the Christian if the world gets the best of him.

ANONYMOUS

I don't know if there are men on the moon, but if there are they must be using the earth as their lunatic asylum.

GEORGE BERNARD SHAW

If Christians withdraw from society because of the bewildering nature of its problems, they will soon lose the right to be heard.

GARY R. COLLINS AND JAMES F. JEKEL

To deny the prevalence of pain in the world and the perennial popularity of evil. To abdicate responsibility for them by assuming that God will take care of them very nicely on his own.... To dismiss them or to encourage others to dismiss them by stressing the promise of pie in the sky.... To maintain your faith by refusing to face any nasty fact that threatens it. These are all ways of escaping reality through religion and should be denounced right along with such other modes of escape as liquor, drugs, TV, or any simplistic optimism such as communism, anticommunism, jingoism, rugged individualism, moralism, idealism, and so on, which assume that if everybody would only see it our way, evil would vanish and all would be sweetness and light.

FREDERICK BUECHNER

Great men are they who see that the spiritual is stronger than any material force.

RALPH WALDO EMERSON

The view we entertain of God will determine our view of the world.

CHRISTOPH ERNST LUTHARDT

Whoever marries the spirit of this age will find himself a widower in the next.

W. R. INGE

Secularism has this age by the throat.

WALTER LOWRIE

In this society we save whales, we save timber wolves and bald eagles and Coke bottles. Yet, everyone wanted me to throw away my baby.

VICTORIA, A PREGNANT WOMAN

The world hopes for the best but Jesus Christ offers the best hope.

JOHN WESLEY WHITE

O Lord, support us all the day long, until the shadows lengthen and the evening comes, and the busy world is hushed, and the fever of life is over, and our work is done. Then in Thy mercy grant us a safe lodging, and a holy rest, and peace at the last.

BOOK OF COMMON PRAYER

The world is charged with the grandeur of God.

GERARD MANLEY HOPKINS

What the soul is in the body, this the Christians are in the world. Christians hold the world together.

LETTER TO DIOGNETUS

See also: Matthew 5:13–16; Romans 6:23; James 4:4; 1 John 2:15–17

WEEK

39

▪▪ RUN THE RIVER

> *I will lead the blind by ways they have not known,*
> *along unfamiliar paths I will guide them; I will turn the*
> *darkness into light before them and make the rough*
> *places smooth. These are the things I will do; I will not*
> *forsake them.*

Isaiah 42:16

At the beginning, the water is calm, the paddling easy. You watch the terns fly above the canoe and take a few pictures of the towering gorge through which the river cuts. Suddenly you hear a distant roar—not unlike the rumbling of a sixty-car freight train. You swallow hard and grip your paddle until your knuckles turn white. The gorge narrows and the canoe sweeps faster. So does your adrenalin-charged blood.

Then, before you're ready for it, you're bouncing amidst haystack waves. Spray whips your face and four inches of water slosh in the canoe at your knees. "Pry on the left," your partner screams as a giant boulder looms directly in your path. But you only have time to shove off with your paddle.

Now the canoe is rocketing through a narrow chute. Aluminum canoes, bent like accordions, litter the banks and indicate what can happen if you get off course. You shudder but paddle furiously as the rapids kick and heave like a Brahma bull. Rocks scrape the bottom and bang the sides until ... *WHOOOOMPHH!* ... the current spits you headlong over the falls and into a quiet pool.

In many ways, life is like running a wild river in a canoe. It has its slow spells, its threatening spurts, its seat-of-the-pants thrills, its waterfalls, its tragedies. It keeps rushing by—sometimes at a roar, sometimes at a whisper—and if you're not careful you can get tossed around like a cork and go straight to the bottom. Or you can follow the guides and navigational charts and keep straight on course. You'll still go through the waterfalls and rapids, but you'll be on *top* of the water.

The only true guide, of course, is Jesus Christ. He's mastered the river; he knows it like the back of his hand. And he's left behind a helper and navigation maps for you. If you pay attention and study faithfully, you'll come out on top.

See also: John 14:26; 2 Timothy 3:16–17; Hebrews 12:1–3

TONGUE POWER

Pleasant words are a honeycomb, sweet to the soul and healing to the bones.

PROVERBS 16:24

Congratulations.
The test is canceled.
I love you.
You've been accepted.
You look great.
Don't bother eating the vegetables.
I am sorry.
You are right.
The growth is benign.
You're on the team.
I forgive you.
You'll do better next time.
Stay out as long as you want.
Keep the change.
I'll write you.
Yes.
Happy birthday.
I'm praying for you.
You're hired.
There are seconds on dessert.
You have no cavities.
The car is yours.
Ball four.
Take a break.
You're right.
Get well.
You've done a good job.
Have a safe trip.

Sweet dreams.
My treat.
Let me help.
God bless you.

As Christian Nestell Bovee once said, "Kindness is a language the dumb can speak and the deaf can hear and understand."

See also: Proverbs 15:1–4; Philippians 4:8; Hebrews 3:13

:: REAL TEARS

I say to every one of you: Do not think of yourself more highly than you ought.

ROMANS 12:3

I thought prejudice was something you only read about in old newspapers and history books, something that happened back in the fifties in places like Alabama. After all, our school was a salad bowl of people of color—and everybody mixed well. Prejudice just didn't seem to exist.

Things changed when Samir started school in May, just before the summer break. At that time of year, the kids were looking for diversions to help get them through the last few weeks of school. Samir became that diversion. He was from Syria or Iran or someplace you only heard about on the evening news. It didn't really matter. What mattered was that he spoke broken English, dressed funny, and looked different.

A couple of the football players had a heyday with him, slipping drugs into his food when he wasn't looking. The next hour in class he was like a parakeet on speed, and nobody could shut him up. The teacher finally sent him to the office, but somebody steered him instead into the girl's locker room.

On another occasion, he was preparing a short speech about his country and sought help from students whom you wouldn't trust to walk your dog if you cared about your dog. As a joke, they peppered his script with four-letter words. When he gave the speech, everybody but Samir roared with laughter. He just stood there with a pained look on his face and then did something nobody had ever done before in English class. He began to cry.

All along people treated Samir like he was different. And difference led to prejudice. It was bigotry, pure and simple. But when they saw his tears, understanding began to sink in. You could see it on people's faces as they looked around at each other, and then looked down. He wasn't an animal, but a real live human being. They had sense enough to recognize that his hurt, his tears were no different from their own.

More important, they had sense enough to be ashamed.

See also: Psalm 131:1; Isaiah 5:21; Romans 12:16

■■ ROUND TUIT

Obey what I command you today.

EXODUS 34:11

One Round Tuit
This is yours! Cut it out and keep it!

There is finally a sufficient quantity of these for all Christians to have their very own. Guard it with your life. Never lose it, and don't let anyone take it away from you.

These tuits have been hard to come by, especially the round version. But there are now enough to go around, and the timing couldn't be better because the demand has been overwhelming. At long last, many of your problems concerning your relationship with God and really getting down to serious, daily Bible study and prayer time will be solved. You can expect your attention span to double and your interest level to increase dramatically now that you have your own round tuit.

As you have often said, "I will start spending regular time alone with God once I get a round tuit." You have also commented, "I know I should read my Bible more, but I just haven't been able to get a round tuit."

Well, now that you've got it, use it!

See also: 1 Timothy 4:13–16; Hebrews 4:7; 6:11–12

■■ BIG DREAMS

> *Jabez was more honorable than his brothers. His mother had named him Jabez, saying, "I gave birth to him in pain." Jabez cried out to the God of Israel, "Oh, that you would bless me and enlarge my territory! Let your hand be with me, and keep me from harm so that I will be free from pain." And God granted his request.*

1 CHRONICLES 4:9–10

Compared to all the big-time, high-profile saints and scoundrels who show up in the Bible, Jabez is a small fry, a bit player. Placed side by side with the prophets, potentates, and assorted nabobs, he's a nobody.

Though his role in the Bible is limited to a paragraph buried amidst genealogy records in 1 Chronicles, it makes fascinating reading. It's a cameo appearance which you'd miss if you blinked at the wrong time.

All that's known about him is conveyed in the verses above. To rehash the facts, he acquired his funny name (which sounds like the Hebrew word for pain) because his birth practically did his mother in. Although he was a good, clean-living kid, he seems to have had a rough life—perhaps because other kids teased him about his name and gave him periodic black eyes.

But the day came when he decided enough was enough, and he asked God to help keep him safe and to give him bigger challenges—to "enlarge his territory."

That's about all the Bible has to say about Jabez, other than to report that God answered his prayer. Jabez wanted bigger challenges and more opportunity, and he got it.

I believe God is eager to do the same for any one of us, providing our ambition is not motivated by selfish desire. The problem is, we're often too content in our own little ruts. It's never crossed our minds to pray that God would enlarge our horizons. Or, to crib a thought from Jesus' brother James in the New Testament, "You wouldn't think of just asking God for it, would you?" (James 4:2 *The Message*).

See also: Psalm 37:4; Matthew 25:14–30; John 16:24; James 4:3

■ HEMMED IN

Make the most of every opportunity.

COLOSSIANS 4:5

If the characters in the Bible were thought of as movie actors and rated according to their prominence in the Scriptures, individuals such as Jesus, Abraham, Moses, Paul, and David would get top billing. Their presence is felt throughout the Bible. Others such as Mary, Absalom, Goliath, Sarah, Herod, and Rahab would be cast in supporting roles.

Jabez, whom you read about yesterday, would be an "extra." He felt hemmed in by circumstances and people, and longed for bigger and better. But God heard his plea for broader horizons and, knowing his motives were honorable, gave him the desires of his heart.

Perhaps you know the claustrophobic feeling of being hemmed in by people and their attitudes toward you. To them you're a nobody because you don't turn heads in a swimsuit, can't slam-dunk a basketball, or won't play by their rules. Maybe others look down on you because of your age.

Or perhaps you feel hemmed in by circumstances; you know you are missing growth opportunities because you live on the wrong side of town, don't have the "right" contacts, or can't afford the "right" school.

One thing is certain, however. Despite what others say or circumstances allow, God has given you abilities and spiritual gifts that are being under-utilized. All you need is the opportunity....

For starters, ask God to help you make the most of every opportunity that now lies before you at home, school, church, or work—and in every area of your life, whether spiritual, emotional, social, or mental. Once you're sure you are being faithful within your present confines, then ask God to begin knocking down a few walls. Thankfully, he isn't bound by the barriers that surround us.

See also: 1 Corinthians 15:58; Philippians 2:1–3; 1 Timothy 4:12

▪▪ POINTS TO PONDER – AMBITION AND SUCCESS

> *If anyone would come after me, he must deny himself and take up his cross daily and follow me. For whoever wants to save his life will lose it, but whoever loses his life for me will save it. What good is it for a man to gain the whole world, and yet lose or forfeit his very self?*
>
> LUKE 9:23–25

If you wish to reach the highest, begin at the lowest.

PUBLILIUS SYRUS

The true goal of the Christian life is heaven: nothing more, nothing less, and nothing else.

SHERWOOD ELIOT WIRT

An ambitious farmer, unhappy about the yield of his crops, heard of a highly recommended new seed corn. He bought some and produced a crop that was so abundant his astonished neighbors asked him to sell them a portion of the new seed. But the farmer, afraid that he would lose a profitable competitive advantage, refused. The second year the new seed did not produce as good a crop, and when the third-year crop was still worse it dawned upon the farmer that his prize corn was being pollinated by the inferior grade of corn from his neighbors' fields.

RALPH L. WOODS

Everybody wants to harvest, but nobody wants to plow.

ANONYMOUS

He who dies with the most toys wins ... nothing. Luke 9:25.

BUMPER STICKER

God give me work till my life shall end, and life till my work is done.

WINIFRED HOLTBY

All you need in this life is ignorance and confidence, and then success is sure.

MARK TWAIN

There are two tragedies in life. One is to not get your heart's desire. The other is to get it.

GEORGE BERNARD SHAW

A life spent in constant labor is a life wasted, save a person be such a fool as to regard a fulsome obituary notice as ample reward.

GEORGE JEAN NATHAN

Aim high. It is no harder on your gun to shoot the feathers off an eagle than to shoot the fur off a skunk.

TROY MOORE

It seems to me we can never give up longing and wishing while we are thoroughly alive. There are certain things we feel to be beautiful and good, and we must hunger after them.

GEORGE ELIOT

If we make it our first goal always to please God, it solves many problems at once.

PHILIP E. HOWARD, JR.

To his dog, every man is Napoleon; hence the constant popularity of dogs.

ALDOUS HUXLEY

He is rich or poor according to what he is, not according to what he has.

HENRY WARD BEECHER

Success has always been a great liar.

NIETZSCHE

See also: Proverbs 3:5–6; Ecclesiastes 1:2–11; Luke 9:46–48

WEEK

40

■ SEASONS OF LIFE

The body that is sown is perishable, it is raised imperishable; it is sown in dishonor, it is raised in glory; it is sown in weakness, it is raised in power; it is sown a natural body, it is raised a spiritual body.

1 CORINTHIANS 15:42–44

Every year about October, my favorite oak catches fire and the leaves explode like Fourth of July fireworks. It is a wondrous display of God's creativity: a flash of red up one branch, a burst of orange down another.

And then, quite suddenly, the leaves wither and dry. A couple of weeks later, the oak is bare and its black tree bones will stand like a skeleton through the long, cold winter until spring.

I can't think of that old weathered oak and its black tree bones without picturing some very special friends who are facing the winter of their lives. I think of Crystal, whose faith is as radiant as autumn leaves despite being trapped in a body withered by cerebral palsy. Despite the disease, she smiles bigger and sings praises louder than anybody I know. And not a day goes by when she doesn't roll her wheelchair into a corner to pray—for those less fortunate than her.

I also think of Harold, who met the Lord in prison while serving a double life sentence for crimes he didn't commit. He was eventually paroled and pardoned, but just when things were looking up he contracted throat cancer. To stay alive, he must now dilate his throat twice daily with an inch-thick, two-and-a-half foot long rubber tube. Despite his suffering, there's not a day he doesn't thank God for his tube, which enables him to keep breathing and to continue ministering to hurting people.

After the winter comes the spring, and every spring brings a miracle to my favorite tree. Its black tree bones, which seem so absolutely barren, suddenly burst with tiny green banners of life. It's an annual reminder that a similar miracle awaits me, my friends, and others who know Christ as Lord. Suffering and disease will be no more, our bodies will be transformed, our tears will be dried, and for the first time we'll discover life as it was meant to be lived.

Think of it like this. It will be as dramatic as watching new leaves erupt from old, withered, petrified tree stumps. It will be the Spring of springs. And on that day, that glorious, magnificent, long-awaited day, we'll finally stand face-to-face with our Lord, our Savior—the King of kings.

See also: 1 Corinthians 15:35–58; Revelation 21:2–4

▪▪ RAMPAGE

We are therefore Christ's ambassadors, as though God were making his appeal through us.

2 CORINTHIANS 5:20

Kevin came from a model family. The kids were very studious and, for the most part, great athletes. His two older brothers were basketball stars and went to college on athletic scholarships. Kevin wanted to follow in their footsteps. But, though he had their brains, the poor guy couldn't have hit a basket if it was hanging from his head.

It was a courtesy to the family that the coach let Kevin try out for the team. As expected, he didn't make it past the first cut. He had tears in his eyes when he headed out of the gym, which was understandable considering his dreams. At that moment, all he needed was for somebody to offer him an encouraging word, or maybe even a slap on the shoulder. Instead, one of the players tossed a grenade.

"Hey, Kevin, don't cry," he chided. "There's always the girls' team."

That afternoon, Kevin went on a rampage in his family's home, using a bat to smash windows, mirrors, lamps, appliances, and furniture. He then took his father's rifle and began shooting holes in the walls. By the time the cops got there, he'd done an estimated $30,000 in damage.

It was all pretty strange, especially since Kevin was the last guy you'd expect to go nutzoid. But it happened—in a nice neighborhood, to a good kid.

In actuality, however, Kevin's Dr. Jekyll/Mr. Hyde conversion is not isolated. Similar though less spectacular transformations occur every day. A cruel remark can force an insecure person into a neurotic shell. A biting put-down can deeply mar one's self-esteem. On the other hand, a kind word can give a person a boost he'll never forget, and loving encouragement can heal a multitude of hurts.

The amazing thing is that it's often within our power to decide which way the transformations will go. With a snub we can create horrors; with charity we can work miracles. It's a power that probably best belongs in the hands of God. But he has entrusted it to us as his representatives to the human race.

See also: 2 Corinthians 1:3–4; James 3:1–10

■■ DESTINATION: HEAVEN

Since, then, you have been raised with Christ, set your hearts on things above, where Christ is seated at the right hand of God. Set your minds on things above, not on earthly things. For you died, and your life is now hidden with Christ in God. When Christ, who is your life, appears, then you also will appear with him in glory.

COLOSSIANS 3:1–4

As you read yesterday, you control an incredible power that can be used to change lives, whether for the positive or negative. That's what Christ was getting at when he said, "You are the light of the world" (Matthew 5:14). We're here to shine, to bring out the God-colors in the world. In other words, we've been empowered with a serious and very sacred task: to help illuminate people's way toward heaven—out of their living hell. We are God's light-bearers.

As C. S. Lewis wrote, "It is a serious thing to live in a society of possible gods and goddesses, to remember that the dullest and most uninteresting person you talk to may one day be a creature which, if you saw it now, you would be strongly tempted to worship. Or else he may be a horror and corruption such as you now meet, if at all, only in a nightmare. All day long we are, in some degree, helping each other to one or the other of these destinations."

If you take the Bible seriously, everybody you know, every person you see at school or work, every member of your family, the president of the United States, the queen of England, the gas station attendant—*everybody* will one day arrive at one of two destinations: heaven or hell. Your role in their lives will help determine that eternal destiny.

Chances are, you don't run in the same circles as the president or the queen. But you do encounter dozens of other people who, by the light of Christ living in you, can be guided toward heaven. Before you do anything else today, think long and hard about the people you bump into who are not now heaven-bound. Pick the four you feel you can have the most influence on—and write their names below:

1. _____

2. _____

3. _____

4. _____

In the days and weeks ahead, pray daily for each of them. Ask God to soften their hearts toward the love and saving power of Jesus Christ and to convict them of their sins. More important, pray that God will empower you to help light up their lives ... and thereby help them toward heaven.

See also: Matthew 28:18–20; 1 Corinthians 10:31–33

■■ IMAGINARY WORLD

He will command his angels concerning you to guard you in all your ways.

PSALM 91:11

The phone rang late at night, much later than people normally call. I knew I didn't want to hear whatever I was about to be told. As suspected, the news was tragic.

Vicky and Jim were returning from a fishing trip, and while driving along a mountain road they were blinded by the sun. For a split second, Jim wasn't sure where the road was—and then it was too late. The car went airborne, and they didn't have a chance.

Vicky and Jim were devout Christians whose young lives centered around their church. My natural inclination was to ask why God let such a senseless tragedy occur to them, of all people. After pondering this question, I tried to imagine a world in which bad things didn't happen to good people.

In such a world, I suppose the car would have sprouted a parachute and drifted to the valley floor. And what about other Christian friends I'd lost recently in an airplane crash? Couldn't God have gently lifted the plane so it cleared the mountain peak?

In that kind of imaginary world, everybody would want to have a Christian along for the ride ... just in case. Every airline would require a Christian on board, as would every ship. Buddy systems would be formed which paired Christians with others just to cross the street. Why risk injury or death when all you had to do was walk in the shadow of a Christian?

The scenario is ludicrous, of course. Yet the thought persists that somehow Christians receive a special dispensation from God which limits the extent to which they suffer. After all, doesn't the Bible clearly say God "will command his angels concerning you to guard you in all your ways"? Guard you from what? Sickness and death? No. Illness and death are intimate parts of the fallen world in which we live, and Christians are not immune from either.

Rather, his angels guard us from separation from God, which is the greater concern. For apart from God, we cannot say we have truly lived.

See also: Luke 9:25; Revelation 21:4

⚏ SUNSHINE SOLDIER

For I will yet praise him, my Savior and my God.

PSALM 43:5

It wasn't that Steve didn't believe in God. He did—provided God met his expectations and *acted like God.* That meant God would be a sort of celestial Daddy Warbucks and dole out health and happiness (plus an occasional bonus for good behavior) in lavish proportion at just the right moment.

For a while there, Steve was really quite the believer. He got good grades, even when he didn't crack a book the night before ("I prayed, and God just refreshed my mind!" he'd say); his acne was manageable ("A face made in heaven!"); he drove a fast car ("Praise God for freeways!"); and dated a girl who could have stopped a train with her looks ("After God made her, he threw away the mold!").

But then cracks developed in Steve's porcelain life that he wasn't able to patch over too well. In one six-month period, his father ran out on his mom, his train-stopping girlfriend took an interest in a member of the varsity swim team, and he jumped a curb in his car and crashed into a eucalyptus tree.

Suddenly God just wasn't acting much like God anymore. Or so it seemed to Steve. From his perspective, how much of a God could God really be if he couldn't solve Steve's problems? No God that Steve was interested in.

In the end, Steve's beliefs were entirely conditional: He'd go through the motions with God *if* God blessed him and kept things running smoothly. Unfortunately, life isn't always so smooth and neat. In some countries, becoming a Christian means nothing but heartache: you lose your job, get disowned by your family, and face jail or death. Not all Christians are born in Beverly Hills; some live in dumps.

In today's verse, the psalmist says, "I will *yet* praise him, my Savior and my God"—regardless of circumstances. God calls us to love him, no strings attached.

That's a tall order, but it's not one-sided. God made the same pledge to us and backed it with Jesus Christ.

See also: Deuteronomy 6:5; Psalm 44:22; Romans 5:6–8

☷ IF ONLY ...

This is how God showed his love among us: He sent his one and only Son into the world that we might live through him. This is love: not that we loved God, but that he loved us and sent his Son as an atoning sacrifice for our sins.

1 JOHN 4:9–10

Robin had heard all the talk about Jesus and how he'd supposedly vacated heaven and become a man. The whole idea seemed rather farfetched, and she just smiled every time her friends tried to raise the subject with her.

Then one winter night she was sitting home alone as it began to snow. The flakes seemed to float down at first, but the wind kicked up and the snow began falling like there'd be no tomorrow. As she was watching the storm from the warmth of the house, a bird suddenly flew smack into the plate-glass window in front of her and fell back into the snow. The *thump!* startled her, and she felt her heart racing. And then, just as suddenly, another bird hit the glass, followed by another and another.

Staring outside into the dark storm, Robin spotted a swirling flock of birds cutting against the wind and then pelting the window. She'd never seen anything like it before and couldn't figure it out. And then it struck her: caught in the violent storm, the birds were trying to seek shelter.

They'll all die out there! she thought as she grabbed her heavy jacket, pulled her gloves and boots on, and then ran outside. She made her way across to the big barn, threw open the door and turned on the floodlights. She waited expectantly, but the birds did not come inside. She jumped up and down, waving her hands in the doorway, but the birds ignored her.

As a last resort, she grabbed a broom and circled behind the house, trying to come at the birds from the opposite direction and shoo them into the protective shelter. But the birds did not understand.

If only I could become a bird, she thought. *Then I could lead them to safety and warmth; then I could save them—or at least communicate with them.*

Unable to do anything more, she gave up her lifesaving efforts and returned to the house, where she watched the birds continue slamming into the glass and dying in the cold.

If I could only become a bird! she thought again.

A sudden faraway look clouded her eyes, and for a moment it was not the birds she was thinking of, but Jesus. Maybe, just maybe, her friends were right.

See also: John 3:16; Romans 5:6–8; Philippians 2:5–11

■■ POINTS TO PONDER – DOUBT AND UNBELIEF

The fool says in his heart, "There is no God."

PSALM 14:1

The difference between the unbelieving fool described by the psalmist and the "God is dead" theologian is that the Old Testament fool said in his heart there was no God; the modern fool brays it all over the countryside.

MARTIN P. DAVIS

It takes more credulity to accept the atheistic position than most men can muster.

GERALD KENNEDY

Doubt is a pain too lonely to know that faith is his twin brother.

KAHLIL GIBRAN

To be a true atheist is to acknowledge no rule except the rule of thumb.

FREDERICK BUECHNER

An atheist does not find God for the same reason a thief does not find a policeman. He is not looking for him.

WENDELL BAXTER

Two men please God—who serves Him with all his heart because he knows Him; who seeks Him with all his heart because he knows Him not.

NIKITA IVANOVICH PANIN

An atheist is a man who has no invisible means of support.

FULTON J. SHEEN

Nobody talks so constantly about God as those who insist that there is no God.

HEYWOOD BROUN

There are no atheists in the foxholes of Bataan.

DOUGLAS MACARTHUR

In all affairs it's a healthy thing now and then to hang a question mark on the things you have long taken for granted.

BERTRAND RUSSELL

An agnostic is somebody who doesn't know for sure whether there really is a God. That is some people all of the time and all people some of the time.

FREDERICK BUECHNER

Every effort to prove there is no God is in itself an effort to reach for God.

CHARLES EDWARD LOCKE

Many an atheist is a believer without knowing it just as many a believer is an atheist without knowing it. You can sincerely believe there is no God and live as though there is. You can sincerely believe there is a God and live as though there isn't.

FREDERICK BUECHNER

If there is a God, atheism must seem to Him as less of an insult than religion.

GONCOURT

I think the trouble with me is lack of faith. I have no rational ground for going back on the arguments that convinced me of God's existence: but the irrational deadweight of my old skeptical habits, and the spirit of this age, and the cares of the day, steal away all my lively feeling of the truth, and often when I pray I wonder if I am not posting letters to a non-existent address. Mind you I don't think so—the whole of my reasonable mind is convinced: but I often feel so. However, there is nothing to do but to peg away. One falls so often that it hardly seems worth while picking oneself up and going through the farce of starting over again as if you could ever hope to walk. Still, this seeming absurdity is the only sensible thing I do, so I must continue it.

C. S. LEWIS

See also: Matthew 14:22–31; Mark 9:17–24; John 20:24–29

■■ A LOVE STORY

He is the image of the invisible God.

COLOSSIANS 1:15

In a dark corner of my garage, tucked inside a grocery bag and sealed within a cardboard box, are untold dozens of letters I exchanged with the girl whom I eventually married. Not all are love letters. Quite a few are hesitant get-to-know-you letters which were signed, *Sincerely, Rick.*

We didn't fall in love the usual way. While I was in England studying and traveling for a year, a girl named Julie sent me a letter. I sent one back, and she wrote another. Before long we were writing every week. She'd tell me about her life and send me little things like pressed flowers, and I'd relay my escapades half a world away.

After about the twenty-fifth letter, my *Sincerely, Rick* had changed to *Love, Rick,* and I didn't want to write another word. For all I knew, the girl weighed three hundred pounds and didn't shave. But I was in love and wanted to hop the next plane home to check her out. I'd carried the relationship about as far as possible by mail; to go any further, I needed to *see* her.

People in past centuries felt the same frustration in their dealings with God. He maintained a strictly long-distance relationship, and nobody could really get close. Nobody ever got to *see* him.

Then something amazing and totally radical happened. God became visible. It wasn't a case of *Presto! Change-o!* where he was here one moment, gone the next. He lived on earth for thirty years, mingling with people and developing personal, face-to-face relationships. The world has never been the same since.

It is, truly, the world's greatest love story. A story not only told and written about, but the greatest ever *seen.*

See also: John 1:18; Ephesians 2:4–5; 1 John 1:1–3

THE UNVEILING

When John heard in prison what Christ was doing, he sent his disciples to ask him, "Are you the one who was to come, or should we expect someone else?"

MATTHEW 11:2–3

As if to prepare for his grand appearance on Planet Earth, which you read about yesterday, God arranged various sneak previews over several thousand years.

Early on, he appeared incognito—as an angel to Jacob, for example. But it was like trying to recognize somebody in a Halloween costume, and Jacob wouldn't have known who it was had not God finally just told him.

Later, with Moses, God used the disguise of a dust cloud and burning bush. Moses didn't mind the special effects and spoke with God "as a man speaks with his friend," but he eventually asked God to unveil himself. Even then, God only let him see his back, not his face.

It may have appeared that God had a case of stage fright and wouldn't come out of the dressing room. But I believe he was warming people up for the time he would put himself on public display; for the time people could walk right up and talk to him, or ask him any kind of stump-God question they could think of.

When that moment came, however, most people still didn't recognize him. One of Jesus' favorite questions to ask his disciples was, "Who do people say that I am?" I suspect he roared to hear some of their answers.

People were so mixed up that some thought John the Baptist was Christ and Christ was John the Baptist. Poor Johnny B.—who was supposed to "Make straight the way for the Lord"—was as befuddled as anybody and wasn't sure who he was fronting for. Through go-betweens, he finally just asked: "Are you the one who was to come, or should we expect someone else?"

You'd think the religious leaders would have had some inkling as to who Jesus was, but they charged him with capital crimes *against* God. And when he was on trial for his life and needed all the friends he could get, his own disciples scattered.

Still, a few did recognize him. And to them God gave the right to be his body—through which he could reveal himself and continue providing glimpses of heaven on earth.

See also: Genesis 32:22–32; Exodus 3:1–6; 33:12–23

▪▪ RUNAWAY

The son said to him, "Father, I have sinned against heaven and against you. I am no longer worthy to be called your son." But the father said to his servants, "Quick! Bring the best robe and put it on him. Put a ring on his finger and sandals on his feet. Bring the fattened calf and kill it. Let's have a feast and celebrate. For this son of mine was dead and is alive again; he was lost and is found."

LUKE 15:21–24

As far back as Danny could remember, he'd been prepped to follow in his father's footsteps and take over the family's insurance business. But at seventeen he was tired of the china-and-crystal lifestyle he'd grown up with, so he cashed in the savings bonds his parents had given him and, "over his father's dead body," hopped a train for Hollywood.

Though he stayed in a dingy motel and ate only once a day at the corner greasy spoon, Danny's money was gone in four months. A couple of young thugs he'd met on the street offered him a corner in their living room along with a candy jar of drugs, and the next two weeks were a constant high. Then they got him making cocaine drops, which seemed like no big deal until his "friends" accused him of skimming money, beat the bejeebers out of him, and left him bleeding in the gutter.

When the train whistles finally quit blasting in Danny's head, he wandered around an area of Tinseltown crowded with neon Budweiser signs and blinking marquees of raunchy theaters. He asked about getting work at the bars and strip joints—anything to make a little money. But one look at his split lip and broken nose, and he was shooed away.

Without a dime to his name, Danny finally did the only thing he could think of. He called home—collect. His father, overjoyed to hear his voice, promptly wired him money. The next morning when Danny stepped off the plane in his dirty, blood-stained clothes, his father was there at the gate with open arms and tears in his eyes. Danny walked into his father's embrace, and for the first time in a very long time felt safe and warm and loved.

"We thought you were lost . . . forever," his father said, his tears brimming over.

"I thought I was lost, too," Danny finally said. "I've made a fool out of myself and have blown everything. But I'm home now if you'll take me; if you'll forgive me."

His father flashed a million-watt smile and, in a voice that seemed to come straight from heaven, said, "The family is waiting, son. Welcome home."

See also: Isaiah 1:18; Matthew 6:14–15; 1 John 1:8–9

■■ TUG-OF-WAR

My Presence will go with you, and I will give you rest.

EXODUS 33:14

There are times when, looking back, I'd give anything for the chance to relive my high school years . . . but with the benefit of hindsight. That's not possible, I know. To paraphrase Longfellow, high school comes but once in a lifetime.

For me, high school was runaway hormones, acne, secret notes, student council, smelly gym socks, swimming pools, acne, a late-model Chevy, tennis courts, minimum-wage jobs, acne, and first loves. Did I say anything about acne? It was the absolute best, absolute worst, absolute most confusing of times.

A large part of my confusion had to do with figuring out who I was. If you asked people who knew me, they'd have said I was almost perfect. I was the student body president, newspaper editor, and letterman in tennis and swimming. I got mostly A's, had decent looks, came from a good home, and got along with most of my teachers. I suppose I was the person that others wanted to be. But I didn't want to be me.

I was tired of the words "responsibility" and "opportunity." All I wanted was the chance to be a normal kid who got into trouble just often enough to have fun. I wanted to take a break from being a leader and follow for a while. So I started doing things I normally wouldn't have done but thought I should do to fit in. For starters, I discovered what a hangover was.

However, I didn't enjoy waking up with train whistles blowing in my head or not being able to look myself square in the eye in the mirror. And I didn't enjoy the confusion of trying to be Mr. America on school days and Mr. Party Hearty on weekends. I felt torn in two, as though I was the object of a massive tug-of-war and the ref had just yelled, "Pull!"

About that time I met Becky. She was a leader type, but she knew how to have fun—without the headaches. Most of all, she had a sense of peace about her that I didn't share. One day she invited me to a Christian youth rally and there I discovered the source of her peace: the Prince of Peace. And I heard his two-thousand-year-old beckon, which changed my life: "Come to me, all you who are weary and burdened, and I will give you rest" (Matthew 11:28).

It was an outrageous, audacious claim. Yet all these years later, those words have the same power as when they were first spoken. "Come to me."

Are you listening?

See also: Joshua 24:15; Isaiah 40:28–31; Revelation 3:20

■■ EXPERIENCED ONLY

> *"Not by might nor by power, but by my Spirit,"* says the Lord Almighty.
>
> ZECHARIAH 4:6

Looking for a job, Rebecca opened the Sunday paper and flipped through the want ads. The little boxes shouted at her:

Experienced Only! Even entry-level jobs seemed to require a Ph.D. or five years of prior experience.

Sometimes it may seem like the world is conspiring against you. Everywhere you turn, you are not old enough, smart enough, talented enough, experienced enough. At a time when you feel very adult and deal regularly with adult-sized concerns, you are constantly belittled and reminded of your youth.

It may help to know that some of the biggest biblical big shots faced similar struggles. Take Timothy, for example. A very close friend of Paul's, he was young enough that the apostle called him son and others ridiculed him about his age. Paul tried to console him by writing, "Don't let anyone look down on you because you are young, but set an example for the believers in speech, in life, in love, in faith and in purity." In other words, *physical* maturity matters less than *spiritual* maturity ... regardless of the world's standards.

That's the same message conveyed in the verses above to Zerubbabel. He was a bit player compared to leading man King Solomon. But God seems to enjoy apparent mismatches, and chose the young, ninety-eight-pound weakling to rebuild his temple. To ease Zerubbabel's feelings of insecurity, the Lord assured him that he was not working alone. The job would get done, he said, "Not by might nor by power, but by my Spirit."

In another instance, Jeremiah complained he wasn't old enough to do what God had in mind for him. But he was promptly reminded by the Lord, "Do not say, 'I am only a child.' ... for I am with you."

Then as now, God can use your life in extraordinary ways if you trust him in very ordinary ways. Forget about age and talent and limitations. Put aside your feelings of insecurity and inexperience.

The Lord has big-time plans for those who care about their stature in God's eyes more than their appearance in man's eyes.

See also: Jeremiah 1:4–10; 1 Timothy 4:12

▪▪ MEMORY CHALLENGE

I have hidden your word in my heart that I might not sin against you.

PSALM 119:11

As you read yesterday, our limitations are not liabilities to God. He recruits the young and inexperienced. There is no handicap that hinders our Lord.

No passage in Scripture explains that as well as the verses below, written by Paul. Read them over and over. And if you are up to a big challenge, commit the passage to memory.

It might help to know that actors memorize dozens of pages for a single stage performance. And some people have memorized entire books of the Bible. Even if you can't remember your social security number and struggle to recall your parents' birthdays, work at the following passage. It will take some time to get it down. But just what are you doing this week that's more important?

Take a good look, friends, at who you were when you got called into this life. I don't see many of "the brightest and the best" among you, not many influential, not many from high-society families. Isn't it obvious that God deliberately chose men and women that the culture overlooks and exploits and abuses, chose these "nobodies" to expose the hollow pretensions of the "somebodies"? That makes it quite clear that none of you can get by with blowing your own horn before God. Everything that we have—right thinking and right living, a clean slate and a fresh start—comes from God by way of Jesus Christ. That's why we have the saying, "If you're going to blow a horn, blow a trumpet for God" (1 Corinthians 1:26–31 The Message).

See also: Deuteronomy 6:6–9; Luke 18:27; James 2:1–9

POINTS TO PONDER – YOUTH

Remember your Creator in the days of your youth, before the days of trouble come and the years approach when you will say, "I find no pleasure in them."

ECCLESIASTES 12:1

Youth is preeminently the forming, fixing period, the spring season of disposition and habit; and it is during this season, more than any other, that the character assumes its permanent shape and color, and the young are wont to take their course for time and for eternity.

JOEL HAWES

The first sign of maturity is the discovery that the volume knob also turns to the left.

"SMILE" ZINGERS, CHICAGO TRIBUNE

Almost everything that is great has been done by youth.

BENJAMIN DISRAELI

Young people will respond if the challenge is tough enough and hard enough. Youth wants a master and a controller. Young people were built for God, and without God as the center of their lives they become frustrated and confused, desperately grasping for and searching for security.

BILLY GRAHAM

The sins of youth are paid for in old age.

LATIN PROVERB

The youth of a nation are the trustees of posterity.

BENJAMIN DISRAELI

A youth becomes an adult when he realizes he has a right not only to be right but also to be wrong.

THOMAS SZASZ

I, for one, hope that youth will again revolt and again demoralize the deadweight of conformity that now lies upon us.

HOWARD MUMFORD JONES

Experience is a wonderful thing; it enables you to recognize a mistake every time you repeat it.

ASSOCIATED PRESS NEWS SERVICE

For God's sake, give me the young man who has brains enough to make a fool of himself.

ROBERT LOUIS STEVENSON

It is better to be a young june bug than an old bird of paradise.

MARK TWAIN

There is a feeling of eternity in youth.

WILLIAM HAZLITT

It is not possible for civilization to flow backwards while there is youth in the world.

HELEN KELLER

At almost every step in life we meet with young men from whom we anticipate wonderful things, but of whom, after careful inquiry, we never hear another word. Like certain chintzes, calicoes, and ginghams, they show finely on their first newness, but cannot stand the sun and rain, and assume a very sober aspect after washing day.

NATHANIEL HAWTHORNE

Youth comes but once in a lifetime.

HENRY WADSWORTH LONGFELLOW

See also: Psalm 25:7; Ecclesiastes 11:9; 1 Timothy 4:12

WEEK

42

■ PERSONAL DELIVERY

In the beginning was the Word, and the Word was with God, and the Word was God. He was with God in the beginning. Through him all things were made; without him nothing was made that has been made. . . . The Word became flesh and lived for a while among us. We have seen his glory, the glory of the one and only Son, who came from the Father, full of grace and truth.

JOHN 1:1–3, 14

I once worked for a company headed by a man who liked his privacy. As the founder, he didn't mingle with the employees, chat in the cafeteria, or wander the hallways. He remained secluded in his office behind closed doors.

When I was first hired, I was told by a couple of other employees that the founder didn't really exist.

"The silhouette you see through his lighted office at night is just a dummy, a mannequin." I knew they were putting me on, of course. I'd received a "welcome aboard" memo from him upon my hiring. But they shrugged it off.

"Dorothy thought the Wizard of Oz was real, too," they said.

Finally, three weeks after joining the company, I met the man face-to-face. I even shook his hand. The occasion? He had something important to tell me that he wanted to convey personally. What he had to say required my immediate attention. So we sat in my office talking for quite some time.

God, too, was something of a mystery. As you might expect of the world's founder, he more or less kept to himself. As you also might expect, many people doubted his existence because he seldom showed his face. He didn't mingle like one of the boys.

But then one day he threw the doors of heaven open wide and visited Planet Earth. Once and for all, the sound barrier was broken as the Word—the sum of all that God wanted to communicate—became flesh.

What he had to say could only be conveyed personally, and he did so in the person of Jesus. Just as God spoke creation into existence in Genesis 1, Jesus spoke salvation into existence. Forgiveness and freedom, judgment and joy, grace and love—it all became real. During his time on earth, he communicated his salvation message through leisurely conversation, intimate personal relationships, and, ultimately, his sacrificial death.

We don't casually walk away from his words. They require our personal attention. Our response to his message marks the difference between life and death.

See also: Galatians 4:4–5; 1 Timothy 3:16; Hebrews 2:14–15

■■ BIT PLAYERS

The race is not to the swift or the battle to the strong.

ECCLESIASTES 9:11

When I go to the movie theater, I am generally one of the last out the door. The clean-up crews are already scraping gum, swabbing spilled Cokes, and sweeping popcorn off the floors as I sit and watch the last of the credits roll across the screen.

For most people, the movie ends when the couple kiss and walk off together into the sunset. But for me it's not over until I've seen the bit players credited: the "Screaming Lady" whose only line was a shriek when "Hoodlum #3" stole her purse, or the "Postman" whose five-second role consisted of being treed by a dog.

By staying until the projector shuts off, I make a social statement that is so subtle I am probably the only one who realizes I am making a social statement. Nevertheless, it's my way of saying there's no such thing as bit players—*everybody* is important.

That's the opposite of the world's view. The way you generally hear and see things, the only people who really matter are those with all of the looks and abilities, those who win gold medals and get elected, those who have large bank accounts and can remember punch lines. As for the rest, well . . . they are relegated to the background.

Every opportunity he got, Jesus thumbed his nose at those standards. You can see that in who he picked as his inner circle: not men who'd earned advanced theological degrees, but backwater lugs who could gut fish in three seconds flat. He kept his distance from the white-collar crowd, preferring instead the company of drunks, cheats, and assorted lowlifes.

When Christ wanted to demonstrate the power of God he healed the street-corner bum, and when he wanted to illustrate the grace of God he forgave the woman who'd warmed the bed of someone other than her husband. The poor, the meek, the runny-nosed kids—theirs is the kingdom of God, Christ said. As for those with Swiss bank accounts and MBA's from Harvard, they stand as much chance of making it through the pearly gates as a double-humped camel does of passing through the eye of a needle.

In the end, bit players received star treatment from Christ. And he challenges us to follow his lead by feeding the hungry, giving water to the thirsty and clothes to the poor, befriending strangers, nursing the sick, and even visiting the imprisoned.

It's not really a choice, but a command. And the extent to which you obey probably says more about you and your Christianity than anything else.

See also: Matthew 5:3–10; 19:13–14, 24; 25:31–46

▮▮ LACK OF TRUST

Do not lie. Do not deceive one another.

LEVITICUS 19:11

Terri was a good friend through high school, but the relationship never held much promise because I never knew exactly how much I could trust her. All too often I caught her lying through her teeth.

Hers were not big, black, soap-opera lies, but little white ones—spread lavishly around whenever she needed to smooth things over or get out of a squeeze.

When a guy she didn't care about asked her out, she concocted some explanation about her parents having grounded her or long-lost relatives flying in to visit that particular night. If he phoned her at home, she stepped outside for a moment … and had her kid sister say she wasn't home. It was better to fib a little than crush a guy's ego, she reasoned.

What she didn't realize was that it hurt the guy more to be strung along with lame excuses than simply to be told from the outset she wasn't interested. The naked truth always hurts less than a lie in fancy clothes. But she never learned that.

When she blew an exam, Terri thought nothing of telling the teacher her grandmother had died and asking her to disregard the grade. Or when she was pulled over for speeding, she told the cop without flinching that her same grandmother was in an accident, and asked for a police escort to the hospital.

In a nutshell, truth wasn't an absolute standard for Terri, but more of an adjustable justification she used when convenient. As such, her word was worth about as much as a used movie ticket.

Ultimately, she developed a reputation for being superficial and insincere, and I always found myself second-guessing her. When she gushed praise, I questioned her motives. When she expressed absolute certainty about something, I figured she was merely trying to convince herself.

The sad thing about Terri was that she thought her white lies hurt nobody. But they did. And they hurt one person more than anybody else: Terri. She lost her integrity over these little matters, and her reputation never quite recovered.

See also: John 1:17; Ephesians 4:25

■■ WEEDS OF DECEIT

> *Lord, who may dwell in your sanctuary? Who may live on your holy hill? He whose walk is blameless and who does what is righteous, who speaks the truth from his heart.*
>
> PSALM 15:1–2

The first recorded sin in the New Testament church was a lie (Acts 5:1–11). It happened when a man named Ananias sold a piece of property and, with his wife's full knowledge, pocketed some of the proceeds for a rainy day. The rest he donated to the church.

So far, so good. The problem is, he bragged around that he'd given the whole wad to charity.

When it came to matters of the heart, the apostle Peter was more sensitive than a lie detector. And as a former fisherman, he could smell a fish story a mile away. Something about Ananias's tale of largesse didn't ring true, so he eyeballed the church chiseler, told him he had not lied to man but to God, and then stepped back as Ananias dropped dead at his feet.

The second recorded sin was also a lie, courtesy of Ananias's wife, Sapphira. She showed up at church about three hours later, unaware she was a widow. Peter asked whether the amount Ananias donated represented the full proceeds of their real estate deal.

"Yes," Sapphira said, without batting an eye, "that is the price."

It was, of course, the couple's prerogative to hold money back. Since the property was theirs, they could have banked all of the proceeds and taken early retirement. They chose instead to give a big chunk of it to the poor box, and tell an even bigger lie. That was their mistake: they were pious frauds. And if the newborn Christian church was to prosper and grow, the weeds of deceit had to be pulled. Peter went right for the root.

"How could you agree to test the Spirit of the Lord?" he asked. "Look! The feet of the men who buried your husband are at the door, and they will carry you out also." And then Peter again took a step back as Sapphira, like her deceased mate, did a face plant at his feet.

"Lying to God is like sawing the branch you're sitting on," Frederick Buechner has written. "The better you do it, the harder you fall."

See also: Joshua 7:16–26; Psalm 73:27

■ MATTERS OF CONSCIENCE

Do not lie to each other, since you have taken off your old self with its practices and have put on the new self, which is being renewed in knowledge in the image of its Creator.

COLOSSIANS 3:9–10

As you might expect, the young Christian community in Jerusalem was scared stiff by the sudden deaths of Ananias and Sapphira, whom you read about yesterday. As Luke tells it in Acts 5, "Great fear seized the whole church and all who heard about these events." A few verses later he adds, "No one else dared join them, even though they were highly regarded by the people." That is, nobody would go near the church for fear God would get literal about the wages of sin being death.

I suppose there would be a lot fewer people in church today if God punished sin by triggering an occasional heart attack in the middle of the service. Imagine if every now and then your pastor asked people to raise their hands if they'd cheated on their income tax or slept around outside of marriage. And imagine if those people who didn't raise their hands, but should have, suddenly gave a little whimper and slumped to the floor, dead. No doubt people would start taking their conscience a little more seriously.

In thinking about this, I recall a story I once read about the government's "Conscience Fund." The special account, which now totals more than several million dollars, was set up in 1813 for people like the woman who couldn't sleep at night because she'd reused an uncanceled stamp. This nagged at her periodically until she sent two stamps to the United States Treasury, along with a letter explaining what she had done. Then there's the individual who contributed $3,485 to make up for what he figured his laziness cost the government while he worked at a Veterans' Administration hospital.

I am ashamed to say it, but the "small wrongs" these people couldn't live with are not that different from the ones I often ignore or rationalize. Like Ananias and Sapphira, I sometimes fool myself into thinking that only the "big" transgressions matter and that true Christianity can be separated from following Christ's righteous pattern of life in very literal, everyday ways.

See also: Zechariah 8:16–17; Acts 24:16

■■ WHAT THE WORLD NEEDS

Blessed is the man who does not walk in the counsel of the wicked or stand in the way of sinners or sit in the seat of mockers. But his delight is in the law of the Lord, and on his law he meditates day and night. He is like a tree planted by streams of water, which yields its fruit in season and whose leaf does not wither. Whatever he does prospers.

PSALM 1:1–3

The following words, written more than a century ago by Josiah Gilbert Holland, still seem appropriate today. No doubt they'll continue to be quoted one hundred years from now:

The world needs young men and women who cannot be bought; whose word is their bond; who put character above wealth; who possess opinions and a will; who are larger than their vocations; who do not hesitate to take chances.

The world needs young men and women who will not lose their individuality in a crowd; who will be as honest in small things as in great things; who will make no compromise with wrong; whose ambitions are not confined to their own selfish desires.

The world needs young men and women who will not say they do it because everybody else does it; who are true to their friends through good report and evil report, in adversity as well as in prosperity; who do not believe that shrewdness, cunning, and hard-headedness are the best qualities for winning; who are not ashamed or afraid to stand for the truth when it is unpopular.

The world needs young men and women who say no with emphasis, though all the rest of the world says yes.

See also: Psalm 34:19–22; 37

■■ POINTS TO PONDER – CHARACTER

A good name is more desirable than great riches.

PROVERBS 22:1

Character is what you are in the dark.

DWIGHT L. MOODY

Merely going to church doesn't make you a Christian any more than going to a garage makes you an automobile.

BILLY SUNDAY

Reputation is what folks think you are. Personality is what you seem to be. Character is what you really are.

ALFRED ARMAND MONTAPERT

There is no such thing as a "self-made" man. We are made up of thousands of others. Everyone who has ever done a kind deed for us or spoken one word of encouragement to us, has entered into the make-up of our character and of our thoughts, as well as our success.

GEORGE MATTHEW ADAMS

If your absence doesn't make any difference, your presence won't either.

ANONYMOUS

Character is not made in a crisis—it is only exhibited.

ROBERT FREEMAN

It is one thing to go through a crisis grandly, but another thing to go through every day glorifying God when there is no witness, no limelight, no one paying the remotest attention to us.

OSWALD CHAMBERS

A good name, like good will, is got by many actions, and lost by one.

LORD JEFFREY

The reputation of a man is like his shadow: gigantic when it precedes him, and pygmy in its proportions when it follows.

ALEXANDRE DE TALLEYRAND-PERIGORD

The person who talks most of his own virtue is often the least virtuous.

JAWAHARLAL NEHRU

What people say behind your back is your standing in the community.

ED HOWE

When God measures a man, he puts the tape around the heart, not around the head.

ANONYMOUS

I have never felt that football built character. That is done by parents and church. You give us a boy with character and we will give you back a man. You give us a character—and we will give him right back to you.

JOHN MCKAY

A man is what he thinks about all day long.

RALPH WALDO EMERSON

The character of Jesus has not only been the highest pattern of virtue, but the strongest incentive to its practice, and has exerted so deep an influence that it may be truly said that the simple record of his three short years of active life has done more to regenerate and soften mankind than all the disquisitions of philosophers and the exhortations of moralists.

WILLIAM LECKY

See also: Acts 17:11; Romans 5:3–5; 1 Corinthians 15:33–34

▪▪ LOOKING AROUND

Do not merely listen to the word, and so deceive yourselves. Do what it says. Anyone who listens to the word but does not do what it says is like a man who looks at his face in a mirror and, after looking at himself, goes away and immediately forgets what he looks like. But the man who looks intently into the perfect law that gives freedom, and continues to do this, not forgetting what he has heard, but doing it – he will be blessed in what he does.

JAMES 1:22–25

Irene didn't have to look far to see some pretty pathetic examples of Christianity in action. For starters, there was the evening news broadcasts about the scandals involving prominent Christians. Closer to home, the wife of a church leader left her husband – not for another man, which would have been bad enough, but for another woman. On the school front, a group of teens who chirped about their Christianity maintained a clique that was pure bigotry toward outsiders. Not to mention Mr. Football, who acted like Jesus, Jr., during the week, but lived like the devil come Friday night.

Irene pointed out these phony Christians as a reason for not believing in Christ. I had to admit, she made a good case. But I also explained that these hypocrites did more to *prove* rather than disprove the existence of God.

To explain, I told her I'd started piano lessons a couple of weeks earlier. Though I'd never played before, my goal was to surprise my fiancée, who was a piano whiz, by memorizing just one song by Mozart. My efforts were pretty dismal, however, and the end result was not music. When I'd bang on the keyboard, dogs barked.

My awful example didn't mean everybody was equally bad at imitating Mozart. Nor did it mean others should think less of Mozart because of me, or doubt Mozart's existence. The fact that so many people, including lugs like myself, were trying to imitate his music indicates his true greatness.

A similar argument can be made about Jesus Christ. He has many imitators – some good, others bad. The fact that people don't imitate him perfectly is, of course, no reflection on him. Rather, as François de la Rochefoucauld has said, it is "the homage that vice pays to virtue."

In other words, bad people will always try acting like saints, which is a credit to Christ, not a detraction.

See also: Psalm 119:9–16; Matthew 7:17–23; Romans 2:21–24; 2 Corinthians 5:17–20

▞ "FINE."

Encourage one another daily, as long as it is called Today, so that none of you may be hardened by sin's deceitfulness.

HEBREWS 3:13

It was easy to feel good about Sharon. All we ever did was go to movies, concerts, and football games. We scrambled from one date to another, too busy to spend much time talking or listening to each other about deeper things. When our dating relationship fizzled, I didn't feel I had ever really known her.

Shortly after we broke up she began dating somebody else. That romance soured before long, and I lost track of her for several months. When we eventually bumped into each other again, I asked how she was.

"Fine," she said, forcing a smile.

However, she wasn't fine. Another friend told me Sharon hadn't been around because she'd been fooling with razor blades, wondering how much she would bleed if she slashed her wrists. She experimented with a small cut and found that even a slight wound bled a lot. That scared her, so she swallowed a bottle of colored pills instead. Thankfully, her parents found her in time and called an ambulance.

I couldn't figure out why Sharon would do something that stupid. She was a Christian and always seemed to have everything under control. But it was obvious I only knew the shell—the always-smiling, even-tempered, everything's-fine Sharon. On the inside she was a bloody mess.

The more I thought about her, the more I wondered about my other friends. None of us talked about our inner needs, doubts, or failings, so I naively assumed nobody had any. Was Sharon an exception, or were others struggling amidst their own private hell? If so, who? Who else needed my honest love and encouragement?

I didn't really know, so I had to suppose the answer was *everybody*. And then I asked God to help me be more caring in my friendships, indiscriminate in my love, and liberal in my compassion.

See also: Hebrews 10:24–25; 1 John 3:18

∷ THE INNER CHAMBER

A man of many companions may come to ruin, but there is a friend who sticks closer than a brother.

PROVERBS 18:24

When it comes right down to it, most of us make pretty lousy friends. That probably has a lot to do with our desire for others to think we're better than we are.

Most of us want to be liked, but think nobody in their right mind would give us the time of day if they knew what we were really like. And so we keep most people at arm's length. That way they see just enough of us to think we're wonderful. And we don't risk them breaking through our high-gloss facade and bursting into that inner chamber where we sometimes think, feel, and act awfully desperate, unfriendly, and lonely.

Think about how conversations have gone with your friends during the past week. All too often they are shallow and cursory—the equivalent of caveman grunts:

"Dude!"

"Hey!"

"How's it going?"

"Not bad."

"Gotta blitz."

"Cool."

"Later."

As discussed yesterday, the end result of surface relationships is that we're appalled when someone like Sharon stumbles and behaves like an honest-to-goodness, imperfect human being. We somehow expect Christians to be always calm and emotionally controlled.

Unfortunately, we forget that each of us—you, me, your mom and dad, the new kid in town, your pastor—is in desperate, daily need of a Savior . . . not to mention a good, old-fashioned friend to encourage us, talk about things that matter, help build our faith, and even explore the dark side of our souls.

Try making the first move. Ask God to help you select another mature individual with whom you can begin discussing your own areas of vulnerability. It will take time to develop this kind of close personal relationship. But it's a lot faster than waiting for somebody else to let down their guard first. In the latter case, the unfortunate reality is you'll likely be waiting the rest of your life.

See also: Proverbs 27:10; Romans 12:9–10

▪▪ LOOKING FOR LOVE

He has rescued us from the dominion of darkness and brought us into the kingdom of the Son he loves, in whom we have redemption, the forgiveness of sins.

COLOSSIANS 1:13–14

It was summertime and the living was easy. As gorgeous weather raged outside, Bill Crawford was working on his second plate of ribs. Then he felt a tug on his sleeve and looked down at a four-year-old girl he'd never seen before. She was wearing a leopard-print bikini, and her arms were raised to be picked up.

He shook his head. "Not now, I'm eating," he said.

She tried the same thing with the other eighteen partygoers, but everybody was covered with barbecue sauce and wouldn't hold her.

A few minutes later somebody screamed. A man raced outside and dove into the pool. When he surfaced, he held the limp body of the little girl in his arms. Somebody started mouth-to-mouth, but she was dead before the ambulance arrived.

"She did the same thing last week," somebody whispered as they carried away her body.

"And twice the week before that," another said quietly.

Before long, Bill had pieced together the story. She was illegitimate and unloved, and a couple of months earlier she'd accidentally fallen into the pool. Upon being rescued, she'd won instant love and attention which she never experienced at home. So she tried the trick three more times in subsequent weeks, and it always worked.

On the day of the barbecue, when nobody picked her up, she resorted to the only sure way she knew to capture attention. Unfortunately, this time it didn't work.

Bill couldn't think of the girl without concluding she wasn't alone. Many other people he knew were desperate for love and acceptance. Perhaps they didn't throw themselves into backyard pools, but they did plunge into drugs, alcohol, sex—anything that would give them the feeling of belonging. But the very thing they saw as the solution eventually destroyed them.

"It wasn't the swimming pool that provided that little girl with love and acceptance," Bill said, looking back on the tragedy. "It was the person who jumped in and saved her from it."

I believe that's the great thing about Christianity. Jesus Christ jumped into the world to save us from drowning. He wants to offer us the love and care and feelings we're searching for.

"Unlike those of us at the party," he added, "Jesus won't ignore or turn away anyone."

See also: Luke 19:10; Romans 7:24–25; 1 Timothy 1:15

:: SOUNDS OF SILENCE

Be still before the Lord, all mankind.

ZECHARIAH 2:13

In the middle of the Indiana woods sits a tiny hut constructed of rubble scrounged from nearby building sites. Resembling a toolshed more than anything habitable, it represents the major turning point in the life of John Michael Talbot, a born-again, guitar-playing Franciscan monk who called the shack "home" for one bone-numbing winter after everything in his life fell apart. Alone, in solitude, he sought God.

At first he had romantic thoughts about living as a hermit and being "spiritual," but he was cured of that the first day his beard froze.

"I spent a good part of the morning just trying to get a flame kindled," he told me. "And most of the rest of the day revolved around chopping wood, nursing fires, praying, and watching squirrels."

But after you've seen a squirrel do everything a squirrel does, what else is there? Before long he began to experience good, basic boredom. And he discovered the true meaning of loneliness.

"I'd read the Scriptures and think, 'I've read this before. I don't need to read it again.' But it was during these basic, boring days that I experienced a deeper sense of just *being*. And in my silence I heard God's most profound words."

John Michael admitted that people aren't going to rush out and build Daniel Boone huts in the woods just to experience some spiritual dimension of silence. But he also said they don't have to. They can easily experience it where they are.

"There's always things that compete with that stillness," he said. "It can be a stereo or TV. The key is not necessarily to build a hermitage. It may start with discovering how to use a stereo and TV properly, or learning how to turn them off. It may be taking a walk around the neighborhood, looking and listening, contemplating what you see in light of God. It might be to spend some time near a creek or park, learning how God communicates through silence. 'It's taking time to be still.'"

See also: Psalm 23:1–3; 37:7; Zephaniah 3:17

■■ SOLITARY CONFINEMENT

My soul is downcast within me. Yet this I call to mind and therefore I have hope: Because of the Lord's great love we are not consumed, for his compassions never fail. They are new every morning; great is your faithfulness. I say to myself, "The Lord is my portion; therefore I will wait for him." The Lord is good to those whose hope is in him, to the one who seeks him; it is good to wait quietly for the salvation of the Lord.

LAMENTATIONS 3:20–26

Being alone can be the worst feeling in the world. It's watching everybody else pair off at the party while you keep the corner company. It's trying to figure out how you'd respond if your parents ever said they loved you. It's breaking up and suddenly spending weekends in the solitary confinement of your room.

Being alone is running for the phone every time it rings, hoping that just once somebody will ask for you. It's hearing yourself referred to over the loudspeakers: "Fumble, number thirty-two." It's looking down into the casket of a friend or relative. It's being stranded on the freeway at eleven o'clock at night. It's being pregnant and unmarried.

Being alone is looking in the mirror, trying to imagine yourself looking like anybody but yourself. It's watching the taillights of your best friend's car as her family moves two thousand miles away. It's telling a door-to-door salesman about your life because nobody else seems to care.

Being alone forces you to confront yourself. It loosens your grip on all surroundings and props, and temporarily frees you from things you generally rely on or deem important.

Being alone drives you to examine what really matters. It forces your values and fears and insecurities out of the shadows and into the light, enabling you to see things about yourself and others that you might not otherwise get to know. For example, why do your parents find it so hard to express love? Maybe they never really learned how. Maybe they need you to take the first step.

As such, being alone is an *opportunity* — an opportunity to listen to yourself and to God, to let the fog in your life lift and the mud settle, to get your bearings and again draw near to God.

The opportunities are pretty common; they're before you every day. It's the people who recognize and know how to seize them that are rare.

See also: Psalm 68:5–6; Luke 5:16

■ POINTS TO PONDER –
LONELINESS

> *Where can I go from your Spirit? Where can I flee from your presence? If I go up to the heavens, you are there; if I make my bed in the depths, you are there. If I rise on the wings of the dawn, if I settle on the far side of the sea, even there your hand will guide me, your right hand will hold me fast.*
>
> PSALM 139:7–10

The soul hardly ever realizes it, but whether he is a believer or not, his loneliness is really a homesickness for God.

HUBERT VAN ZELLER

If you were not strangers here, the hounds of the world would not bark at you.

SAMUEL RUTHERFORD

The whole conviction of my life now rests upon the belief that loneliness, far from being a rare and curious phenomenon, peculiar to myself and to a few other solitary men, is the central and inevitable fact of human existence.

THOMAS WOLFE

The deepest need of man is the need to overcome his separateness, to leave the prison of his aloneness.

ERICH FROMM

It is easy in the world to live after the world's opinions; it is easy in solitude to live after your own; but the great man is he who in the midst of the crowd keeps with perfect sweetness the independence of solitude.

RALPH WALDO EMERSON

Loneliness is the first thing which God's eye nam'd not good.

JOHN MILTON

The mission of Jesus cannot be defined without speaking of man being lost.

HENRI BLOCHER

In cities no one is quiet but many are lonely; in the country, people are quiet but few are lonely.

GEOFFREY FRANCIS FISHER

Solitude is essential to man. All men come into this world alone and leave it alone.

THOMAS DE QUINCEY

The heart is a lonely hunter that hunts on a lonely hill.

WILLIAM SHARP

The surest cure for vanity is loneliness.

THOMAS WOLFE

Man's sin problem is never cured until his alienation from God is overcome, until the rebellion of the human against the divine is ended, until God and man are brought back together.

MYRON S. AUGSBURGER

I was never less alone than when by myself.

EDWARD GIBBON

Shakespeare, Leonardo da Vinci, Benjamin Franklin, and Lincoln ... were not afraid of being lonely because they knew that was when the creative mood in them would work.

CARL SANDBURG

The more affluent a society is, the more pronounced is the sense of ultimate emptiness and alienation on the part of its members.

BILLY GRAHAM

Language has created the word loneliness to express the pain of being alone, and the word solitude to express the glory of being alone.

PAUL TILLICH

See also: Joshua 1:5–9; Psalm 25:16–18

WEEK

44

■■ SOLEMN VOWS

*As a bridegroom rejoices over his bride, so will
your God rejoice over you.*

ISAIAH 62:5

Behind me rose the church altar. Before me sat a crowd of
three hundred friends and relatives. Beside me stood the young
woman, gowned in white and bearing a wisp of a smile, who would
soon be my wife. But first there was the matter of vows. Slowly, and
with a somewhat trembling voice, I turned to Julie and said:

"I take thee, Julie, to be my lawfully wedded wife, to have and
to hold from this day forward; for better, for worse; for richer, for poorer;
in sickness and in heath; to love and to cherish, till death us do part."

My voice wasn't shaking because of the crowd, but because
I was unsure of what the future held. At twenty-one I was making a
vow of love that would bridge the bad times, the lean times, the ill
times until we were parted by death—and only by death.

There was no guarantee our lives would be rosy and bright.
That was the risk. Nevertheless, I vowed to love her, *no matter what.*
I did it with a fair share of nervousness, yes; but a bigger share, by
far, of unadorned, stand-up-and-holler enthusiasm.

As soon as the words were out of my mouth, however, the
most amazing thing happened. Julie vowed the exact same thing!
She pledged her very life—to *me!*

As I look back on that very special day, I can't help but think
how similar my marriage vows were to my commitment to Christ.
When I made that decision at seventeen, I was nervous then, too. I
didn't know what lay ahead. And there were risks. But I vowed to love
God with all my heart, with all my mind, and with all my soul—*no
matter what.* Likewise, God pledged to accept me unconditionally,
for better, for worse, for richer, for poorer, in sickness and in health.

The difference, of course, is that my bond with God lasts
forever. It's not a case of "until death us do part." That's just when
things start looking up—the point I finally meet the bridegroom
face-to-face.

See also: Matthew 25:1–10; Revelation 21

INSIDE OUT

God does not judge by external appearance.

GALATIANS 2:6

Gregg and Shelly were probably the happiest couple I ever knew. They became friends through church in their junior years, and their relationship grew to be "more than friends" over the summer when they shared a biology class.

Shelly was Miss Personality and had cover-girl looks to match. She was the kind of person you could talk to for five minutes and feel like you'd known her all your life. She oozed enthusiasm and talked with exclamation points. As for Gregg, he was no slouch in the personality department, though he tended to have a quieter disposition than Shelly and a subtler sense of humor. But when it came to looks, he was far from being the major, all-American stud that Shelly normally hung around with. On the surface at least, they were a clear mismatch.

However, Shelly was enormously happy in Gregg's company and didn't give a second thought to his bird legs or his honk of a nose or anything else. Nor did she think twice about the guys she stopped dead in their tracks whenever she passed. For her, looks were superficial. Though her friends sometimes commented about Gregg's appearance, she let it be known that she loved and respected him for who he was on the inside. That is, for his integrity, his compassion, the way he encouraged her when she was down, and his deep Christian roots. "As for the legs," she'd say, "I think they're kind of cute."

In the Bible, surface appearance doesn't count for much. Samuel was reminded of that when he went to anoint a new king over Israel. Samuel wanted a Sylvester Stallone; God wanted David.

"Do not consider his appearance or his height," the Lord said to Samuel. "The Lord does not look at the things man looks at. Man looks at the outward appearance, but the Lord looks at the heart."

It's a classic message—one well worth remembering.

See also: 1 Samuel 16:7; Psalm 147:10−11; Luke 16:15

▪▪ BLAME IT ON BOOZE

Wine is a mocker and beer a brawler; whoever is led astray by them is not wise.

PROVERBS 20:1

Like a jug of Gallo wine, King Xerxes was all neck and belly. He had no head. Historians of his day portrayed him as impulsive, wild, dangerous. When a bridge he had erected was wiped out by high water, it's recorded that he ordered the sea to be whipped three hundred times, and then had the bridge builders beheaded. When he sobered up, he probably blamed his ridiculous actions on booze.

Being married to an alcoholic can be sheer hell on earth. And the life of Xerxes' wife, Vashti, was no exception. When he headed for the wine cellar, she headed for the door. He interpreted such behavior as feminist independence; Vashti saw it as survival. She probably just didn't want to get beaten up.

Perhaps to generate points with the menfolk in town, or maybe just because he didn't like to drink alone, King Xerxes threw open both the palace and wine cellar doors to every male in town. For an entire week, drinks were on the house: "wine was served in goblets of gold, each one different from the other, and the royal wine was abundant, in keeping with the king's liberality" (Esther 1:7). In addition, "each guest was allowed to drink in his own way, for the king instructed all the wine stewards to serve each man what he wished" (Esther 1:8).

About the time Xerxes started seeing pink elephants, he summoned his wife to parade in front of his pie-eyed male friends. Vashti had a figure that would stop a chariot, but she also had a brain to match and wasn't about to strut in front of a bunch of drunk, male chauvinist pigs. So she did the only thing she could think of: she sent a message to the king, politely telling him to take a flying leap.

With his ego now as smashed as he was, Xerxes decided to make an example of Vashti in case other women got any funny ideas and refused to let their alcoholic husbands humiliate them in public. He divorced her on the spot.

For Vashti, it wasn't much of a loss; Xerxes had always preferred the company of a bottle over her, anyway. And though suddenly stripped of her crown, she wore her integrity like a golden tiara.

See also: Esther 1; Romans 13:11–14; Ephesians 5:18

EMPTY EYES

For this reason a man will leave his father and mother and be united to his wife, and they will become one flesh.

GENESIS 2:24

The way Elisa told it, it was really "no big deal." When she first learned she was pregnant by Chuck, she began psyching herself up to have the baby adopted. So she was mostly ready when the big moment arrived and the nurses took away the newborn without letting her see whether it was a boy or a girl.

Elisa had quit school to live with Chuck and wait for the delivery. He teased her about "playing house" when she refinished the dresser and patched a gash in the window shade. But any suggestion that they get married was treated more like a joke than anything else. The nine months dragged along, as did their relationship, and most of their time together was spent arguing and fighting and watching television on hot sticky nights in his hole-in-the-wall apartment.

When Elisa came home from the hospital, Chuck was living with another girl—somebody from work. So Elisa took a job working tables at a little cafe and rented a room with a half bath and hot plate. "It was no big deal," she said.

Before long she began sleeping with Glen, an Army private who was passing through on a short leave. Their relationship was pretty uncomplicated, in part because it didn't have time to get complicated. She was just happy to have somebody hold her through the long nights and promise to write her from overseas.

Elisa more or less took things as they came, and did her best to laugh it off when she talked about the problems and emptiness and hurts in her life. But they were choking, panicky laughs, which caused her eyes to flood. She dabbed away the tears with a strand of hair while trying hard to convince herself that everything would be fine if she just laughed a little more and kept her eyes dry and tried not to think about life or love all that much, or about the Cinderella dreams and white picket fence hopes she'd had for herself as a little girl.

Aside from the tears, her eyes were as empty as any of the old boxes that cluttered her closets, waiting for the next move. She said it was all really no big deal, but her eyes gave her away. They spoke sermons about what happens when sex is separated from love and commitment.

And if you'd ever want to know why God created the protective haven of marriage, a look deep into Elisa's eyes would give you a pretty good idea.

See also: Proverbs 5:18–23; 1 Corinthians 6:18–20; Philippians 1:27

▪▪ LOVE FOR A LIFETIME

> *If I speak in the tongues of men and of angels, but have not love, I am only a resounding gong or a clanging cymbal. If I have the gift of prophecy and can fathom all mysteries and all knowledge, and if I have a faith that can move mountains, but have not love, I am nothing. If I give all I possess to the poor and surrender my body to the flames, but have not love, I gain nothing.*

1 CORINTHIANS 13:1–3

Romantic love is probably the biggest lift in life. It gives you a buzz clear to the bones and brightens the landscape around you. Even in the dead of winter, you feel like the middle of spring. Trees seem greener, the flowers brighter, and tomorrow's history exam less threatening.

But true love, if it is indeed true, is more than emotional rush. Good-time feelings come and go, but love endures only if it's nurtured in an environment of *trust, respect,* and *sacrifice.*

Without trust, love erodes. Trust says: I will remove all "No Trespassing" signs from our relationship, not demand we spend every minute together, and give you the freedom God does—to return my love if you so choose. I will allow you to be yourself—at the risk of knowing others may be attracted to the very things that attracted me.

Without respect, love withers. Respect says: I will honor your privacy, listen to your thoughts, learn from our differences, and treat your body like God does—as the temple of the Holy Spirit. I won't try to mold you in my image; doing so would merely ensure one of us isn't needed.

Without sacrifice, love dies. Sacrifice says: I will relinquish the masks that shield my deepest, most confusing emotions; surrender my pride that refuses to be hurt; and share completely the roller-coaster adventure of seeking God's highest calling for each of our lives. I will forget about love being a fifty-fifty proposition, and contribute my *best* to the relationship—even if you're unable to love me back.

Yes, I will love you completely—in an environment of trust, respect, and sacrifice—no strings attached. After all, that's how God first loved us.

See also: John 13:34–35; 1 Corinthians 13:4–7; 1 John 3:11–23

▪▪ THE PERFECT GIFT

Marriage should be honored by all, and the marriage bed kept pure, for God will judge the adulterer and all the sexually immoral.

HEBREWS 13:4

Talking on the phone with Patti was so natural that John felt they were made for each other. And after a half-dozen dates which ended with neither of them wanting to say good-night, he knew he was in love.

To express the depth of his love for Patti, John decided to make something special. And so he bought an expensive block of imported wood from which he began carving a pair of lovebirds. For weeks he worked long into the night, cutting, shaping, and sanding. When finished, the lovebirds were so beautiful he cried. Patti cried, too, when she opened the box. It was the perfect gift.

Spring approached, and with it came the promise of warmer weather. But ice was forming on John and Patti's relationship, and they didn't survive the chill. On the rebound John fell head over heels in love with Laura. He waited a few months, and then considered ways to display his feelings. He searched the malls, but no store-bought present would do. In the end, he could settle for nothing less than making another pair of lovebirds.

A few years and several sets of lovebirds later, John met the woman he wanted to marry. Lisa was everything he'd hoped for in a mate, and all of his other relationships seemed like puppy loves by comparison. Some of their happiest times were spent picking out wedding rings together, and even though John splurged in a big way, he longed to do something more for Lisa.

And so it was that he labored long into the cold nights with his chisels and blades. When he finally presented the lovebirds to Lisa on their wedding night, she smiled broadly and told him there wasn't a happier woman in all the world.

He watched her eyes closely, wondering if she knew of the other lovebirds. And when she held her pair up into the light, he couldn't help thinking of Patti and Laura and all of the other girls he'd given the same present to.

He'd wanted to give his bride something more special and unique. But how could he have improved on the perfect gift?

See also: 1 Corinthians 6:18–20; Ephesians 5:3; 1 Thessalonians 4:3–8

:: POINTS TO PONDER – LOVE AND SEX

At the beginning of creation God "made them male and female." "For this reason a man will leave his father and mother and be united to his wife, and the two will become one flesh." So they are no longer two, but one. Therefore what God has joined together, let man not separate.

MARK 10:6–9

There is no surprise more magical than the surprise of being loved. It is the finger of God on a man's shoulder.

CHARLES MORGAN

Sex is a flame which uncontrolled may scorch; properly guided, it will light the torch of eternity.

JOSEPH FETTERMAN

A successful marriage is an edifice that must be rebuilt every day.

ANDRE MAUROIS

There are three kinds of love: false, natural, and married. False love is that which seeks its own, just as one loves gold, goods, honour, or women outside of matrimony contrary to God's command. Natural love is between father and children, brother and sister. But above them all is married love. It burns as fire, and seeks nothing more than the mate. It says, "I wish not yours; I wish neither gold nor silver, neither this nor that. I want only you."

MARTIN LUTHER

In marriage, being the right person is as important as finding the right person.

WILBERT DONALD GOUGH

Modern man refuses to recognize that God has set certain standards, certain absolutes for sex, as he has for behavior generally. To be ignorant of these absolutes, or to deny them or rationalize them, in no way invalidates them.

L. NELSON BELL

The difficulty with marriage is that we fall in love with a personality, but must live with a character.

PETER DEVRIES

If there is anything better than to be loved, it is to love.

ANONYMOUS

Contrary to Mrs. Gundy, sex is not sin. Contrary to Hugh Hefner, it's not salvation either. Like nitro-glycerine, it can be used either to blow up bridges or heal hearts.

FREDERICK BUECHNER

We may, indeed, be sure that perfect chastity—like perfect charity—will not be attained by any merely human efforts. You must ask for God's help. Even when you have done so, it may seem to you for a long time that no help, or less help than you need, is being given. Never mind. After each failure, ask forgiveness, pick yourself up, and try again. Very often what God first helps us towards is not the virtue itself but just this power of always trying again. For however important chastity (or courage, or truthfulness, or any other virtue) may be, this process trains us in habits of the soul which are more important still. It cures our illusions about ourselves and teaches us to depend on God. We learn, on the one hand, that we cannot trust ourselves even in our best moments, and, on the other, that we need not despair even in our worst, for our failures are forgiven. The only fatal thing is to sit down content with anything less than perfection.

C. S. LEWIS

There is a tendency to think of sex as something degrading; it is not, it is magnificent, an enormous privilege, but because of that the rules are tremendously strict and severe.

FRANCES DEVAS

I never knew how to worship until I knew how to love.

HENRY WARD BEECHER

We pray that the young men and women of today and tomorrow will grow up with the realization that sex is a beautiful flame they carry in the lantern of their bodies.

DEMETRIUS MONOUSOS

Love is not blind—it sees more, not less. But because it sees more, it is willing to see less.

RABBI JULIUS GORDON

See also: Matthew 5:27–30; 1 Corinthians 13; Ephesians 5:1–17

■■ FITTING THE MOLD

> *For it is by grace you have been saved, through faith – and this not from yourselves, it is the gift of God – not by works, so that no one can boast. For we are God's workmanship, created in Christ Jesus to do good works, which God prepared in advance for us to do.*
>
> EPHESIANS 2:8–10

Keith thought he knew exactly how a Christian should look and behave. For starters, he looked harried because he was always running late to a blur of Bible studies, discipleship classes, choir practices, and prayer meetings. He described himself as a "one-hundred-percent-sold-out-for-Jesus, born-again believer."

As such, Keith behaved like a stage-ten idiot. He referred to various teachers as "pagans" and to students he passed in the hall, he'd blurt, "You must be born again!" And he said it with a straight face. One day he outdid himself and tried to command an "evil spirit" to come out of another student during lunch, but only succeeded in being slugged in the jaw. After he picked himself off the ground, he walked away muttering, "Bless those who curse you, pray for those who mistreat you."

His behavior reminds me of a story told by Richard Foster about a wealthy man who ordered a handmade suit from Hans, a renowned tailor. When the man stopped by to pick up the suit, he noticed that one shoulder caved in, while the other bulged out. The sleeves were sewn to the back and front rather than the sides of the coat. And the pant legs were cockeyed and short. But the man didn't want to make a fuss, so he said nothing. He stepped into the dressing room and, after a long period of painful twisting and shoving, managed to fit the convoluted pattern.

After admiring himself in the mirror, he paid the tailor and caught a bus home. Fellow passengers kept staring at the man, until one finally tapped him on the shoulder and asked if Hans hadn't made his new suit. Receiving a nod, he replied, "Amazing! I knew Hans was a great tailor, but I had no idea he could make a suit to fit someone as deformed as you!"

Like Keith, we all appear somewhat deformed whenever we think of Christianity as a set of external actions, as a way to look or act. Too often we bruise and batter ourselves to fit illogical molds of behavior. But thankfully we are human *beings*, not *doings*. Even more thankfully, Christianity is not based on anything we do. We can't push and shove our way closer to God.

As Paul wrote in the verses above, true spirituality isn't a matter of works and willpower on our part, but grace on God's part. He simply draws close to our side. Almost unaware, we're overcome by a growing sense of awe and reverence, and we begin to experience a lifechange—from the inside out.

See also: Romans 3:10–12; Ephesians 2:1–10; Philippians 2:13

■■ ONLY THE FACTS

There is no one righteous, not even one; there is no one who understands, no one who seeks God. All have turned away, they have together become worthless; there is no one who does good, not even one.

ROMANS 3:10–12

Just about everything these days has been quantified, surveyed, indexed, tabulated, and spewed out in one official document or another. This torrent of data informs us, often to our dismay, what we are truly like. For example, I recently read in the paper that:

- Exactly 68 percent of American children live with both of their biological parents; the percentage of Americans who don't recognize CBS News Anchorman Dan Rather is 55; and 42 percent of Americans regularly attend religious services.
- The probability of dying from unnatural causes on your next commercial jet flight is about one in seven million. Even if you fly daily, you can expect to meet the grim reaper aboard only once in every 19,000 years.
- Of white-collar workers in America, 49 percent say they are cyberphobic or resistant to new technology; 66 percent

don't use electronic mail or carry beepers; 65 percent use personal computers; and 58 percent haven't heard anything about the Internet.

- There are 105 different familial relationships for which Hallmark makes cards; when conversing with the opposite sex, males make 96 percent of all interruptions; and the number of schools that invited Lee Iacocca to speak at their graduation in June 1986 was 150.

It is common knowledge that ours is the best informed generation in history—even though 82.6 percent of us probably can't locate Iran on a map, explain exactly what a catalytic converter does, or name the second president of the United States.

What is important is not so much the volume of information that bombards us (we're hit by far more than anyone could absorb, anyway) but *which* statistics we act on. For example, it's unimportant whether you know the name Lee Iacocca and how many speaking invitations he received way back when. There are no consequences if you ignore such information. But some statistics are a matter of life and death. For example:

- The number of people who have sinned and fall short of the glory of God is 100 percent;
- The number of people who are destined to die once, and after that to face judgment is 100 percent;
- At the name of Jesus, the number of knees that will bow, in heaven and on earth and under the earth, and the number of tongues that will confess Jesus Christ as Lord is also 100 percent.

With God, there are no loopholes. It's all or nothing—100 percent of the time.

See also: Romans 3:23; Hebrews 9:27; Philippians 2:10–11

▦ NO EXCUSE

You, therefore, have no excuse, you who pass judgment on someone else, for at whatever point you judge the other, you are condemning yourself, because you who pass judgment do the same things.

ROMANS 2:1

It has been quite some time since I thought much about the hypocrisy around me. Sure, I know it's there. I read the newspapers, listen to the news, hear snatches of gossip. But there's enough hypocrisy in my own life to consume most all of my attention and, presumably, quite a bit of God's as well.

While we tend to judge each other based on outward appearances (whether we act secure, witty, spiritual, etc.), the Lord judges the heart. And we can't mask our innermost thoughts and feelings to fool him. He knows even the best of us harbor secret thoughts of hatred, pride, and lust—inner sins that only he can deal with. Who are we to pretend they don't exist?

Because of this perspective, Christ levels the boom on those who worry about others' problems: "Don't pick on people, jump on their failures, criticize their faults—unless, of course, you want the same treatment," he challenged. "That critical spirit has a way of boomeranging. It's easy to see a smudge on your neighbor's face and be oblivious to the ugly sneer on your own. Do you have the nerve to say, 'Let me wash your face for you,' when your own face is distorted by contempt? It's this whole traveling road-show mentality all over again, playing a holier-than-thou part instead of just living your part. Wipe that ugly sneer off your own face, and you might be fit to offer a washcloth to your neighbor" (Matthew 7:1–5 *The Message*).

It's not that God wants us to be blind to sin and hypocrisy around us. The Bible repeatedly urges believers to evaluate people and situations carefully, to choose between good and evil. We are warned about sexually immoral people (1 Corinthians 5:9) and "angels of light" (2 Corinthians 11:14), among others, and urged to "test everything" (1 Thessalonians 5:21).

Nevertheless, we should quit focusing our binoculars on others' sin and hypocrisy when we have trouble seeing the same things in the mirror.

See also: Luke 6:37–38; Romans 14:10–13; 1 Corinthians 4:5

▪▪ INTELLECTUAL HONESTY

Where is the wise man? Where is the scholar? Where is the philosopher of this age? Has not God made foolish the wisdom of the world? For since in the wisdom of God the world through its wisdom did not know him, God was pleased through the foolishness of what was preached to save those who believe.

1 CORINTHIANS 1:20–21

As Maxine Hancock tells the story, she was on her way to Anthropology 378 when her friend, Dave, invited her to a noon Bible study on campus. About half a dozen others would be there, he said.

"Bible study?" she hooted. "Why study *that?*"

Dave smiled, mumbled something about how if she'd come once or twice she'd understand why, and just kept walking. Not wanting to end the conversation so abruptly, Maxine tried another angle.

"You know, Dave, I don't really think that an intellectually honest person can take the Bible seriously anymore." He didn't respond, so she continued. "Let's face it, everybody knows about the contradictions." She did a quick mental search for an example in case Dave asked, but couldn't think of anything offhand. No matter; he let it pass. "And the myths like Adam and Eve and Noah and the boys. I just don't see that it's honest to go on taking an outmoded book so seriously. That's all."

By the time they were almost to class, Dave had still not responded. She figured she'd gotten his goat, and that it would be a long while before he asked her to something similar again. Maybe he'd even skip the noon study himself and take her out to lunch instead—something she was more interested in.

When Dave finally spoke up, he cleared his throat as if he was going to talk about something else. "Say, Maxine," he said, "speaking of intellectual honesty..."

She fell for it hard. "Yeah?" she said, glancing up.

"What do you think about somebody doing a critical review of a book she's never read?"

See also: Isaiah 29:14–16; 1 Corinthians 1:26–31; 2:6–16

■■ CARRYING ON THE JOB

*The body is a unit, though it is made up of many
parts; and though all its parts are many, they form one
body. So it is with Christ. For we were all baptized by one
Spirit into one body–whether Jews or Greeks, slave or
free–and we were all given the one Spirit to drink.*

1 CORINTHIANS 12:12–13

I once had a boss who agreed to contribute an article for a
book but couldn't find time to write the piece. The day before it was
due, something came up and he had to catch a plane out of town. I
asked him about the article. "Why don't you write it for me," he said.
And then he was gone.

The assignment was an act of trust more than anything else.
He could have written the article on the plane or in his hotel room
that night, but he wanted to involve me. And he knew he could trust
me to speak for him.

Christ entrusted us with a similar assignment shortly before
he returned to heaven. For thirty-three years he walked the earth,
providing people with a close-up look at God. If you wanted to know
what God was like, all you had to do was take a good look at Jesus.
For the first time, God was more than a voice in the clouds or a dusty
concept in a scroll. He had a body, a face.

When Jesus ascended into heaven, he did not vacate Planet
Earth. Rather, he left his followers behind, filled them with his
Spirit, and asked them to serve for him, love for him, speak for him.

We carry on that job–in his name. Now, as then, we are his
body, his hands, his eyes, his heart. Our actions, words, morals, and
thoughts should all mirror his character. If we are successful, people
around us will recognize God and want to know him. If they fail to
recognize him, could it be we're not doing our job?

See also: Matthew 28:18–20; Acts 1:8; Colossians 3:17

▦ THE PERFECT JOB

> *Your attitude should be the same as that of Christ Jesus: Who, being in very nature God, did not consider equality with God something to be grasped, but made himself nothing, taking the very nature of a servant, being made in human likeness. And being found in appearance as a man, he humbled himself and became obedient to death–even death on a cross!*
>
> PHILIPPIANS 2:5–8

The job description seemed easy enough: live in Hawaii and play Santa Claus to the poor. But it turned out harder than Linda imagined.

The work took her into the poorest sections, where the flies outnumbered people one hundred to one, where a stench hung in the air because the streets were treated like one big dumpster, where the worry of parents who didn't have enough to feed their children was almost palpable, and where the hungry children had stopped crying because crying only made them hungrier.

With barking dogs on her heels and a burning sun on her back, Linda trudged into the barrios to tell immigrants about the no-cost services provided by the government: free driving lessons, medical insurance, Kung Fu classes, even free college education–not to mention dental care at less than a dollar per visit. She thought it was an offer nobody could refuse. But in the end, most of the people she was supposed to help didn't want help. They were suspicious and afraid, and time after time they shut their rickety doors in her face.

Why not spare the hassle and drudgery and just print up a flyer? she thought. A little brochure describing all of the services could easily be left on people's doorsteps. That way it wouldn't be any sweat off her back if people didn't want help. As it was, the person-to-person visits were *killing* her.

But then another thought struck her. What if Jesus had skipped the visit and sent flyers instead? What if all you had to do to become a Christian was return a postage-paid coupon? It would have been so much easier than hassling with the crowds. It would have been so much easier than bothering with the cross.

See also: John 15:13; Romans 5:6–8; 1 John 4:9–10

▪▪ POINTS TO PONDER – JUDGMENT

Since you call on a Father who judges each man's work impartially, live your lives as strangers here in reverent fear. For you know that it was not with perishable things such as silver or gold that you were redeemed from the empty way of life handed down to you from your forefathers, but with the precious blood of Christ, a lamb without blemish or defect.

1 PETER 1:17–19

He who has spoken in love will soon be obliged to speak in judgment.

KAY GUDNASON

The New Testament proclaims that at some unforeseeable time in the future God will bring down the final curtain on history, and there will come a Day on which all our days and all the judgments upon us and all our judgments upon each other will themselves be judged. The judge will be Christ. In other words, the one who judges us most finally will be the one who loves us most fully.

FREDERICK BUECHNER

There is no fear of judgment for the man who judges himself according to the Word of God.

HOWARD G. HENDRICKS

You shall judge a man by his foes as well as by his friends.

JOSEPH CONRAD

Truly at the day of judgment we shall not be examined on what we have read, but what we have done; not how well we have spoken, but how religiously we have lived.

THOMAS À KEMPIS

The average man's judgment is so poor, he runs a risk every time he uses it.

ED HOWE

Don't wait for the Last Judgment. It takes place every day.

ALBERT CAMUS

Hesitancy in judgment is the only true mark of the thinker.

DAGOBERT D. RUNES

We judge ourselves by what we feel capable of doing; others judge us by what we have done.

HENRY WADSWORTH LONGFELLOW

History shows that Christ on the cross has been more potent than anything else in arousing a compassion for suffering and indignation at injustice.

F. J. FOAKES-JACKSON

Romantic love is blind to everything except what is lovable and lovely, but Christ's love sees us with terrible clarity and sees us whole. Christ's love so wishes our joy that it is ruthless against everything in us that diminishes our joy. The worst sentence Love can pass is that we behold the suffering which Love has endured for our sake, and that is also our acquittal. The justice and mercy of the judge are ultimately one.

FREDERICK BUECHNER

A man's judgment of another depends more on the one judging and on his passions than on the one being judged and his conduct.

PAUL TOURNIER

I believe the troubles that have come upon us are in part a judgment of God on us for our sins; and that unless we repent and turn to God we are finished as a free democratic society.

BILLY GRAHAM

See also: John 3:16–17; 8:3–7; Romans 2:1–6; Hebrews 9:27–28

▪▪ THIRD GRADE MATH

Caiaphas, who was high priest that year, spoke up, "You know nothing at all! You do not realize that it is better for you that one man die for the people than that the whole nation perish."

JOHN 11:49–50

Caiaphas was essentially the Jewish equivalent of the pope. As the religious boss man of Israel, he presided over the high court of the Jews, called the Sanhedrin. For the most part, he kept things quiet on the home front, and the Roman feds pretty much stayed out of his hair and left him to his cushy job.

However, Caiaphas began to sweat as Jesus headed toward Jerusalem after three years of stirring up controversy and converts around the countryside. By the time he'd fed the five thousand and raised Lazarus from the dead, he was a household name. So the throngs were waiting when he hit Main Street, and they gave him the equivalent of a ticker-tape parade.

Caiaphas and members of the Sanhedrin were also waiting —not to celebrate, but to capture; not to congratulate, but to crucify. They had their reasons to be hot and bothered by the blue-collar Jew. These probably had less to do with his claiming equality with God and healing people on the Sabbath than his habit of talking about religious honchos in less than complimentary terms. He'd singled out these sanctimonious sourpusses as being proud and petty, and they had their fill of it.

"If we let him go on, pretty soon everyone will be believing in him and the Romans will come and remove what little power and privilege we still have," they fretted (John 11:48 *The Message*).

The way they figured it, with Christ out of the way, people would calm down, Rome would stay off their backs, and they could continue living in the style to which they'd grown accustomed. As Caiaphas suggested, it was a matter of third grade math: For the sake of many, it was better that one man die.

Interestingly enough, Christ reached the exact same conclusion. But he fulfilled Caiaphas' prophecy in a way Caiaphas never could have imagined.

See also: Matthew 23; John 12:24; Hebrews 10:14

■■ WOE IS ME!

Woe to you, teachers of the law and Pharisees, you hypocrites! You are like whitewashed tombs, which look beautiful on the outside but on the inside are full of dead men's bones and everything unclean. In the same way, on the outside you appear to people as righteous but on the inside you are full of hypocrisy and wickedness.

MATTHEW 23:27–28

It would be nice to think Christ's words above were a scathing rebuke aimed solely at the religious stuffed shirts of his day. The way he laid into them, there's no question they were a dastardly bunch of pious old poops. But do his comments have other targets? Consider a sampling of his "Woe to you" charges:

"You travel over land and sea to win a single convert, and when he becomes one, you make him twice as much a son of hell as you are ... You give a tenth of your spices—mint, dill and cummin. But you have neglected the more important matters of the law—justice, mercy and faithfulness ... You clean the outside of the cup and dish, but inside they are full of greed and self-indulgence ... You snakes! You brood of vipers! How will you escape being condemned to hell?" (Matthew 23:15, 23, 25, 33).

Those were fighting words to the Pharisees, the particular Jewish sect which Christ singled out because of their extreme legalism and hypocrisy. But they didn't have a corner on the market of snooty pride or vile greed. The same traits Christ fingered are all around us—and in us—today.

Take a few minutes and identify examples of hypocrisy in the church—attitudes or actions which conflict with the Spirit of God as you know it:

_____

_____

_____

Finally, jot down any Pharisee-like qualities you find in yourself:

_____

_____

_____

See also: Luke 6:37–42; 12:1–5; 1 John 1:8–10

▪▪ A BORN WINNER

> *Don't you know that friendship with the world is hatred toward God? Anyone who chooses to be a friend of the world becomes an enemy of God.*

JAMES 4:4

Cindy was a living, breathing masterpiece. She was the prettiest girl I ever knew, the equal of any cover-girl model or actress. You name it: blond hair, blue eyes, a gorgeous tan, all the curves in all the right places. She not only stopped guys dead in their tracks, other girls even looked twice when she passed.

She was a shoo-in for homecoming queen and was the cheerleader everybody watched through binoculars. But she was more than a body. Cindy pulled straight A's in practically every class, earned honors in public-speaking competition, got elected to every school office she ever ran for, and had her choice of scholarship offers. She even lived in a nice house and had a pet dog that didn't shed. What more could anybody ask?

From time to time as the opportunity arose, I talked with Cindy about the Lord. I knew she was interested because she listened— *intently*. She even came right out and said she wanted to believe. But she always held back because she wasn't certain God wouldn't somehow ruin her life if she became a Christian. I think she secretly believed she might wake up ugly the next morning or contract some dreaded disease.

In the end, Cindy figured God needed her more than she needed him. And in that moment of decision, she fell for the lie of the devil, who whispered in her ear that she already had what really mattered—popularity, achievement, looks—and so why chance messing up a good thing by messing around with God-thoughts.

There's a reason Jesus said it's much easier for the poor and needy to enter his kingdom. A hungry, pregnant, fifteen-year-old girl living on a steam grate in New York and hustling quarters from passersby has no question about her needs. When you're at the bottom, things can only improve.

But Cindy, who had it so good already, feared things could only get worse. She essentially was right: hell loomed just around the corner.

See also: Matthew 5:3–10; 16:24–26; 19:24; 1 Timothy 6:6–10

■ MY FAVORITE TREE IS GONE

Then I saw a new heaven and a new earth, for the first heaven and the first earth had passed away, and there was no longer any sea. I saw the Holy City, the new Jerusalem, coming down out of heaven from God, prepared as a bride beautifully dressed for her husband. And I heard a loud voice from the throne saying, "Now the dwelling of God is with men, and he will live with them. They will be his people, and God himself will be with them and be their God. He will wipe every tear from their eyes. There will be no more death or mourning or crying or pain, for the old order of things has passed away."

REVELATION 21:1–4

Jeff had a voice that was straight from heaven, and when he sang "The Lord's Prayer" at my wedding I had tears in my eyes. We were great friends all through high school and college. We surfed together, studied and prayed together, took weekend trips to the mountains together, and discussed first loves and future dreams together. As the scenario developed in our minds, he'd be a great lawyer, and I'd write the Great American Novel.

But then one day before the dreams had a chance to come true, Jeff noticed a little bump behind his ear. It seemed like nothing really, but he finally had it checked out—only to be told he had cancer ... and six months to live.

Jeff is the first true friend I've lost. It's difficult to describe what it feels like afterward. It's sort of like having an awesome view of the Pacific Ocean—the cliffs and sweeping sands of La Jolla, the distant peaks of Catalina Island, and in the foreground a favorite shade tree. And then a building is constructed that partially blocks the view. I can stand in that same spot and look out where I used to see the beautiful evergreen, always full of birds, and my spirit falls.

Maybe the tree is still there, but it is hidden behind an impenetrable barrier. All I know is that I can't see it anymore.

I can stand there for hours, reminding myself of how the tree had balanced the view and given me so much pleasure. And I can optimistically think, It's *still* a gorgeous view. I can still see in the distance the breaking waves, the white sweeping sands, the gulls coasting on the wind, the faraway island peaks. Yes, it's still a gorgeous view. But the tree, my favorite tree, is gone.

That's how it feels.

Some days I'd give anything to be able to talk with him again. But I know he's happy where he is and wouldn't want to be back. Where he is now, every tear has been wiped from his eyes, and there is no more death or crying or pain. Where Jeff is now, he's healed.

Yet I still think of the view and the tree. I can't get it out of my mind. My favorite tree is gone.

See also: Isaiah 35; 65:17–25; 1 Corinthians 15:35–58

:: THE INSIDE STORY

> *These are written that you may believe that Jesus is the Christ, the Son of God, and that by believing you may have life in his name.*

JOHN 20:31

As a journalist and author, I've had the opportunity to meet and interview many famous people. I've talked with Capitol Hillers, Hollyweirdos, Rock 'n' Rollers, and Super Bowlers.

If I want to know what the person is really like when they're not running (ruining?) the country, acting up a storm, blowing out eardrums, or making hamburger of other human beings, I don't just speak with the individuals themselves. For a well-rounded story, I spend time with their friends and associates as well. By utilizing other sources, I'm able to balance and interpret the quotes and material I get from the primary subject.

In trying to get to know more about Jesus Christ, the same methods apply. You must spend time reading what he said about himself—from his earliest recorded comments as a young boy (Luke 2:49), to his parting words before his ascension (Acts 1:7-8). A Bible which prints all of Christ's words in red is particularly helpful for this kind of study. But for a more fleshed-out look at who Christ is and how he behaved at the end of a long, hot day, you must turn to those who knew him best.

John was one of those people. A member of Christ's inner circle, John was probably his best friend. In his gospel, John skips over many of the basics about Christ's life (no blow-by-blow account of his birth, for example), because he figures you can get that elsewhere. Instead of focusing on the readily available facts, he interprets Jesus' life and ponders the meaning of what Jesus said and did as only a close friend can.

His words are full of reflection and commentary, and all for one express purpose: "That you may believe that Jesus is the Christ, the Son of God, and that by believing you may have life in his name" (John 20:31). In other words, he wants you to get to know Christ as well as he does, and thereby share eternity.

If you want the inside scoop on Jesus, spend a quiet evening this week with John.

See also: John 19:35; 1 John 1:1-3

■■ GOOD-BYES

I have chosen you out of the world.

JOHN 15:19

I stood on the porch with my mother before me, my car behind me. The car was loaded down with all of my belongings and was riding low. I glanced at my watch. And then I looked up at my mother.

Her eyes were clouded, and there was a lone tear on her cheek. She didn't try to wipe it away, but just let it fall at her feet. There wasn't much that could be said, so she just opened her arms, and for several long moments we stood there holding each other and thinking about so many happy memories and how hard it was now to say good-bye. I was moving five hundred miles away, and she knew what I didn't: that I wouldn't be back again, except to visit; and probably then with a wife.

"Good-bye, son," she said. Her eyes were wetter.

"Be sure to write," I managed. And then I squeezed the tears from my own eyes and walked to the car. A few moments later I was a set of taillights to her, and she was a distant, waving figure in my rearview mirror.

Good-bye is never an easy word. As far as words go, it ranks near the bottom of my list. At the top are such phrases as "Keep the change," "The exam's been canceled," and "Welcome home." Good-bye is in the dregs, along with "The basement's flooded," "I hope you're sitting down..." and "Call an ambulance."

"Good-bye" is a frequent word in the Christian's vocabulary because ultimately our roots and citizenship are in heaven. So we live as pilgrims, awaiting that still small voice of God that beckons, "Follow me." When it comes, we must be willing to leave family and friends and security behind, to live out of a duffel bag, to sleep anywhere but in our own bed—to say good-bye again and again and again.

For Christians, life is a journey that's homeward bound. And though on this side of eternity the partings don't become any easier, there is a bright side: Those who live in the Lord will never see each other for the last time.

See also: John 13:1; 18:36; Philippians 3:20; Colossians 3:1–3; 1 Peter 2:11–12

POINTS TO PONDER - ETERNITY

I tell you the truth, he who believes has everlasting life.

JOHN 6:47

The choices of time are binding in eternity.

JACK MACARTHUR

When you are with somebody you love, you have little if any sense of the passage of time, and you also have, in the fullest sense of the phrase, a good time. When you are with God, you have something like the same experience. The biblical term for the experience is Eternal Life. Another is Heaven.

FREDERICK BUECHNER

Faith is building on what you know is here, so you can reach what you know is there.

CULLEN HIGHTOWER

I thank Thee, O Lord, that Thou hast so set eternity within my heart that no earthly thing can ever satisfy me wholly.

JOHN BAILLIE

The average man does not know what to do with this life, yet wants another one which will last forever.

ANATOLE FRANCE

Eternity is not an everlasting flux of time, but time is a short parenthesis in a long period.

JOHN DONNE

The worst feeling in the world is the homesickness that comes over a man occasionally when he is at home.

ED HOWE

We think of Eternal Life, if we think of it at all, as what happens when life ends. We would do better to think of it as what happens when life begins.

FREDERICK BUECHNER

The thought of eternity consoles for the shortness of life.

LUC DE CLAPIERS

On earth there is no heaven, but there are pieces of it.

JULES RENARD

God, as Isaiah says "inhabiteth eternity" but stands with one foot in time. The part of time where he stands most particularly is Christ, and thus in Christ we catch a glimpse of what eternity is all about, what God is all about, and what we ourselves are all about, too.

FREDERICK BUECHNER

See also: Ecclesiastes 3:11; Isaiah 57:15; Mark 10:17–31; John 6:47

■■ THE WAR WITHIN

> *"Come now, let us reason together,"* says the Lord. *"Though your sins are like scarlet, they shall be as white as snow; though they are red as crimson, they shall be like wool."*
>
> ISAIAH 1:18

For as long as Andy could remember, there had been one very personal area of his life he didn't discuss with anybody. It was marked "Private—No Trespassing," and not even God could get through.

Andy prided himself on his openness in every other area of his life. It didn't bother him to talk about pride or greed or any other "safe sins." But that one private area of his life—that hidden corner of lust—was different. For Andy, lust dealt with fantasy thoughts and bewitching urges that were simply too personal to discuss with anybody.

Not wanting others to think he was some kind of Neanderthal lug, he kept his private lusts sealed off—only to have them fester and grow in the darkness. He soon graduated from the *Sports Illustrated* swimsuit issue to *Playboy*, and then to *Penthouse* and *Hustler*, and then to living a lie that extended beyond pictures in glossy magazines.

Andy was so concerned what people would think if they knew the true depths of his innermost thoughts that he maintained a thicker and thicker facade of outward spirituality. He was the first to quote a Bible verse, the first to pray, the first to share what God was doing in his life. He was the Christian whom others measured themselves by; the one whom parents wanted their daughters to marry.

But the mask eventually got too heavy, and before long Andy joined the list of Christian "has-beens." He just stopped coming to church and hanging around with other Christians. He began running with a faster crowd and drifting further and further and further from God. It didn't happen overnight, of course. Erosion of the heart is a slow process—so gradual that most of us hardly notice the problem.

But for Andy, as for anyone, that process began when he blocked off an area of his life as private; when he didn't seek God's help and cleansing forgiveness in *every* area of his life. Like Ananias and Sapphira (see Acts 5), he held something back.

The thing is, God wanted his whole heart. Not just a part—not even the biggest part. *All* of it. That's what Moses was getting at when he told the Israelites: "The Lord our God, the Lord is one. Love the Lord your God with all your heart and with all your soul and with all your strength" (Deuteronomy 6:4–5).

As Andy discovered, when you love God with less than all your heart, and when you keep him at a distance, God soon enough becomes a distant memory.

See also: Mark 2:17; Acts 24:16; James 4:8

■■ THE WINNABLE WAR

> *Everything in the world—the cravings of sinful man, the lust of his eyes and the boasting of what he has and does—comes not from the Father but from the world. The world and its desires pass away, but the man who does the will of God lives forever.*

> 1 JOHN 2:16–17

It's not as if you plotted the evil; as if you woke up in the morning with some devious scheme contrary to God's plan for your life. It just sort of . . . well, *happened*.

It started innocently enough, as you were flipping through the latest issue of *Time*—a *news* magazine, for goodness' sake. Suddenly, you spot a picture of the latest lean teen queen, with her peek-a-boo blouse opened down to here and a come-hither look on her face that melts every good thought you've tried to think about the opposite sex. There is magic on the page, and you stare at the image until every curve is burned into your mind. There, safely tucked away, you fondle it mentally for hours.

Lust of the eye, as the Bible calls it, is not merely a guy's problem, consisting of leotards, bikinis, suggestive photographs, and lingerie ads in the Sunday paper. As the dictionary defines it, "lust is an overmastering desire or craving."

Thus, you can lust for popularity just as easily as you can lust for the latest lean teen queen. You can also lust for power and money and fame, as well as for a second helping of coconut cream pie, a red convertible, or Mr. Romeo's arms to hold you.

There is seldom anything wrong with the object of the lust itself. Women look the way they do because that's the way God designed them. Likewise, there is nothing inherently evil about money or cream pie or automobiles. Power, when channeled correctly, can create jobs and end wars. As for money, it is a necessary tool. It's the "love of money"—or the "lust" of money, the overmastering desire and craving for it—that the Bible decries.

As the verse above says, the cravings and lusts of sinful man come from the world. That is, they're fueled straight from hell. Presumably, that includes everything that promotes and encourages those cravings, such as the *Playboy* philosophy, the Miller Lite philosophy, or the Marlboro philosophy.

Until the Lord's promised return, we must wage a constant, internal war against these worldly desires. "In this world you will have trouble," Christ says in John 16:33. But, thankfully, he adds the clincher: "But take heart! I have overcome the world." In other words, it's a winnable war. Christ has set the enemy on his ear, and he's there to help you do the same in your very personal, daily struggles.

You can almost picture his open arms as he calls you close: "Come to me, all you who are weary and burdened, and I will give you rest" (Matthew 11:28).

See also: 2 Corinthians 7:1; James 4:4

:: FINDING RELIEF

Blessed are the pure in heart, for they will see God.
MATTHEW 5:8

Ever since Adam and Eve were booted out of Eden, there has been constant combat between the world in which we live and the kingdom of God. As you've been reading the past two days, that war is often waged in the innermost corners of our heart.

St. Augustine once described our condition here on earth as a simultaneous citizenship in two cities—the city of man and the City of God. Man's city is neon-lit, action-packed, lust-filled. It feels real and immediate. God's city is invisible and shrouded with mystery; some doubt whether it exists at all. Consequently, the whisper of the City of God is often overpowered by the siren call of the city of man.

What is the city of man, to be specific? The warm, intimate smile of Miss September is that city. As is lust in whatever form it takes. For you it may be the girl with the silky blouse opened a button too far; the lure of a buy-now, pay-later Visa card; the all-you-can-eat diner; a six-pack at a hot party; or the guy with expensive cologne and bedroom eyes who makes promises he can't keep for a night of love.

There are many good reasons for casting a deaf ear to the beckoning city of man and heeding the call of the City of God, but most of them sound extremely negative. People will tell you to be pure—or else you'll feel dreadfully guilty or die of AIDS or some such thing. There's truth to that, of course; short-term illicit pleasures generally do have long-term negative consequences, as any child of an alcoholic or coke-head can tell you.

But the best reason for seeking purity has nothing to do with the "live right, or else" rationale. Rather, it's the reason Christ gave in his Sermon on the Mount: "Blessed are the pure in heart, for they will see God."

Think about it: *The pure in heart will see God.* It's a staggering thought. But simply put, if you play by God's rules, he will reveal himself to you so that the City of God will become as real to you as the downtown skyline. Or to put it another way, you will be granted a glimpse of heaven right here on earth.

That promise may seem to lose its luster when compared with the warm glows and immediate thrills offered by Miss September or Mr. Romeo. But that's the deceiver whispering lies. The City of God is as real as the front of your face. And what you become as you build your citizenship in that city is far more inviting, fulfilling, and everlasting than if all your fantasies in the city of man were somehow fulfilled.

See also: Psalm 24:3–4; 73; John 10:10; Ephesians 3:14–21

⊞ BREAKING UP

Cast all your anxiety on him because he cares for you.

1 PETER 5:7

As soon as Kimberly picked up the phone, I knew we had problems. She sounded distant and tight. When I asked what was wrong, she didn't say anything. So I told her I'd drive over to talk about it.

"No, you'd better not," she hedged. There was a long, awkward silence. "Mike's here," she finally said.

"Mike?" I choked. "What—"

"Please, don't make this any harder than it already is," she said, and then for the next ten minutes she explained that she still loved me but wanted to start seeing other guys. Her words were like daggers, and when I hung up there were tears of pain in my eyes. Who was she fooling? She didn't still love me. Our relationship was over.

The first week was sheer torture. I tried to pray, but I found myself asking God to help Kimberly change her mind. I knew that was as futile as asking God to turn Mike into a duck, so instead I just prayed a single word: *hate.* Over and over I repeated that word to God because I couldn't see them together without burning up inside. After a couple of weeks, my rabid-dog feelings began to cool. I moved on to pray about *anger* and *revenge* and then *jealousy.*

Though praying didn't remove the hurt of breaking up, it kept the communication lines open with God and helped me reach the point where I could see Kimberly and Mike together without dwelling on breaking his knees. It also helped me see something else: just how much I had depended on another person for security—and how much more I needed to depend on God.

When my world began spinning out of control, my natural inclination was to focus on myself and my blur of emotions. With God's help, I learned to let him work things out inside of me—to be the still point of my turning world.

See also: Psalm 46:10; Philippians 4:6–7; James 5:13

■■ LOVE TESTS

> *Test everything. Hold on to the good. Avoid every kind of evil.*
>
> 1 THESSALONIANS 5:21–22

When you're sick, you know it. It's a matter of taking your temperature or going to the doctor. Knowing when you're in love is a more confusing matter. There's no gauge to measure this most confusing of emotions. But in his book *I Married You*, Walter Trobisch provided the following practical tests to help you get a handle on love:

The sharing test. *Real love wants to share, to give, to reach out. It thinks of the other one, not of himself. When you read something, how often do you have the thought, I would like to share this with my friend? When you plan something, do you think of what you would like to do or what the other one would enjoy? . . .*

The strength test. *I got a letter once from a worried lover. He had read somewhere that one loses weight if one is truly in love. In spite of all his feelings of love, he didn't lose weight and that worried him. It is true that the love experience can also affect you physically. But in the long run, real love should not take away your strength; instead, it should give you new energy and strength. It should fill you with joy and make you creative, willing to accomplish even more . . .*

The respect test. *There is no real love without respect, without being able to look up to the other one. A girl may admire a boy when she watches him play soccer and score all the goals. But if she asks herself the question: "Do I want this boy to be the father of my* children?" very often the answer will be in the negative. A boy may admire a girl when he sees her dancing. But if he asks himself the question: "Do I want this girl to be the mother of my children?" she may look very different to him.

It would be easier, of course, if love could be determined as easily as measuring the air pressure in your tires. The above-mentioned guidelines may help you sort out your feelings. But in the end, you must rely on God to know best. You must also believe that he knows what is best and will help you decide "Who's the one" when the time is right.

See also: Psalm 37:4; 139:1–12; Jeremiah 29:11

▪▪ THE CONFUSING EMOTION

Be imitators of God, therefore, as dearly loved children and live a life of love, just as Christ loved us and gave himself up for us as a fragrant offering and sacrifice to God. But among you there must not be even a hint of sexual immorality, or of any kind of impurity, or of greed, because these are improper for God's holy people.

EPHESIANS 5:1–3

Are you in love? There's more to this human emotion than mushy feelings, sweet dreams, and a rosy outlook on life whenever your "significant other" is in the vicinity. As you read yesterday, there are common-sense ways to test your feelings about love. Listed below are three more tests that Walter Trobisch provided in his book, *I Married You:*

The habit test. *Once a … girl who was engaged came to me and was very worried. "I love my fiancé very much," she said, "but I just can't stand the way he eats an apple" … Love accepts the other one with his habits. Don't marry on the installment plan, thinking that these things will change later on. Very likely they will not …*

The quarrel test. *When a couple come to me and want to get married, I always ask them if they have once had a real quarrel—not just a casual difference of opinion, but a real fight. Many times they will say, "Oh, no! Pastor, we love each other!" Then I tell them, "Quarrel first—and then I will marry you." The point is, of course, not the quarreling, but the ability to be reconciled to each other. This ability must be trained and tested before marriage ...*

The time test. *A young couple came to me to be married. "How long have you known each other?" I asked. "Already three, almost four weeks," was the answer. This is too short. One year, I would say, is the minimum. Two years may be safer. It is also good to see each other ... at work, in daily living, unshaved and in a T-shirt, or with hair that needs to be washed ..., in situations of stress or danger."*

Trobisch made a final statement in his book. And that is: "Sex is no test of love ... If a couple wants to use the sex act in order to know whether they love each other, one has to ask them, 'Do you love each other so little?'"

See also: John 13:34–35; 1 Corinthians 6:18–20

■■ POINTS TO PONDER – THE OPPOSITE SEX

So God created man in his own image, in the image of God he created him; male and female he created them.

GENESIS 1:27

A person who despises or undervalues or neglects the opposite sex will soon need humanizing.

CHARLES SIMMONS

If all hearts were open and all desires known—as they would be if people showed their souls—how many gapings, sighings, clenched fists, knotted brows, broad grins, and red eyes would we see!

THOMAS HARDY

Where there is no God there is no man. Man without God is no longer man.

NICHOLAS BERDYAEV

The woman was formed out of man—not out of his head to rule over him; not out of his feet to be trod upon by him; but out of his side to be his equal, from beneath his arm to be protected, and from near his heart to be loved.

MATTHEW HENRY

There is a woman at the beginning of all great things.

ALPHONSE DE LAMARTINE

There are only two kinds of men: the righteous who believe themselves sinners; the rest, sinners who believe themselves righteous.

BLAISE PASCAL

Whatever women do, they must do twice as well as men to be thought half as good. Luckily, this is not difficult.

CHARLOTTE WHITTON

An honest man's the noblest work of God.

ALEXANDER POPE

It was Christ who discovered and emphasized the worth of woman. It was Christ who lifted her into equality with man. It was Christ who gave woman her chance, who saw her possibilities, who discovered her value.

ARTHUR JOHN GOSSIP

What a chimera, then, is man! What a novelty! What a monster, what a chaos, what a contradiction, what a prodigy! Judge of all things, feeble worm of the earth, depository of truth, a sink of uncertainty and error, the glory and the shame of the universe.

BLAISE PASCAL

You see, dear, it is not true that woman was made from man's rib; she was really made from his funny bone.

JAMES MATTHEW BARRIE

It is becoming more and more obvious that it is not starvation, not microbes, not cancer, but man himself who is mankind's greatest danger.

CARL GUSTAV JUNG

She is not made to be the admiration of all, but the happiness of one.

EDMUND BURKE

In short, the Man Jesus Christ has the decisive place in man's ageless relationship with God. He is what God means by "man," He is what man means by God.

J. S. WHALE

Man is always looking for someone to boast to; woman is always looking for a shoulder to put her head on.

H. L. MENCKEN

See also: Genesis 2:24–25; 3:1–24

■■ THOSE WERE THE DAYS

You are my friends if you do what I command.

JOHN 15:14

The best time of year is June when an exam or two is all that stands before that big door opening onto a glorious summer. It's at that time yearbooks are distributed. These yearbooks record your year in pictures: the candid young-and-crazy times, the formal try-and-look-cool times, the big-smiling best of times, the eyes-closed worst of times.

What the camera doesn't capture, your friends do. They scribble comments in the margins of their pictures about the times you shared: "Remember when..." or "I'll never forget the time that ..." Maybe some say, "I wish we could have gotten to know each other better, but ..."

Consider for a moment that you've entered a sort of time warp. Instead of this being, well, *this* year, you're back in the year A.D. 18. And instead of attending your school, you're actually a student at Nazareth Prep Academy. One of your schoolmates, a graduating senior, is a young man named Jesus Christ. Your yearbooks have just been distributed, and you've exchanged yours with him.

Put yourself in his shoes for a few minutes. If you had the same relationship with him in person that you have with him now, what would he write about you? What would he remember about the past year and the times the two of you spent together? Were those times memorable? What would he say about your relationship? Were you close? Or were you always just passing each other in the halls, so to speak?

Take some time to write what you think *he* would write beneath his picture in your yearbook:

_____

_____

_____

_____

What do these comments say about your friendship? Are there ways you could improve your relationship?

See also: John 15:15; James 4:4

▦ THE JUDGMENT

> *If, by the trespass of the one man, death reigned through that one man, how much more will those who receive God's abundant provision of grace and of the gift of righteousness reign in life through the one man, Jesus Christ.*

ROMANS 5:17

It was an open-and-shut case. The old man had been caught red-handed, heading out of the grocery store with a loaf of bread stuffed beneath his jacket. The facts were clear enough, and he even admitted his guilt. As he stood trembling before Judge LaGuardia in New York, he simply explained he stole the bread because his family was starving.

"Well, I have to punish you," Judge LaGuardia said. "The law makes no exception, and I have no choice but to fine you ten dollars."

The man swallowed hard, and his eyes grew moist. Where was he supposed to get that kind of money if he couldn't even afford a loaf of bread? The judge's sentence was beyond his ability to pay.

"The law is the law," he said curtly. But then the judge did something unexpected. He pulled out his wallet and extracted a bill. "But here's the ten dollars to pay for your fine.

"Furthermore," he said, tossing another dollar into his hat, "I am going to fine everyone in the courtroom fifty cents for living in a town where a man has to steal bread in order to eat." So he passed the hat up the aisle, and the old man, with the light of heaven in his eyes, left the courtroom with $47.50.

There's one word that describes the judge's action that day in New York: *grace*. Grace is when you get the opposite of what's deserved. It's the same word that describes God's action toward us. According to the laws of God, established from the foundation of the earth, the penalty of sin was death. And each of us, from Adam to ourselves and everybody else in between, has been caught red-handed. The law is the law, and the penalty had to be paid. But God did the unexpected. He paid the penalty himself. As Romans 5:8 says, "God demonstrates his own love for us in this: While we were still sinners, Christ died for us."

But he didn't stop there. As with the New York judge, he took matters one step further. He gave us a free gift of eternal life to boot.

It was a magnanimous act—so totally unexpected that the world hasn't gotten over it yet.

See also: Genesis 2:17; Romans 6:11–14, 23; Philippians 2:5–8

▪▪ OPEN MY EYES, LORD

Why do you look at the speck of sawdust in your brother's eye and pay no attention to the plank in your own eye? How can you say to your brother, "Let me take the speck out of your eye," when all the time there is a plank in your own eye? You hypocrite, first take the plank out of your own eye, and then you will see clearly to remove the speck from your brother's eye.

MATTHEW 7:3–5

Open my eyes, Lord, that I may see . . .
My haste to say, "You are wrong,"
My hesitance to say, "I am to blame,"
My frowns when the other guy or other team wins,
My smiles when I cross the finish line first;
My 20/20 vision at finding cracks in others' character,
My halfhearted efforts to spot any flaws in myself.

Open my ears, Lord, that I may hear . . .
My laughter at the expense of others,
My cries when tables turn and the joke's on me;
My whoops when something awful happens to those I don't like,
My sighs when I'm the one who is kicked in the teeth;
My shouts when I detect sin in others,
My whispers when I am confessing my own sin.

Open my mind, Lord, that I may know ...
My hardheadedness toward those who think I'm El Jerko,
My open-mindedness toward those who know I'm Mr. Right;
My recall of "place and time" when I've been wronged,
My forgetfulness of "when and how" I've hurt others;
My doubt that others have a snowball's chance of escaping hell,
My belief that I deserved heaven all along.

Open my heart, Lord, that I may feel ...
My hatred of sin when others are doing the sinning,
My love of sin when it's my hand in the cookie jar;
My judgment of those whose skin or beliefs differ from mine,
My compassion toward those who are basically just like me;
My rejection of those with a smudge on their cheek,
My acceptance of myself, despite the mud on my face.

See also: Luke 6:37–38; Romans 14:10–13; 1 Corinthians 4:5

■■ NEW BOUNDARIES

> **Be kind and compassionate to one another, forgiving each other, just as in Christ God forgave you.**
>
> **EPHESIANS 4:32**

It was another time and another place; during the early 1940s in France, to be exact. As Rita Snowden tells the story, some men carried the body of a dead friend to a church cemetery for burial. There they encountered unexpected problems.

The priest gently asked if their friend had been baptized in the Roman Catholic Church. When they said they weren't sure but figured he probably hadn't been, the priest said he unfortunately could not permit the burial in his churchyard. He apologized, but explained that rules were rules.

So the men sadly took their friend and buried him just outside the cemetery fence. It was dark when they finished the job, so they returned the following day to check on the grave. However, to their astonishment they could not locate it. Search as they might they could find no trace of the freshly dug soil.

Bewildered, they were about to leave when the priest approached and said he'd been troubled about not allowing their friend to be buried in the churchyard. So early in the morning he had risen from bed and *moved the fence* to include the body.

I think about that story whenever I get slighted in some awful way and feel tempted to seek revenge or shut the person out of my life. Perhaps you know the feeling: somebody wrongs you— blatantly—and you respond by erecting an emotional fence that leaves the person stranded and unforgiven on the other side.

That's a perfectly natural response. But what's natural and normal is not good enough in God's eyes. He would have you move the fence, just as he did for us. Even though we fell short of his standard by a country mile, God demonstrated his own love for us in this: "While we were still sinners, Christ died for us." That is, we deserved to be locked out of heaven, but Christ moved the barriers at Calvary.

Dwell on his supreme act of forgiveness today. And if there is somebody in your life who has done you wrong, ask God to help you forgive them, and thereby move the fence.

See also: Matthew 5:43–48; Romans 5:6–10

■ THE LONG SILENCE

> *We do not have a high priest who is unable to sympathize with our weaknesses, but we have one who has been tempted in every way, just as we are—yet was without sin.*

HEBREWS 4:15

The following story by A. T. L. Armstrong is well-known, but I hope you'll agree it is worth retelling:

At the end of time, billions of people were scattered on a great plain before God's throne. Most shrank back from the brilliant light before them. But groups near the front talked heatedly—not with cringing shame, but with belligerence.

"How can God judge us? How can he know about suffering?" snapped a young woman, who jerked back a sleeve to reveal a tattooed number from a Nazi concentration camp. "We endured terror, beatings, torture, death!"

In another group, a young black man lowered his collar. "What about this?" he demanded, showing an ugly rope burn. "Lynched for no crime but being black! We have suffered in slave ships, been wrenched from loved ones, toiled till only death gave release."

Far out across the plain were hundreds of such groups. Each had a complaint against God for the evil and suffering he had permitted in his world. How lucky God was to live in heaven where there was no weeping, no fear, no hunger, no hatred. Indeed, what did God know of what man had endured in this world?

So each of these groups sent forth a leader, chosen because he had suffered most. There was a Jew, a black, an untouchable from India, an illegitimate, a horribly deformed arthritic, a victim of Hiroshima, and one from a Siberian prison camp. In the center of the plain, they consulted with each other.

At last they were ready to present their case. It was rather simple. Before God would be qualified to be their judge, he must endure what they had endured. Their decision was that God should be sentenced to live on earth—as a man!

But because he was God, they set certain safeguards to be sure he could not use his divine powers to help himself: Let him be born a Jew. Let the legitimacy of his birth be doubted, so that none will know who is really his father. Give him a work so difficult that even his family will snicker when he tries to do it. Let him try to describe what no man has ever seen, tasted, heard, or smelled. Let him try to describe God to man. Let him be betrayed by his dearest friends. Let him be indicted on false charges, tried before a prejudiced jury, convicted by a cowardly judge. At last, let him see what it means to be terribly alone, completely abandoned by every living thing. Let him be tortured, and then die!

When the list of conditions had been finalized, the thought seemed to strike all of the representatives at the same time. Slowly they backed away, and then disbanded altogether. They had no case. God, they realized, had already served the sentence.

See also: Romans 5:7–11; Philippians 2:8; 1 John 4:10–12

■ SEEKING AND SAVING

When Jesus heard what had happened, he withdrew by boat privately to a solitary place. Hearing of this, the crowds followed him on foot from the towns. When Jesus landed and saw a large crowd, he had compassion on them and healed their sick.

MATTHEW 14:13–14

Again and again throughout the Gospels, you read of Christ's compassion. When you come to a passage about him healing the sick, the blind, or the lame, it often is preceded with the statement: "He had compassion on them." Compassion is what motivated him to act.

Compassion has carried a divine flavor ever since. Compassion is, however, not the same thing as sympathy. Like pity, sympathy costs nothing and is worth nothing. Sympathy is the *thought* of love; compassion the *act*. When sympathy shrugs, "I might," compassion shouts, "*I will*."

I can better illustrate the difference between the two by describing an incident that occurred when I took a wild adventure deep into South America. One night after pitching camp, three of us headed down to the banks of the Beni River to hunt alligators for dinner. But on the way I stepped into a mud-filled sinkhole. I whooped it up like a little kid—until I noticed that the once ankle-deep mud was covering my knees. By the time it reached my thighs I pictured myself as a target for a hungry alligator and began calling for help.

One of my friends ran up to my side and began pulling hard on my arm. Before long we were sinking side by side. I really started yelling for help then. Another of my friends ran up, calmly surveyed our situation, then extended a thick branch that we grabbed and used to pull ourselves free.

That's the way it is with sympathy and compassion. Misery loves company, and a sympathetic person is quick to provide it—and soon sinks into the misery, too. A compassionate person works to *alleviate* trouble.

Thankfully, our Lord is filled with compassion toward us, rather than just sympathy. Compassion paved the way to heaven and got us saved; sympathy would merely have gotten us a consoling pat on the back.

See also: Isaiah 54:7–10; Matthew 15:29–38; 2 Corinthians 1:3–4

■■ POINTS TO PONDER – COMPASSION

As God's chosen people, holy and dearly loved, clothe yourselves with compassion, kindness, humility, gentleness and patience.

COLOSSIANS 3:12

The dew of compassion is a tear.

LORD BYRON

The root of the matter is a very simple and old-fashioned thing, a thing so simple that I am almost ashamed to mention it for fear of the derisive smile with which wise cynics will greet my words. The thing I mean—please forgive me for mentioning it—is love. Christian love, or compassion.

BERTRAND RUSSELL

Tell me how much you know of the sufferings of your fellow men and I will tell you how much you have loved them.

HELMUT THIELICKE

The best portion of a good man's life is his little, nameless, unremembered acts of kindness and of love.

WILLIAM WORDSWORTH

Compassion is the sometimes fatal capacity for feeling what it's like to live inside somebody else's skin. It is the knowledge that there can never really be any peace and joy for me until there is peace and joy finally for you, too.

FREDERICK BUECHNER

If you quit loving the moment it becomes difficult, you never discover compassion.

DAVID AUGSBURGER

The value of compassion cannot be over-emphasized. Anyone can criticize. It takes a true believer to be compassionate. No greater burden can be borne by an individual than to know no one cares or understands.

ARTHUR H. STAINBACK

Compassion is the basis of all morality.

ARTHUR SCHOPENHAUER

Not a sigh is breathed, not a pain felt, not a grief pierces the soul, but the throb vibrates to the Father's heart.

ANONYMOUS

There is no exercise better for the heart than reaching down and lifting people up.

JOHN ANDREW HOLMER

When you are in trouble, people who call to sympathize are really looking for the particulars.

ED HOWE

Man may dismiss compassion from his heart, but God never will.

WILLIAM COWPER

Cleverness will enable a man to make a sermon, but only compassion for lost men will make him a soul winner.

LEONARD RAVENHILL

Should we feel at times disheartened and discouraged, a simple movement of heart toward God will renew our powers. Whatever he may demand of us, he will give us at the moment the strength and the courage we need.

FRANÇOIS DE SALIGNAC DE LA MOTHE FÉNELON

See also: Isaiah 54:10; Zechariah 7:9–10; Mark 8:1–8

WEEK

49

■■ IN GOOD HANDS

The Lord will go before you, the God of Israel will be your rear guard.

ISAIAH 52:12

When you're a senior in high school, you're supposed to feel invincible. Everybody says you have your whole life ahead of you and can be anything you want to be—even the president. Right. Then how come a simple little question from your aunt like, "By the way, what are you going to do next year?" causes a major panic attack?

Far from feeling invincible, you feel as if you're about to be swallowed by the great big world you're supposed to have by the tail. What are you going to do with your life? Marriage? College? Career? You haven't the foggiest, and that fact alone scares you to death.

While you can't know where the future will lead, God can because he has scouted up ahead. "The Lord will go before you," Isaiah says in the verse above. You need not worry. "For I know the plans I have for you," declares the Lord, "plans to prosper you and not to harm you, plans to give you hope and a future" (Jeremiah 29:11).

If that's not security enough, Isaiah also offers the assurance that God follows behind you: "The God of Israel will be your rear guard." This is military lingo. The Israelite army always had a vanguard and a rear guard. The vanguard preceded the soldiers and scouted unexplored territory. The rear guard followed behind, helping stragglers, and more or less picking up the pieces.

God does the same thing. He understands that you are sometimes hesitant to move forward because of past failures, bad memories, nagging sins, and old wounds. No problem. God follows behind, forgiving your sins, and helping you back on your feet. He picks up the pieces of your life, mending and restoring hurts and sorrows, and even creating positive results from negative incidents.

As the psalmist writes, "You hem me in, behind and before; you have laid your hand upon me. Such knowledge is too wonderful for me, too lofty for me to attain" (Psalm 139:5–6). Indeed, God has a magnificent plan for your life that exceeds your wildest imaginings. And he's willing to both guide and guard you toward that destination. Why? He simply wants you to experience the "riches of his glory," which he has planned for you from the beginning of time.

See also: Deuteronomy 31:8; Ephesians 1:18–2:7

SURPRISE ENDINGS

No eye has seen, no ear has heard, no mind has conceived what God has prepared for those who love him.

1 CORINTHIANS 2:9

As discussed yesterday, people are sometimes hesitant to draw closer to God and discover his unique plan for their lives because of past failures. Maybe you feel this way, too. Others may look at you and see a pretty decent Christian on the outside—but you know there's a monster lurking inside.

You know your innermost feelings and secret thoughts— thoughts that if flashed on a TV screen would send you running in embarrassment. Or perhaps you feel like you've let God down—not once or twice, but so many hundreds of times that you're beyond forgiveness. And now you're at the point where it seems that his magnificent plan for your life is but a mirage. Your life is full of regrets. Hounded by old wounds and bad memories, you think, "If only I had ..."

If you think your life is shattered because of something you've done or neglected to do, consider Rahab. One of the more illustrious characters in the Bible, she is listed as being a key part of the family tree leading to Christ's birth (Matthew 1:5). And both the author of Hebrews (Hebrews 11:31) and the author of James (James 2:25) commend her for her great faith. Yet a peek at her resume in Joshua 2 indicates that she was the first of the red-hot mamas, operating the best little whorehouse in Jericho.

Do you think she had regrets? Assuredly so. But she was smart enough that in her moment of greatest need, she turned toward God rather than turning away. And surprise of surprises: God welcomed her with open arms! It's the kind of "happily ever after" ending that makes you want to jump to your feet and applaud, to kick up your heels and holler, "Way to go, God!"

But save your applause for the grand finale. As the verse from 1 Corinthians above indicates, the Lord is saving the best for last. He's got a surprise up his sleeve that will boggle your most bizarre imaginings. It's a homecoming party reserved for those who, like Rahab, can quit stewing about the past and proceed to kick up their heels in the sunshine of God's love and forgiveness.

See also: Psalm 103; Romans 5:20

■■ PLAIN EVERYDAY KINDNESS

Love is kind.

1 Corinthians 13:4

I woke up this morning like I usually do, with my mouth feeling like a sweater and the rest of me feeling like a bad accident. I proceeded through my usual morning routine of showering and shaving and got to the point when I was just about to nick myself in the usual place on my chin when something rather nice happened. My wife quietly set a cup of coffee on the sink beside me, touched me gently on the arm, and then slipped away.

I don't know why that particular action made such an impression on me; my wife is normally pretty nice. But as I stood there with the razor poised to cut myself, it struck me that she didn't *have* to get me the coffee. I didn't even ask her to. Acting entirely on her own free will, she had chosen to be ... well, kind. Not major kind, or automatic kind. Just plain everyday kind.

Early in our marriage we established a sort of rule that we would always try to be just plain everyday kind to each other. In the early years, however, we pretty much kept score. I knew when I was being kinder than she was, and she noticed when her acts of kindness went *un*noticed. But after a while, these everyday courtesies became a habit.

So now, if I'm in bed at night and my wife asks me to slip downstairs and turn off the cuckoo clock, I just get up and do it. I don't think much about it because the next day I might ask her to get me an aspirin from the medicine cabinet. I sometimes clean her hairbrush; she sometimes straightens my desk.

These are all things we could just as easily do for ourselves, and probably nine times out of ten we do. But by gladly doing them for each other, we demonstrate our love in very plain, ordinary ways. I can't help but think that has something to do with the fact that we're still married.

This isn't a particularly cosmic thought, I know. But this morning I experienced a small moment of unexpected kindness that set my day off. And in that moment I realized that kindness makes a difference.

See also: Matthew 20:25–28; 2 Corinthians 9:12–13

▟ REACHING OUT

Always try to be kind to each other and to everyone else.

1 Thessalonians 5:15

I sometimes wonder if kindness isn't becoming as extinct as dinosaurs. That thought crossed my mind the other day when I pulled into what used to be called a "service" station for help, and the guy watching TV in the bullet-proof booth growled, "Sorry, no mechanics, only gas!"

All too often I feel like comedian Jay Leno, who says he once chided a supermarket clerk for failing to say thank you, only for her to snap back, "It's printed on your receipt!"

As discussed yesterday, a little kindness goes a long way. And the Bible indicates that plain everyday acts of kindness are noticed in heaven. Welcoming a little child or giving the weary a cup of cold water (Mark 9:37, 41), are specific acts commended by Christ.

Kindness means you smile. You look cheerful. You talk. It means you write an encouraging note on paper rather than just thinking about it in your head.

Kindness means sitting next to the new kid from Kentucky or offering your bus seat to the lady with three screaming kids. It's opening the door for your mom.

Kindness means listening to your grandmother tell the same story for the zeptillionth time, or laughing politely when your dad repeats his stale jokes for the zillyzeptillionth time. It's wishing your teacher a nice weekend.

Kindness means going the second mile, turning the other cheek, and loving people more than they deserve. It's not pretending you're asleep when your dad peeks in your room and wants to talk.

Kindness means opening your home to strangers and your heart to people who think, look, and act differently than you do. It's passing on a compliment, keeping a secret, and hushing up a rumor.

When you have more hassles in your day than hours, it's easy for kindness to get lost in the squeeze. When faced with stress, most people stay close to home base, worrying about their own concerns before thinking about making somebody else's day. It takes time and effort to be kind. And it's usually not convenient.

But that's what kindness is all about. It's being willing to take the time and give the effort—even when inconvenient. And at the end of your life, you can say you've lived well if you've been generous with those "little, nameless, unremembered acts of kindness" (Wordsworth). You might even go so far as to think of them as stepping-stones toward heaven.

See also: Acts 20:35; 1 Peter 3:8–9

:: AGAINST THE WALL

A cheerful heart is good medicine, but a crushed spirit dries up the bones.

PROVERBS 17:22

Whenever I'm faced with tough times or a gut-deep case of the gloomies, I find hope in the following story by G. W. Target. Place a copy in your locker or on your bathroom mirror. Or pass it along to a friend who is struggling:

There were once two men, both seriously ill, in the same small room of a great hospital. Quite a small room, it had one window looking out on the world.

One of the men, as part of his treatment, was allowed to sit up in bed for an hour in the afternoon (something to do with draining the fluid from his lungs). His bed was next to the window. But the other man had to spend all his time flat on his back.

Every afternoon when the man next to the window was propped up for his hour, he would pass the time by describing what he could see outside. The window apparently overlooked a park where there was a lake. There were ducks and swans in the lake, and children came to throw them bread and sail model boats. Young lovers walked hand in hand beneath the trees, and there were flowers and stretches of grass, games of softball. And at the back, behind the fringe of trees, was a fine view of the city skyline.

The man on his back would listen to the other man describe all of this, enjoying every minute. He heard how a child nearly fell into the lake, and how beautiful the girls were in their summer dresses. His friend's descriptions eventually made him feel he could almost see what was happening outside.

Then one fine afternoon, the thought struck him: Why should the man next to the window have all the pleasure of seeing what was going on? Why shouldn't he get the chance? He felt ashamed, but the more he tried not to think like that, the worse he wanted a change. He'd do anything!

One night as he stared at the ceiling, the other man suddenly woke up, coughing and choking, his hands groping for the button that would bring the nurse running. But the man watched without moving—even when the sound of breathing stopped. In the morning, the nurse found the other man dead, and quietly took his body away.

As soon as it seemed decent, the man asked if he could be switched to the bed next to the window. And they moved him, tucked him in, and made him quite comfortable. The minute they'd gone, he propped himself up on one elbow, painfully and laboriously, and looked out the window.

It faced a blank wall.

I've known people whose lives have "faced a blank wall"—of tight finances, intense pain, or a broken family—yet they somehow managed to convey hope and joy to those around them. Their joy was not dependent on circumstances, but on the Lord. As Nehemiah wrote, "The joy of the Lord is your strength" (Nehemiah 8:10). Indeed, joy is soul deep. And if you know the Lord, it should be evidenced in your life . . . even when there is nothing to smile about.

See also: Habakkuk 3:17–19; 1 Thessalonians 5:16–18

▪▪ SERIOUS BUSINESS

May the God of hope fill you with all joy and peace as you trust in him, so that you may overflow with hope by the power of the Holy Spirit.

ROMANS 15:13

One of my best friends in high school didn't want to become a Christian for one main reason. It wasn't that she didn't believe in God; she basically did. But she had this fear that he would take away all her fun. For her, life was a party. And her gut feeling about God was that he was something of a party pooper. At least that's the impression she got from most of the Christians she knew.

Over and over she heard the testimonies of how new Christians had given up things like booze and cigarettes and sex. Some had even quit dancing and going to movies. But if you asked her, they also seemed to have sworn off smiling and laughing and having genuine stand-up-and-holler good-old-times. She had one word which described the whole bunch: boring. It was a broad generalization, to be sure. But it came close to the mark.

Jesus had similar complaints about the religious people of his day. The synagogues were filled with stuffy starched-togas who thought they knew all about God but didn't know a thing about living or laughing. On days of fasting, they assumed the personality of soggy oatmeal and advertised their holiness by moaning and groaning on street corners.

Holiness was important to Christ, but so was happiness. And if you take his life as an example, you see that the two characteristics are not mutually exclusive. Having one doesn't mean you can't have the other. It simply cannot be said that during his time on earth Christ didn't enjoy kicking up his heels a little. He liked parties and fun and swarms of kids—and it was for these things that the sour-puss Pharisees criticized him most.

Christ was a storyteller, and the tales he spun were often of joyous feasts and celebrations. He wanted people to know that heaven was not something to dread, but something to look forward to, something that ought to get your blood pumping with excitement. In fact, he likened the kingdom of God to a rollicking banquet and a wedding feast—tremendously happy, joyous occasions. His first miracle, that of turning water into wine, was done for the pure, unadulterated pleasure of those around him.

Isaiah may have described Christ as being "a man of sorrows, and familiar with suffering" (Isaiah 53:3), but that doesn't mean he was a stranger to joy and happiness. And there's every indication that he's preparing a major, foot-stomping bash for his children in heaven. Indeed, joy is serious business with Christ. And if you seek to be conformed to his image, you might consider kicking up your heels and shouting "Whoopee!" at least once before the day is out. Twice, if you mean it.

See also: 1 Corinthians 2:9; Hebrews 12:2

POINTS TO PONDER – JOY AND HAPPINESS

If you obey my commands, you will remain in my love, just as I have obeyed my Father's commands and remain in his love. I have told you this so that my joy may be in you and that your joy may be complete.

JOHN 15:10–11

What I am anxious to see in Christian believers is a beautiful paradox. I want to see in them the joy of finding God while at the same time they are blessedly pursuing him. I want to see in them the great joy of having God and yet always wanting him.

A. W. TOZER

The moments of happiness we enjoy take us by surprise. It is not that we seize them, but that they seize us.

ASHLEY MONTAGUE

Be happy while you're living, for you're a long time dead.

SCOTTISH PROVERB

You cannot read the Gospels without seeing that Jesus did not tell men how to be good in the manner of the moralists of every age, he told them how to be happy.

SIR THOMAS TAYLOR

This is the secret of joy. We shall no longer strive for our own way; but commit ourselves, easily and simply, to God's way, acquiesce in his will and in so doing find our peace.

EVELYN UNDERHILL

There is no happiness for people at the expense of other people.

ANWAR EL-SADAT

We hold these truths to be self-evident: that all men are created equal; that they are endowed by their Creator with certain inalienable Rights; that among these are Life, Liberty and the pursuit of Happiness.

THE DECLARATION OF INDEPENDENCE

A "right to happiness" . . . sounds to me as odd as a right to good luck. For I believe—whatever one school of moralists may say—that we depend for a very great deal of our happiness or misery on circumstances outside all human control. A right to happiness doesn't, for me, make much more sense than a right to be six feet tall, or to have a millionaire for your father, or to get good weather whenever you want to have a picnic.

C. S. LEWIS

The foolish man seeks happiness in the distance, the wise grows it under his feet.

JAMES OPPENHEIM

There are joys which long to be ours. God sends ten thousand truths, which come about us like birds seeking inlet; but we are shut up to them, and so they bring us nothing, but sit and sing awhile upon the roof, and then fly away.

HENRY WARD BEECHER

May we never let the things we can't have, or don't have, or shouldn't have, spoil our enjoyment of the things we do have and can have. As we value our happiness let us not forget it, for one of the greatest lessons in life is learning to be happy without the things we cannot or should not have.

RICHARD L. EVANS

See also: Psalm 30:4–5; Ecclesiastes 2:26; 1 Thessalonians 5:16–18

WEEK
50

∷ LAWS OF THE LAND

> *I have chosen the way of truth; I have set my heart on your laws. I hold fast to your statutes, O Lord; do not let me be put to shame. I run in the path of your commands, for you have set my heart free.*
>
> **PSALM 119:30–32**

We all know about laws such as those that prohibit us from running red lights or having target practice on a downtown street or disrobing in public. But there are some amazing regulations still on the books that might not be so familiar.

For instance, did you know that you cannot make ugly faces at anyone in Zion City, Illinois, bite your landlord in Rumford, Maine, or mistreat a rat in Denver? Not to mention that you can't wear a false mustache in an Alabama church if it's likely to make people laugh, or grow a real one in Indiana if you are one who "habitually kisses human beings."

In San Jose, California, it is still illegal to sleep in your neighbor's outhouse without his permission. It's also illegal to hang men's and women's underwear on the same clothesline in Minnesota, to spit on your laundry in San Francisco, or to tickle a girl under the chin with a feather duster in Portland, Maine.

Though these laws remain in the various penal codes, we recognize how silly and outmoded they are. Yet we often perpetuate other nonsensical laws in our society—laws that are regularly adhered to though they are not formally recognized.

For instance, we still subscribe to the unwritten law that people are valued more for what they are (good-looking, talented, bright) rather than for who they are in God's eyes (unique creations whom he loves infinitely). In a similar fashion, we undervalue the outcast, the handicapped, the poor—the very people to whom Christ devoted special time and attention.

An additional belief we often hold is that success is determined by the size of your bank account, the worth of your car, the prestige of your job—though in God's eyes these are all nonessentials that you can spend your whole life seeking, only to lose your soul in the process.

Someday . . . yes, someday we will recognize that these unwritten laws are as silly as those which forbid you to swim on dry land in Santa Ana, California, hunt ducks from an airplane in Colorado, or punch a bull in the nose in Washington, D. C.

See also: Psalm 146; Matthew 5:3–10; 6:19–21; Luke 12:13–34

■■ GET OFF MY BACK!

There will be terrible times in the last days. People will be lovers of themselves, lovers of money, boastful, proud, abusive, disobedient to their parents, ungrateful, unholy.

2 TIMOTHY 3:1–2

It's been said that you should treat your parents with all the respect, patience, and understanding you'd show a friend. Tim Stafford figured that's how he'd always treated them, but then he had a little daydream. What if his best friend came over, and he treated him like he commonly treated his parents . . .

"Hi," Ernie said. "Are you ready to go to the basketball game?"

"Would you get off my back?" I said in my most exasperated tone. "What difference does it make if we're a little late?"

"None, I guess. What did you do this afternoon?"

"Nothing," I grunted.

"Did you have practice after school?"

"Nah."

"So what did you do?"

"Why do you always pry into my private life?" I exploded.

"Sorry," Ernie said. He looked a little hurt and tried to change the subject. "Hey, I saw you talking to Charlotte today. How do you rate? She's really something, isn't she?"

"Look, I can't see that it's any of your business."

"Hey, I was just trying to . . . Aw, forget it. Let's go."

"Can I have five bucks?" I asked.

"Well, I don't know," Ernie said doubtfully. "I don't have much money. Don't you have any money of your own?"

"Where would I get it?" I asked sarcastically. "I suppose you want me to get a job on top of everything else I do."

"Who said anything about a job?"

"Everybody always wants you to get terrific grades and practically be an Einstein, but they won't loan you the money to go to a basketball game and relax once in a while. I suppose you'd prefer I went out drinking. That's cheaper, you know."

"Forget I said anything," Ernie said. "You can have the money. Let's just go to the game. We're late already."

"You're always pushing me," I grumbled on the way out the door. But I stopped. "Ernie, do we have to go in that crummy car? It looks so old. Everybody else drives a new car, and I have to go in that beat-up refugee from a junkyard. Can't you get something new?"

"I would if I had the money," Ernie mumbled.

"That's the trouble with you," I said. "All you think about is money. You're so tied up in cash that you don't take time to think about what's important to the rest of us."

"Yeah, right," Ernie said, his head down.

"You bet I'm right," I said. "And if you think I'm going to sit with you at the game, you're crazy!"

See also: Proverbs 15:20; 20:20; 23:25; Ephesians 6:1–2

■■ PERSONAL CONCERN

You shall not misuse the name of the Lord your God, for the Lord will not hold anyone guiltless who misuses his name.

EXODUS 20:7

I was one hundred miles out to sea, trying to hook up with a school of halibut making their way from Japan. But it looked like there would be no fishing because, despite the zeptillion gallons of ocean all around me, there didn't appear to be any fish. And so after a couple of hours I lay back and tried to do something worthwhile, like work on my tan.

I was drifting off to never-never land when all of a sudden a crew member screamed, "Hook up!" at the top of his lungs. The engine was cut, and as the boat coasted into the middle of a school of fish, everybody raced for the bait tank and then flung their lines overboard.

Moments later, even as I was grabbing for a bait fish, one of the fishermen bellowed excitedly, "Jesus Christ, I hooked a whale!"

I've been around enough to know people don't mean anything by using Christ's name in that way. He might just as well have said, "Wow!" or "Man alive!" or some other such phrase to convey his excitement. But he didn't.

Upon hearing the name of Christ shouted across the ocean like that, I immediately looked up. It was like the way I react when I hear somebody calling the name of a good friend across the parking lot—I glance up, scan the aisles of cars, and half expect to see my friend standing nearby—but more often than not, the person is calling somebody else. I had that same reaction that day out at sea. It was almost as if I expected Christ to be standing right there. I take the name Jesus Christ that personally.

I thought about saying something to the man, but let it pass—until a short time later when he GD'd up a storm after accidentally snagging his finger on the tip of the hook. I walked over, told him I was sorry about his finger, but then said something to the effect of, "Contrary to popular belief, God's last name is not Damn."

People use his name without really thinking about it, and maybe that's the problem. God is picky about how his name is used, and he doesn't want it profaned by loose usage. He wants you to think about it, to ponder it. His is a holy name—a name the Bible says should cause every person to worship him: "At the name of Jesus every knee should bow, in heaven and on earth and under the earth, and every tongue confess that Jesus Christ is Lord" (Philippians 2:10–11).

Right now people have a choice in that matter. Ultimately, however, all people will worship him as Lord—whether willingly or not: "'As surely as I live,' says the Lord, 'every knee will bow before me; every tongue will confess to God'" (Romans 14:11).

I think it's important to remind people about that from time to time.

See also: Leviticus 19:12; Ezekiel 39:7; Matthew 5:33–37

:: LOVING GOD

> *You see, at just the right time, when we were still powerless, Christ died for the ungodly. Very rarely will anyone die for a righteous man, though for a good man someone might possibly dare to die. But God demonstrates his own love for us in this: While we were still sinners, Christ died for us.*

ROMANS 5:6–8

"If" love is conditional. It says I love you, Lord ...

if you get my parents off my back;
if you give me the inside track with the babe of my dreams;
if you do something about my boss;
if you cure my acne;
if you get me accepted to the college of my choice;
if you arrange my life like I feel it ought to be arranged.

"Because" love is easy love. It says I love you, Lord ...

because I just got a pay raise and can finally start living;
because I aced an exam I didn't even study for;
because my car repair bill was only $57.60;
because things are looking good with Blue Eyes;
because my creep brother actually got saved;
because things are basically going well for me right now.

"Anyhow" love is hard, unconditional love. It says I love you, Lord ...

anyhow, even if the lab tests are positive;
anyhow, even when the only person I can talk to moves away;
anyhow, even though people die because of hunger and war;
anyhow, even if Grandpa doesn't make it through the night;
anyhow, even when you don't answer my prayers like I want;
anyhow, even when my life is crumbling and you feel distant;

Lord, I desperately want to love you *anyhow*, with no strings attached ... because that's how you love me. I am trying, honestly trying, to learn to love and worship you the same way.

See also: Mark 12:28–30; John 14:15; 1 John 2:3–6

◨ MAYBE NEXT WEEK

> **Let us not give up meeting together, as some are in the habit of doing, but let us encourage one another – and all the more as you see the Day approaching.**
>
> **HEBREWS 10:25**

Lord, I keep telling myself I need to go to church more, but after a whole week of racing around mornings to get ready for school, and then having to show up for work at the crack of dawn Saturday ... well, Sunday is the one day of the week I've got to sleep in. You don't mind if I take a little break, do you? Just this Sunday?

You're an understanding God, right? One who knows that church is just another item on my pressure-cooker list of things to do. I'm fifty pages behind the class in history, I've got a five-pager to write for English, and I'm looking down the barrel at a big test in biology. Not to mention that my mom's hounding me to paint the fence, my radiator needs flushing, and my girlfriend hasn't been called in two days. No offense, Lord, but I just don't think my schedule can handle any additional strain.

I'm not making excuses here, but ... I don't think I *can* get out of bed. After last night's party, there's this feeling I have of train whistles blowing in my head. If Sunday morning came at any other time of the week, I could probably cope with it. But it comes so early after Saturday night, which is the one night I can stay out late and have a good time and ... oh, my aching head!

Okay, Lord, I'm getting up. See? The covers are off and my right foot is touching the ground. Maybe with a couple of aspirin I can make it through the service without falling out of the pew and grabbing my head. There, now, both feet are ... *Yawn!* ... on the ground, and ... *Stretch!* ... Give me just five more minutes to sleep, and then ...

Lord, I must have overslept! Oh, no—it's already 10:05 and I've missed church! Well, not exactly. There's always the second service, but I probably wouldn't know anybody. And then there's the matter of the playoffs starting in just a couple hours, which is just enough time to shower and eat and ...

Lord, maybe things will be different next week. Yeah, maybe.

See also: Genesis 2:2–3; Matthew 18:20; Acts 2:42

■■ TOP SECRET

Keep watch, because you do not know on what day your Lord will come.

MATTHEW 24:42

The world stopped to listen a few years ago when Chicago's mayor announced plans to move into the city's Cabrini Green housing projects. It seemed like a nutty thing to do.

The high-rise neighborhood is a virtual hell on earth—a world where thirteen-year-olds tuck sawed-off shotguns beneath their beds at night; a world where if you don't join a gang, you mortgage your life for "protection"; a world where court cases are regularly dropped because witnesses suddenly "forget" what they saw or mysteriously "disappear"; a neighborhood where you wouldn't take your dog for a walk—if you cared for the dog.

The mayor wanted to establish peace in the neighborhood once and for all by moving in. Reporters around the world wanted to know the date of the move, but calls were not returned. Repairmen, police, exterminators—everyone sought information about when the mayor would arrive so they could prepare, get things polished up, put their best foot forward. But the mayor stonewalled.

"My arrival will be a secret. No one will know until I'm there," the mayor said, not wanting people to start cleaning things up the day before. Without a move-in date, there would be daily anticipation. Everybody would have a better quality of life if The Day could happen any old day.

And so it was some 2,000 years ago when Christ promised to return to earth, but declined to say exactly when. Had he pinpointed the date, people would have circled it in red on their calendars and then ducked into church the day before to repent.

But nobody knows the hour or the day of his arrival. He intended that we live each day as if his arrival were imminent. He wants to be greeted by saints, not whitewashed pretenders.

See also: Matthew 24:37–44; 25:1–13

▪▪ POINTS TO PONDER – WORSHIP

Come, let us bow down in worship, let us kneel before the Lord our Maker; for he is our God and we are the people of his pasture, the flock under his care. Today, if you hear his voice, do not harden your hearts.

PSALM 95:6–8

It cannot be that the instinct which has led to the erection of cathedrals, and of churches in every village, is wholly mistaken and misleading. There must be some great truth underlying the instinct for worship.

SIR OLIVER LODGE

Measure not men by Sundays, without regarding what they do all the week after.

THOMAS FULLER

Rejoice in him and make a fool of yourself for him the way lovers have always made fools of themselves for the one they love. A Quaker Meeting, a Pontifical High Mass, the Family Service at First Presbyterian, a Holy Roller Happening—unless there is an element of joy and foolishness in the proceedings, the time would be better spent doing something useful.

FREDERICK BUECHNER

When Christian worship is dull and joyless, Jesus Christ has been left outside—that is the only possible explanation.

JAMES S. STEWART

O my Lord! If I worship Thee from fear of hell, burn me in hell, and if I worship Thee from hope of Paradise, exclude me from it;

but if I worship Thee for Thine own sake, then withhold not from me Thine Eternal Beauty.

RABIA AL-ADAWIYYA

The glory of God is a living man; and the life of man consists in beholding God.

ST. IRENAEUS

It is only when men begin to worship that they begin to grow.

CALVIN COOLIDGE

Many of today's young people have little difficulty believing that God was in Christ. What they find hard to accept is that Christ is in the church.

ERNEST T. CAMPBELL

As you worship, so you serve.

THOMAS L. JOHNS

To worship God means to serve him.

FREDERICK BUECHNER

Some people in church look like guests at a royal banquet, who couldn't afford to be left out, but have been forbidden by their doctor to eat anything.

W. R. MALTBIE

The true inner life is no strange or new thing; it is the ancient and true worship of God, the Christian life in its beauty and in its own peculiar form. Wherever there is a man who fears God and lives the good life, in any country under the sun, God is there, loving him, and so I love him too.

GERHARD TERSTEEGEN

See also: 1 Chronicles 16:29; Luke 4:5–8; John 4:23–24

**W
E
E
K**

51

■ THOSE "IMPOSSIBLE" POSSIBILITIES

> *I am the Lord, the God of all mankind. Is anything too hard for me?*

JEREMIAH 32:27

For high school graduation, I was given an "indestructible" scuba-diving watch. It worked fine—until I accidentally smashed it.

Bits of the fluorescent hour and minute hands were jarred loose and jammed the inner workings. After that the watch never kept proper time. So I got a small screwdriver, pried the timepiece open, and began tinkering. That's when my *real* trouble began. Tiny gears soon littered the table—gears that are infinitely easier to take apart than put back together.

When I finally took the impossible mess to a specialist, his eyes popped. "What on earth have you *done?*" he asked, clucking his tongue. I just shrugged my shoulders and grinned sheepishly.

Our problem as Christians is that we hang onto our problems. This quirk isn't related only to mechanical things such as watches and cars—it's carried over into our everyday spiritual life as well. When problems hit, we probe and ponder, seeking our own solution. We worry and calculate. We simply don't go to the Specialist soon enough. When we finally turn the matter over to God, he gets the leftovers—the mishmash *left over* after our tinkering is done.

Yet the problems we fret most about are the very things we ought to trust God with. Nothing is too difficult for him.

"Yeah, but you don't know my situation," you think.

Reread the end of Jeremiah 32:27: "Is *anything* too hard for me?" Where you see the word "anything," substitute the concern you are carrying now. Fill in the blank: Is _____ too hard for me?

Your impossibility may be about finances or parents or feelings of inferiority or an old habit or your school plans next year or your job. A friendship healed, a bad memory erased, a sin forgiven, a family reconciled—*nothing* is too hard for the Lord.

Release your grip on your worries now. For as Christ said, "What is impossible with men is possible with God."

See also: Jeremiah 32:17; Luke 18:27

■■ JUST ANOTHER SOMEBODY

Be gracious to me, for I am lonely.

PSALM 25:16

I sometimes wondered what it would be like to be student-body president, to look good in a swimsuit, to have people call my name and wave across the cafeteria, to have my picture in the school newspaper.

But that's just for other people, I figured. It would never happen to me.

I sat behind a cheerleader in geometry. She always had a ribbon in her hair—sometimes red, sometimes blue, sometimes yellow. It was always pressed and perfectly tied on a braid of her chocolate hair.

One day I saw her with her mom at the nearby mall. It was a Saturday, and I nearly bumped into her as I rounded the corner out of the music shop.

"Excuse me," I quickly muttered. When I looked up and saw it was her, I nearly died of embarrassment. But I forced a smile and said "Hi." She said "Hi" back, but in a real nonchalant way, then kept walking.

"Who was that?" I heard her mom say as they passed by.

"I don't know," the cheerleader said. "Just somebody from class."

Just somebody from class. That made me sound so anonymous, so faceless. I'd been sitting behind her the entire year, and she didn't even know my name. I knew hers ... even her middle name.

Why does school have to be such a lonely place, Lord? The question popped into my mind one day on a bus ride home from school. It was so crowded that there were two, sometimes three to a seat. Some freshman girl I didn't know was crammed beside me.

You'd think with all these kids, school would be one great party. Maybe it is for others, but not for me, I thought. *You know my name, don't you, Lord? I just wish you weren't the only one.*

I glanced at the girl next to me. On any other day, I probably would not have given her a second thought. But she looked as lonely as I felt. When our eyes unexpectedly met, I forced an awkward smile. I didn't know what to say, but I mumbled something that made her smile. She said something back, and I responded.

It was a brief exchange with somebody I didn't know, but in those moments I got out of my skin and didn't feel so lonely. I think it was the same for the girl, who probably got on the bus feeling like a sardine and left feeling like somebody noticed her.

That's when it struck me: the antidote for loneliness is to build bridges with other people instead of walls. That's not a particularly cosmic thought, I know. But it's something to remember on those blue, just-another-somebody days.

See also: Matthew 5:46–47; John 15:9–17; Revelation 21:1–4

██ LOOKING FOR CHANGE

O Lord, you have searched me and you know me. You know when I sit and when I rise; you perceive my thoughts from afar. You discern my going out and my lying down; you are familiar with all my ways.

PSALM 139:1–3

By the time I graduated from high school and completed two years of college, I was ready for a change. I wanted to get away from old friends, my family, from textbooks and Friday nights at the library, from the same old nickel-and-dime striving to get better grades. And I was bored with myself. So I went to Europe for a year. I thought that would solve all my problems.

At first, boredom didn't exist. New friends seemed more interesting than the old. They skied the Alps and spoke three languages. And there was always something different to do: restaurants and theaters and beaches I'd never been to before. It was exciting not knowing my way around—unlike back home where I had the city map memorized. Even getting lost was fun. And if I got the least bit bored with one city or tired of one beach, I hopped the next train to a new destination and started all over again.

Europe was everything travel posters said it would be, but after three months that wasn't enough. I got tired of living out of my backpack and hopping trains every few days. Soon I was as lonely and bored as I'd ever been at home. I actually got tired of all of the variety and newness. I longed for what I knew: home.

During that time, I began to realize I couldn't escape my problems. Sure, I could change my geography. I could change my hotel or hostel. I could change my friends, my school, my church, my wardrobe, my hairstyle. But none of that did much good because I was still stuck with myself.

My predicament was like the standard plot from an old sci-fi thriller: You see the monster and flee down the alley, duck into an open doorway, and double-bolt the door. Then you hear a noise and spin around, only to find you've locked yourself in with the monster. The monster, you see, is yourself.

When I've tried to change myself, I've gone about it wrong. In a sense, I'm much like a woman who has cosmetic surgery. A tuck here and an implant there will make her look different in the mirror, but inside she's still the same person. That's why God doesn't focus on externals. The surgery he conducts to make us more like him is done from the inside out—he starts with the heart, the monster's cage.

As I allow God to tame the monster within, that's when true change occurs; that's when I can begin living an abundant, forgiven, fulfilling life.

See also: Ezekiel 11:19; 2 Corinthians 5:17

■■ DIAMONDS IN THE ROUGH

We are God's workmanship, created in Christ Jesus to do good works, which God prepared in advance for us to do.

EPHESIANS 2:10

Picture God as a master jeweler and yourself as a priceless diamond in the rough. Paul probably had something like that in mind when he wrote, "We are God's workmanship." Each of us is of infinite value to the Lord. And he is at work, shaping, cutting, filing, grinding, buffing, and polishing until every facet of our lives reflects his artistry.

The shaping process is not a pleasant task, because a lot of coarse material first needs to be cut away. These rough areas may be our attitudes toward others, the way we talk, a persistent bad habit, our anger, lust, jealousy, pride, or ambition. Yet God is a gentle craftsman. He doesn't pound away with a cold chisel and sledge hammer. He works delicately and slowly, with small, precise strokes, through the convincing power of his Spirit.

So we must be patient. Gross feelings of inadequacy and inferiority will develop if we dwell on the rough sides of our character. And if we compare ourselves to other Christians, there will always be someone who seems more polished. Remember, God's work is a *process*—to be completed over a long period of time.

We are his workmanship, but as yet we're uncompleted projects. So be patient. We can't expect to be perfect and always act the right way or say the right things. We may lose our temper when provoked, talk behind someone's back, or covet another's looks, abilities, or success. God doesn't ignore these things—it's just that cutting and shaping take time. Philippians 1:6 says we can be confident "that the God who started this great work in you would keep at it and bring it to a flourishing finish on the very day Christ Jesus appears" (*The Message*).

In other words, God *will* complete the job.

See also: Philippians 2:12–13; Galatians 5:19–26

▪▪ BORN AGAIN

I tell you the truth, unless a man is born again, he cannot see the kingdom of God.

JOHN 3:3

Some would describe Christians as people who *believe* certain things. For example, that Jesus was born in a Middle Eastern cow stable. That he turned water into wine. That church is a good place to hang out on Sundays.

Others would describe Christians as those who *do* or *don't do* certain things. They talk to God. They don't tell dirty jokes. They read the Bible. They don't smoke in school restrooms.

Still others would describe Christians as basically *good* people. They send birthday cards to their grandma. They actually sing the "Star-Spangled Banner" at ball games. They turn in homework on time. They smile a lot.

But Jesus had something else in mind. He described Christians as those who have been "born again." When he first used the term, he was speaking with Nicodemus, a head Jew who was big in religious politics. At first, Nicodemus didn't understand what Jesus was talking about. It triggered a ridiculous image in his mind of a grown person curling into a fetal ball and reentering his mother's womb to be reborn. But Christ was not trying to be funny when he used the analogy. He wanted to convey some key spiritual concepts.

For one thing, your spiritual birth (like your physical birth) marked a new beginning for you in a new world. As W. A. Criswell notes, "Christianity is the land of beginning again." You were given a new father, a new home, a new family. That is, a whole new identity. As the early Christians said of each other, you've become a "new creation."

Sure, you still look the same in a mirror. Your outer characteristics don't change. But your inner characteristics do. As you get to know God better, some of his personality and traits rub off on you. It's not a conscious thing. One day you simply notice that some things you once enjoyed now seem empty and pointless. Things such as attending wild parties, getting plastered, or making crude jokes about others no longer have the same attraction they once might have. You also notice things such as a new-found sense of hope and peace about the future. Or perhaps a changing attitude toward others—your parents, for example.

At the heart of the "born again" analogy is the idea that there's nothing you could ever have done to "earn" or "deserve"

God. Being a Christian is not something you do or think. Being a Christian is not living idealistically and doing good deeds. It's a relationship. Like physical birth, spiritual birth stems from an act of love that precedes delivery. It's through Jesus, and Jesus alone, that we've become sons and daughters of God.

Welcome to the family!

See also: 2 Corinthians 5:17; Ephesians 2:1–10; 4:17; 5:21

▪▪ GROWING UP

> *Though by this time you ought to be teachers, you need someone to teach you the elementary truths of God's word all over again. You need milk, not solid food! Anyone who lives on milk, being still an infant, is not acquainted with the teaching about righteousness. But solid food is for the mature, who by constant use have trained themselves to distinguish good from evil.*

> **HEBREWS 5:12–14**

When I was a kid, we had a doorway in our house etched with pencil marks. Each year on my birthday, I'd cram my heels against the door frame, stretch my neck as long as possible, and have Mom mark how much I'd grown during the preceding year. Some years there were great spurts. Others, I hardly grew at all. Finally, at 6'-1/2" my growth stopped.

I often think about that doorway. I wonder what it would look like if, instead of my physical growth, it measured my *spiritual* growth. Would the chart mark me as a believer who has "fought the good fight, holding on to faith and a good conscience," or one who has "forsaken my first love."

Some years my growth would have skyrocketed because I was hungry to know more about the Lord and *practice* what I'd learned. I got involved in helping others and saw my friends become Christians. But I'm ashamed to say there would be other years when those growth spurts slowed to an inch or two, and those dark times — signifying periods when I ignored God — when I didn't grow at all.

Thinking back over the years I've been a Christian, I realize you don't just grow old in the Lord. You must also *grow up*. That's what Paul is getting at in the verses in Hebrews. There are some Christians whose spiritual bodies are atrophied and squat. They're still at the Gerber stage, when they should be digesting steak and potatoes.

The result: their spiritual "muscle" is correspondingly misshaped—appearing more like Barbie's than Hulk Hogan's.

How about you? Have you *grown up* and claimed the power that is yours? Or are you living more like a 98-pound weakling—with a spiritual physique to match?

See also: Proverbs 2; Luke 8:5–15; James 1:23–25

∷ POINTS TO PONDER – LOOKS

The Lord does not look at the things man looks at. Man looks at the outward appearance, but the Lord looks at the heart.

1 SAMUEL 16:7

It is our own vanity that makes the vanity of others intolerable to us.

FRANÇOIS DE LA ROCHEFOUCAULD

Vanity keeps persons in favor with themselves, who are out of favor with all others.

WILLIAM SHAKESPEARE

Vanity is the quicksand of reason.

GEORGE SAND

Vanity is the foundation of the most ridiculous and contemptible vices—the vices of affection and common lying.

ADAM SMITH

Vanity is the fruit of ignorance. It thrives most in subterranean places, never reached by the air of heaven and the light of the sun.

ALEXANDER ROSS

We are so presumptuous that we wish to be known to all the world, even to those who come after us; and we are so vain that the esteem of five or six persons is enough to amuse and satisfy us.

PASCAL

Vanity may be likened to the smooth-skinned and velvet-footed mouse, nibbling about forever in expectation of a crumb; while self-esteem is too apt to take the likeness of the huge butcher's dog, who carries off your steaks, and growls at you as he goes.

WILLIAM GILMORE SIMMS

Vanity is a strong temptation to lying; it makes people magnify their merit, over-flourish their family, and tell strange stories of their interest and acquaintance.

JEREMY COLLIER

Every one at the bottom of his heart cherishes vanity; even the toad thinks himself good-looking.

JOHN WILSON

Vanity makes men ridiculous, pride odious, and ambition terrible.

SIR RICHARD STEELE

Vanity is the weakness of the ambitious man, which exposes him to the secret scorn and derision of those he converses with, and ruins the character he is so industrious to advance by it.

JOSEPH ADDISON

When a man has no longer any conception of excellence above his own, his voyage is done; he is dead; dead in the trespasses and sins of blear-eyed vanity.

H. W. BEECHER

She neglects her heart and studies her glass.

JOHN CASPAR LAVATER

See also: Psalm 147:10–11; Romans 3:24–25

WEEK

52

■■ NEW LIFE

Forget the former things; do not dwell on the past.
See, I am doing a new thing!

ISAIAH 43:18–19

When I lived in Indiana, my backyard was landscaped with large trees, including several maple and birch, a couple each of apple, cherry, and pear, and one or two oak. With the onset of the cool autumn weather, they all dropped their leaves. Those that didn't fall on their own accord were knocked off by the howling wind, rain, and biting snow of winter. Mother Nature, along about January and February, used brute force to strip the trees to bare-bark skeletons.

Walking through that boneyard backyard one winter, I noticed a few leaves had somehow survived intact—they'd resisted the season's strong-arm tactics and clung tenaciously to branches here and there. The icy winds hadn't blown them off. The snows hadn't knocked them off. The pelting rains hadn't forced them off.

We sometimes have problems like that—problems that cling on and on and on, refusing to let go. Despite what we do to shake them, they persist in plaguing us. It may be a problem with a friend we can't quite clear up, a nagging doubt or inferiority. Maybe it's an ornery boss who won't ease off, or a bad habit that haunts us endlessly. Perhaps it's hassles at home or school that are never-ending. We simply can't get rid of them.

But wait—new life comes! With the onset of spring, the tree's roots extend deeper and pump new life up the trunk to the tip of every branch. Buds appear, pushing the wind-whipped leaves off. At last: every leaf that has clung through winter is pushed off by new buds in the spring.

Our problems are the same. Blue days can turn to weeks and months as depression hangs on. We feel doomed by defeats. Our drive is deflated. These problems can't be blown off, shaken off, knocked off. But they are forced off with the help of new life. Christ said, "I am the vine; you are the branches."

He's the new life that surges into our lives, pushing off the old and making room for the new.

See also: John 15:1–8; Romans 6:4; 2 Corinthians 5:17

▪ TEAM EFFORT

> *When Jesus looked up and saw a great crowd coming toward him, he said to Philip, "Where shall we buy bread for these people to eat?" He asked this only to test him, for he already had in mind what he was going to do.*
>
> JOHN 6:5–6

The apostle John estimated that there were 5,000 men in that great crowd. But that figure didn't include women and children. So there were probably some 10,000 people milling about—people who had followed Christ's boat around the Sea of Galilee and waited for him to land. They were desperate for his help, and Christ spent the day healing their sick and ministering to their special needs. As nightfall approached, another more basic need arose: The people had nothing to eat. And all of the Burger Kings were closed.

It was at this point Christ approached Philip. "Where shall we buy burgers for these people to eat?" Jesus asked. The question seemed absurd. Didn't Christ know the situation was hopeless?

"Eight months' wages would not buy enough Whoppers for each one to have a bite," Philip quickly responded. Other disciples rallied around Philip by urging Christ to "send the crowds away." *Come on, Jesus. Be serious. What you ask is crazy. Utterly impossible!*

Christ probably felt a twinge of sadness in his heart. The Bible says Jesus asked Philip the question simply as a test, *for he already had in mind what he was going to do.* The question was a way of asking, "Philip, will you trust me with this seemingly impossible situation? Will you refuse to trust your own understanding and allow me to work out a solution?"

That's the same question you face every day in myriad ways. Perhaps your family is on the rocks, or maybe there's a situation at school that seems hopeless. Your "impossibility" might concern your future, a bad habit you've been unable to kick, or a serious problem with a friend. Regardless of the specifics, the question Christ raised with Philip is unchanging: *"What are we going to do?"* Jesus wants to work with you in a team effort.

In the story above, Christ already had a plan worked out. He knew the solution. And he always does. What may seem impossible to you is possible to God.

See also: Proverbs 3:5–6; Matthew 19:26

▪▪ THE FIRST MOVE

Love your neighbor as yourself.

LUKE 10:27

When the divorce papers were filed, Randy's father loaded his belongings into a U-Haul and pulled out of Randy's life in a cloud of dust. He settled in a small house nearby, but he might as well have moved to another continent, because he never called or stopped by.

At night Randy often did his homework by the phone, hoping his father might decide to call. But as days blurred into weeks without word from his dad, Randy sensed it was a case of out of sight, out of mind.

Then one day Randy decided he wouldn't wait for his father to make the first move. He might not see him again if he did. So he screwed up his courage and stopped by his dad's new house.

"How long's it been?" he asked Randy when his son entered.

"Three months."

"No kidding. Has it really been that long?" His father muttered something about being so busy, then showed him his place: lawn chairs as living room furniture; TV on a crate; cheap foam pads thrown down as a mattress, no dresser.

"It's not much, but it's livable," his father said.

Randy nodded and forced a smile. It hurt to see his father living like that. And in that moment, he saw his dad not as his own father, but as a person in desperate need. He probably hadn't called because he felt no one really cared about him. Maybe he thought everyone blamed him for the divorce.

Suddenly Randy turned to his dad and hugged him tightly. And in the middle of the embrace, he silently asked God to help him love his father with the love of the Lord.

In the Bible, Christ says we are to love our neighbor as ourselves. It's presented not as a suggestion, but as a command. And it's no less of a command when your "neighbor" happens to be your own father.

See also: Colossians 3:12–14; 1 John 3:16–18; 4:19–21

■ TWO OLD GEEZERS

I give you this charge: Preach the Word; be pre-pared in season and out of season.

2 TIMOTHY 4:1–2

If anyone needed to know the Lord, I figured it was old man Chambers and his wife, Gladys. They lived two doors down, and when I'd leave for church on Sunday mornings, I'd see them sitting in lawn-chair rockers beneath the shade of their dying elm tree. He'd be reading a copy of some movie magazine; she'd be chain-smoking Winstons and watching jays through a pair of opera glasses.

Mr. Chambers had worked highway construction, and I used to marvel at his strength when I was a kid. "Go ahead, feel the muscle," he'd say, and would then pump his biceps till it seemed his arm would pop. But his arms had grown thin and veiny over the interven-ing fifteen years, and his once-smooth voice grated like a cement truck in low gear. The neighborhood gossip now was that they both had liver and lung problems—too much booze and too much smoking.

I found it easy to wave as I drove by their house. It was the polite thing to do—you know, "Be nice to old people." But I could never get up the courage to actually stop the car, get out, and talk with them. After I became a Christian, I often thought of how God could fill their lives with purpose. They always looked so lonely sitting out front, but I was busy and, well, there were things to do, places to go, people to see. Besides, what would I say? "Hi, sure is nice to talk with you after fifteen years. Great weather, uh, by the way, do you know Jesus loves you?"

As months passed, I convinced myself I was just on a guilt trip, feeling overly weird about two old people who really didn't matter to me. And then one winter night as I was getting ready for bed, I heard the wail of fire engines nearby. I grabbed my jacket and darted out the door. Flames were shooting from the Chamberses' house, and a crowd was gathering.

I thought, great, the Lord will show me some way to befriend them after the fire. All the waving I'd done would finally pay off. Then I saw the firemen drag two bodies from the house and cover them with blankets until the county coroner could arrive.

I will never forget that scene. To this day it's tattooed on my brain. I see the snow, feel the cold, smell the smoke. And then there are the bodies—a vivid reminder that doors of opportunity God opens for us don't stay open forever.

See also: Isaiah 52:7; Matthew 28:18–20

:: SHUT OUT

Peter said to Jesus, "Lord, it is good for us to be here. If you wish, I will put up three shelters—one for you, one for Moses and one for Elijah."

MATTHEW 17:4

He was the ultimate mystery man—so reclusive that getting a picture of him was like trying to get a formal portrait of Bigfoot. During his later years, he never saw outsiders, so his appearance was unimportant to him. His hair and scraggly beard curled halfway to the floor. His nails were long and twisted, like two-inch corkscrews. He seldom bathed.

A skid row bum? No, Howard Hughes—one of the wealthiest men in the world before his death in 1976.

Why was he so enigmatic, so isolated? His closest aides reported that Hughes simply wanted to keep his environment sanitized, to maintain germproof sterility. People carried disease, so he locked them out. But he died from disease anyway—the *loneliness* disease.

The Howard Hughes story reminds me somewhat of Peter, who one afternoon hiked up a high mountain with Jesus and two other disciples. Upon reaching the summit, something strange happened. While Jesus was praying, Matthew reports, his face shone like the sun, and his clothes became as white as light. Mark, who today could make a killing doing Clorox commercials, says Jesus' clothes dazzled as if he'd used supernatural bleach. Moments later, Jesus was joined by Moses and Elijah.

Peter's toes tingled so much he couldn't contain himself. "Lord," he blurted, "isn't it great we're here!" Translation: "Thank God it's *us* and no one else." And then he volunteered to construct a mountain lodge so they wouldn't have to leave the holy peak. They could stay there and have a male bonding experience—apart from people and the dirt of their problems. It would be germproof living.

Jesus didn't answer him. But God did. Speaking from a cloud, he boomed that the wisest thing Peter could do was to zip his lip. And that scared Peter so badly he fell on his face and nearly knocked himself out.

In each of us is a touch of both Howard Hughes and Peter. We hoard our privacy, hiding behind locked doors—and not just physical ones. We shut people out as easily with harsh words and looks. The same is true when we hang out in cliques or post those invisible banners: "SENIORS ONLY" or "WHITES ONLY" or "CHRISTIANS ONLY." We don't want to get *too* involved in others' problems or lives. There are times when, as Mark Twain said, we'd like to hang the whole human race, and finish the farce.

But isolation is anathema to Christianity, which was built on relationship. That's why Christ admonished his followers to be the salt of the earth. To do the job right, salt can't stay in the shaker.

See also: Matthew 25:31–46; Luke 10:25–37; Hebrews 10:25

■■ BLESSED ARE SMASHED BURRITOS

Blessed are they whose ways are blameless, who walk according to the law of the Lord. Blessed are they who keep his statutes and seek him with all their heart. They do nothing wrong; they walk in his ways.

PSALM 119:1–3

It sometimes feels like fun and good times and happiness are for others. Everybody *else* seems to get the attention, the applause, the dates, the acclaim. It's *they* who smile and fill locker halls with happy talk and laughter, and who chatter on and on about weekends full of things you can't even imagine. As for you, what's to smile about? Your life is a smashed burrito.

You're at the end of your rope. Maybe you've lost what is most dear to you. Or perhaps you've simply grown tired of fighting life's toughest battle: trying to live a Christian life. You're weary of the daily struggle with sin. You're worn out by saying *no* to temptation. You're ready to throw in the towel.

If so, consider yourself blessed.

And consider Christ's words of comfort in his "Sermon on the Mount," as conveyed in the popular version of the Bible known as *The Message* (Matthew 5:3–12). It's God's message to *you*:

"You're blessed when you're at the end of your rope. With less of you there is more of God and his rule.

"You're blessed when you feel you've lost what is most dear to you. Only then can you be embraced by the One most dear to you.

"You're blessed when you're content with just who you are—no more, no less. That's the moment you find yourselves proud owners of everything that can't be bought.

"You're blessed when you've worked up a good appetite for God. He's food and drink in the best meal you'll ever eat.

"You're blessed when you care. At the moment of being 'care-full,' you find yourself cared for.

"You're blessed when you get your inside world—your mind and heart—put right. Then you can see God in the outside world.

"You're blessed when you can show people how to cooperate instead of compete or fight. That's when you discover who you really are, and your place in God's family.

"You're blessed when your commitment to God provokes persecution. The persecution drives you deeper into God's kingdom.

"Not only that—count yourself blessed every time people put you down or throw you out or speak lies about you to discredit me. What it means is that the truth is too close for comfort and they are uncomfortable. You can be glad when that happens—give a cheer, even!—for though they don't like it, *I* do! And all heaven applauds...."

See also: Isaiah 40:28–31; Matthew 11:28–30; Galatians 6:7–10

■■ POINTS TO PONDER – WISDOM

The fear of the Lord is the beginning of wisdom, and knowledge of the Holy One is understanding. For through me your days will be many, and years will be added to your life. If you are wise, your wisdom will reward you; if you are a mocker, you alone will suffer.

PROVERBS 9:10–12

God grant me the serenity to accept the things I cannot change, courage to change things I can, and wisdom to know the difference.

REINHOLD NIEBUHR

There are but two classes of wise men: the men who serve God because they have found him, and the men who seek him because they have found him not.

RICHARD CECIL

Wise men learn more from fools than fools from the wise.

CATO THE CENSOR

It is easy to be wise after the event.

ENGLISH SAYING

Some are weather-wise, some are otherwise.

BENJAMIN FRANKLIN

Wisdom is only found in truth.

WOLFGANG VON GOETHE

The doorstep to the temple of wisdom is a knowledge of our own ignorance.

CHARLES SPURGEON

Common sense in an uncommon degree is what the world calls wisdom.

JOHN DUKE COLERIDGE

There is one person that is wiser than anybody, and that is everybody.

ALEXANDER A. TALLEYRAND

Much wisdom often goes with the fewest words.

SOCRATES

The wise man endeavors to shine in himself; the fool to outshine others. The first is humbled by the sense of his own infirmities, the last is lifted up by the discovery of those which he observes in other men. The wise man considers what he wants, and the fool what he abounds in. The wise man is happy when he gains his own approbation, and the fool when he recommends himself to the applause of those about him.

JOSEPH ADDISON

A wise man looks upon men as he does on horses; all their comparisons of title, wealth, and place, he considers but as harness.

RICHARDS CECIL

A man begins cutting his wisdom teeth the first time he bites off more than he can chew.

HERB CAEN

We can be knowledgeable with other men's knowledge, but cannot be wise with other men's wisdom.

MICHEL DE MOITAIGNE

God has placed no limit to wisdom.

FRANCIS BACON

See also: 2 Chronicles 1:1–12; Jeremiah 10–12

SCRIPTURE INDEX

SUBJECT INDEX

(Subjects are indexed to the page on which the devotional starts; persons to the page on which the mention occurs.)

We want to hear from you. Please send your comments about this book to us in care of the address below. Thank you.

ZondervanPublishingHouse
Grand Rapids, Michigan 49530
http://www.zondervan.com